# SCOTTISH COOKERY

## Catherine Brown

MERCAT
PRESS

First edition published in 1985 by Richard Drew Publishing Ltd.
This revised edition published in 1999 by Mercat Press
James Thin, 53 South Bridge, Edinburgh EH1 1YS

ISBN: 1 873644 930

Illustrations by Jane Glue

Typeset in Windsor Lt BT and Ehrhardt at Mercat Press

Printed and bound in Great Britain by
Redwood Books, Trowbridge, Wiltshire

# CONTENTS

INTRODUCTION                                    ix

ACKNOWLEDGMENTS                                 xiii

WEIGHTS, MEASURES and TERMINOLOGY               xv

1    OATS & BARLEY                              1

Oatcakes—Traditional Girdle Oatcakes with Fine Meal; Oven Oatcakes with Butter and Pinhead Oatmeal. Porridge. Brose—Oatmeal Brose; Pease Brose; Atholl Brose; Mixed-Grain Porridge; Mixed-Grain Girdle Scones. Bannocks—Old-fashioned Bannocks; Barley Bannocks; Modern Barley Bannocks; Oatmeal Bannocks. Mealie Puddings and Skirlie. Oatmeal and Barley Breads—Oatmeal Bread with Molasses; Oatmeal Bread Rolls; Sour Dough Oatmeal Bread; Cooked Potato Starter; Buttermilk Bread with Oatmeal. Other Uses of Oatmeal and Barley—Clootie Dumpling; Sweet Oaten Pudding with Raspberries; Buttered Oats; Walnut and Oat Biscuits; A Swiss/Scots Breakfast.

2    FISH                                       25

Atlantic, Wild Scottish and Farmed Salmon—Baked Salmon in Butter; Grilled Salmon Steak with Parsley and Lemon Butter; Potted Salmon; Salmon Soup; Tay Salmon in Pastry with Vermouth and Dill Sauce. Smoked Salmon. Salmon Trout, Brown Trout—Baked Trout with Herbs and Lemon. Herring—Fresh Herring Fried in Oatmeal; Fresh Herrings as Dressed at Inveraray; Open Arms Herrings with Drambuie Butter; Grilled Herring with Mustard; Soused or Potted Herring; Sweet Spiced Herring. Atlantic Mackerel—Potted Mackerel. Kipper—Potted Kipper; Grilled; Fried; Jugged; Baked; Uncooked. Salt-Pickled Herring—Tatties and Herring; Marinated Salt Herring; Salt Herring Salad with Beetroot and Mushrooms. Haddock, Cod and Whiting—Baked Fish; Haddock and Chips; Fresh Haddock in a Light Creamy Mustard Sauce; Grilled Fresh Haddock. Rizzared Haddock (Blawn Whiting). Finnan Haddock— East Coast Fishwife's Broth; Finnan Haddock with Melted Cheese and Eggs; Baked Smoked Haddock with Cream and Poached Egg; Smoked Haddock with Bacon; Smoked Haddock Flan. Arbroath Smokie—Baked

Arbroath Smokie with Baked Potato; Arbroath Smokie Poached in Milk. Potted Arbroath Smokie with oatcakes.

## 3    SHELLFISH & SEAWEED                                    58

Molluscs, Scallops—Scallops in Butter with Shallots and Garlic; Steamed Scallops in a Creamy White Sauce. Oysters—Served Raw in Their Shells; Oysters with Whelks; Oysters in a Crust; Oysters on Skewers with Bacon. Mussels—Mussel Stew with Crusty Bread and Butter; Mussels and Cockles in Garlic and Olive Oil; Mussels Grilled in Their Shells with Wine. Horse Mussels—Clabbie Dhubs with Leeks and Tomatoes. Periwinkles—Cooking and Eating. Razor Shell Clams. Other Scottish Molluscs. Crustaceans. Crab—Partan Pies; Partan Bree. Lobster—Grilled Lobster; Boiled Lobster; Lobster Soup. Norway Lobster—Grilled Norway Lobster. Other Scottish Crustaceans. Other Shellfish Recipes—Fruits of the Sea; Arisaig Seafood Pastry; Shellfish Broth; Shellfish Sauce; Orkney Squid. Seaweeds. Caragheen—Caragheen Chocolate Pudding; for Thickening. Dulse and Tangle—Dulse Broth with Lamb or Mutton; Dulse Cakes. Sloke.

## 4    GAME                                                   87

Venison—Braised Shoulder or Haunch of Red Deer with Sloe Gin; Roast Saddle of Venison; Venison Collops with Oysters and Lemon; Venison Pasty with Claret or Port; Venison Liver; Venison Tripe (*Poca Buidhe*). Red Grouse—Roast Young Grouse; Grouse Soup. Pheasant—Roast Pheasant with Fresh Herbs; Braised Pheasant with Whisky and Juniper. Hare—Bawd Bree. Rabbit—Elsie's Rabbit with Onions; Honeyed Rabbit. Other Game dishes—Rich Game Stew Garnished with Brambles and Choux Pastry. Other Scottish Game.

## 5    BEEF AND LAMB                                          105

Beef—Boiled Beef; Scotch Barley Broth; Minced Collops; Bacon Dumplings; Beef Olives; Grilled Beefsteaks with Whisky and Shallot Butter; Spiced Beef; Beef Cooked in Claret; Forfar Bridies; Tripe Suppers; Kidney Puddings; Veal Sweetbreads and Kidneys; Sweetbread Pie; Potted Hough; Potted Tongue. Other Traditional Beef Products—Lorne Sausage; Sassermaet; Suet; Dripping. Lamb—To Boil a Gigot with Turnips; Roast Rack of Lamb; Grilled or Barbecued Leg of Lamb; Braised Lamb Shoulder with Carrots and Turnips; Lamb and Kidney Pie. Scotch Pies. How to Use up a Whole Sheep; Grilled Flank with Tomato Sauce; Lamb's Fry; Haggis.

# SCOTTISH
# COOKERY

## CATHERINE BROWN

A Glaswegian, journalist and author, her early career involved teaching and professional cooking in hotels and restaurants.

During postgraduate research at Strathclyde University, she wrote the thesis which was published as *British Cookery* and since the early 1980s has written a food column in *The Herald* which has been credited with several Glenfiddich food-writing awards.

She is also co-presenter, with Derek Cooper, of *Scotland's Larder* for STV and Grampian Television.

Previously published books:

*Scottish Regional Recipes*
*Broths to Bannocks*
*Food Trails of Scotland*
*Feeding Scotland*
*A Scottish Feast* (Co-editor)
*A Year in a Scots Kitchen*
*Traditional Foods of Britain* (Co-author)

## 6    FRUIT, SWEETS, PUDDINGS & CAKES    137

Scottish Soft Fruits (Raspberries, Strawberries, Blackcurrants, Brambles, Red Currants, Blaeberries). Fruit and Cream—An Ashet of Fresh Fruit. Fruit, Cream and Sauce—Gourmet Strawberries; How Escoffier Served Strawberries at the Carlton; Brandied Fruit Cup; Raspberry Vinegar. Using Wine with Soft Fruit—Marinated Strawberries and Raspberries with Whipkull. Fruit Puree and Cream—Whipped Fruit Pudding. Iced Fruit Puree with Cream—Rich Ice Cream; Ettrickshaws Home-made Ice Cream; Clear Sharp-flavoured Water Ice; Peach Highland Cream. Fruit, Cream and Cheese—Cranachan (Cream-Crowdie). Other Sweets—Trifle; Caledonian Cream; Biscuits and Cream; Rhubarb Custard Tart; Rhubarb and Bananas; Syllabub; Butterscotch Sauce; Blackcurrant and Apple Pudding; A Rich Strawberry Tart; Hazelnut Meringue Cake; Lemon Pudding.

## 7    VEGETABLES, SOUPS & OTHER DISHES    160

Potatoes—Stovies; Stovies in the Oven with Bacon; Chappit Tatties; Oatmealed Potatoes; Dripping Potatoes; Fried Potato Cake; Tattie Scones; Potato Soup; Potatoes and Hard Boiled Eggs. Leeks—Cock-a-Leekie; Sauteed Chicken and Leeks with Skirlie; Leek Salad; Leek and Bacon Pie; Roasted Leeks; Leeks Served Cold with Vinaigrette and Hard-boiled Eggs. Carrots—Carrot or Turnip Soup; Carrot and Bacon Soup; Carrot Cake; A Rich Moist Carrot Cake; Glazed Carrots. Cabbage—Rumbledethumps; Red Cabbage with Apples. Turnip—Mashed Turnip. Kale—Buttered Kale; Kale and Crowdie Pie; Green Kale Soup with Bacon. Broccoli—Creamy Broccoli Salad. Peas—Buttered Peas with Mint; Puree of Green Peas Baked in a Mould. Mixed Vegetable Dishes—Hotch Potch; Lentil Soup.

## 8    SUGAR & SPICE & BAKING, SCOTTISH
SWEETIES & PRESERVES    186

Scottish Baking. Shortbread—Rich Shortbread. Scones—Soda Scones; Sweet Milk Scones; Sultana Scones; Treacle Scones; Honey Scones; Cream Scones; Fresh Fruit Scones; Herb Scones; Cheese Scones; Onion Scones. Scottish Pancakes and Crumpets. Scottish Cookies—Plain Cookies; Cream Cookies; Iced Cookies; Currant Cookies; James Burgess' Spiced Cookies. A Special Yeast Cake; White Floury Baps. Gingerbread—Dark Gingerbread. Black Bun; Selkirk Bannock; French Toasts with Rum; Ecclefechan Butter Tart; A Rich Almond Tart. Easy-to-Make Rich Cakes—Dundee Cake; A Cake with Apples in It; Mincemeat Sandwich Cake; Maple Syrup Cake; Chocolate Drop Cake; Seville Orange Chocolate Cake.

Biscuits—Almond Biscuits; Broken-Biscuit Cake. Other Baking Specialities. Sweeties—Tablet; Tablet Variations; Toffy for Coughs; Traditional Scottish Sweeties Past and Present. Preserves—Marmalade; Chip Marmalade; Fortingall Marmalade; Raspberry Jam; Strawberry Jam; Rowan Jelly; Herb Jelly; Spiced Damsons; Mincemeat; Mince Pies; Mincemeat Tart; Apple Chutney; Raisin Chutney; Mrs Beeton's Plum Chutney; Store Mustard; Pickle Vinegar.

## 9    CHEESE    225

Methods of Cheese Production. Buying and Storing Cheese. Cheese Types. Toasted Cheese; John Thorne's Toasted Cheese; Cheese and Eggs. Milk-Related Traditions—Hatted Kit. Cheese Salad; Cheesecake.

## 10    CULINARY INTERCHANGE    237

Italians—O Ragu di Mama. French—Gratin Dauphinois; Tarte Tatin. English—Roast Sirloin of Beef and Yorkshire Pudding; Sussex Pond Pudding. Irish—Irish Stew; Colcannon. Scandinavians—Salt Herring with Leeks; Marinated Fried Herring. Pakistanis/Indians—Pakora; Mrs Anwar's Chicken. Chinese—Stir-Fried Vegetables. Jews—Challah (Plaited White Bread). Americans—Original Southern Crisp Fried Chicken with Cream Gravy; Brownies; Strawberry Shortcake.

## SCOTTISH REGIONAL RECIPES    259

## EARLY SCOTTISH COOKERY WRITERS    261

## HOUSEHOLD BOOKS, LETTERS & DIARIES    266

## SELECT BIBLIOGRAPHY    270

## GENERAL INDEX    274

# INTRODUCTION

It was a cold, wet, inhospitable day and the wild West Highland scenery looked unfriendly and menacing from where we sat inside the warm croft-house. As the light began to fade, Alistair lit the paraffin lamp and Maggie brought crisp oatcakes, butter, cheese, home-made jam and soft floury bannocks from a cupboard in a corner of the room. These North West Highlanders had lived on this croft all their lives and were now into their seventies. They were too old now to benefit from the road which had been built a few years earlier in 1972, linking the communities on this remote Applecross peninsula which had depended on the sea as a means of communication for centuries. The peat fire burned with a comforting steady glow, the wind and rain raged audibly without, while inside we warmed ourselves with whisky, and talked. Then Alistair got up and took the lid off the pot sitting on the fire in the black iron range which dominated one wall. A rich smell of broth suddenly pervaded the room. It had been cooking so slowly, and for so long, that only the faintest whiff of its existence had been noticeable till then. He removed the piece of mutton (from a Blackface sheep he had killed and salted himself) and sliced the meat off the bone in rough chunks. Then he threw a few handfuls of chopped leeks into the broth and we ate the meat first with a knife and fork and some oatcakes, while the broth finished cooking. It was thick with vegetables and barley and had the exquisite flavour only possible with a piece of well-flavoured salt mutton from a mature sheep which has grazed long on the heather hills.

The memory remains vivid. So many hardships and such isolation, yet they were always so cheerful. Considering their difficult conditions, and limited resources by today's standards, the food they put on the table was remarkable—simple, sustaining, flavoursome and ingenious. As I sat with them, it seemed like stepping backwards into the past. But not a deprived past. Everything was here for comfort and survival, except wealth. Alistair and Maggie were content.

I made my farewells and left.

Driving back along the winding single-track road round Loch Torridon, I made no declaration of intent to write about Scottish food and its history. But thinking about it later, I realised that being a part of their lives for a short while had given me a valuable benchmark, a starting point, which eventually resulted in this book. Many other experiences in many other parts of Scotland, by the sea, in the mountains, in remote places, in cities, from childhood, and brought to me through the writing of others, often distant in time, have contrasted and blended together and shaped my perception of Scottish cookery. The structure and theme of this book has been dictated by distinct primary Scottish raw materials and the chapters explore their place in the Scottish diet, past and present.

The fact that in Scotland the emphasis of primary food production has been mainly on barley and oats rather than wheat, and mainly on sheep, cattle, fish and potatoes and to a lesser extent on pigs, poultry, fruit and vegetables, has influenced my approach. I have also taken into account the fact that this food production is not quite uniformly reflected in what is eaten since Scots consume (per head) more beef, fish, eggs and potatoes, but less lamb, pigmeat, poultry, fruit and vegetables, than the rest of Britain.

Of vital importance to the Scottish economy is its export trade in food with the rest of the UK and beyond. Scotland has been increasing its primary food production since the Second World War at a greater rate than domestic consumption, so while it has become more self-sufficient there is also more produce to trade with. As in the past the rest of Britain, and the world, continues to recognise the value of primary Scottish food and food products. But making the best use of this asset at home is equally important.

While domestic cooking is more likely to retain a stronger loyalty to the national food culture, a distinct national style in the marketplace can only become established when professional chefs take the lead. But from the early 1900s to the 1980s, professional kitchens and menus were dominated throughout the UK by a classical French style. It may have suited grand Edwardian hotels like Gleneagles, but it sat awkwardly on menus in the majority of smaller hotels, country houses, city restaurants and country pub diners around Scotland. Only when this style began to decline did the opportunity to establish a stronger Scottish flavour on the professional menu develop. Remnants of the old attachment to *à la Française* remain. But those who avoid foreign phrases where perfectly good English or Scots words will do instead, provide a more easily understood blueprint for the meal.

Throughout the 1990s the movement to define Scottish cooking more clearly and confidently on professional menus has continued in partnership with the fashion for a a multicultural approach to modern sophisticated eating. Dominated by rustic Italy—taking over where classical France left off—the 'Mediterranean style' has become the current fashion, with many chefs choosing to avoid committing themselves to either native or foreign by describing their style as 'fusion' or 'eclectic'.

But the trick, for those who choose to stay loyal to the national food culture, is to create a menu which provides a balanced choice with clearly defined Scottish dishes. Highlighting Scotland's food potential can be done in a number of ways. Primary produce—beef, lamb, fish, soft fruits and cheeses—is already well recognised for its quality. But there are also good reasons to highlight the local tag and satisfy environmental concerns about the damaging effects of transporting food for miles. Making the best use of this asset also provides a valuable platform for local producers: Arbroath smokies, Perthshire raspberries, West Coast shellfish are just a few of the colourful local foods which deserve top menu billing. If they can be eaten in their own locality so much the better, for there is the added bonus of freshness and ripeness. No matter how sophisticated the transport facilities are, the fact is that fish and shellfish are at their best immediately after landing, while soft fruits, in particular, have a much better flavour if they are allowed to ripen on the plant before picking.

Another way national dishes can take a more prominent place in the food culture is when traditional dishes such as haggis and Cullen skink are presented in their original rustic simplicity. If there has been an advantage in the change of fashions, from classical French to rustic Italian, it has been that peasant dishes have become more valued for their simplicity, honesty and native worthiness. Which is what Robert Burns was on about in his *Address to a Haggis* when he questioned those—even in his time—who were less than loyal to the rustic simplicity of native foods:

> Is there that ower his French ragout,
> Or olio that wad staw a sow,
> Or fricassee wad make her spew
>     Wi' perfect sconner,
> Looks down wi' sneering, scornfu' view
>     On sic a dinner?

And if inventive Scots are inspired to create new combinations, there is always the opportunity to take something like a fine black pudding from Stornoway and marry it with a Scottish pancake and a wild mushroom sauce, as they do at Café Gandolfi in Glasgow, where a mix of rustic and refined modern Scottish cooking sits confidently alongside fashionable Mediterranean. Finding what conventions of form and detail can be dispensed with, while preserving the spirit of the whole through balance, best exploits the unpretentious quality of Scottish food. I have tried to illustrate this through a mixture of approaches, both formal and informal as well as traditional and modern. They reflect my own flexible approach to ingredients and the way we put them together. First and foremost, we should recognise their potential and let them dictate. Spending time wandering round food shops and markets, searching out the excitement of quality and freshness is the best inspiration. And as developments in the Farmers' Markets movement begins to spread throughout the country, with local farmers selling their produce direct to the public in a city or town centre venue on a regular basis, there is a better opportunity to make more of the Scottish food potential and establish its own clearly defined style.

The recipes in this book reflect my liking for cooking from scratch— which need not necessarily be more time-consuming than reaching for other alternatives. Things like one-pot meals which cook by themselves are an essential and constant part of my life, as is the need to get meals on the table in a hurry, without compromising on quality. Having worked in the hotel and catering industry, I recognise that the short-order aspect of feeding people is also important. A range of foods which will combine in a variety of ways to suit individual tastes is essential. A large joint, for instance, which will sit in the refrigerator for several days, and can be instantly teamed up with interesting chutneys, preserved fruits or vegetables and served with good bread and butter, is just one way of avoiding the worry of what to have for the next three days.

While I have made the selection, many others from all kinds of cooking philosophies have influenced the finished result. Some have had a more direct influence than others, while many appear frequently throughout the text in their writings and recipes. But it is to Alistair and Maggie— both gone now from their croft in Wester Ross—that the book is dedicated. For they provide the most revealing glimpse of the past, sitting at their peat fire with their pot of amazing broth, mutton, oatcakes, cheese, butter, jam and floury bannocks: the essence of Scottish cookery.

Catherine Brown, 1999.

# ACKNOWLEDGEMENTS

Thanks to a multitude of people this book has taken shape. It is the harvest of many people's creativity, imagination, knowledge and experience, and recognition of them all on a single page is impossible.

To everyone, I am sincerely grateful.

To each of the following I am particularly grateful for the time, information and encouragement which they gave while I was researching the first edition of the book. I hurled many awkward questions at them which they patiently answered: Dr J.J. Connell, Director, Torry Research Station, Aberdeen; Martha Crawford, Secretary of the British Deer Farmers Association, Cluanie, Beauly, Inverness-shire; Keith Dunbar of Summer Isles Foods, Achiltibuie; Sheila Harley, Scotch Quality Beef and Lamb Association; Peter Hick, Director, Reawick (Shetland) Lamb Marketing Company; Professor George Houston, Department of Political Economy, University of Glasgow; James Keay, Torry Research Station, Aberdeen; D.S. MacDonald, Oatmeal Miller and Grain Merchant, Montgarrie Mills, Alford, Aberdeenshire; Elizabeth MacIntosh, Scottish Milk Marketing Board; Professor A.D. MacIntyre, Director, Marine Laboratory, Aberdeen; Donald MacLean, Chairman of the National Vegetable Society, Dornock Farm, Crieff, Perthshire; Dr Donald McQueen, Marketing Director, Scottish Milk Marketing Board; Dr David Mann, United Biscuits, Glasgow; Rosemary Marwick of Howgate Cheeses, Penicuik, Midlothian; I.G.A. Miller, Oatmeal and Pearl Barley Miller, Kelso Mills, Roxburghshire; George Motion, Assistant Secretary, The Red Deer Commission, Knowsley, Inverness; Hamish and Livingston Neil of S.L. Neil Glasgow; Douglas Ritchie of Strathaird Sea Foods; J. Russell, Manager of the Company of Scottish Cheese Makers; Archie Sinclair, Caithness Smoking Company, Latheronwheel; Stewart Sloan of Robert Sloan, Butchers; Susanna Stone of Highland Fine Cheeses, Tain, Wester Ross; Dr Charles E. Taylor, Director, Scottish Crop Research Institute, Invergowrie, Dundee; Richard Van Oss, Director, The Game Conservancy, Fordingbridge, Hampshire; Joseph Walker of Walkers Shortbread, Aberlour; Gillan Whytock of the Advisory and Development Service, Agronomy Department, The West of Scotland Agricultural College, Auchincruive, Ayrshire.

Sincere thanks also to Antony Kamm for editing the first edition and to Iseabail MacLeod, Editorial Director of the *Scottish National Dictionary*, for editing the revised edition, also to Bruce Lenman, Professor of Scottish History at St Andrews University, and to Tom Johnstone of the Mercat Press for his helpful support during the revision.

For the use of their kitchens, as well as their stimulating company and help, reading and correcting recipes, my thanks to Joan Campbell and Catherine Braithwaite (my mother). And to many others who have helped in a practical way I am deeply grateful, for without their help also the book would simply not have been written.

# WEIGHTS, MEASURES & ANGLO-AMERICAN TERMS

## Quantities produced by the recipes

While I have given some indication for each recipe, it can only be an approximation since so much depends on serving size and on the position in the meal, not to mention individual appetites. A dish used as a starter will usually provide double the servings than if it is used as a main course. The yield for scones, biscuits, etc. will depend on unit size; again my quantities are only an approximation.

## Converting from one system of measuring to another

Do not mix measures—stick to one system throughout a recipe.

Any conversion from one system to another can only be an approximation, not an exact equivalent. While one does not wish to appear unduly careless, weighing out for everyday cooking does not need the same kind of measuring precision necessary for weighing out gold or silver. The odd half ounce here and there will not ruin the recipe.

In any case basic items like flour, sugar, butter and margarine vary in moisture content and also air content, which matters if you are measuring by volume, while results can also depend on whether the day is dry of wet, the kitchen hot or cold.

## Converting from Imperial to Metric

Scales and measures are usually graduated in multiples of 25g. If the conversion of 1 oz to 25 g is made (1 oz = 28.35 g), it is inevitable that there are illogical jumps, for example when you move from 3 to 4 oz, and instead of going up by 25 g I have mostly taken the jump to 125 g simply because then the metric measurements can be compared proportionately: i.e. ¼ lb = ⅛ kilo; ½ lb = ¼ kilo; 1 lb = ½ kilo, etc.

For liquid measurements the same proportional system can apply with ¼ pt = ⅛ L; ½ pt = ¼ L; 1 pt = ½ L, etc.

The main advantage of this method is that it makes measuring easier, quicker and more convenient; especially if you are using ingredients which are packaged in metric.

Where it matters, and each recipe has to be judged separately as to the effects of this method, then the quantities can be rounded up or down as appropriate, remembering that 500g is actually about 2 oz more than 1 lb; and 1 litre is about ¼ pt less than 2 pts. When working in large quantities, special adjustments have to be made, since obviously the discrepancies become greater with increasing quantities to the extent that when using, say, the metric equivalent to 1 gallon according to this system, it would be 4 litres, which would be about 1 pint short of a gallon. In the recipes I have adjusted accordingly.

## Imperial to American cups

I have to confess that I like the way Americans weigh ingredients and when not testing recipes, would always prefer to use American cups, unless cooking in large quantities, when they become too time-consuming. American butter is packaged in 4 oz sticks, 4 to a box of 1 lb, which makes for easy and quick measuring, especially since they are usually graduated on the wrapping paper.

The main point to remember when using the American system is that they have actually retained the old British measure for 1 pint at 16 fl oz (UK = 20 fl oz), which was originally the same as the solid measure and which the British abandoned in 1825. American cups are graduated in fractions of 16 fl oz. Sets of cups are available (I use a set made by CUISENA). There are five sizes in the set—⅛; ¼; ⅓; ½ and 1 cup.

I have used the following table as a basis for conversion though on occasions in the recipes I have had to adjust quantities to produce comparable results. Where the cup is described as scant then I have filled it to about ¼ in of the rim of the cup, while generous means that it was slightly heaped.

American names for commodities, where different from the British, are in brackets.

| SOLID INGREDIENTS | IMPERIAL | METRIC | AMERICAN |
|---|---|---|---|
| **Dry ingredients** | | | |
| Beans, dry | 8 oz | 250 g | 1 c |
| Barley, flour | 3 oz | 75 g | 1 c |
| Breadcrumbs, | | | |
|     dry | 4 oz | 125 g | 1 c |
|     fresh | 2 oz | 50 g | 1 c |
| Cocoa Powder | 4 oz | 100 g | 1 c (gen) |
| Cornflour (Cornstarch) | 4 oz | 100 g | 1 c (gen) |
| Currants | 5 oz | 150 g | 1 c |
| Flour—Plain | | | |
|     (All-purpose flour) | 4 oz | 125 g | 1 c (gen) |
| Self-raising | | | |
|     (All-purpose Self Rising) | 4 oz | 125 g | 1 c (gen) |
| Wholemeal | | | |
|     (Whole Wheat) | 4 oz | 125 g | 1 c (gen) |
| Gelatine | ¼ oz | 7 g | 1 envelope |
| Glace cherries | | | |
|     (Candied) | 4 oz | 125 g | ¾ cup |
| Ground almonds | 3 oz | 75 g | 1 c |
| Nuts—broken or | | | |
|     coarsely chopped | 4 oz | 125 g | 1 c |
| Oatmeal, fine, medium | 4 oz | 125 g | 1 c (scant) |
| Coarse—Pinhead | | | |
|     (Irish Oatmeal) | 4 oz | 125 g | 1 c (scant) |
| Rolled Oats (Oatmeal) | 3 oz | 75 g | 1 c |
| Pearl Barley | 6 oz | 175 g | 1 c |
| Rice | 6 oz | 175 g | 1 c |
| Suet (shredded) | 4 oz | 125 g | 1 c (scant) |
| Sugar—caster, granulated | 7 oz | 200 g | 1 c |
| | 8 oz | 250 g | 1¼ c |
|     Brown | 5 oz | 150 g | 1 c (scant) |
|     Icing (Confectioner's) | 4 oz | 125 g | 1 c (gen) |
| Sultanas and Raisins | 6 oz | 175 g | 1 c |
| Yeast, dry | 2 level tsp | 7 g | 1 package |
|     fresh | ½ oz | 15 g | 1 package |
| | | | or cake |
| **Fruit, Cheese, Vegetables, etc.** | | | |
| Butter and other fats | 8 oz | 250 g | 1 c |
| | 4 oz | 125 g | 1 stick |
| Cabbage, raw, shredded | 3 oz | 75 g | 1 c (scant) |
| Carrot, 1 medium, sliced | 5 oz | 150 g | 1 c |
| Cheese, Cheddar, grated | 4 oz | 125 g | 1 c |
|     Cream, crowdie, cottage | 8 oz | 250 g | 1 c |
| Herbs, fresh | 2 oz | 50 g | 1 c |

| SOLID INGREDIENTS | IMPERIAL | METRIC | AMERICAN |
| --- | --- | --- | --- |
| Mayonnaise | 6 oz | 175 g | 1 c |
| Meat, raw or cooked, chopped or minced (Ground beef) | 8 oz | 250 g | 1 c |
| Mincemeat | 10 oz | 275 g | 1 c |
| Mushrooms, raw, sliced | 2-3 oz | 50-75 g | 1 c |
| Onion, chopped | 5 oz | 125 g | 1 c |
| Potatoes, cooked, mashed | 8 oz | 250 g | 1 c |
| Treacle, black (Molasses) Golden Syrup (Light corn syrup) | 12 oz | 350 g | 1 c |

| LIQUID | IMPERIAL | METRIC | AMERICAN |
| --- | --- | --- | --- |
| Water, milk, vinegar, oil, etc. | 8 fl oz | 250 ml | 1 c (½ pt US) |
| | ¼ pt (5 fl oz) | 150 ml | ¾ c (scant) |
| | ½ pt (10 fl oz) | 300 ml | 1¼ c (scant) |
| | ¾ pt (15 fl oz) | 450 ml | 2 c (scant) (1 pt US) |
| | 1 pt (20 fl oz) | 600 ml | 2½ c |
| | 1¼ pt (25 fl oz) | 700 ml | 3 c |
| | 1½ pt (30 fl oz) | 850 ml | 3¾ c |
| | 1¾ pt (35 fl oz) | 1000 ml | 4¼ c |
| | 2 pt (40 fl oz) | 1150 ml | 5 c |

## AMERICAN STANDARD MEASURING SPOONS

These are the same as the metric measuring spoons now widely available in Britain.

All spoon measures are taken as level.

### For Liquids:

1 teaspoon = 5 ml
1 tablespoon = 15 ml
2 tablespoons = ⅛ c = 1 fl oz = 25 ml (approx)
5 tablespoons = ⅓ c = 2½ fl oz = 60 ml (approx)
8 tablespoons = ½ c = 4 fl oz = 100 ml (approx)
1 tablespoon = 3 teaspoons

# ANGLO-AMERICAN COOKING VOCABULARY

| BRITISH | AMERICAN |
|---|---|
| **Cooking Terms** | |
| Fry | Pan Broil (without fat) |
| | Pan Fry (with fat) |
| Grate | Shred |
| Grill | Broil |
| Gut | Clean |
| Knock Back | Punch down |
| Prove | Rise |
| Sieve | Sift |

## Commodities not already mentioned in conversion table

| | |
|---|---|
| Anchovy essence | Anchovy paste |
| Bannock | Flat, round cake |
| Bicarbonate of soda | Baking soda |
| Biscuits | Cookies or Crackers |
| Boiling fowl | Stewing fowl |
| Broad beans | Lima beans |
| Cake mixture | Cake batter |
| Caster sugar | Granulated sugar |
| Cornflour | Cornstarch |
| Desiccated coconut | Flaked coconut |
| Double cream | Whipping cream |
| Dripping | Meat dripping |
| Essence | Extract |
| Flaked Almonds | Slivered almonds |
| Haricot Beans | Navy beans |
| Hough | Shank of Beef |
| Icing | Frosting |
| Jam | Preserves |
| Jelly (sweet) | Gelatin dessert |
| Rasher | Slice |
| Roast Potatoes | Oven-browned potatoes |
| Scone | Shortcake, biscuit |
| Single Cream | Light cream |
| Soft brown sugar | Light brown sugar |
| Spring onion | Green onion |
| Stewing steak | Braising beef |
| Sultanas | Seedless white raisins |

| BRITISH | AMERICAN |
|---|---|
| **Cooking equipment** | |
| Ashet (Scottish) | Meat dish |
| Baking sheet or tray | Cookie sheet |
| Frying pan | Skillet |
| Greaseproof paper | Waxed paper |
| Stewpan or pan | Kettle |
| Large pot | Dutch Oven or deep cooking utensil with a tight fitting lid |
| Liquidiser | Electric blender |
| Roasting tin | Roasting pan with rack |
| Sandwich tins | Round-layer pans |

# 1
# OATS

Original and frequent use of oatmeal was a mark of Scottish nationality to the extent that the English lexicographer Dr Johnson described the Scots in his dictionary as 'oats eaters'. The English thought oats only fit for horses and Dr Johnson did not spare the sarcasm in saying so—'a grain which in England is generally given to horses, but in Scotland supports the people'.

Yet the people appear to have survived on this frugal diet, even been quite healthy, if travellers' tales are to be believed. Thomas Pennant, one of the most eminent naturalists of the eighteenth century, made a tour of Scotland in 1789 and described the men as 'thin but strong'. Travelling people like drovers who herded the cattle around the country seem to have subsisted almost totally on oatmeal carried in 'great wallets' hung round their 'broad and sturdy backs'. They mixed the oatmeal with water and baked cakes on stones heated by the fire. Soldiers were more sophisticated, carrying a 'flat plate' strapped to their saddle. Presumbably foot soldiers made do with the heated hearth stones. A legendary figure is the ascetic Scottish student from a humble cottage, living a subsistence existence in his sparse garret on the bag of oatmeal which he brought from home at the beginning and middle of the term.

It is not known where or when cultivated oats originated. Wild oats are said to have been cultivated before 1000 BC by cave-dwellers in Switzerland. The carbonised grains of both wild and cultivated oats, along with wheat and barley, were found at digs along the Forth and Clyde Canal and at Camphill in Glasgow and were dated to a hundred or so years BC. Specimens are kept at the Museum of Scotland in Edinburgh, and it is generally agreed among authorities that, although oats thrive best in cool climates, they originally came from some warmer country in the East, from south-east Europe, central or western Asia or North Africa, and were certainly cultivated on the European continent before they arrived in Britain. The fact is that a cool climate is much more suitable for growing oats. When the growth is comparatively slow, the kernels get the best chance of filling out. In warm climates, where the

*...Oatmeal with milk, which they cook in different ways, is their constant food, three times a day, throughout the year, Sundays and holidays included...*
J. Donaldson
*A General View of the Agriculture of the Carse of Gowrie, 1794*

1

growth is faster, the kernels are poorly filled and even oats grown in the south of England are not nearly so well filled as those in Scotland.

The flavour of oats depends on a number of factors. The variety is important but also the amount of moisture; the district where it is grown; the kind of season; the kind of soil; the manuring; the time of cutting the crop; and how the grain is threshed, dried and milled. Varieties of oats are continually changing and have a relatively short life compared with some of the varieties grown in the past. Around 1900 an old variety of oats known as Sandwich was favoured for its well-flavoured oatmeal. This was due to a high oil and protein content compared with the oats which are grown today—the higher the oil content the better the flavour. Oats today contain around 5-7% oil compared with only 1-2% in other cereals while oatmeal has an oil content of 6-10% compared with around 1% in other cereal flours. Oats not only have fat in the 'germ' but also in the 'endosperm'.

From a practical storing and cooking point of view the amount of moisture is important. Most samples of newly milled meal have 6-8% moisture and this is generally recognised as too high. At this level the meal lacks flavour and this is the reason why certain recipes say—'Toast the oatmeal lightly in the oven before use.' It is simply to concentrate the nutty flavour. Similarly, oatcakes were always toasted before the fire to 'harden off'. Oatmeal used to be much 'harder dried' to only 3-5% moisture and the slower the process, the better the flavour. If it is dried too quickly the flavour can be harsh and fiery. This applies also to oatmeal being dried off in the oven before use.

Since it does absorb moisture readily it is better to store oatmeal in an airtight container and press it well down. Oatmeal which is kept in open bags in shops for some time cannot be of the best quality. Scots used to keep their oatmeal in a 'girnal' (wooden chest)—the freshly milled oatmeal was tramped into it in the spring and lasted through the summer till harvest.

All the traditional oatmeal dishes such as porridge, oatcakes, brose and skirlie depend so much on the natural flavour of the meal that it is very important to use freshly milled meal if possible. If stored for too long it absorbs moisture and may develop a bitter taste or 'nip'. This is caused by 'lipase' enzymes which break down the fat into a bitter, unpleasant-tasting, fatty acid.

## TRADITIONAL MILLING

First the grain is dried out or 'conditioned' to a moisture content of around 15%. It is then kiln-dried: spread out on the kiln floor, consisting of perforated metal sheets with a smokeless-fuel-fired furnace some 20-30 feet below. The oats are turned by hand with large shovels until the moisture content is reduced to around 4-5% when the meal will have taken on its mild, nutty flavour. The milling begins with shelling the husks, then the grains are ground between stone-mill wheels to the required 'cuts' or grades.

There are five water-powered, stone-ground mills and several factory mills where kiln-drying and stone-grinding is the method used.

## OATMEAL 'CUTS' OR GRADES

**Pinhead**—used for haggis, oatmeal loaves.
**Rough**—used for porridge or brose, sometimes rough oatcakes.
**Medium/Rough**—used by butchers for mealie puddings.
**Medium/Fine**—porridge, brose, skirlie, baking.
**Super-fine**—used in baking and in oatcakes along with a coarser grade.

To make Pinhead oatmeal the whole kernel is cut in half with any floury meal sifted out. Medium/Rough is also known as Coarse Medium. Medium and fine grades are the most popular. There is also Oat flour which is distinct from Super-fine which still has a granule.

## OTHER OAT PRODUCTS

Rolled oats or Oatflakes were developed in America by the Quaker Oat Company in 1877 and are made by steaming and rolling pinhead oatmeal. While they have the obvious advantage of cooking more quickly than regular meal they have been specially heat-treated with some loss of flavour and nutrients and this also applies to the other 'instant' oat porridges now on the market. Jumbo Oatflakes are made by steaming and rolling the whole groat.

## DIETETIC VALUE

It has taken an American professor, James Anderson of the University of Kentucky College of Medicine, to find a good reason why we should eat more oats in future. Namely, that oats contain a gummy fibrous material (evident when porridge is made) which reduces blood cholesterol, blood sugar and fats. Researching the problems of diabetics, he discovered that oat bran is particularly rich in this 'water-soluble' fibre, much more so than wheat bran, which contains the 'unsoluble' cellulose and very little of the gum. Oats also score on value for money since they contain more protein, more fat, more iron, more of the B vitamins, more calcium and also slightly more calories.

# Barley

Despite the fact that today barley is mainly malted and used for distilling whisky, it was the chief crop in Scotland for all purposes from neolithic times till the introduction of oats in the Roman period. From this time onwards the oat crop developed but did not start to compete with barley till about the seventeenth century. By the end of the eighteenth century, oatmeal was the predominant food crop and barley used for distilling, making barley broth and bannocks. In the Highlands and Islands, and among the lower classes in the Lowlands, barley continued to be used for making bread and is still used today in the Hebrides and in Orkney.

This distinct Northern variety of barley grown in upland areas of Scotland since ancient times is known as 'bigg' or 'big' (*hordeum vulgare*) and makes a dark greyish-brown bannock. Barley from 'bigg' is called 'bere' (pronounced 'bare'). There is no sweetening in the Beremeal bannock, which allows the natural flavour of the meal to predominate. It has a stronger, more definite flavour than oatmeal with a slightly astringent 'earthy' tang which combines well with creamy Orkney Farmhouse cheeses. Bere is ground and made into Beremeal Bannocks by the local bakers. Stoneground Orkney Beremeal is sold in Orkney and also in many specialist shops, as well as butchers' shops and small village shops in rural areas in the rest of the country. It is mostly stone ground at the water-powered mill in Golspie, Sutherland.

Pearl barley, which is used for thickening Scotch Broth, is commonly available in all food shops. Barley flour is more of a specialist item but can be found in grain shops. Like oatmeal, they should both be bought in small quantities and stored in an airtight container. The flavour of this barley flour is not as strong as the northern variety but it still has the distinctive, earthy tang.

# Peasemeal

Roasted milled peas are used to make this very fine flour much loved for making brose (see p.10). Yellow field peas are first roasted which caramelises some of the sugar and darkens the colour. They are then ground through three pairs of water-powered millstones becoming successively finer with each grinding. Peasemeal was originally used in a mix with other meals in bannocks and scones.

# Wheat

In fertile, lowland areas, wheat flourished, but the rest of the country grew mostly oats and barley. South-east Scotland, the Laigh of Moray, parts of Fife and Easter Ross were all developed by monastic farmers in the eleventh and twelfth centuries and wheat was grown in these parts, but mainly as a cash crop. Not much seems to have been eaten by the common people except at feasts and festivals. Higher up the social ladder, wheaten bread was initially something of a prestige food, but it made its social descent gradually till some time in the early twentieth century when it became a staple item for all people.

# Oatcakes

Burns meant, of course, land of oatcakes and not the sweet-flavoured cakes that have long been associated with the word. But why should the oatcake have come about, and why wasn't it just called oat bread or oat biscuit? It's an etymological jigsaw puzzle of a problem, and to see the whole picture more clearly, it's necessary to go back to the original meanings of loaf, bread, cake and biscuit.

*Hear, Land o' Cakes, and brither Scots...*
Robert Burns (1759-1796)

## LOAF, BREAD, CAKE AND BISCUIT

'Loaf' is simple—it has always meant the undivided article. 'Bread' is more complicated since it originally meant only a 'piece or bit', later referred to as 'broken bread'. Finally it became known as the substance, 'bread'. The Lowland Scots and the Northern English have retained the original meaning of 'piece' when they say 'Gie's a piece'—meaning a piece of bread.

When bread, meaning the substance, was baked in a comparatively small flattened, round, oval or otherwise regularly shaped form, this was known as a 'cake of bread'. It was usually baked hard on both sides by being turned in the process. We still talk of something being 'caked' hard, or of making something into a hard, round, flattish 'cake' like a cake of soap. In Wales, the North of England and Scotland (all oat-growing areas) this meaning survives in the oatcake.

'Biscuit' seems to have had a different meaning, though the end result is also a small, round, flattened, unleavened item which was eaten as 'bread'. The word, though, has the meaning 'baked twice' and seems to have been applied to something which was made for its keeping qualities. In England, at any rate, about the middle of the sixteenth century, it had these features—'The bread was such as was provided to serue [sic] at need, or in Wars, for it was BISCUIT, this is twice baked and without leaven or salt'. Sailors ate 'sea biscuit' which they sometimes called just 'bread'. And that makes our modern biscuits and oatcakes direct descendants of the oldest form of bread, the ground grain plus water, shaped thin

5

and dried out, which also survives in things like Mexican Tortilla, Indian Chapati, American Johnnycakes and Chinese Pancakes.

## SCOTS OATCAKES—SHAPE AND FLAVOUR

In their most basic and primitive form, Scots oatcakes are made with ground oatmeal, salt, a little dripping and water to mix. The Hebridean oatcake (*Bonnach Imeach*) is usually made with fairly fine oatmeal and is rolled out to between a quarter and half-an-inch thick, making it a fairly substantial cake. The Highlanders prefer a thinner, crisper variety usually rolled out to less than a quarter-of-an-inch thick and made with medium oatmeal. Lowlanders often add some wheaten flour, which makes the texture less brittle, but they may also prefer a coarser oatmeal (pinhead) mixed with medium oatmeal, which makes an oatcake with a good bite to it. The taste in the north-east is for a rough oatcake. The heavier Hebridean variety is the exception to the general preference throughout the country for a crisp, crunchy cake, which means it must be rolled out as thinly as possible.

A quarter-of-an-inch is usually quoted in most cookery books; I find an eighth difficult to handle. They perhaps hit the right thickness in the Borders if C. Lowther is to be believed when he says in his diary, *Our Journal into Scotland*, 1629—'Three travellers in the Borders had oat bread cakes, baked a fifth of an inch thick on a griddle....' At the other extreme there was the 'mill bannock' which was made twelve inches round and one inch thick, with a hole in the middle to simulate the mill wheel.

The usual shape is a round bannock (the size depends on the diameter of the girdle) cut with a cross into four. In pagan times, the Greeks and Romans cut crosses on their buns to represent the four seasons. Today we continue the custom, with a different symbolism, when we put crosses on hot cross buns.

A three-cornered piece of oatcake, scone or shortbread, the fourth part of a bannock, is known as a 'farl'. Old-fashioned, girdle-baked oatcake 'farls' are not sold commercially today since they curl up at the edges and break easily. Most commercial oatcakes are oven baked and sold in packets.

The fat which is used will affect the flavour of the oatcake. Bacon fat is preferred for flavour, though other drippings from beef and lamb roastings are also good. Dripping of one form of another is better from the point of view of making a shorter cake. Butter and oil may also be used.

# OATCAKES IN THE DIET

'Oatcakes are especially good with herrings, sardines, cheese, curds, buttermilk, broth, and kail; or spread with butter and marmalade to complete the breakfast,' says F. Marian McNeill (*The Scots Kitchen*, 1929). Like porridge, oatcakes do not marry well with sweet things except perhaps with marmalade—but only when it is a bitter one. The delicate, mealy flavour goes well with unsalted butter and some crowdie (traditional Scottish version of cottage cheese) mixed with a little cream, the soft-cheese texture complementing the crunchy cake. All traditional soft cheeses are good with oatcakes (see p.229). Heather honey is often eaten with oatcakes. It doesn't have the sickly sweetness of other honey but a particular bitter-sweet tang which goes well with the oatmeal.

Records of meals show that oatcakes were commonly eaten at breakfast, dinner and supper as well as with tea at four o'clock in the afternoon. 'Oatcakes with milk' appears frequently in the diet charts of farm workers. In his *Description of Scotland*, in 1629, G. Buchanan says: 'They make a kind of bread, not unpleasant to the taste, of oats and barley, the only grain cultivated in these regions, and, from long practice, they have attained considerable skill in moulding the cakes. Of this they eat a little in the morning, and then contentedly go out a hunting, or engage in some other occupation, frequently remaining without any other food till evening.' Highland crofters who went up into the mountains with their flocks during the summer months and stayed in primitive 'sheelins' or 'bothies', made butter and cheese with cows' and sheep's milk which they ate with oatcake, according to Thomas Pennant writing in 1772.

Burns says that they 'are a delicate relish when eaten with warm ale'. Whether this means that amongst the very poorest classes they were regarded as a luxury is not clear, but in the poorhouse diets oatcakes are never mentioned. Porridge with milk, more quickly and easily made than oatcakes, were their basic fare.

*For Breakfast...the cheese was set out as before, with plenty of butter and barley cakes, and fresh baked oaten cakes, which no doubt were made for us: they were kneaded with cream and were excellent.*
Dorothy Wordsworth
*Recollections of a Tour Made in Scotland, 1803*

## TRADITIONAL GIRDLE OATCAKES
### with fine meal

These attractive, curled triangles have a crisp, 'short' bite to them. They can be cut into 4, 6 or 8 depending on when they are to be eaten, the largest size usually served at breakfast.

Mix and roll out only enough for one girdleful at a time. Making up large quantities means that the mixture cools, making it difficult to roll.

*Girdle Oatcakes*

*Quantity for one girdle*

**4 oz/125 g medium and fine oatmeal (about half and half or all medium oatmeal) (1 c)**

**1 tablespoon melted dripping***

**Large pinch of salt**

**Boiling water to mix (about ½ c)**

*Bacon fat is the most popular but lamb and beef dripping is also used. Oil and butter are not traditional but may be used.

## Mixing and Shaping

Mix the meals and salt. Add the dripping; stir this through the meal. When well mixed, make a well and add enough boiling water to make the whole come together into a soft, firm ball. The less water used the crisper the oatcake. Knead into a round, dust with fine oatmeal and roll out on a board dusted with fine oatmeal to a circle about ⅕ in (½ cm) thick. Keep bringing together round the edges to keep it from cracking. Cut with a cross into four or into 6 or 8. Leave to dry for about ½ hour before cooking—not necessary, but it helps to make the oatcakes curl.

## Heating the girdle

(A large, heavy-based frying-pan will do instead)

Heat the girdle slowly to get an even heat. It should be moderately hot for oatcakes, and the best way of testing is by holding your hand about 1 in (2½ cm) from the surface. It should feel hot, but not fiercely so. A steady, slow heat is needed for drying out oatcakes.

## Firing

Put the oatcakes on the girdle and leave till they have curled—they will curl upwards. If the cakes are too thick, they will not curl. Turn and leave for another five minutes till thoroughly dried out. This was originally done on a special toaster in front of the fire. Like toast, they should be put upright to cool since they continue to lose moisture till cold. Put in a toasting rack in front of the fire if you wish.

**Note:** Sometimes oatcakes were simply 'toasted very slowly at a distance from the fire, first on one side and then on the other on a toaster of open bars to let the moisture escape.' Meg Dods (1826).

## Storing

Keep in an airtight tin or buried in oatmeal, which gives them a nice mealy taste. If they have been kept for more than a week it is a good idea to dry them off slightly in the oven or in front of the fire to improve the flavour.

## Serving

They can be served slightly warm but not so hot that they make the butter run.

# OVEN OATCAKES
## with butter and pinhead oatmeal

This is a rougher-textured oatcake which is best eaten with a smooth, creamy cheese. Shorter in texture than a traditional girdle oatcake, wheaten bread flour is used to prevent them from breaking too easily. These oatcakes will not curl in the oven.

### To make

Preheat the oven to 350F/180C/Gas 4.

Put the meals, flour and sugar into a bowl. Mix thoroughly. Put the butter into a pan and melt with the water. When almost boiling, add to the meal and mix to a stiffish dough. It should come together easily. If it is too crumbly, add more boiling water. The less water that is added, the shorter the oatcake, but too little will mean the finished result will be too crumbly. Roll out and cut into rounds or squares, using oatmeal to prevent sticking. Bake slowly without browning for 30-40 minutes.

### *Oven Oatcakes*

8 oz/250 g medium oatmeal (2 c)

4 oz/125 g coarse oatmeal (1 c)

4 oz/125 g plain flour

3 oz/75 g salted butter

1 tsp sugar

4 fl oz/ 125 ml boiling water

# PORRIDGE

Goldilocks stole her porridge in the morning, soldiers marched on their morning porridge, and the Scottish peasant for many centuries started the day with a bowl of this sustaining food.

It is a morning ritual, porridge making: the handfuls of oatmeal running through your fingers into a large, iron pot filled with boiling water, while the other hand stirs with the long, tapered stick (spurtle); then the pot left at the side of the fire giving the familiar 'plot' every few minutes just to show it is still cooking.

It is true that it was also eaten for supper, and that leftovers were poured into the 'porridge drawer' in the Scotch dresser. The cold porridge set like a jelly and slices were cut off, known as 'caulders'. These were taken to the fields and eaten in the middle of the day, or slices were fried and eaten at night with eggs, fish or bacon.

### Type of meal

Porridge is usually made with medium-ground oatmeal, sometimes with pinhead added, which gives it a rough texture. Fine oatmeal produces too smooth a porridge for most Scottish tastes.

### Many ways of cooking but only one way of eating

Wooden bowls (china or earthenware plates lose heat too quickly) were filled from the central pot, often placed in the centre of the table, and the porridge was eaten with a carved horn spoon. The spoon was dipped into the hot porridge, leaving enough room for the milk or cream on the spoon. The traditional carved horn spoon is quite large, round and deep, at least the size of a large tablespoon. The milk or cream bowl or cup was placed beside the larger one and the spoonful of hot porridge was then

*I took my porridge i' the morning an' often got naething again till night, because I couldna afford it.*
W. Anderson
*The Poor of Edinburgh*, 1867

dipped into the cold milk/cream and eaten. This way the porridge remained hot till you had finished, whereas if the milk/cream is added to the porridge it cools it down too much. The essence of porridge eating is hot porridge, cold milk/cream.

There is nothing sacred about flavouring it only with salt. Robert Louis Stevenson made maps with golden syrup on top of his porridge as a child and many people like it with honey. The point about sticking to a savoury taste is that the flavour of the oatmeal, otherwise overpowered by sweetness, is preserved. The sharp, bitter flavour of molasses is good with porridge; a habit of many farm workers in the north-east was to eat their porridge flavoured with some of the molasses which had been bought in drums to feed the horses.

## To make porridge

**4 servings**

Put 2 pts/1¼ L water (5 c) into a pot and bring to the boil. Sprinkle in 4 oz/125 g medium oatmeal (1 c) with one hand, while stirring with a spurtle (long wooden stick) to prevent lumps forming. Lower the heat, cover and leave to simmer for anything up to 30 minutes.

It does reduce and thicken so it is very much a case of how thick you like it. I prefer it cooked for a shorter rather than a longer time, about five minutes. Apart from saving time, it is less jelly-like in texture and the grains still have some bite to them (reduce water by half).

Season with a generous pinch of salt and serve in bowls with a smaller bowl of milk, cream or buttermilk. Natural yoghurt, especially the Greek variety made from ewes' milk, is good with porridge and it is even better with a spoonful of molasses on top.

# BROSE

Brose is distinguished from porridge by its method of making. Single men living in bothies made brose in the morning: country people working in the fields or shepherds in the hills made brose. It was the quickest, cheapest way of making a meal.

In rural areas day began at daybreak, about five o'clock, with perhaps a bowl of brose, then four or five hours later, workers would return for breakfast. Dinner was in the middle of the day, supper at night.

Meal was put into a bowl—oatmeal, barley, pease meal, in whatever proportions available, and boiling water, hot milk or the liquid from cooking vegetables or meat was poured over. Often a piece of butter was mixed in and perhaps some dried fruit. This was frequently a supper first course, the meat and vegetables eaten after with oatcakes. Today we eat

*In these barracks the food is of the plainest and coarsest description: oatmeal forms its staple, with milk, when milk can be had, which is not always; and as the men have to cook by turns, with only half an hour or so given them in which to light a fire, and prepare the meal for a dozen or twenty associates, the cooking is invariably an exceedingly rough and simple affair. I have known mason-parties engaged in the central Highlands in building bridges, not unfrequently reduced by a tract of wet weather, that soaked their only fuel the turf and rendered it incombustible, to the extremity of eating their oatmeal raw, and merely moistened by a little water, scooped by the hand from a neighbouring brook.*
Hugh Miller
*My Schools and Schoolmasters,*
1854

Swiss Muesli for breakfast which is after all only a sophisticated version of Scottish Brose (see A Swiss/Scots Breakfast p.24).

## OATMEAL BROSE
### for breakfast

Put a handful of medium oatmeal or rolled oats into a bowl and pour over 1 cup of hot milk to cover the oatmeal, add a small piece of butter and stir while pouring. Season to taste with salt.

## PEASE BROSE
### as eaten in the bothy

This is made in the same way as oatmeal brose, but instead fine peasemeal is used which gives it a richer flavour. Lots of currants and butter can be added as well as honey or sugar for sweetening.

## ATHOLL BROSE

It was common to mix whisky with honey in the past and equally common to mix liquid with oatmeal. Bringing the two together in this potent way is credited to a Duke of Atholl during a Highland rebellion in 1475, who is said to have foiled his enemies by filling the well which they normally drank from with this ambrosial mixture, which so intoxicated them that they were easily taken.

Some traditional recipes leave in the whole oatmeal while this one, reputed to have come from a Duke of Atholl, uses only the strained liquid from steeping the oatmeal in water.

### To make

Put the oatmeal into a bowl and add the water. Leave for about an hour. Put into a fine sieve and press all the liquid through. (Use the remaining oatmeal for putting into bread or making porridge—see p.10). Add honey to the sieved liquid and mix well. Pour into a large bottle and fill up with the whisky. Shake well before use.

### Uses

May be drunk as a liqueur; is often served at festive celebrations such as New Year, or may be mixed with stiffly whipped cream and served with shortbread as a sweet.

*Atholl Brose*

**6 oz/175 g medium oatmeal (1½ c)**

**4 tablespoons heather honey**

**1½ pt/¾ L whisky (3¾ c)**

**¾ pt/450 ml water (2 c)**

## Mixed Grain Porridge

*Mixed Grain Porridge*

8 oz/250 g each of: oatmeal or rolled oats; wheat flakes; rye flakes; whole barley; sunflower seeds mixed with pumpkin seeds and mixed nuts; raisins

4 oz/125 g dried milk powder

2-4 tablespoons of drinking chocolate

# MIXED-GRAIN PORRIDGE/BROSE
## (Muesli)

This mix is made up by a mountaineer friend who takes it to the hills and uses it as survival food for long trips. The drinking chocolate is his innovation.

### To make

Mix ingredients and reconstitute with water or milk as required. It should be soaked overnight or at least for a few hours before eating. It can also be cooked as for porridge.

# MIXED-GRAIN GIRDLE SCONES

The leftover porridge mix can be mixed with self-raising flour (1 cup porridge mix to 2 cups flour) and mixed with an egg and water or milk to a soft consistency and cooked as for pancakes on both sides on a hot girdle.

# BANNOCKS

*...bannocks and a shave of cheese Will make a breakfast that a laird might please.*
Allan Ramsay
(1682-1758)
*The Gentle Shepherd*

A bannock is something large and round, which was originally cooked on the girdle, thicker and softer than an oatcake. In the past the type of meal used depended on what was available, with great variations throughout the year and from district to district. Despite this, there is constant reference to barley bannocks by travellers describing their meals.

Thomas Pennant, in 1772, talks about the 'fresh eggs, fresh barley bannocks, and tolerable porter, together with some smoked salmon' which they enjoyed in an Inn at 'Cree in La Roche' (presumably Crianlarich since he was travelling up Glen Falloch).

James Russel, writing in the nineteenth century, says that 'Oatcakes and bannocks of barley meal with an admixture of pease, were the ordinary table fare. Wheaten bread was scarcely known.'

Thomas Somerville, a minister in Jedburgh from 1741 to 1830, writes in his diary that—'Though wheaten bread was partly used, yet cakes or "bannocks" of barley and peasemeal, and oatcakes formed the principal household bread in gentlemen's families; and in those of the middle class on ordinary occasions, no other bread was ever thought of.'

## OLD-FASHIONED BANNOCKS
### without rising agent

Early forms of bannocks were made without raising agents, which may sound unpalatable to modern tastes, but the barley bannock which F. Marian McNeill describes in *The Scots Kitchen* as the 'old method' produces a bannock which is more like an Indian chapati in style.

Its charm lies in the barley flavour, and in the contrasts of texture; the soft inside and harder, but not quite crisp, outside.

Pre-heat the girdle till fairly hot. Flour lightly.

### Making up the dough

Put the milk into a pan, add the butter and heat through to melt the butter; add the salt. Stir in the meal; it should come together into a softish paste a bit like the consistency for choux pastry. Turn out onto a floured board and knead lightly to a smooth ball, dusting well on top with barley flour. Press out to about 6 in (15 cm) in diameter.

### Firing

Place on girdle, press out evenly with your knuckles to about 10 in x ½ in (25 x 1 cm) thick and cook on a moderate girdle till brown on one side, about 10–15 minutes. Turn, using two fish slices, or cut in half and turn in two pieces. (Bannock spathes, now only to be found in museums, were used in the past for this job.) Cook on the other side for 10–15 minutes. Place on a cooling rack and eat warm.

*Old-Fashioned Bannocks*

½ pt/300 ml milk (1¼ c scant)

1 oz/25 g butter (¼ stick)

4 oz/125 g barley flour (may be mixed with peasemeal) (1 c)

Salt to taste

## BARLEY BANNOCKS
### wafer thin

Another early form was made with a much thinner mixture poured onto the girdle like large Breton pancakes (*crêpes*). Franco-Scottish connections may have had something to do with this, since there is a striking resemblance between the large Scottish girdles (a woman in Edinburgh had one five feet across which was used on a flat open hearth), and the large iron plates used in Brittany for making *crêpes*.

In his *Travels in England and Scotland in 1799*, Faujas de St Ford talks about 'barley cakes, folded over'—it is possible these are the cakes he was referring to.

Mix ingredients to a pouring consistency and cook on both sides, as for French *crêpes*. Roll up with cream cheese, honey or preserves.

*Barley Bannocks*

4 oz/125 g beremeal or barley flour (1 c)

3 eggs

1 oz/25 g melted butter (¼ stick)

Water to mix

## *Modern Barley Bannocks*

4 oz/125 g Beremeal or barley flour (1 c)

1 tablespoon plain flour

1 teaspoon baking soda

Pinch of salt

Buttermilk to mix

---

# MODERN BARLEY BANNOCKS
## with raising agent

These are the round, light bannocks which bakers in Orkney make usually about the size of an outstretched hand. (6 in/15 cm approx.)

### To make

Heat the girdle till moderately hot and flour well.

Sift the dry ingredients together and mix with the buttermilk to a soft dough. Put onto the hot girdle; dust the top with flour and press down lightly with your fingers into a 6-in (15 cm) round. Bake on both sides, turning once, about 5-10 minutes each side.

---

## *Oatmeal Bannocks*

12 oz/350 g fine oatmeal (3 c)

1 teaspoon salt

1 teaspoon bicarbonate of soda

1 tablespoon sugar

1 tablespoon syrup

1 pt/600 ml milk (2½ cups)

2 eggs

---

# OATMEAL BANNOCKS

This sweet, crumpet-style bannock comes from the north-east where they call it a 'Sauty Bannock'. The name is thought to come from the old superstition of adding some magic soot from the fire on special festive nights such as Halloween and Fastern's Een. They are thicker and heavier than the barley ones and should be eaten warm from the girdle.

### To make

Dissolve the syrup in the milk and add to the oatmeal, salt, and sugar. Soak overnight. When ready to cook add the eggs and soda.

Mix in more milk if necessary to make a thickish, creamy mixture.

Pre-heat the girdle till fairly hot and grease lightly.

Drop the mixture in spoonfuls onto the hot girdle—they should spread to 5-6 in (12-15 cm). Fire on both sides; pile on top of one another and wrap in a cloth to keep them soft. Serve hot, with butter and jam or crowdie.

---

*It fell about the Martinmas time
And a gay time it was then, O
that oor guidwife had puddens to mak'
And she boiled them in a pan, O.*
Anon.

---

# MEALIE PUDDINGS AND SKIRLIE

In the days before the turnip was used as winter feed for animals, Martinmas, 11 November, was the time for killing the animals which people could not afford to keep during the winter. 'Mairt' was an incredibly busy time though several families would work together to get the job done. Every scrap of the beast was used—the meat mostly salted down and puddings made from the innards. Pudding is the original name for the innards of an animal, and Pudding Lane in London got its name, not because people ate puddings there, but because this was where the butchers used to wash out the innards of the animals (see Haggis Pudding p.135).

Mealie puddings, black and white, were made when beef cattle were killed. This is now mostly a butcher's job though some people still make their own. The oatmeal, onions, suet from the animal and salt and pepper were mixed in a large basin. Blood from the animal was added to make the 'bleedy' ones. The intestines were thoroughly washed, usually in a burn, and then stuffed loosely with the mixture. A writer in the *North East Review* writes nostalgically of the puddings his mother used to make— 'Come time the skins were a' filled up, and tied, and jabbit wi' a darner, and they were ready for the pot. They were biled an oor. It wis easy the langest oor I mind on. My teeth wid be watering till I slivert again, and when they lifted the lid o' the pot to see the water wisna biling in—oh! the guff that filled the kichie. The tastings, or the preens as my mother ca'ed them, were first oot and nae wirds could tell ye fit they tastit like— as the poet his't—"warm-reekin', rich," ye dinna see the like the day.'

Skirlie is made with the same ingredients as mealie puddings but the mixture is fried in a pan. The noise of the frying or 'skirl' as in skirl of the pipes gave it its original name of 'skirl-in-the-pan'.

Skirlie has several uses. It can be served with roast meat and is particularly good with game. It can also be used as a stuffing for any kind of poultry or game or made into a steamed pudding using either a cloth or bowl.

Medium or coarse oatmeal is used. The type of fat varies, though fresh beef suet, meat or bacon dripping make the best-flavoured Skirlie. Chopped onions are most commonly used, though an expatriate Scot told me recently of a Skirlie she makes using leeks, instead of onions.

## To make Skirlie

Melt the fat in a frying pan. When hot, add the onion and cook till soft and transparent but not coloured. (Some people add water at this point to soften the onion, but this seems to be a regional variation. It is a good idea if it is to be used for stuffing, since it helps to hold the mixture together.) Now add enough oatmeal to absorb the fat (about 4 oz/125 g/ 1 c), season well with salt and pepper and serve.

*Skirlie*

**2 oz/50 g fat**

**1 medium onion, finely chopped**

**4 oz/125 g/1 c oatmeal**

**Salt and pepper**

# OATMEAL AND BARLEY BREADS

Challenged by one of the leading bakers of good bread in Glasgow to make an oatmeal loaf—he thought it impossible since oatmeal has no gluten—the following breads are the results of my experiments, with some help from Bernard Clayton's *The Complete Book of Breads* (Simon and Schuster, 1973).

## Oatmeal Bread

6 oz/175 g rolled oats (2 c)

2 oz/50 g lard/butter (½ stick) or 4 tablespoons oil

2-3 teaspoons salt

6 oz/175 g molasses or treacle (½ c)

¾ pt/450 ml lukewarm water (2 c, scant)

1 oz/50 g fresh yeast (1 tablespoon dried or 1 pkt Easy Bake)

1¼ lb/625 g strong white bread flour (5 c)

2 eggs

2 tablespoons rolled oats to coat tins

2 x 1 lb/500 g loaf tins

# OATMEAL BREAD
## with molasses or treacle

### Makes 2 loaves

This striking loaf, richly brown on the inside, has a light, speckled crust produced by lining the tin with rolled oats.

Pre-heat the oven to 375F/190C/Gas 5.

### To make

Put the oats, lard/butter or oil and salt into a bowl. Dissolve the molasses in the lukewarm water and pour over the oats. Activate the yeast if dried by mixing with a little of the warm molasses water or mix the fresh yeast with a teaspoonful of sugar. Add the yeast (just stir in the packet of Easy Bake) to the oats and stir in half of the flour. Beat well for three or four minutes—this can be done with the mixer. Beat in eggs and then work in the remaining flour gradually till the dough is soft and sticky but not too dry. Leave for 10 minutes to rest.

### Kneading and rising

Turn onto a board and knead till the dough is smooth and elastic. Cover and put to rise in a warm place for about 1½ hours or until the dough has doubled in size.

### Shaping

Grease tin well with lard or oil and coat the base and sides with rolled oats. Knead dough for a few minutes and then divide into two. Shape into loaves and put into tins. Cover with cling-film and put back in a warm place till they have risen to double their size again. Brush with milk and sprinkle on top with rolled oats. Bake for ¾ to 1 hour or until they make a hollow sound when tapped on the base.

Cool thoroughly.

# OATMEAL BREAD ROLLS

### 6-8 rolls

These moist, well-flavoured rolls are sprinkled on top with rolled oats before they are baked.

Pre-heat the oven to 375F/190C/Gas 5.

### Mixing the dough

Dissolve the dried yeast in a little of the water and leave in a warm place till it froths, or blend the fresh yeast with a little sugar, or sprinkle the packet of Easy Bake yeast in with the flour.

Put half the flour, along with the oats, sugar, yeast, salt, butter and water into a bowl and beat for at least 2 minutes either by hand or with the mixer. Then add the remaining flour gradually, mixing in by hand till the right soft, sticky consistency is reached.

## Kneading

Turn the dough onto a lightly floured board and knead till it becomes smooth and elastic and leaves the hand cleanly. Add more flour if it is too sticky.

## Rising

Put in a bowl, cover and stand in a warm place till it has risen to double in size.

## Shaping and proving

Knock back the dough and knead for a few minutes. Divide into 6 or 8 pieces. Leave to rest for a few minutes. Shape into rolls, place on baking tray, cover with lightly oiled cling-film and put in a warm place till they have risen again to double in size.

## Baking

Brush the tops with milk and sprinkle with rolled oats. Bake for about 30 minutes. Test by tapping the bottom of one—it should sound hollow.

### *Oatmeal Bread Rolls*

**5 oz/150 g rolled oats (1½ c)**

**12 oz/325 g strong white bread flour (3 c)**

**½ oz/15 g fresh yeast, ¼ oz/7 g dried (1 packet of Easy Bake)**

**2 tablespoons sugar**

**1 tablespoon salt**

**2 oz/50g softened butter (½ stick)**

**12 fl oz/50 ml warm water (1½ c)**

## SOUR DOUGH OATMEAL BREAD

Pioneer Americans perfected this idea of rising the dough, not by commercial yeast which was unavailable, but by a bubbling pot of aromatic starter, making use of the wild yeasts which are all around us. It seems that the Scots in remote areas had also discovered this phenomenon— 'What some of them did was to twist an oak rod, four to eight inches long, boil it in wort (unfermented beer) and dry it well; then, when they steeped it in wort a second time, it fermented and made yeast'. *Domestic Life of Scotland in the Eighteenth Century*, Marjorie Plant 1952.

The dough is firstly a flour and liquid mixture which is allowed to ferment naturally in a warm place. Then more starchy substance is added for the yeast to feed on, making a 'sponge'—now it is thoroughly fermenting and the yeast cells multiplying by the million. The life and movement in this dough is a constant source of wonder—the finished loaf, with its unique flavour and aroma, a great delight.

## Cooked Potato Starter

*Cooked Potato Starter*

4 tablespoons cornmeal (fine)

5 tablespoons sugar

3½ teaspoons salt

8 fl oz/250 ml milk (1 c)

3 medium potatoes and
   cooking liquid

## Sour Dough Oatmeal Bread

*Sour Dough Oatmeal Bread*
*Day before baking*

¾ pt/450 ml boiling water (2 c)

8 oz/250 g medium oatmeal
   (2 c)

8 oz/250 g strong white flour
   (2 c)

3 tablespoons brown sugar

12 fl oz/50 ml Cooked Potato
   Starter

*Add the next day*

12 fl oz/50 ml warm water
   (1¼ c)

4 tablespoons dried milk
   powder

½ teaspoon ginger

5 teaspoons salt

4 oz/125 g butter (1 stick)

6 tablespoons syrup (maple)

2 tablespoons brown sugar

## How to make a Cooked Potato Starter

Blend the cornmeal with milk and add 2 tablespoons of sugar and 1½ teaspoons of salt. Put into a pan and bring to the boil, stirring constantly. Pour into a small bowl, cover and leave in a warm place for 2-4 days till it ferments and looks light and frothy.

Reserve the liquid from boiling the potatoes and make up to 2 pts/ 1.15 dl (5 c). Purée or sieve the potatoes and add to the liquid. Mix through 3 tablespoons sugar and 2 teaspoons salt. When cool, stir in the fermented cornmeal. Cover and leave in a warm place overnight, stirring down when it becomes bubbly. Next day put into a large jar, cover with some foil rather than a lid, since it continues to give off gas, and put into the refrigerator to age for about 3 days before using. Stir well each time before using. Replenish when the starter has been reduced to 1½-2 cups adding a new potato, potato water, sugar and salt mixture made as before.

## Day before baking

Pour boiling water over oatmeal and when lukewarm add flour, sugar and starter. Stir well, cover and leave overnight in a warm place.

## The next day

Pre-heat oven to 350F/180C/Gas 4.

Prepare 4 x 1 lb/500 g loaf tins.
   Add the water, milk powder, ginger, salt, butter, syrup and sugar.

## Mixing and kneading

Stir well then start adding flour—2 lb/1 kg (8 c). Add half to begin and mix for about two minutes, then add remaining flour gradually till the dough forms a soft mass. Turn out and knead till it is smooth and elastic and comes away easily from your hands.

## Rising

Put dough back into the bowl, cover and put in a warm place till it has risen to double its size.

## Knocking back and shaping

Knock down the dough and turn out onto a floured board. Divide into loaf-sized pieces. Knead for a few minutes, shape and put into tins. Brush the tops with melted butter, cover with lightly oiled cling-film and leave in a warm place to rise to double their volume.

## Baking

Bake for about 1 hour, test by removing from tins and knocking on base when it should sound hollow. Cool thoroughly.

**Note:** May also be rolled out into a rectangle and spread with a layer of maple syrup, about 2 tablespoons, cover with 1 tablespoon ground cinnamon and sprinkle a few currants on top. Roll up and put in loaf tin.

# BUTTERMILK BREAD
## with oatmeal and barley

This is a moist, aromatic bread which is best eaten with cheese or a thick soup-stew. It can be baked in a round bannock shape and cut in wedges. I bake it in a 10-in (25 cm) cast iron pot with a lid in the style of the Irish bastible pot (see p.195). A chicken brick also works well though the finished loaf is a slightly odd shape.

## To make

Pre-heat the oven to 350F/180C/Gas 4.

Put all the meals, the wheatgerm and the bicarbonate of soda into a large bowl and mix well.

Grease the tin—2 lb/500 g loaf tin or 7 in (12 cm) round pot with lid which can be put in the oven or a chicken brick. Coat the sides with sunflower and/or sesame seeds.

Make a well in the centre and add the honey, egg, oil, salt and buttermilk/soured milk. Mix this together with the outstretched fingers of one hand. Once it is well mixed, begin bringing in the flour from the sides. The mixing should be done as quickly as possible and it is important to have a large enough bowl. When the mixture comes together as a soft, but not sloppy, elastic dough it is ready. If it is too stiff the bread will be heavy.

Either shape into a round, divide into four, and bake on a greased baking tray, or make into a loaf and bake in a tin or pot with a lid. Bake the round for 30-40 minutes. The covered loaf will take longer, about an hour. To test, remove from tin and knock on the base: it will make a hollow sound if ready. Remove and cool thoroughly.

*Buttermilk Bread*

**4 oz/125 g medium oatmeal (1 c)**

**4oz/125 g beremeal or barley flour (1 c)**

**12 oz/350 g wholemeal flour (3 c)**

**2 oz/60 g wheatgerm**

**1 heaped teaspoon bicarbonate of soda**

**1 tablespoon heather honey**

**1 egg**

**2 tablespoons extra-virgin olive oil**

**1 teaspoon salt**

**1 pt/600 ml buttermilk or fresh milk soured with the juice of a lemon (2½ c)**

**Oil for greasing/sunflower and/or sesame seeds for coating tin/pot**

*A huge pot hung over the fire which leapt in a shining black-and-steel range. A black kettle stood on one hob, a brown teapot on the other. Steam rose gently from the kettle and thickly from the great black pot, whence also came a continuous 'purring' noise and the wonderful smell.*

Jennifer Gowan
'Friendship is a Clootie Dumpling', *Scottish Field*, July 1966

## *Clootie Dumpling*

4 oz/125 g beef suet, finely chopped, or Atora pre-prepared (1 c)

4 oz/125 g self-raising flour (1 c)

6 oz/175 g fine white breadcrumbs

2 oz/50 g fine oatmeal (½ c)

1 teaspoon bicarbonate of soda

12 oz/350 g raisins/sultanas mixed (3 c)

2 teaspoons each—cinnamon, ginger

1 grated nutmeg

2 tablespoons black treacle

2 tablespoons golden syrup

2 eggs

4 oz/125 g tart cooking apple, grated

10 fl oz/300 ml buttermilk or fresh milk soured with the juice of a lemon

# OTHER USES OF OATMEAL AND BARLEY

## CLOOTIE DUMPLING

### 8-10 servings

Not as spicy rich as a Christmas pudding, or even as sweet, this delicately flavoured, misshapen mound with its shiny skin is as good fried with bacon the next day as when it first comes steaming from the pot. Traditional for birthdays and other festive occasions, my childhood memories remain vivid of my white-haired grandmother dishing out a huge steaming dumpling to her large family New Year gathering, its aroma wafting across the table as we waited for our plateful which always had a 'surprise' silver coin. We ate it with creamy custard. It is named after the cloth 'clout' (pronounced cloot) which the pudding is boiled in.

To cook in the traditional way, it should be boiled in a large cloth, though it can also be cooked in a greased pudding bowl but the result will not have the 'skin' so greatly loved by dumpling fans.

### Preparing the cloth

Half fill a very large pot with water and bring to the boil. Place a metal grid or upside-down saucer in the base to prevent the dumpling sticking. Add a large piece of white cotton or linen cloth approx. 22 in (55 cm) to the boiling water and leave for a few minutes. Lift out with some tongs, allow excess water to drip off then lay out flat on table. Dust a layer of flour over the cloth (this forms the 'skin').

### Making the dumpling

Put all the dry ingredients into a large bowl. Mix well together. Make a well in the centre. Add the treacle, syrup, eggs, grated apple, and buttermilk/soured milk. Mix to a soft, but not sloppy, consistency. If it is too soft, the dumpling may split when you turn it out. If too stiff the dumpling may turn out too firm and solid. Put the mixture into the centre of the prepared cloth, draw up the edges and tie with some string, leaving an extra length of string to hold the dumpling in position with, also leaving some room for the dumpling to expand. Pat it round the edges to make it a good, round shape

### Steaming

Add the dumpling. The water should come about three-quarters of the way up. If possible, tie the string to the handle so that the dumpling is held up in the pot and will keep its shape better. Bring to simmering point, cover and cook for 4-5 hours. Check the water level occasionally.

(Alternatively use a 3 pt/1½ L pudding bowl [English: pudding basin], cover the top with foil or greaseproof paper and tie securely.)

## To turn out

Fill a large basin or sink with cold water. It should be large enough to hold the dumpling. Have ready another bowl that the dumpling will just fit into. Also a large, round, heated plate or ashet. First dip the pudding into cold water for about 60 seconds. This releases the skin from the cloth. Now put it into the bowl and untie the string. Open out the cloth and hang over the sides of the bowl. Put the serving dish over the bowl, invert it and then remove the cloth carefully.

## Drying off and serving

Dry off in the oven or in front of the fire. Sprinkle with caster sugar and eat with cream or custard. Leftovers provide useful breakfasts when fried with bacon, or slices may be wrapped in foil and reheated in the oven.

## SWEET HAGGIS

A simple savoury-sweet boiled pudding which is made using the same method as a Clootie Dumpling, but the mixture depends not on spices for flavouring but on the oatmeal combined with dried fruit, suet, and sugar. It is eaten as a main course with fried bacon and eggs when hot. Cold it can be sliced and fried like a mealie pudding.

## To make

Put all the ingredients into a bowl and mix with water to a fairly stiff paste. Cook as for Clootie Dumpling.

**Sweet Haggis**

12 oz/350 g medium oatmeal

4 oz/125 g plain flour

10 oz/300 g beef suet, finely chopped

4 oz/125 g currants

4 oz/125 g raisins

Salt and pepper

Water to mix

## SWEET OATEN PUDDING
### with raspberries

All old Scottish cookery books have versions of this pudding. Mostly, the recipes are for a kind of rich custard pudding which has been thickened with oatmeal and well-flavoured with nutmeg, mace, lemon and brandy. The mixture was usually boiled in a cloth, as in the clootie dumpling, though it was also baked in a pie shell.

The following recipe is a modern adaptation using the original flavourings and ingredients, plus raspberries for colour and flavour, but changing

## Sweet Oaten Pudding

¾ pt/450 ml milk (2 c)

2 oz/50 g medium oatmeal (½ c)

1 large egg, beaten

1 small lemon, zest and juice

2 tablespoons caster sugar

½ oz/15 g gelatine (2 envelopes)

¼ pt/150 ml double cream,
   lightly whipped (¾ c, scant)

Blade of mace

A little grated nutmeg

the method to make a light cream sweet.

Soak the oatmeal and blade of mace in milk overnight (or at least for a few hours).

### To make pudding

Put the oatmeal mixture into a pan and bring to the boil, simmer for 3-4 minutes. Pour into a bowl and add the beaten egg, grated lemon rind, grated nutmeg and sugar to taste. The heat of the mixture will thicken the egg. Put the gelatine and lemon juice into a cup and set in a pan of simmering water. Dissolve gelatine and allow to cool a little, add to the mixture then fold in the cream.

### Serving

Put some fresh raspberries into individual glasses and pour the mixture on top. When set, garnish with raspberries and cream or make a raspberry purée (p.144) and pour a layer on top when set.

## Buttered Oats

1½ oz/40 g butter

2 oz/50 g brown sugar (2
   tablespoons)

4 oz/125 g rolled oats (1¼ cup)

4-5 medium cooking apples

½ lemon

# BUTTERED OATS

I first came across this very useful oatmeal mixture as 'Oatmeal Topping' (an Oat Information Council recipe, 1984), renaming it to something which more effectively captures the richness of its character. Its popularity has now been assured as mainstream breakfast-cereal manufacturers have cottoned on to its sales potential, renaming it 'crunchy'. It is very simple to make and can be made in quantity then stored in an airtight jar and used as a handy 'crumble' top for cooked or uncooked fruits.

Making it yourself also means you can regulate the sugar and fat content, since some of the manufactured versions have a very high sugar content as well as flavourless oils and fats. Nuts can be added and it can also be mixed, Cranachan-style, through cream and soft fruit. It is also good as a layer in the base of the tin when making particularly moist cakes, or as a cake topping. (See Mincemeat Sandwich Cake, p.209) I have used it mostly in layers with stewed apples, something in the style of a Danish Apple Cake, using buttered oats instead of breadcrumbs.

### To make

Melt the butter in a pan and add sugar and oats. Mix well.

Spread out in tin and toast in a moderate oven till golden brown.

### Apple purée

Peel, core and slice the cooking apples. Toss them in the juice of ½ lemon and put into a casserole with a tight-fitting lid. Bake in a moderate oven till apples are soft and fluffy. They should take about 30 minutes. Beat up with sugar to taste. Cool.

## Finishing the dish

Using a straight-sided soufflé dish or any other suitable sweet-dish or pie-dish, arrange a layer of oats, then apples, and so on, till all are used up. Finish with a layer of oats and leave at room temperature for about an hour for the flavours to blend.

# WALNUT AND OAT BISCUITS

A coarse-textured, hearty biscuit, richly flavoured with walnuts, vanilla and oats.

## To make

Pre-heat the oven to 350F/180C/Gas 4.

Prepare a greased baking tray.

Beat together the butter, sugar, egg, water and vanilla essence till creamy.

Mix in the flour, salt, bicarbonate of soda, rolled oats and walnuts.

Using some extra rolled oats on the board, roll out the mixture into a long sausage shape about 2 in (5 cm) in diameter and then put in a cool place for an hour to harden. Cut with a sharp knife into ¼-in (1 cm) slices and place on baking tray. Bake for 15-20 minutes till lightly brown.

*Walnut and Oat Biscuits*

6 oz/175 g butter (¾ c)

6 oz/175 g brown sugar (1 c, generous)

4 oz/125 g granulated sugar (½ c)

1 egg

4 teaspoons water

1 teaspoon vanilla essence

4 oz/125 g plain flour (1 c)

1 level teaspoon salt

½ teaspoon bicarbonate of soda

9 oz/250 g rolled oats (3 c)

4 oz/125 g walnuts, finely chopped (1 c)

## A SWISS/SCOTS BREAKFAST

*A Swiss/Scots Breakfast*

4 oz/120 g rolled oats (1¼ c)

½ pt/300 g milk (1¼ c)

1 grated apple

2 oz/50 g chopped hazelnuts
(½ c)

Juice of 1 orange

Juice of 1 lemon

1 orange, segmented

1 banana, sliced

2 oz/50 g fresh pineapple,
sliced (½ c)

A leading exponent of natural food, the Swiss chef Anton Mosimann, created this special blend of fresh fruit flavours as a background to mellow oats (*Cuisine Naturelle*, 1985). As is often the case in the realms of food, similar customs develop in different countries with minor variations: the old-fashioned Scots Brose finding its counterpart in modern Swiss Muesli.

The recipe can be adapted to make it suit any meal with a flexible approach to ingredients and quantities.

### To make

Soak the oats and milk overnight.

Add the grated apple, hazelnuts, orange and lemon juice, the segmented orange, banana and pineapple.

Sweeten to taste with honey.

For a sweet, garnish with

¼ pt/150 ml double cream (¾ cup)
2 oz/50 g brambles (blackberries) (½ c)
A few strawberries
Pineapple leaves

## OTHER RECIPES USING OATMEAL

Fresh Herring or Mackerel Fried in Oatmeal p.38. Dulse Cakes p.86. Minced Collops p.112. Beef Olives p.113. Cream Crowdie (Cranachan) p.150. Oatmealed Potatoes p.167. Sautéed Chicken and Leeks with Skirlie p.172. Buttered Kale p.181. A Cake with Apples in It p.208.

# 2
# FISH

While haddock, herring, mackerel, cod, sole and whiting might make up most of the consumption of fish in Scotland, up to a dozen other species are regularly caught and landed from unpolluted Scottish waters. So where are they? Some are on the slabs of the more enterprising Scottish fishmongers while the rest are exported. Yet this is not to say that the Scots are unenthusiastic about eating fish. The variety may be limited but they continue, as they have in the past, to consume more fish per head of the population than the rest of the UK, and more in a fresh state rather than frozen or processed.

Inbuilt tradition, plus the fact that better prices are to be had elsewhere for such high-quality fish, contribute to the restricted range of Scottish fish consumption. In the last decade or so, however, attitudes have been changing. More fishmongers have taken the initiative to display a more representative selection of fish and more Scots are adventuring into species of fish and shellfish they would previously not have considered eating. Part of this success has been due to fishmongers who are willing to explain the best treatment for unfamiliar fish. But caterers also have made better use of the Scottish catch and awakened appetites to what is an important food asset.

Earliest recorded fishing traditions were on the East Coast where there is an abundance of natural harbours. West Coast fishing was a later development when the people lost their lands and turned to the sea for sustenance. On the Islands, the Hebrides, Orkney and particularly Shetland, people were born and bred to a long tradition of fishing. Shetland fisher-people went to the Faroes, Iceland and Greenland and established fishing in these parts long before fishermen from the rest of Scotland.

Off the Western Highlands and Islands, at one time, there were huge shoals of herring, haddock, whiting and mackerel. There were also good supplies of salmon, cod, ling, eel, turbot and other flat fish, as well as innumerable shellfish, including cockles, oysters, lobsters and scallops in plenty. Round the Hebrides and Orkney, whales and seals were eaten. Whale flesh was thought better boiled than roasted, while the liver was

*There is an element of exotic interest in seafood which is perhaps not sufficiently exploited in this country.*
A.D. McIntyre (Director, Marine Laboratory, Aberdeen) *The Sea and Fresh Waters*, 1985

regarded as a great delicacy—'It smells like Violets, tastes pleasantly, and is very nourishing being salted.' Guy Miege, *The Present State of Great Britain and Ireland*, 1738.

While fishermen in those days had no concern for preservation of the fish stocks, today our established species, especially the top six, are under threat due to overfishing. Herring and mackerel stocks are particularly vulnerable and stocks are now monitored by scientists and the fishing closed (as it was in 1977 for herring) when they reach what is considered a dangerously low level. Though there is little or no other way of managing wild stocks of fish, the possibilities in the future of farming the sea may be one way of stabilising supply. The main fish being farmed in Scotland are Atlantic salmon, while other species being farmed in smaller numbers are sea trout, turbot, Arctic char and rainbow trout. But they make up only a very small percentage of the total fish production from Scottish waters.

I should like to have devoted more of this chapter to the fish which are caught and landed in Scotland but do not reach Scottish fishmongers' slabs. Instead, here is a list of them and and a few of the best books, firstly, for identifying them and, secondly, for cooking them.

**Brill, Catfish, Conger Eels, Dabs, Dogfish, Dover Sole, Flounders, Gurnard, Hake, Halibut, Ling, Lythe, Megrims, Monkfish, Norway Pout, Plaice, Saith, Sand Eels, Shark, Skate, Torsk, Turbot, Witches, Sprats.**

Alan Davidson, *North Atlantic Seafood* (Macmillan, 1979/Penguin, 1980).
Jane Grigson, *Fish Cookery* (Penguin, 1975).
Sonia Stevenson, *A Fresh Look at Fish* (Mitchell Beazley, 1996).

# Atlantic Salmon (*Salmo Salar*)

## LIFE CYCLE

Hatched in the purest of Scotland's freshwater rivers, after two years or so salmon migrate to the sea, grow fat over several years then return to their native waters, fight their way back upstream to where they were hatched and then spawn. The female lays her eggs on the river-bed and the male fertilises them. By this time, both fish are badly run down and either die or go back to sea to return another year.

The terminology for the various stages starts with Fry, which is just after the salmon hatch and come out of the gravel, on to Parr which is the two-year period of growth in their home river. Just before they leave, they change physically to equip them for seawater and at this point are called Smolts. Salmon which come back after one year are called Grilse and weigh 2 lbs-8 lbs depending on the richness of their sea feeding grounds. Fish which come back after two, three or four years are Adult Salmon and the best quality are caught early in the season when still fat and flavoursome from the rich sea feeding grounds. They are likely to weigh from 8 lbs upwards to about 60 lb. When, and if, they reach their place of hatching, the female spawns and the male ejects his milt on top of the spawn. After this, they either die from exhaustion and lack of food (Spent Kelts) or they make it back to sea (Mended Kelts) and return to spawn again. All Pacific salmon spawn and then die, whereas 5% of Atlantic salmon return to spawn again. They usually spend two to three winters in the sea, maximum five. The oldest recorded salmon was caught on Loch Maree in Wester Ross: it was thirteen years old and had spawned four times.

# Wild Scottish Salmon

The early salmon fisheries were on the Tay, Spey, Tweed, Don and Dee, producing large catches which were eaten fresh in summer and 'kippered' (smoked) in winter. While supplies remained plentiful for the best part of the nineteenth century, there has been a gradual decline in the twentieth century. Overfishing and netting have been two of the problems, others have been less easy to define. In top condition, early in the season, their flavour is unbeatable, when they should be served very simply with plain, boiled, floury potatoes, butter, fresh green peas and lemon.

## SEASON

Lasts from February to September with variations for rod-caught fish on some rivers. Most plentiful from May-July.

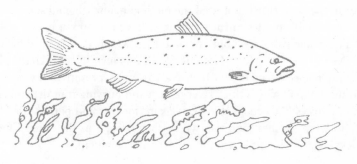

# Farmed Salmon

Salmon farming began on the West Coast in 1969 and has spread to the islands, particularly Shetland and Orkney where they market their salmon separately from the rest of Scotland. Though there have been environmental and commercial problems with farmed salmon, aquaculture provides a vital source of employment in remote areas which have a declining population and much research has been undertaken to find solutions. Skilled salmon farmers can produce high-quality fish. But this depends on a number of factors such as stocking densities and where the cages are positioned.

When there are fewer fish in the cage there is less chance of disease spreading, which has been a major problem. Low stocking density, plus controlled feeding, so that the fish do not get too fatty too quickly, will produce the best-quality salmon. Another factor is the water current round the cages, since it has been proved that those farmed in the fast-running current between the islands in Orkney and Shetland produce a better textured fish—the fish has to swim against the current as it rushes through the cages. Some salmon farms on Orkney have applied for organic status from the Soil Association and, if successful, will produce the first organic-farmed salmon in the UK.

## BAKED SALMON
### in butter

*'Tibby was for cutting it in twa cuts, but I like a saumon to be served up in its integrity.'*
Christopher North,
*Noctes Ambrosianae*, 1822-1835.

To follow Christopher North's method is difficult if you don't happen to have a large enough fish kettle, which may have been Tibby's problem. Working in hotels has meant that I've usually had one available to cook the salmon whole. But it was in a hotel, not a mile from the finest salmon river in the area, that I first used the method below which dispenses with the kettle, with no detriment to finished flavour or texture.

The whole fish is well buttered and then wrapped in foil and baked in the oven in its own juices. Cooking food in its own juices, like this, is an old and respected method which goes back to primitive practices like coating the food with a thick layer of clay and burying it in the embers of a fire. Gipsies liked cooking hedgehogs in this way and potters used their clay to wrap up meat and fish which they cooked in the kilns. Chicken 'bricks' and cooking foil are the modern development.

Don't let any of the moisture escape or the fish will dry out.

## To bake a whole or part of a salmon or salmon trout in foil

Pre-heat the oven to 300F/275C/Gas 1-2.

Clean, gut and wipe salmon. Check that it will fit into the oven. If it is too large try removing the head (it can easily be put back on again). Otherwise, cut off the head and a bit of the shoulders, the less the better. Use double-thickness foil, the thickest, strongest variety. Put foil on the baking tray and brush liberally with melted butter, then place the salmon on top. Brush salmon liberally with more melted butter. Season lightly with salt and put some salt and a few lumps of butter into the body cavity. Now cover with a double layer of foil and secure, not too tightly, round the edges.

Place in a cool oven and bake. Allow 12 minutes per lb (500 g) plus 12 minutes.

If to be served hot, leave for 10 minutes before removing foil, otherwise leave in foil till cold. Skin and garnish with lemon and some greenery—the delicate, green, feathery dill or fennel, if you have them, are lovely with pink salmon but, if not, good fresh parsley will do. Served on an old blue-and-white ashet, the dish needs no more adorning.

## To cook in a fish kettle

If you do happen to have a large fish kettle and want to use it, the fish can be prepared as above, placed into cold water in its foil casing and brought to the boil. Give it about 30 seconds boiling, then turn off the heat. Leave to cool and finish cooking in the latent heat. Not suitable for serving hot.

## GRILLED SALMON STEAK
### with parsley and lemon butter

All the ghillies I've known who fish salmon rivers have had an uncanny knack of cooking salmon to perfection. Most of the fish, mind you, was of the 'poached' variety but their favourite way of cooking, when the salmon was fresh and in prime condition, was by grilling.

Salmon has so much natural richness, especially early in the season, that grilling rather than frying preserves its flavour and texture best. For such a sensitive protein as fish (it coagulates so much quicker than meat and, when over-coagulated, the muscle fibres begin to squeeze the natural juices out of the fish thus destroying both flavour and texture), grilling is a more easily regulated method and the fish can be removed from the

29

heat and the cooking stopped more quickly when it has just set.

All of the cook's art can be revealed in grilling fresh fish. So thought the late Ted Reynolds, of the Scottish Hotel School. While others ordered complicated dishes with elaborate sauces in upmarket restaurants, he used to test out a restaurant by the chef's ability to grill a fish to perfection.

### To grill

Dip the steak in mild-flavoured oil (sunflower or groundnut) and salt lightly. 1 steak = 1½ in (3-4 cm) thick. The best cuts for grilling are from the end of the belly-opening towards the tail, giving a cut of uniform thickness and without the belly flaps.

Place on a very hot grill, cook for about two minutes until it takes colour, turn, grill the second side. Open up the flesh a little to check if cooked through. Remove the central bone and serve.

### To make the butter

Melt 4 oz/125 g butter (1 stick) in a pan and add 1 tablespoon chopped parsley, juice of 1 lemon and salt and pepper. Beat with a wire whisk over a moderate heat for a few minutes till well blended and serve in a heated sauceboat with small steamed potatoes sprinkled with parsley and some skinned diced cucumber tossed in chives.

# POTTED SALMON

**2-4 servings**

Early methods, like the one in Meg Dods (1826), baked the salmon first with butter, seasoning and spices, pounded mace, cloves, black pepper and allspice. Then it was drained and the pieces packed into 'potting cans', covered with clarified butter and kept in the larder for later use. These are recipes which were appropriate when salmon was the commonest and cheapest fish in Scotland. A Highland laird travelling in the south of England in the nineteenth century recalls how he ordered salmon for his servant and beef for himself and was dismayed to find the salmon cost him more than the beef.

A more economical method uses leftover cooked salmon and butter. If keeping for any length of time then clarified butter is necessary for sealing. Clarified butter can be used throughout though is not essential.

### To clarify the butter

Place the butter in a pan and heat gently—it is worth doing 1-2 lb/½-1 kg (4-8 sticks) at a time since it keeps well and can be used for frying since it has had the solids removed which normally cause it to burn. When melted, it will have divided into three parts:

(1) a foam on top
(2) a middle layer of pure clear butter
(3) sediment at the bottom.

Lift off the foam with a wide flat skimming spoon. Decant the clear butter into a bowl, leaving the sediment at the bottom.

Use the sediment and foam for flavouring soups but remember they are very salty.

## Potting

Beat the salmon and butter together to a smooth paste, season and pack tightly into an earthenware pot. Press down well. A pot with a lid is best since the lid prevents the butter drying out and shrinking from the edges. Otherwise, cover with foil. Cover with a very thin film of clarified butter. It will keep for several weeks in a cool place.

Serve for lunch or supper with fresh crusty brown bread and a light, green salad or hot toast.

### *Potted Salmon*

12 oz/350 g cooked salmon, skinned and boned

1 cup melted butter

Salt and pepper

Pinch of grated nutmeg

Clarified butter for sealing

# SALMON SOUP

### 8-12 servings

The delicate salmon-pink and varying shades of green make this an attractive soup. You must be careful not to overcook the greens and spoil their fresh green colour. It is a fairly substantial soup, good as a soup/stew at lunch. It also has the advantage of using up the head and trimmings of the salmon if you happen to have them. (Helpful fishmongers will keep them for you at little or no cost.)

## To cook

Put all the fish trimmings into a pot, cover with 4 pts/2 L (10 c) of cold water and bring to the boil. Skim and simmer for 20-30 minutes. Just before turning off the heat, add the fresh salmon and leave to cook in the liquor. (Do not re-cook if the salmon is already cooked.) When cooled, skim off any excess fat and strain stock. Remove the salmon and break up into flakes.

Meantime, melt the butter in a pan and add the vegetables (the white of the leek only). Gently sweat with the lid on, stirring every few minutes to prevent sticking, for about ten minutes. Add the fish stock and bring to the boil. Simmer gently till the vegetables are tender, about 30 minutes. Add the finely chopped green leek and the flaked salmon. Heat through for a few minutes, add the cream, season and serve.

### *Salmon Soup*

Head, bones, skin and fins of the salmon

Bones from 2 whiting

6 oz/175 g fresh salmon or 4 oz/125 g cooked

2 sticks celery, finely chopped

1 medium onion, finely chopped

1 lb/500 g small diced potatoes

2 leeks, white and green finely chopped separately

2 oz/50 g butter (½ stick)

2 tablespoons double cream

Salt and pepper

# TAY SALMON
## in Pastry with Vermouth and Dill Sauce

*Tay Salmon in Pastry*

6 x 5-6 oz/150-175 g slices fresh Tay salmon

1 lb/500 g puff pastry

1 yolk of egg mixed with 1 teaspoon water

*For the fish mousse*

½ lb/250 g sole

1 egg

1 egg white

½ pt/250 ml double cream (1¼ c scant)

*For the sauce*

3 fl oz/75 ml Chambray Vermouth

¼ pt/150 ml good fish stock (¾ c)

Fresh or dried dill to taste

4 oz/125 g unsalted butter, softened (1 stick)

**6 servings**

Crisp, golden puff pastry envelopes contain a pink salmon layer topped with a creamy sole mousse. They are served with an aromatic dill-flavoured sauce.

Skin sole, chop roughly and liquidise or put in processor. Add whole egg and egg white. Mix well. Refrigerate and when required add cream.

### To prepare the salmon

Pre-heat the oven 450F/230C/Gas 8.

Spread the fish mousse about ¼-½ in on top of each slice of salmon. Roll out the pastry almost paper thin and cut into 6 squares. The size will depend on the shape of the salmon. Each piece of pastry should be large enough to wrap round the salmon slice with about a ¼ in overlap and at the ends it should extend by about ½ in. Place salmon slice on pastry square, mousse-side down. Wet edges of pastry and fold over, making both edges just overlap slightly in the centre.

Press down to seal. Repeat with other slices. Place on baking sheet, reversing so the mousse side is up. Brush with egg wash and bake for about 10 minutes till the pastry is lightly brown and puffed up.

### To make the sauce

Put the vermouth and fish stock into a pan and reduce by about half. Add the cream and gradually the butter in small pieces. Adjust consistency with more butter or fish stock. Add dill and taste for seasoning.

### To serve

Place salmon portions on a warm plate and cut half way through the middle, open slightly, pour sauce round. Garnish with a fine julienne of vegetables on the side of the plate.

(From David Wilson, Peat Inn in Fife, 1984.)

# Smoked Scottish Salmon

Preservation began with a method known as 'kippering' which can be traced back to the fifteenth century and was used to keep the fish during winter. It was a domestic operation as F.M. McNeill describes in 1929: 'To Kipper Salmon: A modern method'. This involved preserving with salt, demerara sugar, olive oil, rum or whisky, and she suggests that the best smoky flavour would be achieved if the fish was smoked in an outside shed without windows used as a 'kiln', over a mixture of peat, oak chips and juniper wood.

Though there are still some domestic smokers who smoke more or less in the way she describes using make-shift garden sheds, there are around a hundred commercial smokers of varying sizes and types. The basic method involves first **SALTING**: may be dry or wet salting to stabilise the salt content to around 3.5% . The most common method is to lay the fish on trays of salt and sprinkle salt over them by hand to varying degrees, depending on the taste required. Depending on size they are left for 12-24 hours. Smokehouses may add their own secret ingredients —sugar, juniper berries, herbs, molasses, rum or whisky—at the salting stage. Small smokehouses will take much longer to salt and dry out the fish while in large-scale, mass-production smokers there may be a fast-injection brining which speeds up the process.

**SMOKING**: fillets are washed and left overnight to dry; laid out on wire mesh trays and wheeled on trolleys into controlled smoking kilns to be cold smoked at 20-30C, usually over smouldering oak chips, though some smokers continue to use traditional peat. During the process, the temperature and moisture content are monitored and controlled. Some curers 'rest' or 'mature' the fish for 3-4 days after smoking in a chilled temperature which will improve the flavour by reducing the water content. In large, automated systems there is less personal control of the fish compared with smaller operations when the 'gut feeling and nose' of the experienced smoker controls more carefully the finished cure. It may be sliced by hand or machine. Hand-sliced will be more expensive but will be a finer cut.

## BUYING

Sweet, salty, woodsy, peaty...what is the best cure? Provided that the texture is as satin, the colour natural, and the balance of oil to flesh perfect, choosing a cure becomes easier when you identify the type you prefer. If you are American, it's likely that you will prefer a cure dominated by woodsy flavours with a slightly sweet edge over saltiness. If you are Italian, however, you are much more likely to go for a saltier cure. In between the two extremes is the Japanese taste for perfect balance. The sweet must cancel out the salt and they are not interested in woodsy flavours.

There has been a trend in the last decade or so, as mass-produced smoked salmon has become much more widely available, to reduce this cure to its lowest common denominator. Wet and flabby smoked salmon

*All smoked salmon is not created equal. Most aficionados give the nod to smoked Scotch salmon as the best...It is as a rule the least oily, the most subtly flavoured, has the firmest and most pleasing texture and the least amount of salt. It is also the most expensive.*
New York Times, *1984*

from quick curing methods which do not mature flavour in the traditional way have been the main problem. Smoking is a craft-skill with a hands-on element which cannot be easily automated on a large scale. Often the worst cures are from salmon which have a bogus Scottish tag. Hijacked for its prestige, there are some which may neither use Scottish fish, nor be smoked in Scotland. They may, or may not, have a label. Of those who have fraudulently labelled their produce as 'Scottish', there have been more than a dozen convictions under the Trade Descriptions Act.

Those who appreciate the subtleties of this delicacy prefer to buy from small Scottish smokers who are within easy reach of the best supplies, or from mail order companies who usually select with care from small rural smokehouses.

'Top-quality wild fish, smoked in Scotland by experienced local smokers with distinctive cures, is to the mass-produced product as "Chateau Bottled" is to "Vin Ordinaire"', says Keith Dunbar, a salmon curer from the Summer Isles Smokehouse, 'and it ought to be labelled as such.'

## ATLANTIC OR PACIFIC

Atlantic salmon is longer and narrower, smaller and thinner than a side of Pacific salmon. Pacific salmon widens towards the middle and is thick and meaty. It is difficult to tell purely by colour, but the Pacific fish is closer to deep coral in colour than the Atlantic fish. In flavour and texture the Atlantic has a much more delicate flavour and a finer more satiny texture, which allows it to be sliced to translucent thinness. Pacific fish have a coarser wider grain and a less subtle flavour.

## FRESH/FROZEN/VACUUM-PACKED

'Fresh' smoked fish will always slice better and taste better but provided that frozen and vacuum-packed are carefully handled, there should not be too much loss of flavour or texture. To defrost, take it out of its sealed pack, then place uncovered in the refrigerator. This allows it to thaw slowly and excess moisture to evaporate instead of going back into the fish. Frozen fish will never slice as thinly as non-frozen. Vacuum-packs will keep in good condition in the refrigerator for about two weeks. Once opened they should be used within the week.

## COLOUR/APPEARANCE

The flesh should be a natural-looking pink—beware of bright pink or orange: it may have been dyed. It should look firm and smooth, not torn or mottled, and should have a natural sheen without looking oily. Smoked salmon does go 'off', when it will have a fairly obvious rancid odour.

## PREPARING

Ready sliced—the supplier should cut the slices wafer thin, almost transparent. For the full benefit of the flavour they should be served at room temperature or very slightly cooler, so remove at least 20-30 minutes before serving. Keep closely covered with cling film since they dry out very quickly.

Whole side—place on a wooden board and prepare by trimming round the edges, if necessary. With tweezers, remove the 'pin' bones which run down the centre of the fillet. Use a sharp knife with a thick flexible blade. Special knives for slicing smoked salmon may be bought from specialist suppliers. They are about 10-in long and have a slightly undulating edge. Keep the knife flat while cutting and make long, even strokes working towards the tail, making paper-thin slices without tearing the flesh, which should be dense and resilient. The slices should be as large as possible, preferably one slice covering the entire plate. Do not slice more than 2 or 3 hours before use.

## TO SERVE

Go for the best quality you can afford. Cut it paper-thin for the best appreciation of the subtle flavour. Serve simply with brown bread and butter and perhaps a little pepper. 2-3 oz/50-75 g should satisfy most palates, though I have known some who could consume 4 oz/125 g at a sitting.

What to drink with it is a matter of taste. Scandinavians drink chilled vodka or schnapps with Gravlax which is superb but somehow anaesthetises the palate for the more subtle flavours of smoked salmon. Champagne has its followers, others go for White Burgundy, while everyone agrees that red wines compete too much.

# Sea Trout, Salmon Trout, Brown Trout (*Salmo trutta*)

The sea/salmon trout has a similar life cycle to salmon; it also eats the same kind of food (among other things, pink crustaceans) and therefore has a similar pink flesh. It is different in size—smaller than salmon and with a more delicate flavour preferred by many. Freshwater brown trout are smaller, and their flavour is entirely dependent on the richness of their feeding grounds, which also applies to the farmed variety.

*This is a confusing species, which embraces the brown trout of rivers: the bull or lake trout of larger inland waters: and the sea trout, which is a migratory fish with a natural range from North Africa to Norway and Iceland.*
Alan Davidson
*North Atlantic Seafood, 1979*

# BAKED BROWN TROUT
## with herbs and lemon

*Baked Brown Trout*

**4 x ½ lb/250 g trout**

**2 tablespoons olive oil or
melted butter**

**Sea salt**

**Freshly ground black pepper**

**4 sprigs fresh herbs (either dill,
fennel, chives or parsley)**

**1 lemon or lime**

**4 servings**

This is the same method as Baked Salmon—encasing the fish in foil and allowing it to cook in its own juices without drying out.

Pre-heat the oven to 450F/230C/Gas 8.

Scale and clean the trout; cut off the fins and wipe with kitchen paper. Season the inside with salt and pepper and put in herbs. Cut 4 pieces of foil into oval shapes long enough to hold the fish plus 3 in (7 cm). Brush the foil with oil or butter and lay the trout up the centre. Brush the fish with oil or butter, season with salt and pepper and place a slice of lemon on the fish. Bring up the sides of the foil to make a boat and pleat over the foil at the top to enclose the fish, pinching together with thumb and forefinger to make a scalloped edge like a Cornish Pasty.

Put on a baking sheet and bake in a hot oven for 8-10 minutes.

Cooking time will depend on the thickness of the fish, so check one by opening up. Gently and carefully ease open the flesh at the thickest part along the lateral line right down to the bone. This should all be opaque. Serve in foil, first making a small slit in the foil for easier opening.

# Herring

*Of all the fish that swim in the sea
The herring is the fish for me.*
Scottish Folk Song

It's not just songs which have been sung about this remarkable little fish. Battles have been fought over them and even towns established on the strength of their availability.

The word 'herring' comes from the Germanic word, 'heer', meaning an army, which is a good description of the shoals of herring numbering many thousands which swim together for protection.

Until 1963 catches had been relatively stable, but then they began to rise rapidly to a peak in 1969 when over a million tons were caught. From then on there was a steady decline, till in 1976 only two hundred thousand tons were caught in Scotland, and in 1977 the Scottish herring fishing was closed. The introduction of the purse seine net, which could catch a whole shoal of herring, meant that they were being caught more effectively than ever before. Even if the whole shoal was not caught, small numbers of remaining fish could not survive from predators without the large shoal's protection. Serious conservation methods of protecting the species were put in operation with scientists monitoring stocks closely, setting quotas and closing down the fishing in certain areas when the fish are under pressure.

# SEASONS AND BUYING

I agree with Meg Dods (1826) when she says that herring should be eaten 'almost alive'. They are like shellfish and deteriorate quickly when dead. For some time I lived in a cottage beside the pier in Ullapool on the West Coast and could pick up a 'fry' of herring from the fish which had spilled onto the pier as the boats unloaded. The luxury of fresh herring straight off the boats makes it impossible for me to buy herring from city fishmonger if its 'bloom' has gone. The same applies to mackerel. Look for firm bright fish, as they have a flabby look when past their best. MacCallum, the Glasgow and Troon fishmonger, sells fish straight from the boxes where fussy fish buyers rummage through the catch, holding whole herring and mackerel up by their tails to see how much they bend over, thus judging freshness.

Herring are available all year round from different sources, but the heavier, fatter, summer fish will have more flavour than the lean winter ones. The amount of fat in the flesh varies throughout the annual reproductive cycle. There is a long period of starvation after spawning followed by a time of intensive feeding while the milts and roes are developing. The fat content can vary from as little as 2% to as high as 20%, so it is important to look for the plump fish which have been feeding and have well-developed roes. They have the highest fat content and the best flavour.

The availability from certain areas around the Scottish coasts is, and always has been, unpredictable, but each ground has its season and the fishery at any one place is rarely exploited outside these periods.

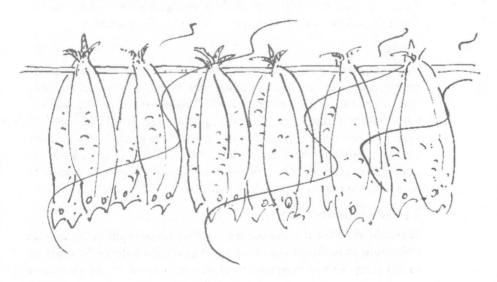

*Fresh Herring in Oatmeal*

**4 fresh herring, whole or filleted**

**2 heaped tablespoons medium oatmeal, lightly toasted**

**Salt and pepper**

**Butter and/or a neutral oil for frying**

# FRESH HERRING
## fried in oatmeal

**4 servings**

One of the great Scottish combinations. The rich herring needs a coating with flavour and bite to it which the oatmeal provides.

All fish cooked with the bone left in will have more flavour, and herrings are no exception. A common breakfast dish when we visited my grandmother was a large ashet piled with whole fried herring. She lived beside an East Coast fishing village and from an early age children had to master the art of removing the bones from cooked fish—or starve. She believed, along with the fisher wives, that removing bones before cooking removed half the flavour and, in any case, given the vast amounts of fish consumed, no one had any time for filleting.

### To prepare whole herring

Slit up the belly and remove the gut, scraping up the backbone with your thumbnail to loosen the spinal vein starting from the tail up. Cut off the head if you wish, though this is not necessary. Cut off all fins with scissors and wash. Make sure all blood is removed from the belly cavity. Salt inside.

### To fillet herring

Place the fish, which has been prepared as above, on a board, skin-side up with the belly flaps spread out, and press with the base of your palm from tail to head along with backbone. The fish will flatten out as you press and when it is fairly flat, without being squashed, turn onto the flesh side and the bone will lift out; cut at the tail to release.

### To fry

Heat the fat in a large frying-pan. Mix the seasonings into the oatmeal and press the wet fish into it, coating both sides—it is not necessary to moisten the fish with anything. Shake off excess oatmeal and fry. Filleted fish should be placed flesh side down first. Whole fish will take longer to cook. Test by opening carefully with a sharp pointed knife at the thickest part right down to the bone: if the flesh is still not opaque, leave for another few minutes. They should take from 5-10 minutes each side depending on the thickness of the fish.

### To bone cooked fish

Removing the flesh is quite simple once you have found the lateral line which runs from the middle of the gill flap to the middle of the tail. Cut with a sharp knife through the skin and right down to the bone in a straight line the length of the fish. Now gently ease away the fillets on either side. If the fish is correctly cooked they should come away cleanly, exposing the bone. To expose the lower fillet, lift the tail and release the skin and flesh at the very end. Then, with your knife, hold down the flesh on the plate and prise off the bone, gradually working upwards towards the head. When you reach the head it should come away easily attached to the bone. Before you discard it, do not forget to pick out the cheeks—a delicacy often overlooked.

## 'FRESH HERRINGS AS DRESSED AT INVERARY
### (and the Highland Sea-Lochs)'

*The best herrings are obtained in these localities almost alive. Cut off the head, fins, and tails; scale, gut, and wash them. Split and bone them or not, dust the inside with pepper and fine salt. Place two herrings flat together, the backs outmost, and dip in toasted oatmeal and fry them for seven minutes. Serve hot. They are delicious; and, in the summer, add much to the breakfasts on the steamers on the Clyde, and round all the northeast and west coasts of Scotland.*

Meg Dods,
*The Cook and Housewife's Manual*, 1826.

This is a useful method for small herring: the two flesh sides fuse together, making a moist juicy centre which contrasts with a crisp outside.

## OPEN ARMS HERRING
### with Drambuie butter

**4 servings**

With fresh East Coast herring, this dish combines traditional Herrings in Oatmeal with a Drambuie-flavoured hard butter and lifts them out of a common, everyday dish with this simple touch.

### To cook

Soften the butter slightly without melting. Beat in the other ingredients. Roll into a sausage shape 1 in (2½ cm) in diameter. Wrap in foil or greaseproof paper and leave to harden slightly. Cut in slices and serve two on each fish just before serving. Garnish fish with lemon wedges and watercress. To store leftover butter for future use, cut all the butter into slices. Place on tray and freeze, then put in small freezer bags and keep frozen till required. Do not keep for more than a few weeks since the

*Open Arms Herring*

**4 herrings, fried in oatmeal (see p.38)**

*Drambuie Butter*

**4 oz/125 g unsalted butter (1 stick)**

**2 teaspoons lemon juice**

**1 tablespoon chopped parsley**

**3 tablespoons Drambuie**

39

Drambuie flavour will begin to deteriorate in time.

From Chef Douglas, the Open Arms Hotel in Dirleton, East Lothian, 1984.

# GRILLED HERRING
## with mustard

*Grilled Herring with Mustard*

**4 whole or filleted herring**

**2-3 tablespoons medium oatmeal, lightly toasted**

**Salt and pepper**

**2 oz/50 g butter (½ stick)**

**Mustard**

**4 servings**

Of the many commercial varieties of mustard the best for herring are those made with the less piquant whole mustard seeds. Or you may wish to make your own: see A Store Mustard (p.224).

### For whole herring

Slash the skin diagonally about three times on either side: this opens up the flesh and makes it cook more evenly. Salt the inside of the fish. Mix the seasonings through the oatmeal. Now press both sides into the oatmeal and place in grill pan. Put pats of butter on top along the centre line and place under a hot grill. Cook on both sides for 5-10 minutes and serve with mustard.

### For filleted herring

Press the wet fish into the seasoned oatmeal, shake off excess. Place skin side up and dot all over with butter. Grill under a hot grill on both sides for about five minutes.

### Serving

Serve with mustard. Also with plain, boiled, floury potatoes skinned, sprinkled with chopped chives and with plenty of butter. Mashed Scottish turnips (known as Swedes in England; Rutabaga in North America) are good with fried or grilled herring. This can all be mashed together and served as Orkney Clapshot (see p.180).

# SOUSED OR POTTED HERRING

**6 servings**

Try potting them whole. If they are cooked slowly for four to five hours the vinegar dissolves all the small bones and the cooking liquor becomes quite thick and full of flavour. A little of it should be served with the fish. Make sure you use good, fatty herring. Poor-quality herring will not stand up to the long, slow cooking, nor will they survive the strong, spicy flavours which characterise this method of cooking herring.

Made with the season's first Loch Fyne herring, gleaming silver fish, plump and full of flavour, they are—once experienced—never forgotten.

## To cook

Pre-heat the oven to 425F/220C/Gas 7.

Clean the herring and remove the heads (optional) and fins. Season the belly cavity with salt and pepper. Lay the fish, heads to tails, in a large casserole with the spices and seasonings in between. Pour over the vinegar and water. It should almost cover them. Cover very tightly and place in a hot oven for 30 minutes till the liquid begins to bubble, then reduce the heat to the lowest possible ( 250F/130C/Gas ½) and leave for 4-5 hours. Leave to cool in the liquid.

### To pot filleted herring

**6 servings**

Pre-heat the oven to 350F/180C/Gas 4.

Clean and fillet the fish. Season flesh surface with salt and pepper.

Roll up from head end to tail and place in shallow casserole closely packed together with the tails sticking up. Sprinkle spices on top and cover with vinegar, cider and water. Cover and bake for 45 minutes. Leave to cool in the liquor. Drain and serve.

Note: To pot correctly, the fish should be drained well, then packed into an earthenware pot and covered with clarified butter. They will keep in a cool place for at least four weeks if treated in this way.

## SOUSED HERRING
### Shetland-style

'He had taken 13 herring, cleaned them, boned them, laid them out open and flat on their backs and applied a little salt and white pepper. He then rolled them up from head to tail and laid them in a shallow casserole large enough to take them all in one layer. He added a cup each of water and ordinary white vinegar and cooked the herrings in a moderately hot oven (400F/200C/Gas 6) for 25 minutes with the lid on and a final five minutes with the lid off "to brown the tops". The result was extremely good.'

Alan Davidson in *North Atlantic Seafood* (1979) describing Jimmy Fraser's method in his Shetland fish shop.

## *Soused Herring*

**6 fat herring**

**½ pt/300 ml malt vinegar (1¼ c)**

**¼ pt/150 ml water (¾ c)**

**1 teaspoon salt**

**¼ teaspoon ground black pepper**

**6 cloves**

**2 blades of mace**

**1 bay leaf**

**12 peppercorns**

**1 oz/25 g butter (¼ stick)**

**1 cayenne pod**

## *Potted Herring*

**6 herring**

**Salt and pepper**

**¼ pt/300 ml malt vinegar (¾ c)**

**¼ pt/300 ml dry cider (¾ c)**

**¼ pt/300 ml water (¾ c)**

**2 bay leaves**

**10 peppercorns**

**2 blades of mace**

**¼ teaspooon grated nutmeg**

**4 oz/125 g clarified butter (1 stick) (see pp.30-1)**

## *Sweet Spiced Herring*

8 fl oz/250 ml pickle vinegar (see p.224) or wine or cider vinegar (1 c)

1 medium onion, thinly sliced

6 oz/200 g granulated sugar (¾ c generous)

1 tablespoon allspice berries

1 tablespoon black pepper-corns

3 small bay leaves

1 lb/500 g fresh whole herring

# SWEET SPICED HERRING

Use good fatty herring for this spicy, sweet/sour cure—lean winter herring will be overpowered by the spice. They are good served slightly chilled with a grated Beetroot Salad (see p.47) and some sliced raw mushrooms and spring onions for garnish.

Put all the ingredients except the herring in a pan and simmer gently for a few minutes to infuse, then leave to cool.

## To prepare the herring

Clean, gut and fillet the herring (see p.38). If possible, skin the fish. If it is in good condition this should be quite easy. Loosen the very thin papery skin at the head end and then push your fingers under it. When you have enough loosened to get a good grip, pull downwards towards the tail and it should all come off in one piece. Separate the two fillets, trim and place flat in an earthenware casserole. Pour over cooled spice vinegar and leave at least overnight but preferably for 2-3 days before use. Keeps well for at least a month in a cool place.

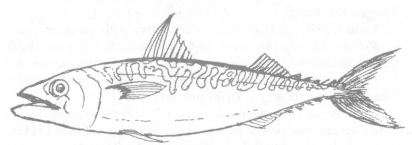

# Atlantic Mackerel (*Scomber Scombrus*)

A muscular fish with a streamlined body which is similar to herring in many respects. It too swims in very large shoals which makes it more liable to overfishing. It also spoils rapidly, and like herring has a rich, oily flesh which also fluctuates according to season. It differs in flavour and in the texture of the flesh which is firmer and freer of the fine bones found in herring.

Traditional recipes serve mackerel with acid fruit sauces, gooseberry being the most common, though it is good with other sharp fruits like rhubarb, cranberries or raspberries.

**Season**—They spawn throughout the spring, early and late summer and stop feeding during the winter, so are at their best from April through to November.

## HOT SMOKED MACKEREL

Because mackerel have a high oil content, similar to herring, this cure became popular in the 1970s when the herring fishery was closed and mackerel were more widely eaten as a result. It is made with summer and autumn fish which are particularly high in oil. The fish are filleted to remove the head and bone. Single fillets with the skin on are cured in salt brine, placed on stainless-steel trays and cold smoked for an hour then hot smoked for two hours. Flavourings of pepper, herbs and spices are sprinkled over before they are smoked.

### POTTED MACKEREL

Soften the butter and place in liquidiser or processor or beat by hand for a slightly coarser result, with the mackerel and garlic. Blend to a smooth paste. Taste and season with salt and pepper and lemon juice. Put into individual pots and cover with clarified butter. Serve with hot toast for high tea or supper or as a starter course for dinner.

# Kipper

Although kippers are not a Scottish invention they make up about a quarter of all the processed fish eaten in Scotland today and there are some fine Scottish cures.

In the 1840s, when the kipper was first developed in Newcastle, it was a saltier, drier and darker cure. It was coloured naturally from the smoke to a dark-brown colour. During the last years of the 1914-18 war a chemical dye, known as brown FK (For Kippers) was used by UK smokers which allowed the smoking times to be reduced without loss of colour or weight. By the 1930s all the large kipper manufacturers had turned to dyed kippers. Only a small, but recently growing, band of independent smokers stuck to the old traditional method. Now a few of the larger curers have made the concession of leaving a few undyed as public concern about unnecessary additives to food has gathered momentum.

The undyed kipper is a paler silvery brown kipper easily distinguished from the richer brown of the dyed variety. Kippers with the bone removed have a consequent loss of flavour and especially so if they are frozen.

*Potted Mackerel*

**10 oz/275 g skinned and boned smoked mackerel**

**5 oz/150 g unsalted butter (1¼ sticks)**

**1 clove garlic, crushed**

**Lemon juice to taste**

**Salt and pepper**

**Clarified butter to cover (see p.48)**

*Some years ago, when staying at a fishing port on Lochfyne-side, I used to watch the herring-boats sail in at dawn and unload their cargo, which was run straight up to the kippering sheds. Here the fish were plunged into a brine bath and thereafter hung up to smoke over smouldering oak chips, while their colour changed slowly from silver to burnished copper.*

F.M. McNeill
*The Scots Kitchen*, 1929

## TRADITIONAL METHOD

They are usually brined for 30 minutes to provide a 'shine' rather than a strong, salty taste, then they are cold-smoked for between 18-24 hours over oak chips (sometimes from whisky barrels). Individual curers have their own brining recipes which give variations in flavour.

## BUYING

For the best flavour and keeping qualities look for plump kippers which have a glossy shine to them, which is partly the result of the brining process but also indicates a good fat content, essential for a well-flavoured kipper.

## POTTED KIPPER

*Potted Kippers*

2 medium to large cooked kippers, giving approximately 8 oz/250 g kipper meat

4 oz/125 g butter (1 stick)

2 tablespoons whisky

4 anchovy fillets

2-3 teaspoons lemon juice

Cayenne pepper

**4-6 servings**

It is essential to use a well-flavoured, fatty kipper.

Put all the ingredients into a liquidiser or food processor and reduce to a fine paste. This will break up all the fine bones in the kipper flesh.

Adjust lemon, cayenne and whisky flavourings to taste. Salt may not be necessary because of the anchovies. Serve with oatcakes which have been slightly warmed in the oven or with hot toast. A good dry cider is excellent with this and other kipper dishes.

Note: I have tried using some of the more interesting peaty malt whiskies but they tend to lose their distinctive characteristics. A good blended whisky will give that faint taste of whisky which is all that is necessary.

## TO COOK KIPPERS

All kipper addicts have their favourite way of cooking. If it is left to the cook, however, she will make sure that the entire kitchen does not reek of kipper for days.

### Grilled Kipper

This is a good method since it concentrates the flavour well, though the grill should be well lined with foil. It is not necessary to baste with butter—there should be enough natural fat in the kipper to keep it from drying out. The head and tail should be cut off before grilling. Place under a medium-hot grill, flesh-side up, and cook for about ten minutes, (depending on size) on the flesh side only.

## Frying

Not a popular method with cooks, since they can't protect the frying pan with foil. It also coats an already fatty fish with another layer of fat. If intent on frying, use the merest film of oil in the pan, just enough to prevent sticking, and place the kipper in flesh-side down. Cook for five minutes on either side and serve.

## Jugging

This is a popular method for cooks and kipper lovers alike since it doesn't involve any cooking as such, and the utensil used is easily cleaned. Place the kipper in a heated jug which is deep enough to hold it, and fill the jug with boiling water. Alternately use a deep pot, but make sure it is well heated. Cover well, and leave for at least 10 minutes. Remove the kipper and serve immediately. Some of the flavour and fat is obviously lost in the liquid but the fish retains its plumpness and the texture of the flesh is soft and juicy.

## Baking

Another method favoured by both cooks and eaters. The whole fish is wrapped in a foil parcel and placed in a moderate oven (350F/180C/Gas 4) for 15-20 minutes. Wrap the fish individually and serve in the parcel to preserve the full aroma till it is opened.

## Uncooked

In the early 1960s, TV chef Philip Harben was an early advocate of this method. He suggested the fish should be boned, sliced thinly and covered in a marinade of oil and lemon juice for several hours before eating. More recently Jane Grigson has suggested that the thinly sliced, raw fillets should be 'arranged in strips round the edge of some well-buttered rye bread, with an egg yolk in the middle as sauce' (*Good Things*, 1971). A deeply chilled glass of vodka or schnapps goes well with this.


# SALT-PICKLED HERRING

Ironically, this is the cure which made Scotland famous for many years as the world's greatest herring-producing country, but is the one we eat least of today. About ninety per cent of the cured fish was exported so perhaps it is not surprising that Scots have not continued to eat it in any great quantity. The Scandinavian countries, to which much of the herring was exported, have maintained a liking for it and still eat pickled herring in large quantities. They have developed an amazing range of ideas for dealing with this fish, while the most common Scots dish is Tatties and Herring.

## Buying

Most traditional fishmongers will have a barrel of salted herring. The herring should be big and fat. The longer they have been in the pickle the saltier they will be.

## Eating

I have seen fishermen eat them raw on the bone, they stimulate the digestive juices like no other food I know, but I prefer, if eating them raw, to have the flavour slightly modified in a sweet vinegar pickle. The raw fish can also be cut in strips and used as for anchovies.

*Salted Herring*

**Coarse salt**

**Fat, fresh herring**

# TATTIES AND HERRING

Remains a popular dish, particularly in Highland areas, the salty fish and the bland potatoes making the sharp contrast of flavours which is so much part of its charm.

## To salt herring

Use a small wooden barrel or large plastic bucket.

Begin by removing the gills and long gut from the fish, leaving on the heads. Begin with a good, thick layer of salt then set the fish in the layer with their backs uppermost, but slightly on their sides. Put in the next layer of salt, then the fish lying in the opposite direction. Continue in layers till the barrel is full. Put a plate on top to keep weighted down when the brine forms. Cover well and store in a cool place. May be used after 1-2 months. Will keep for about a year.

## To cook

Wash fish and soak overnight in cold water. They may be cooked in the same pan as boiled potatoes. Usually they are laid on top of the boiling potatoes or they may be cooked separately well covered with water and simmered for about 10 minutes and then eaten with boiled jacket potatoes. (They are best with a floury potato such as Golden Wonder.)

## To eat

Tatties and herring were traditionally dished up into an 18-in, shallow, square dish, used specially for the purpose, called a 'clar' in Gaelic. They were then picked up and eaten with the fingers—a pinch of herring with a mouthful of potato.

# MARINATED SALT HERRING

**4-6 servings**

A Finnish friend tells me that most of the herring they eat is salted. They appreciate the fact that, once dead, the fish deteriorates so quickly, and instead prefer to eat it preserved by a method which intensifies the character of the fish.

Finns, as well as other Scandinavians, have a highly developed tradition of salt herring dishes. This is one which they describe as Everyday Herring. The Scots have obviously made something similar, according to F. Marian McNeill, *The Scots Kitchen* (1929). It was called a 'Pickled Herring' and the salted herring were simply marinated in vinegar, brown sugar and onions.

This should be made with the gentler, acetic, acid-based condiment they use in Scandinavia, and not vinegar which is too harsh. If the Spirit Condiment (also called Non-brewed Condiment) is not available then chemists sell concentrated acetic acid which can be diluted to taste.

## To make

Bone and skin the herring. Slice into bite-sized pieces and arrange in a dish with sugar, spices, onions and carrots layered in between.

Pour over condiment to cover.

Leave overnight in a cool place. To serve, garnish with some fresh onion (red onions are best) and plenty of chopped fresh dill. Eat with thickly buttered rye bread and ice-cold schnapps or chilled lager.

*Marinated Salt Herring*

8 salted herring

3 tablespoons sugar

3 medium onions, sliced

2 carrots, thinly sliced

Bay leaf

1 tablespoon allspice

1 tablespoon peppercorns

3 cups non-brewed spirit condiment

# SALT HERRING SALAD
## with Beetroot and Mushrooms

**4 servings**

Rich, dark beetroot, shining strips of silvery herring, creamy white mushrooms and green spring onions make a stunning visual impact. You may arrange them as you wish. The flavour combinations are equally powerful.

## To make

Bone and skin the herring and slice into bite-sized pieces. Grate the beetroot finely and mix with the oil and vinegar. Taste for seasoning.

## To assemble

Arrange the beetroot on the dish. Place the herring on top, then a spoonful of soured cream and finish with raw mushrooms and spring onion. Serve with thickly buttered Oatmeal Bread (see p.16) or Barley Bannocks (see p.13) and chilled lager.

*Salt Herring Salad*

8 salt herring

2 lb/1 kg beetroot, boiled

2-3 tablespoons wine vinegar or Red Umeboshi (Japanese Plum vinegar)

4 tablespoons olive oil

Salt and pepper

4 oz/125 g mushrooms, sliced

4 spring onions, chopped

4 tablespoons soured cream (not essential)

# Haddock, Cod and Whiting

More haddock is caught and eaten than any other white fish in Scotland. Cod comes next, and then whiting. These, and other demersel fish, have different habits from the herring; swimming around in much smaller shoals at the bottom of the sea, and therefore in less danger of being wiped out with one net. Even so, overfishing has caused quotas to be put on the landings of these fish too. The chemical composition of the haddock flesh is similar to that of cod and other members of the cod family, and therefore it is quite practical in recipes to interchange fish of this type.

## SEASONS AND BUYING

Plump and firm, top-quality North Sea haddock are available from November through to February and are best during these months. After February, they spawn and from April to June the fish are soft and poor quality, but from about July onwards they begin to recover and after September the flesh firms up rapidly. The cycle for fish from more northern waters is the same but occurs about a month or so later than in the North Sea.

## OTHER WHITE FISH

All these fish are available all year round, but for spawning reasons they are a better-quality fish during the following months.

> **BRILL**—June to March
> **COD**—October to February
> **FLOUNDER**—August to November (also known as Flukie)
> **HALIBUT**—August to April
> **HAKE**—May to February
> **LEMON SOLE**—December to March
> **LING**—November to April
> **MEGRIM, ABERDEEN SOLE**—August to April
> **PLAICE**—May to December
> **SAITH**—September to May (also known as Coalfish, Sillock, Coley and Green Cod)
> **TURBOT**—September to March
> **WITCH**—September to May (also known as Witch Sole or Long Flounder)
> **WHITING**—November to March

Treatment and recipes for haddock may be applied to other White Fish, even small cuts of larger fish such as brill or turbot.

# WHOLE FISH—BAKED

**4 servings**

This is most suitable for sole, plaice, trout, sea bass, salmon, mackerel, John Dory and brill. It is a conservation method which keeps all the flavour of the fish intact in a parcel.

## To cook

Pre-heat the oven to 230F/450C/Gas 8.

Wet the paper thoroughly, spread out two thicknesses. Gut the fish and lay on top. Put herbs around the fish and inside its belly cavity. Dot butter on top. Fold and wrap up as a parcel. Put on a baking tray and bake for 10-15 minutes for thin flat fish and 15-20 for thicker, round fish.

Serve the parcels. The skin usually comes off with the paper.

*Baked Fish*

**8 sheets greaseproof paper**

**4 x 1 lb/500 g whole fish**

**Fresh herbs to taste (tarragon, lemon balm and dill are some options)**

**2 oz/50 g butter**

**1 lemon, juice of**

**Salt and pepper**

# HADDOCK AND CHIPS

**4-6 servings**

'Chippies' (Fish and Chip shops) have a mystique of their own—the smell of the fried fish and vinegar mingling and filtering through the newspaper. It's warming and comforting food for cold Scottish winters which remains a popular tradition despite strong competition from other, more modern, fast-food developments.

## Beer Batter

This is a light, crisp batter. The yeast in the beer has a leavening effect if left for up to 24 hours when the batter will have expanded and the flavours amalgamated. It can be used sooner but should be left for at least 1 hour minimum.

Sift the flour into a bowl and add the other ingredients.

Beat with a wire whisk till well mixed and free from lumps. Cover and leave for 1-2 hours or overnight.

*Beer Batter*

**4 oz/100 g plain flour (1 c)**

**2 egg yolks (reserve whites)**

**1½ teaspoons salt**

**2 tablespoons oil**

**4 fl oz/125 ml beer (½ c)**

**Pepper**

49

## To fry the chips

Heat the fat or oil to 375F/190C. Peel 1-2 lb potatoes and cut into even-sized chips. Pat dry in kitchen towel. Immerse chips in a basket in the heated oil and cook, tossing occasionally, till they have just cooked through without taking any colour—known as blanching. Remove from the oil and drain. Repeat the process if they have to be done in two lots. Leave aside till the fish is cooked when the fat should be reheated to 400F/200C. Plunge the chips into the very hot oil, they will brown very quickly. Remove basket; shake off excess oil and drain on kitchen paper for a few minutes. Salt lightly before serving.

## To fry the fish

Heat the oil to 375F/190C.

First beat egg whites fairly stiff and fold gently into batter. Cut each fillet into two up the centre back line to make pieces of roughly the same size and drop three or four pieces into the batter at a time. Gently shake off the excess. Make sure they are well coated before lowering gently into the hot oil. Fry for about five minutes depending on the size and thickness of the fish. Test by removing a piece and gently prising open with a very sharp knife. Turn with a slotted spoon a few times. When cooked drain on kitchen paper to absorb excess fat and repeat the process with the rest of the fish. Keep hot until the chips have been browned off and serve with salt and malt vinegar.

*Fried Fish*

1½ lb/750 kg firm-fleshed
  haddock fillets

Oil for frying

---

*Haddock in a Mustard
  Sauce*

1 lb/500 g fresh haddock
  fillets

1 tablespoon seasoned flour

4 fl oz/125 ml clarified butter
  or oil (½ c)

1 teaspoon Mustard Store
  Sauce (p.224) or other made
  mustard

8 fl oz/250 ml single or double
  cream (1 c)

# FRESH HADDOCK
## in a light, creamy mustard sauce

**4 servings**

This was a popular Victorian breakfast dish which adapts well to lunch, supper or high tea. Mustard with fish is an old combination.

## To cook

Heat about half of the butter in a frying pan. Coat the haddock in butter/oil and then in flour. Put into the pan and seal quickly on both sides without browning. Add cream and simmer gently till the fish is cooked. Remove some of the cooking liquor and mix with the mustard. Return to the pan and mix through but do not cook any longer since mustard loses its flavour very quickly when cooked. Serve the fish and pour over sauce. Serve with Buttered Kale (see p.181) sprinkled with toasted oatmeal.

## GRILLED FRESH HADDOCK
### served with Lemon and Parsley Butter

**4 servings**

Mix the seasoning through the breadcrumbs. Pass the haddock through the butter, drain off any excess and then press into the breadcrumbs. Place on a buttered tray which will fit under the grill and sprinkle the fish with melted butter. Grill gently till golden brown.

### Serve with Lemon and Parsley Butter

Soften the butter slightly without melting and beat in the other ingredients. Roll into a sausage shape and slice ¼ in thick. These can be deep frozen on a small tray and then stored in small freezer bags.

*Grilled Haddock*

**1 lb/500g fresh haddock fillets**

**4 fl oz/125 ml clarified butter (½ c)**

**4 oz/125 g breadcrumbs (1 c)**

**Salt and pepper**

*Lemon and Parsley Butter*

**4 oz/125 g butter (1 stick)**

**2 teaspoons lemon juice**

**Pinch of cayenne pepper**

**Salt to taste (the butter may be salty enough)**

**2 tablespoons finely chopped parsley**

# Air-dried Salted Fish: Sillocks, Cuiths, Ling, Cod and Saith

These were an important part of the fish preservation process for excess catches before rail transport and refrigeration. Aberdeen now has the largest commercial production, and supplies areas where the cure is still popular. They also continue to be produced in some remote areas, and on Orkney and Shetland, by domestic curers.

Though boiling with potatoes, using the highly flavoured fish as a seasoning, is the most popular dish, the salty, flaked fish is also mixed with mashed potatoes to make 'hairy' tatties.

### Traditional method

The fish are gutted and headed, usually split if large and left whole if small. If large the top part of the backbone is removed, then they are layered in coarse salt and completely covered. They may be left for a few days or up to a fortnight when they are removed from the salt. They may then be washed and pressed, usually between stones, to remove as much moisture as possible or they may simply be hung up by the tails in pairs in a cool place with a good draught until they are very hard.

# RIZZARED HADDOCK
## or Blawn Whiting

*The small whiting, hung up with its skin on, and broiled without being rubbed in flour, is excellent. A wooden frame, called a 'hake', is used for drying fish. In Orkney cuiths (which in Shetland they call piltocks and in the Hebrides cuddies) are prepared in this way, care being taken that the fish are perfectly fresh, newly gutted, and thoroughly cleaned, and that the salt is rubbed well in along the bones from which the guts have been removed. They may be either boiled or brandered—if boiled, the are eaten with butter, melted. They are particularly good with buttered bere bannocks or wheaten-meal scones and tea.*

F. Marian McNeill,
*The Scots Kitchen*, 1929.

## *Rizzared Haddock*

**4 whole fresh haddock or whiting (medium size, about ½ lb/250 g each)**

**8 oz/250 g sea salt (1 c)**

**2 tablespoons seasoned flour**

**2 oz/50 g melted butter/oil (½ stick)**

### To prepare

Gut and clean the fish, remove eyes. Place fish in an ashet and sprinkle over salt. Put plenty in the body cavity and rub well into the skin all over. Leave in a cool place for about 12 hours.

Remove and wipe dry. Hang up in a cool place where there is a good draught, threading a wire through the eyes or tie in pairs tied by the tail for another 12 hours.

### To cook

Make about three slashes into the skin across the thickest part of the flesh about an inch apart. Brush with butter and roll in seasoned flour. Grill till lightly browned on both sides. Serve.

*A good breakfast as usual in Scotland, with Findon Haddocks, eggs, sweetmeats (preserved blackcurrants formed one) and honey.*
Robert Southey
*Journal of a Tour in Scotland in 1819*

# FINNAN HADDOCK—COLD SMOKED

This notable Scottish cure makes up about a quarter of the total amount of smoked fish produced in Scotland. They are descendants of 'speldings' which Robert Fergusson refers to in his poem, *The Leith Races*, 1773—'Guid speldins, fa will buy?'—and in the same year James Boswell in his diaries describes them as: 'salted and dried in a particular manner, being dipped in the sea and dried in the sun, and eaten by the Scots by way of a relish.' He also says that you could buy them in London.

Speldings were a hard, salted, unsmoked haddock, distinguished from the modern Finnans which are only lightly salted and smoked. The name 'Finnan' comes from the Aberdeenshire village of Findon where local fishwives developed a high reputation for the quality of their cure. The advent of the railways in the late nineteenth century was responsible for changing a hard, heavily smoked fish into a much more perishable product with obvious improvements to the eating quality. A fish curer in 1882 complained that the old cures 'fell into disuse as transit improved'.

Alternative modern cures which have developed using artificial dyes are known variously as 'golden fillet' or 'yellow fillet', but should not be used as a substitute for the traditional Finnan. The other variation is the Aberdeen fillet, or Smoked fillet. This is a single fillet which has been traditionally cured with no dyes, but with the bone removed before smoking and the skin left on. There is also some local variations of the basic cure such as the Pales, whose brining and smoking times are shorter than for the Finnan. They are made mainly from smaller haddock and include the Eyemouth cure and the Glasgow Pale. Some Pales are so lightly smoked that they have only the slightest smokey flavour and almost no yellow colour.

## Traditional method

Gutted, headed, split fish, with the bone left in, were dry salted overnight then smoked over soft 'grey' peat for 8-9 hours then cooled and washed in warm, salted water.

# EAST COAST FISHWIFE'S BROTH

**4-6 servings**

This was referred to in F. Marian McNeill's *The Scots Kitchen* (1929) as Cullen Skink, though it was a common dish throughout the area. 'Skink' is an old Scots word for 'soup-stew'.

## To cook

Wash the potatoes and put into a pot with the onion. Bring to a simmer and cook until the potatoes are almost ready. Place the Finnan on top and cook for about 5 minutes until it is cooked through. Remove from the heat and leave to cool

To finish the broth, remove the fish. Take off the skin and remove the bones. Reserve the flakes of cooked fish. Remove the potatoes, skin and cut roughly into bite-sized chunks. Return to the broth with the flaked fish. Reheat and add butter. Adjust the consistency with milk. Season and serve.

*East Coast Fishwife's Broth*

1 lb/500 g floury potatoes

1 onion finely chopped

2 pts/1 L water

1 large Finnan or 8 oz/250 g Aberdeen smoked fillet

2 oz/50 g butter

8 fl oz/250 ml milk

salt and pepper

*Finnan Haddock with
Cheese and Eggs*

½ lb/250 g (2 c) grated Galloway Cheddar

1 teaspoonful of cornflour

6 tablespoons milk

3 egg yolks

8 oz/250 g cooked Finnan
haddock

salt, pepper and/or cayenne

# FINNAN HADDOCK
## with Melted Cheese and Eggs

**4-6 servings**

The cheese and eggs combine to make a richly flavoured sauce which is
very quick and easy to make.

### For the Cheese and Egg Mixture

Put the cheese in a pan with the cornflour which has been mixed into 6
tablespoons milk. Heat, stirring constantly, for five minutes till the cheese
melts. Beat the egg yolks together lightly then spoon some of the hot
cheese mixture into the eggs and beat well. Pour back into the pan and
continue cooking over a low heat till the mixture thickens slightly then
add the Finnan haddock. Season with salt, pepper and/or cayenne. Pour
into heated ramekin dishes.

Serve with toast.

*Baked Smoked Haddock*

1½ lb/750 g smoked haddock*

8 fl oz/250 ml double cream
(1 c)

**Freshly ground black pepper**

**Small piece of butter for
greasing**

4 poached eggs

*Either smoked fillets, Aberdeen fillet
with the skin still on or Finnan haddock on the bone may be used—allow
an extra few ounces/grams if the bone
is still in.

# BAKED SMOKED HADDOCK
## with Cream and Poached Egg

**4 servings**

Classically simple comfort food which can be served for breakfast, lunch
or supper with oatcakes or bread and butter or with boiled floury potatoes, baked tomatoes or buttered spinach.

### To cook

Pre-heat the oven to 350F/180C/Gas 4.

Grease a shallow gratin dish with butter and place the fish skin-side
down. Pour over cream and grind some pepper on top (salt should not be
necessary). Bake for 20-30 minutes giving it a shake in the middle of the
cooking to re-coat the fish. Serve with the cream which will have reduced
slightly and thickened and a poached egg.

# SMOKED HADDOCK WITH BACON
## (HAM AND HADDIE)

*Ham and Haddie*

**4 fillets Aberdeen fillet**

**4-8 rashers of Ayrshire bacon**

Pre-heat the oven to 300F/150C/Gas 2.

Rub a pie dish with butter. Place fillets in a single layer and place
bacon on top. Cover with  greaseproof foil and bake for 30 minutes.
Remove the foil for the last 10 minutes to crisp the bacon. Serve with
mashed potatoes.

54

## SMOKED HADDOCK FLAN

A superb fish pie which is richly flavoured with cheese and smoked fish topped with a thick layer of creamy potatoes. It can also be made into a fish pie, omitting the pastry flan, and putting the mixture into a pie dish.

### To cook

Pre-heat the oven to 350F/180C/Gas 4.

Size of flan tin—9 in (22 cm) round by 2 in (5 cm) deep.

Cut the lard and butter into a bowl and pour over the boiling water. Beat with a wire whisk till the fats are melted and the mixture creamy. It does not matter if it separates. Sift in the flour and salt and pepper and add the cheese. Mix thoroughly and put in the refrigerator for at least one hour to harden. Roll out and line flan tin, bake blind.

Place the haddock in milk and poach gently till the fish is almost cooked. Cool, remove the fish and flake. Melt the butter in a pan and add the flour, cook for a few minutes and then strain in the milk from cooking the fish gradually, stirring as it thickens. Add the haddock and season.

### To assemble the flan

Slice the cheese thinly and put a layer in the base of the flan. Cover this with a layer of thinly sliced, hard-boiled eggs and then pour the sauce on top. Leave this to cool and set before putting the potato on top. Spread over and fork up. Cover with a layer of grated cheese and heat through in a hot oven 425F/220C/Gas 7 for 10 minutes or until top is lightly brown. Serve with a light salad for lunch or supper.

From Chef Paul Booth of the Killiecrankie Hotel, 1984.

*Smoked Haddock Flan*

*Never-fail pastry*

(see p.120 for origin)

6 oz/175 g plain flour (1½ c)

2 oz/50g lard (½ stick)

2 oz/50 g butter or margarine (½ stick)

2 fl oz/50 ml boiling water (¼ c)

2 oz/50 ml grated cheese (½ c)

Seasoning

*For the filling*

1 lb/500 g smoked haddock

1 tablespoon plain flour

1 tablespoon butter

½ pt/300 ml milk (1¼ c)

2 oz/50 g Red Galloway Cheddar (½ c)

2 hard-boiled eggs

2 lb/500 g creamed potatoes

1 oz/25 g grated Red Galloway Cheddar (¼ c)

Seasoning

# Hot-Smoked Arbroath Smokie

Before the smoking process moved to Arbroath, to be nearer fish supplies, rows of blackened barrels were dotted along the edge of the cliff in Auchmithie where the cure originated. The lovely wood smoke mingled with the cooking haddock and wafted up the cliffs filling the tiny village street with enticing aromas. The haddock had a darker, more tarry appearance than the modern cure and also a much more powerful flavour of smoke. They were also more salty. At home they were eaten for tea, heated through in the oven, and served with melted butter and piles of hot toast.

## Traditional method

The fish are gutted, headed and dry-salted for about 2 hours, depending on the size of the fish. This is to draw moisture from the fish and impart a slight saltiness. They are then tied in pairs and hung over wooden rods and left to dry for about 5 hours to harden the skin. Then the fish are placed in the smoke-pit and hot-smoked over a hardwood fire of oak or beech, covered with layers of hessian (the number of layers depends on the weather outside and may be adjusted throughout the smoking to prevent the fish smoking too quickly or too slowly). Smoking time is approximately 45 minutes.

## BAKED ARBROATH SMOKIE
### Served with Baked Potato

*Baked Arbroath Smokie*

2 pairs Smokies

2 oz/50 g melted butter (½ stick)

Freshly ground black pepper

**4 servings**

### To cook

Pre-heat oven to 350F/180C/Gas 4.

Place each Smokie on a piece of buttered foil, brush well with butter on both sides. Grind a few turns of pepper over each one. Wrap up, or omit foil and place in a shallow dish with a tightly fitting cover; or cover with foil. Bake for 15-20 minutes. Serve in individually wrapped parcels or remove from foil, split open along the backbone and remove the bone. Place a pat of butter in the centre, close up and serve with lemon wedges and baked potatoes.

## ARBROATH SMOKIE
### Poached in Milk

*Arbroath Smokie Poached in Milk*

4 Smokies

Boiling water

½ pt/300 ml milk (1¼ c)

Pepper

1 teaspoon cornflour

**4 servings**

This traditional way of cooking sometimes has the milk thickened slightly, though in fishing communities it is more often left plain.

### To cook

If the fish are freshly smoked, the skin will peel off quite easily. Otherwise pour boiling water over the smokies, drain and peel off the skin.

Put in a pan with the milk and heat through. Remove fish to warmed serving dish. Blend the cornflour with some of the milk, add to the sauce and boil up to thicken. It should not be too thick. Pour over the fish and serve.

56

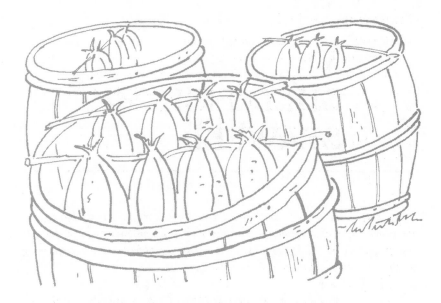

## POTTED ARBROATH SMOKIE
### with Oatcakes

**4 servings**

Remove the skin (as above, with boiling water if necessary). Take the flesh off the bones and place in a bowl. Add softened butter and beat together to a smooth paste. This can be done in a processor which makes the texture a uniform smoothness. Beating by hand produces a roughness without being too coarse. Season with salt, pepper and lemon juice. Pack into one large pot, cover the top with a thin layer of clarified butter (see pp.30-1). Cover with a lid or foil and store in a cool place. They will keep for at least a month.

Serve with slightly warmed oatcakes or hot toast and butter.

*Potted Arbroath Smokie*

**2 medium Smokies (approximately ½ lb/250 g flaked flesh)**

**2-4 oz/50-125 g softened butter**

**Salt**

**Cayenne pepper**

**Lemon juice**

**Clarified butter**

# 3
# SHELLFISH & SEAWEED

---

*Very early in the spring, long before the cold east winds of March have gone, the women take up their positions. Each one has an improvised table, consisting frequently of an orange box, on which are placed saucers containing shellfish, together with the necessary condiments.*

J. H. Jamieson,

'The Edinburgh Street Traders and their Cries' in the *Book of the Old Edinburgh Club*, 1909.

It was industrial pollution which destroyed the huge shellfish beds in Lowland waters which had provided these Edinburgh fishwives with their supplies of street-selling seafood. Taverns too were supplied with vast amounts of shellfish, and a single Edinburgh tavern in the nineteenth century might serve ten thousand oysters a week. But only the remnants of this trade survive, such as the mussels, whelks and clabbies (horse mussels), which are sold at the weekend Glasgow 'Barras' (a Sunday Street Market which began with selling from barrows).

In some parts of the Highlands and Islands, where you would expect it to be most popular, there has been an aversion to shellfish as poverty food. On a West Coast island some years ago, we boiled up a potful of mussels on the beach and some curious local children watching us came back later with some food for the 'starving' people on the beach. Shellfish was 'last resort' food and only eaten in direst poverty. Those displaced from the glens to the coast during the Clearances equated shellfish eating with poverty and it played no part in their everyday diet, though there was an abundance of it free for the taking all round them. Other Highlanders, however, have different attitudes and it would be wrong to think that they all reject it for this reason.

Another factor which has affected recent shellfish eating is the campaign by enlightened fish traders who have recognised the potential of selling seafood at its point of landing. Pioneers have been Loch Fyne

Oysters and Macallums of Troon, both with fish shops and restaurants at the coast selling fish and shellfish straight from the boats. As Scots rediscover the 'buried treasure' which lies beneath the unpolluted waters around their large coastline, shellfish are out in front as top earners for Scottish fishermen. The world wants Scottish shellfish in unlimited quantities and is willing to pay a premium price for it. Now the Scots must value it too. They should make an effort to seek out seafood around the coast, encouraging those who are attempting to change a pattern which deprives Scotland of one of its most valuable eating assets.

**Note on terminology**: because shellfish are sometimes commonly described by a misleading name (eg. a periwinkle called a 'whelk' or a Norway Lobster called a 'prawn' or 'crayfish') I have given the generic name for correct identification.

# Molluscs—Scallops

Their beautifully decorative shell gives them a charm in outward appearance which is only matched by the subtle and delicate flavour of the contrasting creamy muscle and orange coral inside. They call for the simplest methods of cooking since their elusive flavour is easily lost in complicated dishes.

Now a major Scottish shellfish catch, their importance has increased steadily since the 1960s when they were first harvested from natural scallop beds by divers. In the wild they spend most of their life on the sea bed.

## SCALLOP FARMING

This developed in the 1970s and is still developing. It produces a more uniform supply than wild scallops. The young 'spat' are put into 'spat collectors' where they attach themselves to the sides of nets. As their shells begin to grow, they fall off the nets and are gathered into free-floating 'lantern' nets suspended in the sea water where they feed and grow. Queen scallops are left for about one to one and a half years, King scallops for about four to five. Princess scallops are gathered after about a year. Ranching or bottom culture, where the scallops are grown naturally on the sea-bed, is a method favoured by some scallop farmers. This has always been a risky business because it is not possible to protect stocks from dredgers or divers. Recently, however, the first Several Fishery

Orders have been granted to scallop farmers giving their stocks legal protection. The area of production is on the West Coast from Dumfries and Galloway to the Shetlands.

# IDENTIFICATION

The Great or King Scallop (*Pecten maximus*) has a flat-bottomed shell and a concave upper shell with a muscle diameter of approx 5 cm. Minimum legal carapace size is 10 cm. The Queen Scallop (*Chlamys opercularia*), caught in deeper waters, is smaller and the top and bottom shells are both concave. Muscle diameter is approximately 3 cm. Both the Great and the Queen scallop have creamy shells, and a creamy muscle surrounded by an orange roe, both of which are edible, but the 'frill' round the edge of the shell, which is the eyes, should be removed. The Princess scallop is the immature Queen scallop and has a reddish-pink shell with a creamy-white muscle, but the roe has not usually developed fully because of its age.

# BUYING

Scallops may be bought either live in the shell, or shelled. To prevent them drying out if they have been shucked, they may have been soaked in water. 'Soaked' scallops are likely to have considerably less flavour than 'unsoaked' or live in the shell. Soaked scallops are not suitable for frying or grilling where the obvious loss of taste is more obvious. Live scallops should have tightly shut shells. Those which have sprung open have been out of the sea too long and should not be eaten. They can also be bought smoked.

## SCALLOPS IN BUTTER
### with shallots and garlic

**4 servings**

Cooking quickly and lightly preserves their full flavour. Served in their shell with aromatic butter sauce, their natural good looks speak for themselves and need little embellishment.

### To open scallops

Slide the blade of a knife under the flat lid of the shell and cut through the muscle, keeping the blade hard against the shell so that the muscle is removed in one piece. The shell will then open. Scoop out the scallop attached to the hollow shell. Discard the frilly membrane and any brown parts. Reserve 4 good shells, clean well and put to heat through in the oven with a small nut of butter. For shucked scallops, dry well before frying.

## To cook

Heat the oil in a frying pan. Season the scallops with salt and fry in oil for 1-2 minutes on each side. They will cook very quickly. The pan should be hot enough to brown them lightly. Put into heated shells. Finish by adding the butter to the pan. Once it is melted and hot, add the garlic and shallots and swirl around for a minute until they begin to brown a little. Just before pouring over the scallops squeeze lemon juice into the pan and finally the chopped parsley. Serve with crusty bread or hot toast.

### *Scallops in Butter*

8 scallops, preferably live in their shells (16 Queens)

3 tablespoons olive oil

2 oz/50 g unsalted butter (½ stick)

Sea salt

2 large cloves of garlic, crushed

2 shallots, finely chopped

Juice of half a lemon

1 tablespoon parsley, chopped

## STEAMED SCALLOPS
### in a creamy white sauce

**4 servings**

With no competing flavours, and against the neutral background of milk and cream, the natural flavour of the scallops dominates. A crunchy textured breadcrumb-topping contrasts with the soft creamy white sauce. When I make this dish I think of a hotel owner I once worked for in Wester Ross who would have his scallops no other way.

## Cooking the scallops

Prepare the scallops as in the previous recipe or use shucked scallops. Use a double boiler or steamer or plate on top of a pan of hot water. Season the scallops with salt and dot with nuts of butter. Pour over milk and cream. Cover the pan, place it on the heat and bring to the boil. Remove and leave for five minutes with the lid on. The scallops should just cook through, and no more, in the latent heat. It is important not to overcook or too much of the scallop's natural juices will go into the milk if the protein in the flesh coagulates too much.

## Making the sauce

Drain off the cooking liquor and put into another pan. Bring to the boil and reduce slightly. Work the flour into the butter to make a smooth paste and drop very small nuts into the boiling liquid to thicken very lightly. Season.

## Serving

Put scallops into heated shells and pour over sauce. Cover with browned crumbs and serve.

### *Steamed Scallops*

8 scallops, preferably live in their shells (16 Queens)

Sea salt

2 oz/50 g butter (½ stick)

½ pt/250 ml milk (1 c)

2 tablespoons cream

1 tablespoon butter and 1 tablespoon flour, i.e. kneaded butter

Salt and pepper

2 oz/50 g lightly browned breadcrumbs (½ c)

61

# Oysters

Oysters have been eaten with great relish in Scotland for centuries. James Hogg (1770-1835), known as the Ettrick Shepherd, was an avid oyster-eater and complained that 'a month without an R has nae right being in the year'. For centuries they were the central feature of oyster parties in Edinburgh taverns. Genteel Edinburgh ladies with a taste for excitement, and in the days when the centre of city life was still in the Auld Toon, frequented the less-genteel, subterranean Oyster Cellars for dishes of oysters and pots of porter. At the end of the night they would join in the communal drinking of 'a large bowl of brandy punch'.

Oysters were so cheap and plentiful that cooks threw handfuls into sauces, soups and stews (sixty or so at a time) which makes it difficult for us to imagine the kind of flavours they must have created. They were not even the same species as those most common today but were native oysters, mentioned by Martin Martin in his *Description of the Western Islands of Scotland* (1703) as growing on 'rocks and are so big that they are cut in four pieces before they are ate'.

## IDENTIFICATION/BUYING

There are two types of oyster—the wild and the cultivated—but many different species. The original indigenous oyster beds in Scotland were European native oysters (*Sore edulis*). When pollution was destroying the oyster beds at Prestonpans in the Firth of Forth, oyster spat (eggs) was taken from Scotland to Brittany, so that French oysters today have a Scottish pedigree. There are still a few wild beds of native oysters around the coasts but most were overfished when discovered, or became polluted, and are now extinct. Some European native oysters are being commercially cultivated in oyster beds round the Scottish coast.

Breeding oysters retain their eggs and taste unpleasant, though not poisonous. This occurs in most waters from May to August, but Scottish oyster farmers suggest this timing is slightly different for Scotland because of the colder climate and advise that native Scottish oysters will not spawn until well into June.

Pacific oysters (*Crassostrea gigas*) are the most common oysters farmed on the West Coast. They can be sold all year because the water is too cold for them to breed.

Native oysters are fan shaped, almost circular; one half of the shell is flat, the other cupped. The shell of the Pacific oyster is more deeply cupped; rougher and more elongated than the native. All will show variation in colour, texture and flavour according to their origin.

Reject an oyster which is not tightly shut; if buying in a restaurant the sign of a 'good' oyster is that it should be full of liquid and look alive. The bad one is shrivelled and dried up. Despite many claims, there is no scientific evidence that they are aphrodisiacs.

Once the oysters have left the sea they should be kept in a cool place; the salad section of the refrigerator is a good place, under a damp cloth with the flat shell uppermost. They will stay fresh for four to five days but should be eaten sooner if possible since their juices will continue to dry up on keeping.

## FARMED OYSTERS

Scottish farmed oysters are a particularly good flavour since they grow naturally in the very pure sea water in areas which are free from industry and shipping and where population levels are low. They are not put through sterile water tanks in order to make them safe for consumption, but are taken straight from the sea for sale, which retains the natural fresh flavour.

Lochs chosen for oyster farming must have shelter and a rich supply of natural nutrients in the waters. Oysters from different lochs taste differently. The most common method of farming is to put the young seed into mesh bags which are put on metal or wooden trestles at low water mark. Allowing the oysters to be uncovered is considered important since it allows them to close tightly and survive in air, which is essential when they are eventually transported for sale. They are usually harvested after two summers' feeding. They are farmed on the West Coast from Dumfries and Galloway to Shetland, with some in Lothian.

## OPENING

Hold the oyster in a cloth in your left hand with the round side in the palm so that the juice is not lost. Insert a strong knife with a short rounded blade at the hinge end which should be towards you and give a quick upward turn, cutting through the muscle at the hinge. Remove any shell fragments. Loosen round the edge.

## EATING

Oysters are best eaten raw on the half shell. Serve in the deep half to reserve the juice and place on a bed of ice. Serve with brown bread and butter and a chilled dry white wine. Between 8 and 10 are usually regarded as a portion, though a dozen used to be common when they were

*A genuine oyster-eater rejects all additions,—wine, eschalott, lemon, etc., are alike obnoxious to his taste for the native juice.*
Meg Dods
*The Cook and Housewife's Manual,* 1826

cheap and plentiful. (Lemon juice, cayenne pepper, chilli sauce or Tabasco are matters of taste.)

# OTHER WAYS OF EATING OYSTERS

This depends on the type of oyster since some species are large and 'meaty' and lend themselves to cooking. Almost every chef has his own ideas, and whole recipe books have been written on the subject. I like this combination of oysters and whelks which is a version adapted from Troisgros brothers, *The Nouvelle Cuisine*, 1977.

## OYSTERS WITH WHELKS

### *Oysters with Whelks*

24 oysters (8 clabbies)

12 doz whelks (1 pt/1¾ lb/2½ c), washed and steeped overnight in fresh water

*For cooking the whelks:*

2 carrots sliced

1 onion sliced

1 stick celery sliced

1 sprig of thyme

1¾ pts/1 L water (4½ c)

*For the sauce:*

8 oz/220 g butter (2 sticks)

2½ tablespoons distilled vinegar

Juice of half a lemon

Salt, freshly ground pepper

**4 servings**

If oysters are too expensive then Clabbie Dubhs are excellent in this recipe. Their flavour combines well with whelks and their very large deep shells hold the sauce nicely. If the clabbies are large then two per person should suffice. Steam them open first (see recipe p.68).

### To cook the oysters and whelks

Open the oysters over a small pan, catching all the liquid. Detach the oysters and put them into the pan with their liquid. Place the hollow shells in two ovenproof dishes. Put carrots, onions, celery, thyme and vinegar into a pan, add the water and bring to the boil—cook for 15 minutes to develop the flavours. Add the whelks, bring back to the boil and cook for 3 minutes. Take the pan off the heat and let the whelks cool in the liquid. Strain off liquid, reserving about 5 tablespoons. Pick out whelks, remove the eyes (the mica-like plate) and put the whelks into a bowl.

### To make the sauce

Strain the five tablespoons of the whelk-cooking liquid into a small saucepan and place over a fierce heat. Add the butter in very small pieces, working up with a whisk till you have a smooth sauce. Taste for seasoning, add lemon juice.

### To finish the dish

Heat the oysters gently without boiling, about 2 minutes over a medium heat. Heat the empty oyster shells in the oven and put the oysters into their shells. Arrange six whelks in each oyster and cover lightly with the sauce. Place on a bed of coarse sea salt, garnish with a little parsley and add a few whelk shells for decoration.

## OYSTERS IN A CRUST

**4 servings**

Pre-heat the oven to 350F/180C/Gas 4.

Cut the baguette into sixteen slices about one and a half inches thick. Take out some of the bread in the middle (use for breadcrumbs) and put the slices on a baking dish or tray. Drop an oyster in the middle of each slice and cover with a little of the cheese sauce. Bake for 20 minutes, when the oyster should have cooked and the outside become crisp. Serve with ground black pepper or grated nutmeg.

*Oysters in a Crust*

**1 baguette**

**16 oysters**

**Cheese and egg sauce (see p.234)**

**Black pepper**

**Nutmeg, grated**

## OYSTERS ON SKEWERS
### with bacon

(Once known as Angels on Horseback and served as a savoury end to a meal.)

**4 servings**

Pre-heat the grill to moderate. Roll half a rasher of bacon round each oyster and impale 6 on each skewer.

Grill, turning from time to time, until the bacon is cooked. Maximum cooking time about 5 minutes. Season and serve with pepper, crusty bread and unsalted butter.

**Note:** also suitable for clabbies and scallops.

*Oysters on Skewers*

**24 oysters, shelled**

**12 rashers of unsmoked streaky bacon, cut thinly**

**Freshly ground black pepper**

# Mussels
## Common and Horse (Clab-Dubh)

As part of the general foraging for seafood to eke out a meagre diet from the land, both common mussels (*Mytilus edulis*) and the larger horse mussel (*Modiolus modiolus*) were eaten by Scottish peasants living in coastal areas and on islands. Mussel brose was a common dish which, according to a recipe by F. Marian McNeill (1929), was made with cooked mussels and their liquor, plus fish stock and milk. The mussels and the liquid were then poured over a handful of oatmeal in a bowl in the traditional brose style.

## WILD AND FARMED

While some mussels are harvested from rocks, cultivation has been prac- tised throughout Europe for many centuries. First recorded in Scotland

65

in the 1890s, several experiments took place on the East Coast growing mussels on ropes, but the idea was abandoned following a series of disasters. In 1966 experiments were resumed: cultivation was again on ropes and commercial ventures started in the early 1970s using ropes attached to long lines and rafts. Both methods continue to be used with each farmer developing a system which suits his particular site. Once harvested they are washed and graded. Horse mussels are harvested from natural beds lying at extreme low-water mark. Most mussels are harvested from the West Coast though some also come from the East.

## IDENTIFICATION

Usually from 2–3 in (5–8 cm) in length, they have blue-black shells, paler blue turning to pearly white inside with a contrasting orange muscle.

Horse Mussels are known in Scotland by their Gaelic name Clab-Dubh (clabbies) meaning large black mouth. Their flavour is more robust than the small mussel and they are very filling. Small young ones have a more delicate flavour than the larger variety. They are similar in shape and colour to the common mussel, but about 6–8 in (15–20 cm) long.

## BUYING

They should be bought live, all shells tightly shut. Discard any open ones.

They are at their best after summer feeding and before they spawn in the spring. They can be good until February but by March are losing condition.

## PREPARING

Leave overnight in fresh water then scrub clean and remove the beard— the tuft of fibres projecting from the shell which anchors it.

# MUSSEL STEW
## with crusty bread and unsalted butter

**4 servings**

It's simple and quick to cook and serve mussels in their shells. Piled high on plates their steaming aroma captures all the essence of the sea.

## To cook the mussels

Put the water, onion, thyme and bay leaf into a very large pot. Bring to the boil and add mussels. Cover well and cook over a high flame, shaking frequently until the shells begin to open. This will only take a minute, even less if the mussels are small. Remove from the heat, keep the lid on. The remainder of the mussels will open in the latent heat—it is important not to overcook. Pile the mussels high in soup plates. Strain cooking liquor, taste for saltiness and adjust with boiling water if necessary and stir butter in. Season with a few grindings of pepper, add the parsley and ladle over mussels. Serve with crusty bread and butter.

**Using cooked mussels**—Mix through a creamy scrambled egg or warm them through in a little butter and fold into a soft omelette. Add to the sauce with Roast Lamb (p.128).

*Mussel Stew*

4 lb/2 kg mussels in their shells, well scrubbed and cleaned

½ pt/250 ml water (1 c)

1 medium onion, finely chopped

Sprig of thyme

1 bay leaf

1 handful chopped parsley

2 oz/50 g butter (½ stick)

Freshly ground black pepper

# MUSSELS AND COCKLES IN GARLIC AND OLIVE OIL

**4 servings**

Wash the mussels/cockles and soak in salted water for 24 hours.

Heat the oil in a deep pan and cut the garlic in slices. Add to the oil and cook till lightly brown. Add the shellfish and cook over a low heat until they open, stirring from time to time. Remove from the heat, season with pepper and serve with lemon wedges and crusty bread.

*Mussels and Cockles in Garlic and Olive Oil*

2 lbs mussels and/or cockles

3 tablespoons olive oil

3 cloves of garlic

Lemon

White pepper

# MUSSELS
## grilled in their shells with wine and butter

**4 servings**

French friends, visiting us in the Highlands, cooked and served mussels gathered from rocks in the loch in this way. Filling the mussels with a little wine and butter keeps the mussels plump, juicy and full of flavour, but it does not work so well with small mussels.

## Mussels Grilled with Wine and Butter

4 lb/2 kg mussels, well washed and scrubbed

½ pt/250 ml white wine (1 c)

2 oz/50 g butter (½ stick)

1 handful chopped parsley

## Clabbie Dubhs with Leek and Tomatoes

8 clabbies

1 pt/500 ml water (2 c)

1 leek, finely chopped

3 tablespoons olive oil

6 oz/175 g risotto rice (1 c)

3 medium tomatoes, finely chopped

2 cloves garlic, crushed

Salt and freshly ground pepper

### Cooking the mussels

Put a large open pan on to heat. Add about ¼ in (½ cm) water and bring to the boil. Add the mussels and cook over a high heat, stirring and tossing all the time till they open. Remove and take out of shells.

### Serving

Remove beards and split shells. Place half shells on a cooling rack or wire rack and put a mussel into each shell. Fill up shell about three quarters full of wine, add a knob of butter and put under a hot grill for a minute. Sprinkle over some chopped parsley and place (still on rack) on a tray in the centre of the table. Eat with the fingers with crusty bread and butter.

# CLABBIE DUBHS
## with leek and tomatoes

**4 servings**

A robustly flavoured soup-stew which can be made first as a stew, then thinned down with stock and with some more vegetables and served as a soup the next day.

### Preparing

Cook the clabbies in water till they just open. Strain the cooking liquor. Take clabbies out of their shells and remove beards. Cut into two or three pieces depending on size.

### Cooking

Melt the oil in a pan and add the white of the leek, cook for a few minutes and then add tomatoes and garlic. Stir in the rice and then start adding the cooking liquor. Add enough to make a sloppy mixture and cook uncovered till it is absorbed, stirring from time to time. Add more stock as needed without making the mixture too wet. It should take about 20 minutes to cook the rice.

Now add the green leek, stir through till softened and finally add the chopped mussels just before serving. Season well.

# Periwinkles—Scottish Whelks

Local pickers now collect Scottish whelks in large numbers round the coasts. The best Scottish whelks are from the richest feeding grounds: plump juicy morsels with a unique flavour. Market demand for them has been growing steadily as their popularity increases.

## IDENTIFICATION

The periwinkle (Latin name *Littorina littorea*), which is known in Scotland as a whelk or buckie, has a dark grey/black little shell. The true whelk (*Buccinum undatum*) has a whiter shell and flesh and is known to Scots as the Dog Whelk. It is not generally eaten, since it is tough and lacking flavour compared with the black variety.

## PREPARATION

Steep overnight in fresh water to remove sand, etc.

## COOKING

Place in boiling water to cover and simmer for 2-3 minutes. Drain, save liquid for using as stock.

## EATING

Serve with a large pin to pick out the meat. Discard the mica-like plate, 'the eye', at the mouth of the shell.

# Razor-shell Clams—Scottish Spoots

These are a highly esteemed delicacy among coastal communities who catch their own seafood. Difficult to find, razor-shell clams (*Ensis ensis*) take their name from the shape of an old cut-throat razor. The shells have a glossy brown exterior and the inside shell is white, they are very brittle and gape permanently at either end.

## CATCHING/BUYING

They are often found in reasonable numbers at the very edge of the lowest tides and especially where there are spent shells to be seen. The

*'Wanted: Spoots, Spoots and More Spoots,' said a newspaper article when I was last in Orkney, spoots being what they call razor-shells there. I went spooting at the lowest of low tides and with an expert guide, but came back with nothing but mussels.*
Alan Davidson
*North Atlantic Seafood*
(Penguin, 1979)

traditional method of catching is to walk backwards along the beach, watching for the little 'spoot' (spout) of water ejected by them as you walk over the sand. If one is located the spooter inserts a long pronged fork or knife to locate where the shell is, and then catches it and twists it round to bring it to the surface. This must be done very quickly for spoots can burrow into the sand if they sense danger. Both diving and suction dredging are commercial methods for catching them.

Like a number of other Scottish shellfish the catch is largely exported, some to Hong Kong where they are highly prized by the Chinese. Season is from October to May. Hand fishing takes place in March and September when the equinox produces particularly low ebb tides.

## COOKING

The best method is to put them on a hot charcoal grill when they will be ready as soon as the shells open. Otherwise they can be grilled or steamed very briefly, as you would mussels, simply to open the shells, and then either eaten cold or used to make shelfish broth with the cooking liquor. Remove the stomach bag and add the meat chopped finely just before the soup is served. If overcooked they become chewy to the point of being inedible.

# Other Scottish Molluscs— Limpets, Cockles, Clams

These are common on Scottish sea shores though not as widely used or sold as others.

Limpets have an interesting flavour but rather a tough muscle. Chip them off the rocks with a sharp knife or knock them with a sharp stone. They are boiled in the usual way and can then be added to Stovies (p.180). The liquid which they have been cooked in has lots of flavour and should be used as stock for making fish sauces and soups. Small limpets are more tender and once boiled, can be fried with bacon.

Cockles live in sand and have to be raked out and must be steeped in fresh water with a handful of oatmeal or flour to remove the sand. They may be eaten raw or cooked as for mussels.

Clams are usually cooked, but very small ones can be eaten raw.

# Crustaceans—Edible Crab or Common Crab—Scottish Partan, Velvet Crab

The partan (*Cancer pagurus*) was a common item of food for coastal communities. More easily caught than lobsters, they became more integrated into the diet and were used like mussels, to flavour broths. Commercial creel fishing for crabs and lobsters began in the mid-eighteenth century, though crabs were never as highly regarded as lobster. They have, however, experienced a recent revival as their value has been better appreciated. At centres of intensive crab fishing, such as in Orkney, processing plants have been set up to remove the crab meat from boiled crabs. Creel caught, dark brownish red, velvet crabs, are a smaller species than the partan. They are highly regarded in Mediterranean countries and most of the catch is exported, with very small amounts reaching the local market. Crabs have been most appreciated on the East coast, rather than the West where creel fishermen, as recently as the 1960s, were throwing crabs back into the sea considering them not worth the effort of finding a buyer.

## IDENTIFICATION

Partans are reddish brown colour, tinted with purple, legs reddish and claws black. Legal minimum size is 4½ in (11 cm). Size across the back up to 12 in (30 cm).

## BUYING CRAB

Preferably buy live: they should smell fresh with no hint of ammonia and they should be reasonably lively. Lift the crab by its back to check that it is a good weight for its size. Male crabs are a better buy since they have a better quality and higher proportion of white meat than females. They can be distinguished from the female by a smaller tail flap on the underside. They are available all year round but are best from April to September.

## BOILING CRAB

Put live crab in boiling, salted water, press down with tongs for a few minutes and then reduce to a simmer and cook for about 10-15 minutes. Remove from the pan and leave to cool.

71

## TO REMOVE MEAT BEFORE SERVING

1. Remove the claws and legs close into the body shell. Crack the shell of each claw with a wooden mallet without damaging the flesh. Remove the flesh and separate the bony cartilage. Break open the legs at the joints and pick out the flesh with a skewer.

2. To open the crab, pull off the tail flap and discard. Hold the crab in both hands with two thumbs hard against the base at the bottom of the tail flap and press hard. The whole central part should come out, but if it does not, loosen with a knife round where the legs were attached and then press again. Pull central part free and remove the elongated gills (deadmen's fingers) along with edges and discard. Cut down the middle and use a skewer to pick out the flesh from the many crevices on both sides.

3. With a teaspoon, scoop out the meat from inside the shell and reserve it, but remove and discard the small stomach sac which is just behind the crab's mouth.

4. To open out the shell, press round the outer edge where there is a weak line: it should break cleanly. Wash the shell.

## TO SERVE PLAINLY

Mix the brown body meat with the meat from the centre part of the shell. Season and return to the shell on either side, leaving a space in the centre for the claw and leg meat. Garnish with chopped parsley and serve with a lightly flavoured mayonnaise, brown bread and butter.

## PARTAN PIES

*Partan Pies*

4 medium crabs

2 tablespoons soft breadcrumbs

4 oz/125 g butter (1 stick)

¼ grated nutmeg

Salt and pepper

1 handful of chopped parsley

**4 servings**

The crab shell acts as a useful container for all the meat extracted. The strongly flavoured body meat can be flavoured with a little nutmeg and packed into the sides of the shells, leaving space in the middle for the white claw meat.

### To cook

Boil the crabs and remove all meat from claws and body, clean out shell thoroughly, break off pieces of shell on either side of eyes with thumbs. They should come cleanly away to open up the shell more.

Keep the two meats separate. Put the soft body meat in a bowl and add the breadcrumbs, half the butter and nutmeg. Season with salt to taste. Pack this mixture into the sides of the shell. Mix the other meat with softened butter, season with salt and pepper and place in the centre. Cover with foil and heat through in the oven or serve cold garnished with chopped parsley.

## PARTAN BREE

### Serves 4

The crab flavour comes through strongly in this creamy soup which is thickened with rice. It is also good made with razor fish. Bree means liquid or gravy.

### To cook

Remove all the meat from the crab but keep the claw meat separate. Put the rice into a pan with milk and water and cook till tender. Liquidise this with the brown body meat from the crab and then add the white meat. Add cream and re-heat. Taste for seasoning. Adjust consistency with more milk if necessary. Serve garnished with some finely chopped chives.

*Partan Bree*

**1 large cooked crab (see p.87)**

**2 oz/50 g rice (¼ c)**

**1 pt/600 ml milk (2½ c)**

**1 pt/600 ml cooking liquor from boiling the crab (2½ c)**

**¼ pt/125 ml single cream (¾ c)**

**Salt and pepper**

**Garnish—finely chopped chives**

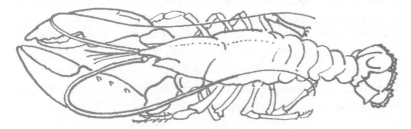

# Lobster—European

It was around the mid-eighteenth century that commercial creel-fishing began for crabs and lobsters. The lobster (*Homarus gammarus*), however, became highly prized by English fish merchants who organised a system for transporting them to the London fish market in a boat fitted with floating chests or 'keep boxes'. By the nineteenth century, however, there is evidence that they had also been taken up by Scottish gourmets, notably the gathering of gastronomes known as the Cleikum Club where their recipe for 'Lobster Haut Gout' involves much spicing and a red wine sauce. Though the style is simpler today, the wholesale exodus of lobster has been halted, slightly, with some appearing more frequently on Scottish menus as native chefs follow the trend to make more use on local menus of local produce.

# IDENTIFICATION

Bluish-black shell, thick round body and two large forward claws. Length up to 18 in (45 cm). In order to protect stocks, a minimum landing size was introduced in 1984 of 85 mm (approx. 3½ in) carapace length (upper body shell). Weight varies from ¾ lb (375 g) to 2¼ lb (1¼ kg).

## BUYING LOBSTER

Choose a live lobster which looks lively, i.e. when prodded it thrashes about with some vigour. If it is sluggish in reacting, then it has probably been kept for several days out of water and without food, with a consequent loss of weight and vitality. Lift up the lobster by the back: it should feel heavy for its size.

Available all year round but best and most plentiful in the summer.

## KILLING LOBSTER

(If possible, ask your fishmonger to kill it for you.)

**Method 1**—Recommended by the RSPCA. Put in the freezer for 2-3 hours and then cut in half through the spinal cord. Hold the lobster on a chopping board, underside down, and using a heavy sharp knife pierce the shell firmly in the centre of the cross-shaped mark behind the head. Press down heavily and cut along the body and tail to halve the lobster. Then cut the head in half.

**Method 2**—To both kill and cook the lobster, fill up a large pot with boiling salted water and plunge the lobster in. Hold it under the surface with tongs for two minutes. Turn down the heat, cover the pan and simmer the lobster, allowing 12 minutes for the first 1 lb (500g) and 10 minutes for the next pound and 5 minutes for each additional pound.

## GRILLED LOBSTER

*Grilled Lobster*

2 x 1½-2 lb (¾-1 kg) live
    lobsters

4 oz/125 g unsalted butter (1
    stick)

1 tablespoon tarragon

Juice of a small lemon

Salt and pepper

**2-4 servings**

Using an uncooked (method 1) lobster, this is the best way to preserve its full flavour. It is important not to overcook and dry out the flesh. The tarragon flavouring comes from Sonia Stevenson: fish cook extraordinary and author of *A Fresh Look at Fish*, 1996.

### Preparing the lobster

Once the lobster is split, remove the sand sac and the coral if it is a hen lobster. This looks like a long, dark greenish-black sac running along the back under the shell. It turns a bright scarlet when cooked. Discard the white gills and the intestinal canal which runs down the middle of the tail.

## Making the butter

Put the butter and the coral into a food processor and blend together. Add the tarragon and lemon juice.

## Grilling

Remove claws from the body. Place claws and body shell on a baking or roasting tin, shell-side up. Put under a hot grill for 2 minutes or until they turn red. Remove. Turn over and spread cut surface with flavoured butter. Turn over the claws. Grill for 3-4 minutes, remove claws and check body. When the meat comes away easily from the shell they are cooked. Serve with the pan juices poured over the meat. Crack the claws and arrange on the plate beside the body shell. Serve with finger bowls and a bowl of fluffy cooked rice.

# BOILED LOBSTER

How to prepare a boiled lobster for serving plainly:

1. Remove the lobster when it is cooked and leave to cool. Snap off the eight legs close to the body. Break legs at joints and pick out meat with a skewer.

2. Remove each claw close into the body, and bang with a wooden mallet to crack the shell. Pull away the shell and remove the meat. Remove the cartilage that runs through each claw.

3. Lay the lobster on its back and cut with a heavy, sharp knife close to the hard outer shell along its entire length on either side. Pull away the bony covering on the underside. Starting at the tail, prise away the tail meat in one piece. Strip off the brown-grey feathery gills.

4. The soft grey-green liver remains in the shell. Scoop it out with a spoon and save. Lift out the inedible gravel sac (stomach) and discard.

5. Lay the tail meat on a chopping board and slice into pieces about ¾ in (2 cm) thick. Scrape out any remaining meat in the lobster shell.

## To serve

Clean the empty tail shell and fill with the meat. Arrange the remainder attractively on a large white plate with the liver and coral (if there is any) as a garnish. Decorate with some cooked and buttered mangetout peas. May be served with a lightly flavoured lemon mayonnaise and brown bread and butter. Chilled dry white wines or Champagne are best with cold lobster.

## Lobster Soup

*Fish Stock*

1 leek

1 onion

1 celery stalk

1 small head of fennel

few sprigs of thyme

1-2 bay leaves

12 black peppercorns

5 fl oz/150 ml dry white wine

2-4 lb/1-2 kg lobster shells
  and white fish trimmings
  including heads

Water to cover

*For the soup*

2 large pinches of saffron

4 tablespoons boiling water

1 tablespoon olive oil

1 oz/50 g butter

2 large beefsteak tomatoes

2 garlic cloves, crushed

2 teaspoons flour

5 fl oz/150 ml soured cream
  or crème fraiche

1 cooked lobster (or 8 oz/250 g
  of other shellfish or fish).

# LOBSTER SOUP

**4-6 servings**

A special occasion soup which takes time to prepare and costs a fortune. But there are never any regrets when you sit down to steaming platefuls of such a remarkable soup. Its secret lies in the deep flavour which saffron brings to any fishy dish plus the system of broth making, which early Scots perfected, of preparing an aromatic 'strong broth' first which extracts the maximum fish flavour from bones, heads, vegetables and herbs.

## Making the stock

Chop all the vegetables roughly and put in a pot with the thyme, bay leaf and peppercorns. Simmer to reduce by half, adding the white wine about halfway through.

Clean fish trimmings, removing the gills, and add to the vegetables. Bring up to simmering point and cook, just simmering, for about 20 minutes. Leave until slightly cooled but not cold and strain.

## Making the soup

Pour boiling water over the saffron. Heat the oil and butter in a pan and add the tomatoes. Cook for a few minutes until the tomatoes are pulped. Stir in the garlic and flour.

Cook for a few minutes and then add the saffron and add 2 pts/1 L of the stock gradually. Bring to the boil and remove from the heat. Purée till fine in a processor. Return to the pan. Add soured cream or crème fraiche to taste. Season with salt. Add the lobster pieces and just heat through. Serve.

# Norway Lobster

Of all Scottish shellfish, this is the one which has 'taken off' most successfully. In the early 1950s it was completely unknown commercially but is now a major shellfish catch either creel-caught or trawled. It is caught in deep, muddy waters on the East and West Coast, particularly in the Firth of Forth, the Moray Firth, the Minch and the Clyde.

It is known by many names, which causes much confusion. The generic name is *nephrophs norvegicus*. A species of the Lobster family, their name has been confused with prawns, initially by the fishermen who refer to 'prawn-boats' and 'prawn-fishing'. This first occurred when Dublin fishermen described *nephrophs* as Dublin Bay Prawns. This is the first name they were popularly known by in the UK. Then the Dublin Bay part was dropped and they became known simply as 'prawns', which was an unfortunate misnomer since the Norway Lobster is really nothing like the common prawn (*Leander senatus*). Perhaps the important point to remember is that *nephrophs* is in fact a true lobster with all the characteristics which distinguish the common lobster. (They are known to the Italians as *Scampi* and the French as *Langoustine*.)

In Scotland, they are also sometimes referred to in the fish trade and on hotel menus as Crayfish. This is correctly the name of a freshwater crustacean (*Astacus fluvuatilis*) no longer common in Britain but a great delicacy in Scandinavia. It is yet another misnomer further adding to the confusion.

# IDENTIFICATION

Whole, they look like small lobsters, but a different colour, for they are pale, orangey pink and when raw the claws are striped with white. Sometimes they are sold alive and this is the best way to buy them. Also sold pre-boiled. Flavour and texture deteriorate with freezing.

# BUYING

You can expect an average of 6-8 whole per pound.

For 4 servings depending on course and other accompaniments— approx. 2 lb/1 kg tails in their shells; 1 lb tails shelled; 3-4 whole per person for a starter, double for main course depending on size. There is a quality difference between creel-caught and trawled, since the creel-caught should still be alive and therefore fresher, while the trawled will almost certainly have died during the trawling process. The better flavour and texture of a creel-caught langoustine is easily recognisable. Available all year round but best in the summer months.

# PREPARING AND COOKING

Boil in salted water for three to four minutes, depending on size, with a few bay leaves and juniper berries—drain. They need little preparation if being served in the shell. If they are whole and have been pre-cooked first pull off the head and claws. Then cut with a sharp knife through the bony cartilage on the underside, but do not cut through the tail meat. Open out and remove the whole tail, pick out spinal cord. Crush the claws with a wooden mallet and pick out the meat with a skewer.

## SERVING

These very pretty, pink-orange shelled creatures need no fancy garnishing.

## TO SERVE HOT IN THEIR SHELLS

They may be tossed in butter for a few minutes till thoroughly heated through then served in the centre of the table in the sauté pan or an a heated ashet and garnished with some colourful fresh fruits—Kiwi fruit, pineapple (use leaves to decorate), mango, strawberry. (As served by Nick Ryan at his seafood restaurant in Crinan Hotel, Argyll, and described as Jumbo 'Prawns' Corryvreckan.)

## TO SERVE AS A COLD SALAD

They may be left in their shells or removed and used to decorate a large, preferably white, plate. Use green salad vegetables and herbs to complement the pink-orange colour. Serve with Shellfish Sauce (see p.81).

## GRILLED NORWAY LOBSTER

As recommended by David Wade of Amazon Seafoods at the wet fish counter on Gairloch pier in Wester Ross. Treat the creel-caught, largest size, he says, as for lobster. Split in half down the back. Open out and place on a baking tray. Brush with butter, sprinkle with a little dry white wine and a crushed clove of garlic. Grill until the flesh comes away from the shell and is cooked through.

# Other Scottish Crustaceans
## —Spiny Lobster (Crawfish/French, *Langouste*), Brown Shrimp, Common Prawn and Squid

These are available from Scottish waters in varying quantities. Least available are the Spiny Lobsters. Their most noticeable feature, in comparison with lobster, is that they do not have claws. They are reddish-brown in colour with yellow and white markings and for cooking they can be treated in the same way as Lobsters.

The catch of 'spinies' or Squat Lobsters (one third the size of Norway Lobsters) has gradually been increasing, as these interesting little shellfish become better known.

Both Brown Shrimps and Common Prawns are harvested from Scottish coasts but not in large quantities. While there is historical evidence of both shrimps and prawns having been eaten by Scots in the past there is no evidence of squid. Abundant supplies are available but it is largely the ethnic communities in Scotland, particularly the Chinese, who have made full use of squid's potential.

# Other Shellfish Recipes

## FRUITS OF THE SEA

**4-6 servings**

Shellfish traders in Scotland complain that native Scots do not appear to appreciate the value of shellfish, at its best, in the shell. To get the full value of their catch it must be exported but they would really prefer to sell more of it in Scotland. Other Europeans, who value the quality of Scottish shellfish, serve it simply on a large tray of crushed ice on what is known as a *fruit de mer* stand.

### To prepare

Pile the shellfish on top of the ice on the tray. Place stand in the centre of the table and put tray on top. Provide plates for shellfish debris and finger bowls.

*Fruits of the Sea*

4 lbs/2 kg mixed shellfish, cooked in the shell (but including some raw oysters)

1 large round tray filled with crushed ice

1 *fruit de mer* stand (available from cook shops)

Bowl of halved lemons

Finger bowls

# ARISAIG SEAFOOD PASTRY

### Arisaig Seafood Pastry

1 lb/500 g puff pastry

2 lb/1 kg selected seafood, shelled

6 oz/175 g butter (1½ sticks)

2 oz/50 g well flavoured Scottish cheddar, grated (½ c)

1 egg yolk mixed with 1 teaspoon water for glaze

Salt and pepper

*For the sauce*

3 oz/75 g flour (¾ c)

3 oz/75 g butter (¾ stick)

1½ pt/850 ml milk and fish stock (3¾ c)

**6-8 servings**

This is made with whatever seafood is fresh and available from local boats at Mallaig. Usually the selection includes Norway lobster, prawns, salmon, clams, monkfish, halibut or turbot, crabs and lobster when they are plentiful and cheaper, and also squid.

Pre-heat the oven to 450F/230C/Gas 8.

## To make the sauce

Make a roux with the flour and butter and then add the milk gradually and cook till thick.

## To bake the pastry

Roll out the pastry to ⅛ in (3 mm) thick and into strips about 3 in (8 cm) wide. Brush top with egg glaze and bake till golden and risen.

## To assemble the dish

Melt the butter in a pan and add the seafood. Sauté lightly till cooked. Mix into the white sauce and add cheese, taste for seasoning. Split the pastry through the middle and fill the bottom half with the seafood. Cover with lid. Slice and serve hot with lemon and green salad.

From Janice Stewart, Arisaig Hotel, Inverness-shire, 1984.

# SHELLFISH BROTH

### Shellfish Broth

Selection of shellfish

1 onion, finely chopped

1 oz/25 g butter

Chopped parsley

Pepper

The smaller crustaceans, taken as a group, have diverse shapes and colours from dark blue mussels to bright orange coral from scallops. To assemble them simply, plainly boiled in their cooking liquor, has a stunning visual effect. Serving can be done in two ways. Either pile all the shellfish in a very large ashet in the centre of the table and serve the broth separately in a tureen with a ladle, or arrange the shellfish in large, round, deep soup plates and pour over the hot broth just before serving.

Selection of shellfish from the following:

(1) **Mussels, whelks, cockles**—Clean well, scraping shells if necessary.

(2) **Norway Lobster, crawfish, spinies**—Wash well.

(3) **Scallops, oysters**—Open shells, loosen them from the shells and reserve the juice in a bowl.

## To cook the shellfish

Put the mussels into a pan with about ½ in of boiling water in the bottom. Keep moving till they open, then remove from the heat. Cover and keep warm. Cook the cockles in the same way—reserve cooking liquid and keep warm. Cook the whelks in boiling water for about 5 minutes. Reserve liquid and keep warm.

If not already cooked, boil the Norway Lobster and crayfish in boiling water, reserve liquid and keep warm.

Cook the oysters gently in their own juice and a little water. The scallops only take a couple of minutes; the oysters about 30 seconds. Return to shells and keep warm.

## To make the broth

Sauté the onion in butter till yellow and soft then add the cooking liquor from the shellfish to make up to 2 pts/1 L/5 c. Some will be saltier than others so balance the combination accordingly. Add chopped parsley. Pour over shellfish in plates or put into tureen. Finish by throwing a handful of freshly chopped parsley over the shellfish and serve.

# SHELLFISH SAUCE
## for serving with all cold shellfish

Leftover shells still hold an amazing amount of hidden flavour, which can be extracted by making this lovely sauce to serve with any cold shellfish.

## To make

Crush soft shells in a liquidiser or food processor. Melt the oil and sauté them for 5 minutes. Add the cognac, flame and then add the white wine followed by the fish stock or water. Simmer for 20 minutes.

Strain through a conical strainer pressing the shells firmly with the back of a spoon to press through all the flavour.

Return stock to the pan and reduce to about 4 tablespoons. Remove from pan and allow to cool. Mix the mustard, cream, vinegar, salt and pepper in a bowl. Whisk together and then start adding the shellfish stock gradually. Season. Serve cold. This is not a store sauce and so will not keep.

# ORKNEY SQUID

**4 servings**

Good supplies of small, tender squid are available in Orkney. These are lightly cooked in a rich tomato sauce and colourfully finished with parsley and chives. Unless squid are very large, they cook as soon as they

*Shellfish Sauce*

*For the stock*

**2 lb/500 g heads of either lobster or Norway Lobster**

**1 tablespoon cognac**

**1½ tablespoons dry white wine**

**1 tablespoon neutral oil**

**¼ pt/150 ml fish stock (¾ c) or water**

*For the sauce*

**¼ pt/150 ml whipping cream (¾ c)**

**1 tablespoon wine vinegar**

**1 teaspoon smooth Arran mustard**

**Salt and freshly ground black pepper**

81

## Orkney Squid

4 small squid, with or without
tentacles, cleaned

2 tablespoons oil

1 medium onion, finely chopped

4-5 large tomatoes, skinned
and chopped

1 clove of garlic, crushed

3 tablespoons red wine

Salt and pepper

1 tablespoon chopped parsley

*In the North, and in many other
places on the coast of this
country, people feed upon Sloke,
that is, the sea lettuce; they make
Broath with it, and sometimes
serve it up with butter. Some of
them eat dils; ...and some eat
that sort of Sea Tangle. It is a
pleasant taste betwixt salt and
sweet; it's eaten as a salade.*

R. Sibbald
*Provision for the Poor in Time of
Dearth and Scarcity,* Edinburgh,
1709

have heated through. Cooking for longer toughens them. Served with
some lemon and a local beremeal bannock they are a unique taste of the
islands.

### To cook

Leave squid whole or cut into rings. Heat the oil in a pan and add the
onion. Cook till soft then add the tomatoes and reduce slightly. Add the
wine and garlic. Simmer for a few minutes to blend the flavours. Season.
Add the squid and heat through. Stir in parsley. Serve with a toasted
Barley Bannock (see p.13).

(From Norma Hasham, Foveran Hotel in Kirkwall, 1984.)

# Seaweeds

'Dulse and Tangel' was a favourite Leith street-cry a hundred years ago.
Around the coastal areas of the Highlands and Islands there is also evidence of the wide use of seaweed with twenty-two different Gaelic names
for it. Gathered from the foreshore it was used, particularly dulse, to
flavour broths, deepening the flavour with the seaweed's high content of
strongly flavoured amino acids. Dulse was eaten raw by children and
was an important source of nutrients. In the Hebrides the blade of sea-
tangle, or redware, was eaten: cut away from the fronds and stalk, it was
roasted on both sides over embers and then placed on a buttered barley
bannock.

Wet and slippery on seaside rocks, it has a lively taste of the sea.
Orientals make the most of seaweed, doing inventive things like changing
the thin, slippery fronds of sloke, which they call *nori*, into crinkly, black,
paper-thin sheets which look and feel nothing like the real thing. Everyone eats it. The same nori can be found in Wales and the West Country,
not in thin, dry sheets but made into a black jelly known as laverbread
and sold from bowls which sit amongst the fresh fish on fishmongers'
slabs. 'Words cannot describe how wonderful laverbread is,' says Jackie
Geer, in *The Best of Breakfasts, Recipes from Radio 4's 'On your Farm'*.
'Rolled in oatmeal and fried in bacon fat—a true gastronomic experience.'

Seaweed is nutritionally very low in fat, almost calorie free, while at
the same time containing more minerals than any other kind of food. It is
high in potassium iodide. Approximately 30% of the mineral content is
lost to the soaking water, so use this water whenever possible.

# GATHERING/BUYING/DRYING

Seaweeds have seasons of growth like other plants. They produce shoots and should be harvested before they become fertile when they build up a bitter content which makes the flavour harsh. The season is spring to autumn. Remove the overlying seaweed and gather the tiny plants from beneath. Do not take too far down the stem since if enough is left the weed will regenerate. Commercial divers harvest autumn dulse, pepper dulse, daberlocks, grockle, sugar ware, finger ware and sloke (wild nori). It is air-dried in a recirculating drying oven at a low heat to preserve the flavour but remove the moisture content. It is then packed in airtight packets.

Fresh gathered seaweed should be washed in running water to remove sand, shells, etc. It is easy to dry and store. Simply lay out in a good cold current of air till thoroughly dry and store in an airtight container. It may be dried in the sun.

Dried seaweed can be bought in specialist whole food shops. Japanese or other Oriental food shops are the best source. Light and cheap to post, mail order is also a good option: the largest and oldest established company (1954) is Carabay Seaweeds, Kylebroughlan, Moycullen, Co Galway, Ireland.

# CARRAGHEEN (*CHONDRUS CRISPUS*)

This is named after the village of Carragheen near Waterford in Ireland where it abounds. It usually grows on a boulder-strewn shore near the low water mark of spring tides, so that sometimes it can be collected only about two hours each side of the low water for a few days each fortnight. Carragheen is high in vitamin A and iodine and it also contains B vitamins and many minerals. It is an important source of vegetable gelatines (alginates) which are used commercially for thickening soups, emulsifying ice creams and setting jellies.

# IDENTIFICATION

Having spent fruitless hours, with frozen hands and feet, gathering Batter Frond which is very similar in appearance to Carragheen but produces no jelly, I recommend buying some to identify it correctly first. The branched fronds can be up to 6 in (15 cm) long, and their colour varies from purple to brown to a bleached browny white when exposed to light.

These have a distinctly flat stalk, and branch repeatedly into a rough fan shape. Batter Frond is different since it has a concave surface with the sides of each segment tending to roll inwards, and older specimens have tiny pimples.

## CARRAGHEEN CHOCOLATE PUDDING

*Carragheen Chocolate Pudding*

½ oz/15 g dried carragheen (¼ c)

1 pt/600 ml milk (2½ c)

1 tablespoon sugar

1 egg

2 oz/50 g bitter chocolate

Almond or vanilla essence or Angostura Bitters

Children in Ireland enjoy this pudding. Carragheen has a bland flavour which can do with some pepping up. In its natural state it was eaten mostly by invalids who were unable to cope with other food and Highlanders still make a natural Carragheen Jelly for the sick. To make this, omit all the other flavourings except the sugar, though without it, the true flavour of the seaweed can be appreciated and some people prefer to eat it like this with lots of whipped cream, even if they are not ill.

### To cook

Wash the carragheen in cold water to remove any grit etc. Put into a bowl and just cover with hot water—about ¼ pt/150 ml (¾ c). Leave for 15 minutes. The seaweed will have softened and the liquid become jellyfied. Put into the milk. Bring to the boil and simmer gently for about 10 minutes or until the mixture is quite thick—about 20 minutes. Strain. If the seaweed is very young and tender much of it can be pressed through the sieve, though this obviously gives a stronger carragheen flavour. Melt the chocolate over a gentle heat and add the mixture with the sugar, egg yolk and flavouring, stirring well. Beat the egg white till stiff and fold in. Pour into a mould or four small dishes and leave till set. Serve with cream.

## CARRAGHEEN
### for thickening soups and stews

To add to soups and stews, soak in cold water for a few minutes and remove from the water leaving behind the grit, etc. chop the carragheen finely or put some of the soup or stew liquid into a liquidiser with the carragheen and blend till smooth. Carragheen gives nice body to a soup or stew; the delicate flavour is not obvious.

# DULSE AND TANGLE

Dulse (*Rhodymenia palmata*) is a broad-leaved seaweed, dark reddish purple in colour, which can grow up to 12 in (30 cm) long. The young fronds are thin and papery. Tangle is a variety known as *Laminaria sacharina*, often found attached to small stones on muddy, sandy flats. Pepper Dulse (*Laurencia pinnatifida*) can be a variety of colours from yellow-green to red-brown and is up to 7 in (18 cm) long. This is the one which Scots like to chew for its pungent flavour and which is sometimes known as Poor Man's Tobacco. It is the kind of eating experience which begins in childhood, beachcombing with parents who encourage the idea of eating seaweed, and a lifelong liking, even craving, is developed, as many Highlanders will testify. Dulse contains the highest concentration of iron in any edible food source, as well as being rich in potassium and magnesium.

# USES

Dulse has a more definite flavour than Carragheen and it combines well with lamb and with most root vegetables. It has an affinity with white fish like haddock, cod and whiting, rather than the stronger-flavoured oily fish, and is good with shellfish, particularly sliced very finely in accompanying salads. It is also good added to Stovies. Soak for 15 minutes then drain. Chop finely and add with the potatoes and meat. (Recipe p.166).

# DULSE BROTH
## with lamb or mutton

Other meats can be used but mutton is traditional. A unique flavour combination can be made with Shetland reestit mutton.

### To cook

Place the neck in a pan and add water. Bring to the boil, simmer till the meat is tender. Strain cooking liquor, remove excess fat. Cut off all the edible meat from the neck and dice finely.

Melt the butter in a pan and add the onion. Cook till the onion is soft and yellow. Add all the other vegetables and dulse and gently sweat, tightly covered, for five to ten minutes, stirring occasionally to prevent sticking. Add the stock from the mutton and seasoning, bring to the boil and simmer gently till the vegetables are cooked.

Just before serving, add the meat and parsley and adjust the seasoning.

*Dulse Broth*

2 lb/1 kg neck of mutton, or reestit mutton

1 onion, finely chopped

1 medium carrot, diced

3 sticks of celery, diced

2-3 medium potatoes, thinly sliced

1 oz/25 g butter or 1 tablespoon oil

2 oz/50 g dulse (1 c loosely packed)

4 pts/2 L water (10c)

Salt, freshly ground pepper

Handful of chopped parsley

*Dulse Cakes*

8 oz/250 g carrots

8 oz/250 g turnip

3 oz/75 g rolled oats (1 c)

1 oz/25 g dulse

2 tablespoons olive oil

Salt and pepper

# DULSE CAKES

I first came across this idea in Roger Phillips' *Wild Food* (1983) but have used Scottish yellow turnips rather than the parsnips which he suggests.

## To cook

Boil the carrots and turnip in water till tender, drain and mash together.

Rinse the dulse and then steep in cold water for 10 minutes.

Drain (reserve the liquid for soups) and chop finely. Add to rolled oats, mix thoroughly. Put half this mixture into the vegetables, season and mix in. Shape into four round cakes. Coat with remaining oat mixture, fry on both sides in hot oil till lightly brown.

Serve as a vegetable with roast lamb.

# SLOKE

This is the Scottish/Irish name for what the Welsh call Laverbread, Latin name *Porphyra purpurea*. There are several species which are very similar. They form large, thin-lobed sheets attached to the rocks by a very small disk. The species vary in colour from brown to purple to greenish. Do not use the common green variety which is bitter. It turns dark bottle green when cooked. Rinse the weed well to remove all sand and dirt, then steep overnight in fresh water with a handful of salt. Drain.

## To make a purée (Welsh laverbread)

Put in a pan with a little seawater and dripping or butter. Bring to the boil and simmer gently, beating well, when it will, like spinach, reduce to a pulp. It should simmer gently for several hours to reduce, when it will turn a very dark and glossy greenish-black. Season according to taste: with pepper and more butter, some vinegar, orange or lemon juice—salt may not be needed—and serve hot or cold as a piquant flavouring for mashed potatoes and roast meats.

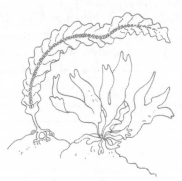

# 4
# GAME

Neither an exotic food, nor an exclusive delicacy of the rich, game was first eaten by prehistoric man whose survival depended on his ability to hunt and catch wild animals. It continued in this role as everyday food of the people, when they could get it, until large-scale shooting estates were set up by the landed gentry in the nineteenth century. Thus began its exclusiveness which brought about a complete reversal of game's role in the diet, as it took on the rich, exotic tag associated with sport and hunting.

In England, game reserves were set up and game laws passed to protect the animals. Game laws also applied in Scotland, but it was much more difficult there to control the wild game. It seems that local people continued to catch and enjoy what had always been part of their diet until at least the nineteenth century. Sir Frederic Eden writing in 1797 on 'The State of the Poor' says that: 'there is no restraint, but 'tis every man's own that can kill it'. But nevertheless, the idea of game as everyday food had been lost.

It is a situation which game dealers and butchers have increasingly made more effort to reverse, making available a much greater variety of game so that it is not only those who hunt who can enjoy the merits of this rich and varied food supply. It provides exciting meat for the cook. In sharp contrast to the more predictable flavours of domestic meat and poultry, it has a huge range of subtle flavours, reflecting the game animal's varied diet. While the meat's intense flavour might lend itself to rich sauces of cream, wine and spirits, it is also a meat which can stand on its own with nothing added and nothing taken away. The truth is that when perfectly cooked and in prime condition, it gains nothing from too many competing flavours.

In Scotland there is so much land that is free from urban pollution that the quality and range of game is unrivalled.

*...Game was so plentiful, red deer, roe, hares, grouse, ptarmigan and partridge; the river provided trout and salmon, the different lochs pike and char; the garden abounded in common fruits and common vegetables; cranberries and raspberries ran over the country, and the poultry yard was ever well furnished.*
Elizabeth Grant of Rothiemurchus, *Memoirs of a Highland Lady,* 1797–1827

# Venison

*...Dined sumptuously upon venison, a piece of Roe, dressed partly in Collops with sauce, and partly on the grid-iron.*
Robert Forbes,
*Diaries, 1708-1775*

Venison originally meant the flesh of anything which was hunted. It comes from the Latin *venatio* meaning hunting, and was used for the flesh of hare and rabbit and for other game meats. The change in terminology seems to have been gradual over several centuries, until the nineteenth century, when it was exclusively applied to the meat from any kind of deer.

Venison is sometimes described as one of the world's last pure food products, and hunting deer on foot in the mountains accompanied by local guides became popular in the nineteeth century, encouraged by Queen Victoria and Prince Albert at Balmoral. It remains a popular pursuit with large areas of the Highlands given over to sporting estates of rough grass, heather and peat bog. The deer are culled in the wild and gralloched (innards removed immediately) then transported on ponies to a collection point where they are then transported in refrigerated vehicles to a production unit where they are skinned, inspected by a vet and hung (time depends on temperature and humidity) before being butchered into cuts.

Domestic consumption of wild red deer venison is rising and has been for several years, though post-World War II and until the 1980s, most was exported to West Germany. Now the game industry in Scotland has begun to tackle the problems of production and marketing which are largely to do with the fact that, while other animals are killed in abattoirs, deer are not. The Red Deer Commission report an annual cull of 60,000 and there are around 600 game estates which operate through a total of 51 co-operatives of varying sizes. All are members of the Association of Deer Marketing Groups. Roe deer are sold commercially in much smaller numbers and there are a few small herds of Sika deer; there are even fewer fallow deer.

## FARMED VENISON

This is the modern equivalent of the early Deer Parks which controlled stocks and allowed for selective breeding. While there are up to fifty farms in Scotland which keep some deer, only a few are actively selling the meat commercially. The herds of deer on these farms are fairly small, the largest is about three hundred, so that while satisfying local needs the impact on the game market of farmed venison is not great. Scottish members of the British Deer Farmers Association may sell their venison to the Deer Producers Society who retail it for them, but it is also available at the farms, with some of them, like Rediehill in Auchtermuchty, developing a considerable trade for both raw meat and made-up venison products. Like farmed salmon, the meat from farmed deer should not be compared with the wild variety. It is an entirely different product. The main differences are in flavour and texture. The grass-fed venison is milder and the meat more tender since they are all shot young. Farmed venison in my experience has always been extremely tender, with a more delicate, less gamey flavour than the wild variety. Cooking methods should be adjusted since heavy, rich sauces and strong marinades are unsuitable.

## RED DEER

The commonest variety in Scotland inhabits rough wild hill country. A stag weighs about 14-16 stone (cleaned): hind 7½-11 stone.

**Scottish season for stags**—1st July-20th October; **for hinds**—21st October-15th February.

**Best time for eating stags**—early autumn; **for hinds**—November to mid-January.

## ROE DEER

Inhabits forests, weighs about 4 stone.

**Scottish season for bucks**—1st May-20th October; **for does**—21st October-28/29 February.

**Best time for eating bucks**—October; **for does**—December to February.

## FALLOW DEER

Inhabits forests and parklands, weighs about 12 stone.

**Scottish season for bucks**—1st August-30th April; **for does**—21st October-15th February

**Best time for eating bucks**—October to November; **for does**—December to February.

## SIKA DEER

Stag weighs 6-7 stone: hind 4½-5 stone.

**Scottish season for stags**—1st August-30th April; **for hinds**—21st October-15th February.

## HANGING/BUYING

Deer must be skinned soon after they are shot then hung in a cool place so that the surface of the carcass is properly sealed. If this is done correctly, the meat can be hung for several weeks without going 'moochie' (mouldy from warmth and/or damp) until tender.

Age and hanging time greatly affect venison meat. Older animals will be tough, sometimes very tough, and possibly also dry (braise or stew rather than roast). Game dealers and butchers should be knowledgeable about the likely tenderness of the meat and should advise accordingly.

Bruce Brymer of Brechin buys his venison from the Dalhousie estate and is invited every year for a day's shooting when he can see for himself the care and attention which is given to handling the carcass. He gets his estate venison when it has been hung for about a week, then he will hang it for another two to three weeks when the joints will be in prime condition. Well dried out and 'sitting up like a good piece of beef', enzyme action will have tenderised it and developed a rich, gamey flavour. The meat should be dark crimson with pure white fat. It is the fat which signals the condition of the meat

## COOKING

'Cooking large game, either wild or farmed is easy,' says Janie Hibler, in *Wild About Game* (1998), 'because there are only two basic rules to follow.

Rule 1: The tender cuts—that is the meat farthest away from the head and feet: the loin, tenderloin, steaks and chops—are cooked hot and fast. Without the fat layers to cook through, the heat penetrates through the muscle, cooking the meat to rare or medium rare in just minutes and minimising the loss of juices. When game meat is over-cooked, the connective tissue in the muscle contracts, squeezing out all the juices, making the meat dry and tough.

Rule 2: The tougher cuts—or those closest to the head and feet, the neck, shoulder, chuck and shank—are cooked slow and low.'

According to these rules, the upper part of the Haunch or Leg is a prime cut for roasting or slicing into collops (steaks). The Saddle is also a prime cut for roasting and it includes the fillets. The Saddle may be divided into loin chops for frying or grilling. The Flank may be boiled or stewed or minced for sausages. The Shoulder may be cut up and stewed or braised in a piece. The Neck may be stewed or boiled for soup. The Head may be used for broth. A good Liver is a great delicacy and can be fried or used for a venison haggis along with the Heart and Flank. Kidneys may be fried. Venison Tripe has a very good flavour but must be removed from the animal and washed out thoroughly within half an hour of killing, otherwise the stomach continues to digest the contents and the flavour of the tripe is spoiled. This can be difficult if the beast has been shot on top of a mountain—farmed deer do not cause the same problem.

90

# BRAISED SHOULDER OR HAUNCH OF RED DEER
## with Sloe Gin

The taste and aroma of sloes, juniper and gamey wild venison combine with admirable results. The sloe gin was not a sweet one—I have also made it with ordinary gin and some port. The idea of using gin comes from the Germans, who are well practised at cooking venison, one of their favourite meats.

Pre-heat the oven to 300F/150C/Gas 2.

### Browning the meat and vegetables

Melt the oil in a heavy pan which will go into the oven and which will contain the meat snugly. Put in the meat and brown it on all sides. Remove. Add the onions, celery and bacon and cook till a light-brown colour. Add the juniper, sloe gin and sloes, scrape up the pan residues and then put the browned meat on top.

### Cooking the meat

Sprinkle the meat with salt and add enough water or stock to come halfway up the meat. Set the pan over a high heat till the liquid comes to the boil. Cover with a piece of buttered greaseproof paper and then a tight fitting lid. If necessary put a layer of foil under the lid, twisting it down the sides of the pot to ensure that moisture does not escape. Put into the oven and cook for about 2 hours, testing for tenderness after an hour and a half.

### Finishing the dish

Remove the meat to a serving dish and keep warm. Strain the cooking liquid into a wide pan. I worked with a chef once who reduced all his sauces in a large frying-pan. It is a good idea, since the greater the surface area the faster the reduction. Reduce to a syrupy consistency—it should be a rich mahogany colour by now. Taste for seasoning. Remove the string from the meat and serve with the sauce.

Carve into thick slices and serve with broccoli, new potatoes, some Spiced Damsons (see p.222) and a robust red wine.

# ROAST SADDLE or HAUNCH OF VENISON

**6-8 servings**

Provided there is enough fat/oil for basting during cooking, I do not find it necessary to either marinade or lard cuts of venison. If it needs either of these treatments, then it ought not to be roasted but cooked by some other more suitable 'slow-and-low' method.

*Braised Shoulder or Haunch of Red Deer*

2 tablespoons oil

4 lb/2 kg shoulder or haunch, boned and rolled

2 medium onions, finely chopped

2 rashers bacon

2 sticks celery, diced

1 tablespoon crushed juniper berries

¼ pt/150 ml sloe gin (¾ c)

1 cup sloes from the gin

Salt and freshly ground black pepper

Water or stock

### Roast Saddle or Haunch of Venison

4 lb/2 kg saddle or haunch of young venison

3 tablespoons olive oil

2 oz/50 g butter (½ stick)

5 fl oz/150 ml robust red wine (¾ c)

5 fl oz/150 ml game stock

Salt and freshly ground pepper

The saddle is the part that lies between the top of the hind legs and the first ribs. Roasting on the bone protects the meat, prevents it drying out and improves the flavour.

Pre-heat the oven 450F/230C/Gas 8.

### Preparing the meat

Put the meat in a dish and rub in olive oil to all surfaces. Grind some black pepper on top.

### Roasting

Allow a roasting time of 15 minutes per pound (500 g) for underdone pink meat. Heat the butter in a roasting tin and put in the saddle. Turn it in the butter and cook, basting frequently. Remove and keep warm on a heated ashet covered with some buttered greaseproof paper or foil.

### Making the sauce

Drain off the excess fat from the pan, add some robust red wine and scrape up all the residues from the pan. Simmer for about five minutes to reduce and concentrate the flavours. Now add the stock and continue reducing, stirring all the time. Some juices will, by now, have dripped out of the saddle and they should be poured into the sauce. When the sauce has a good consistency and flavour, season with salt.

### Carving and Serving

Carve down the centre back on either side of the bone, keeping close into the bone. Then, holding the knife parallel with the board, take thin slices of meat with the grain making slices into long strips. Continue to carve horizontally on both sides. Turn the saddle over and slice out the small fillets—carve at a slant across the grain to give thin escallops. Slice the flank pieces into neat strips and arrange pieces of each type of meat on each plate. (Serve on very hot plates since venison fat congeals at a higher temperature than other fats and is unpleasant to eat as it congeals.) Serve with the sauce and some Rowan Jelly.

### Venison Collops

4 x 6 oz/175 g ½ in (1 cm) thick steaks cut from a well-hung haunch

2 oz/125 g melted butter (½ stick) or 4 tablespoons olive oil

2 oz/50 g white breadcrumbs

Salt

Nutmeg, grated

12 fresh oysters

3 tablespoons double cream

lemon juice to taste

## VENISON COLLOPS
### with oysters and lemon

A tender, young haunch of venison is essential for this very old Scottish way of serving venison. My great-grandmother was noted for her venison collops, which everyone remembers eating but no one can recall her recipe. Mrs McLintock (1736) included 62 shelled oysters for the sauce along with some red wine. The meat was coated in lemon, mace and nutmeg-flavoured breadcrumbs, then fried.

Brush steaks with butter or soak in oil for an hour before grilling. Season breadcrumbs with salt and nutmeg. Coat the steaks in breadcrumbs. Place in a baking tray under a very hot grill. Cook both sides, about five minutes each side.

To make the sauce: Put the oysters into a pan with their liquor and the cream, heat through gently. They should just set. Add grated nutmeg and lemon juice to taste. Serve with the venison.

You may omit the oysters and serve with Raisin Chutney (see p.223).

## VENISON PASTY
### with claret or port

**6 servings**

Some use pork fat with venison but I have always followed Meg Dods' recommendation and used lamb or mutton fat, mainly because I think this fat improves the flavour. Mutton fat, if you can get it, is best. I also agree with her attitude to marinating meat when she says—'Some cooks marinade the meat in the wine and other seasonings for a night, or for some hours previous to baking. This, no doubt, imbues the venison with the flavour of the seasonings, but at the same time drains off the juices, and hurts the natural flavour of the meat, so that we discountenance the practice.'

Pre-heat the oven to 400F/200C/Gas 6 for the first 20 minutes. Then turn down oven and cook for a further 80 minutes at 325F/170C/Gas 3.

### Cooking the meat

Heat the oil in a stewpan and brown the onions. Add the meat and fat. Brown lightly. Mix in the seasonings then the stock, claret or port and vinegar. Pour into an oval 2½ pt/1¼ L pie dish. Season and leave to cool slightly.

### Making the pasty

Place a pie funnel in the centre of the pie dish. Roll out the pastry about 1 in (2.5 cm) wider than the rim of the dish. Place dish on top of pastry and cut round. Use an extra strip for round the rim of the pie dish. Wet the pie dish edge well to seal the edge. Decorate the edge and also the top of the pastry with scraps. Make two holes for steam to escape. Brush with egg yolk and bake.

*A modern pasty is made of what does not roast well, as the neck, the breast, the shoulder. The breast makes the best pasty.*
Meg Dods,
*Cook and Housewives Manual,*
1826

*Venison Pasty*

**2 tablespoons oil**

**3 lb/1½ kg neck, breast or shoulder**

**½ lb/250 g firm fat from the neck or leg of lamb or mutton**

**2 onions, finely chopped**

**Salt, freshly ground pepper**

**½ teaspoon ground mace**

**½ teaspoon ground allspice**

**¼ pt/150 ml good venison stock (¾ c)**

**¼ pt/150 ml claret or port (¾ c)**

**2 tablespoons wine vinegar**

**8 oz/250 g puff pastry (For brushing—1 egg yolk, 1 teaspoon water)**

# VENISON LIVER

*Venison Liver*

**4 rashers of bacon**

**4 slices venison liver about ½ in (2.5 cm)**

**3 tablespoons milk**

**1 tablespoon seasoned flour**

A gamekeeper all his life, Peter MacIntosh, of Braemar and Knoydart, knew a good liver when he saw it. The innards are the keeper's perk and he would fry only the best (the quality of the liver is a good guide to the health of the animal and is judged by a vet before the carcass is exported). But Peter's test of quality was to put his first finger and thumb on either side of the liver and press together. If there was too much resistance then the liver was deemed too old and tough. But if finger and thumb came together easily then it was good for frying. His wife had died and he was no longer stalking the high hills but lived alone in a remote bothy on the Knoydart estate at the head of Loch Nevis, watching the salmon river for poachers and cooking for himself. His timing was always perfect and the liver served up just pink in the middle and well browned and crisp on the outside. He ate it with oatcakes and butter for high tea or for breakfast with crisp fried bacon.

## To cook

Put the bacon into a hot pan and fry till crisp. Remove and keep warm. Meanwhile soak the liver for a few minutes in milk then coat in seasoned flour. Fry very quickly on both sides in hot bacon fat. Serve with the bacon and toast or oatcakes and butter.

# VENISON TRIPE
## (*Poca Buidhe*—Yellow Bag)

*Venison Tripe*

Venison tripe

**4-5 medium onions**

**4 oz/125 g butter (1 stick)**

**4 oz/125 g flour (1 c)**

**2 pt/1 L milk (5 c)**

**salt and pepper**

This was another of Peter's venison delicacies. The tripe must be cleaned (see p.90) then soaked for 24 hours in cold salted water. Rinse out thoroughly and then simmer for 6-8 hours in plenty of water. Drain and cut into 1-inch squares. Fry the onions, finely sliced, in butter till soft and yellow. Add the flour and cook for a few minutes. Gradually add the milk, then the tripe and seasoning, and simmer for about an hour, adding more milk if necessary. Serve with a pile of hot buttered toast.

# Red Grouse
# (*Lagopus Scoticus*)

Red grouse live on the high heather moors eating, besides heather, a number of other herbs and grasses which give them their special flavour. Native to Scottish moors, they are wild birds and cannot be hand-reared. However, their survival can be enhanced by human 'management' of the areas in which they live. To create a mosaic of heather plants at various stages of growth as the grouse habitat, different areas of the hill are burnt each year to help them regenerate. This system provides plenty of young shoots, important for their diet, plus older, well-grown heather as cover for nesting birds. Availability is variable depending on how well grouse moors have been managed and the weather. Cold, wet conditions when the young chicks are vulnerable lead to fatalities. Grouse shoots are usually highly organised with groups of beaters driving the birds forward towards the guns.

Also in the grouse family, though less commonly shot, are the Black Grouse (Blackcock); Wood or Great Grouse (Capercaillie) and the White Grouse (Ptarmigan).

**Season**—12th August to 10th December.

*Nothing is better for a spartan lunch by the spring on a hillside than half a cold grouse with oatcake, and a beaker or two of whisky and water.*
A.I. Shand,
*Shooting*, 1902.

## JUDGING AGE

One method is to look at the two outer primary feathers. If the bird is young they will be pointed, whereas old birds have more rounded, tattered and sometimes faded feathers.

Another method which is recommended by the Game Conservancy is the Bursa test. The Bursa is a blind-ended passage on the upper side of the vent. In all young game birds it becomes much reduced or may close completely when the bird reaches sexual maturity. The presence of a normal Bursa is a certain test for a young bird. Insert a matchstick which has been burnt at one end, so that it is narrow but not too sharp, or a quill.

Yet another guide is to look at the claws. Adult grouse shed their nails between July and September so that if a nail is in the process of shedding then it is an old bird. If it has already been shed there may be a transverse ridge where the old nail was attached, which again indicates an old bird though this may fade after a month or two.

## HANGING

Young birds are often shot and eaten the same day (as they are at the opening of the grouse season on the Glorious Twelfth of August). Game

95

enthusiasts do not recommend this practice, arguing that the real grouse flavour is not tasted when they are so fresh. Among those of this opinion was Winston Churchill, who on one occasion refused to eat grouse caught and served up for him on the twelfth of August. They should not be hung for more than 2-4 days, depending on temperature and humidity. Their distinctive flavour is spoiled if they become too gamey.

# ROAST YOUNG GROUSE

*Roast Young Grouse*

**4 young grouse**

**8 slices of fat bacon or piece of pork fat**

**2 tablespoons oil**

**4 oz/125 g softened butter (1 stick)**

**Salt and pepper**

**4 servings**

Pre-heat the oven to 450F/230C/Gas 8.

## Preparing the grouse

Divide the butter into four pieces and insert into each bird. Lay the pieces of bacon or pork fat on the breasts and truss the bird with a needle and string, securing the fat in the process.

## Roasting

Heat the oil in a roasting tin and when hot, add the birds, turning them to coat thoroughly. Roast for about 15 minutes. Remove the birds from the oven, cut the trussing strings and remove the fat. Return to the oven for about 10 minutes to brown the breast.

## Serving

Grouse is usually served on a round or square of bread sometimes spread with a liver paste (the grouse liver may be used or other livers). Meg Dods serves her grouse on 'buttered toast soaked in the dripping pan' and recommends that the toast be sprinkled first with a little lemon juice. However you decide to serve, the bread under the bird is a good idea since it catches the natural juices which continue to drip out of the meat. Serve on toast, garnished with some watercress. The best way to appreciate all the complex flavours in different parts of the bird is to pick up and chew off the bone. Serve with finger bowls.

*But, oh! my dear North, what grouse-soup at Dalnacardoch. You smell it on the homeward hill, as if it were exhaling from the heather.... As you enter the inn the divine afflatus penetrates your soul. When upstairs, perhaps in the garret, adorning for dinner, it rises like a cloud of rich distilled perfumes through every chink on the floor, every cranny of the wall.*

Christopher North,
*Noctes Ambrosianae*, 1822-35

# GROUSE SOUP

**6-8 servings**

I make this with the debris from roast grouse or with older birds. The same method can obviously be used for other game birds, singly or in combinations. It is certainly the best way to extract every last ounce of flavour from game bones and meat.

## Making the stock

Remove the breast meat from the grouse if using whole birds. Put the carcasses into a pan, cover with water/stock and add herbs and celery. Bring to the boil, cover and simmer gently or at least 1 hour, 2 if possible. Strain, leave to cool and skim off any excess fat. Remove any edible meat from the carcasses and chop finely for adding to the broth at the end. Discard the carcasses.

## Finishing the soup

Melt the fat/oil and butter and begin by sauteing the onions and bacon. When the onions are soft and yellow and the bacon just crisp, add the other vegetables and the rice. The grouse breast meat, chopped finely, may be added at this point or it may be kept for a separate dish. Cover and sweat over a very low heat for ten minutes, checking that it is not burning.

Add the strained stock, bring to the boil and simmer until the vegetables are just tender and the rice cooked. If there is any other edible grouse meat from the carcasses, chop finely and add at this point. Taste for seasoning and add parsley. Serve with boiled potatoes.

### *Grouse Soup*

*For the stock:*

**3 grouse (or the bones and legs from 4–6) or other game birds**

**4 pts/2 L water or poultry stock**

**6 crushed juniper berries**

**Bundle of fresh herbs including parsley**

**2 sticks of celery**

*To finish the soup:*

**2 oz/50 g solidified fat from the stock or 2 tablespoons oil**

**1 oz/25 g butter (1 tablespoon)**

**2 rashers of bacon, finely chopped**

**2 medium onions, finely chopped**

**4 stalks celery, finely diced**

**4 shallots, finely chopped**

**2 tablespoons long-grain polished rice, washed and drained**

# Pheasant

It was called the Phasian Bird when it lived beside the river Phasis near the Black Sea, but the Greeks took it to Rome and the Romans took it with them as their empire expanded and eventually it arrived in Britain. It doesn't frequent the high moorland or eat very much heather so its flavour is milder and less distinct than grouse. Nevertheless, if well hung it has an attractive, mild gamey flavour which becomes stronger, as it does with all game, when eaten cold. It is cheapest to buy during the height of the season and is more generally available than grouse.

**Season**—1st October to 1st February.

## JUDGING AGE

The Bursa test (p.95) can be applied to both the cock and hen bird. In young birds the Bursa will be approximately 1 in (2 cm). In old birds it may be closed completely.

# HANGING

Pheasant should be hung by the head and the time will depend on your own taste, the age of the bird and also the weather. Pheasant which has not been hung very long lacks flavour. This is a matter of taste, but my early training was with a cook on a shooting estate who believed in hanging pheasant for at least a fortnight. These were mature birds which needed the long hanging, not just to tenderise them, but also to develop the rich, gamey flavour which I associate with pheasant.

# ROAST PHEASANT
## with fresh herbs

*Roast Pheasant*

1 x 2½-3 lb/1¼-1½ kg young
   pheasant

4 oz/125 g butter (1 stick)

4 large sprigs of parsley

4 sprigs of fresh tarragon

Sheet of fresh pork fat for
   barding or 2 rashers of
   bacon

**2-3 servings**

The secret of keeping this dry bird moist and succulent is to roast quickly and keep turning it in the oven so that it self-bastes. Most of the roasting time should be on its breast so that the juices are running into it, rather than out. Ideally it should be roasted on a spit. All problems of basting and turning small game birds, which dry out so quickly in the hot oven, vanish if you are able to spit roast, while the results are the best ever.

Pre-heat the oven to 375F/190C/Gas 5.

## Preparing the bird

Put two sprigs of parsley and two of tarragon in the cavity with about half of the butter. Spread the remaining butter over the breast. Put the remaining herbs on top and cover with pork fat. Truss with a needle and string, tying on the pork fat well.

## Roasting

Put the pheasant on its side on a rack in a shallow roasting tin and roast for 10 minutes. Turn onto other side, baste and roast for another 10 minutes. Now turn onto its breast, baste and roast for about 20 minutes. Remove from the oven, take off the barding fat and return to the oven for another 5 minutes, placing it breast side up to brown the skin. It should take about 45 minutes in all. To test the pheasant for doneness, pierce the meat near the thigh and leg joint. If the juices which run out are pale pink the bird will be juicy but slightly underdone. If the juices are clear then it is thoroughly done. This may take up to an hour, so be prepared to continue with the basting since the breast meat loses its juices very quickly if overcooked. Serve with a gravy made from a reduction of the pan juices and a little stock or water and with some oyster mushrooms (ordinary ones will do if they are not available) sliced, sautéed in butter and garnished with chopped parsley and tarragon.

## BRAISED PHEASANT
### with whisky and juniper

**2 servings**

This is a recipe for a mature, two-week-hung bird. I used a mellow Lowland malt such as Auchentoshan. The peaty island malts are too strong, but it is worth experimenting with other malts with a less-dominating character.

Pre-heat the oven to 375F/190C/Gas 5.

### Braising the bird

Melt the fat in a cast-iron enamelled casserole and brown the pheasant on all sides. Remove and add onions and cook till golden brown. Return the pheasant to the pan and pour over half the whisky. Flame, and when the flames die down, add stock and juniper berries. Cover well, and bake in the oven for 45 minutes or until tender. Test after about 40 minutes when the leg should come away easily. It could take up to an hour depending on the age of the bird. Remove the bird and cut into 4 joints (2 legs and 2 breasts).

### Finishing the dish

Keep the joints warm and covered in their serving dish while finishing the sauce. Strain the sauce and then return to the pan. Now add the remaining whisky, cream and lemon juice and reduce to a good consistency. Taste for seasoning and serve round the pheasant.

*Braised Pheasant*

**2 tablespoons oil or butter**

**1 x 2½ lb/1¼ kg pheasant**

**1 medium onion, finely chopped**

**4 fl oz/125 ml whisky (½ c)**

**5 fl oz/150 ml game stock or water (¾ c)**

**1 tablespoon juniper berries**

**4 fl oz/125 ml whipping cream (½ c)**

**1 teaspoon lemon juice**

**Salt and pepper**

# Hare

Not so highly regarded as other game meat, yet Scottish hares which have exercised well on the mountains have a superb flavour. They need a 'slow-and-low' method of cooking which allows their rich flavour to develop to its full potential. Hare is available in season from good game butchers or dealers.

**Season**—no close season but may not be sold March to July inclusive. The best time for eating is October to January.

## JUDGING AGE

A young hare will have soft thin ears which tear easily and white sharp teeth whereas an older hare will have tougher ears and larger, yellower teeth. The coat of an older hare will be rougher.

## TYPES

**Brown Hare**—weighs up to 7 lb/3 kg.

**Mountain Hare** or **Blue Hare**—weighs between 5-6 lb/2-2.4 kg. Regarded as the best flavoured. It has the same open season as the Brown Hare but it is not suitable for roasting and should be stewed or braised or made into soup.

## HANGING

Hares should be hung head downwards, ungutted, for 1-2 weeks, again depending on the weather, taste and toughness of the hare. Place a bowl with a teaspoon of vinegar in it (this stops the blood congealing) underneath the head to catch the blood.

## SKINNING

Make a circular cut through the fur just above the back heel joints. Make a lengthwise cut along the inside of the leg on both sides and pull the skin off both legs. Tie the paws together and hang up somewhere. This is not essential but makes the skinning job easier and means that the blood is collecting at the top end and is therefore less likely to spill out all over the place when the belly is opened up.

Make a slit at the base of the tail from the top of one hind leg to the top of the other. Peel the skin back gently, turning it inside out and leaving the tail attached to the body. Now peel the skin down over the body and forelegs to the shoulders. Make a circular cut through the fur on the front legs just above the paws and then slit the skin along the inside of the leg. Peel back the skin on both legs. Peel the skin from the neck and then over the head as far as the ears, cut off the ears at the base and pull away the rest of the skin. It may be necessary to loosen round the eyes and mouth.

Lay the hare on its back and with a very sharp knife open up the belly. Draw out and discard all the intestines leaving the liver, heart, lungs and kidneys. Now take out the kidneys; remove the liver carefully, remove the gall bladder and discard. Put the liver into a bowl with 1 teaspoon of vinegar. Position the bowl underneath the body and make a slit in the diaphragm at the base of the chest and allow the blood to run

100

out. When you have collected the blood, pull out the heart and lungs and place in the bowl.

## BAWD BREE

A mature, well-hung hare is essential for this traditional soup/stew or 'mouthful soup' as it is aptly described in *The Household Book of Lady Grisell Baillie* (1692-1733). 'Bawd' is the old Scots word for hare and 'Bree' simply means gravy, juice of liquid in which something is cooked.

### Preparing the hare

Skin and clean reserving the blood, liver, heart, and kidneys.

Remove the fleshy pieces from the back and legs and cut into neat pieces. Place the remainder of the carcass in the cold water and leave overnight.

### Making the stock

Bring the carcass and water to the boil, skim and then add the herbs. Simmer for 1 hour and then add the vegetables. Cook for another hour. Strain and remove the vegetables. They may be diced or sieved into the stock.

### Finishing the dish

Flour the reserved hare flesh. Slice the kidneys and heart and flour. Melt butter in a pan and fry till lightly browned. Add to the stock and simmer gently till the meat is tender. Add diced vegetables and any edible carcass meat.

Press the liver through a sieve and mix with the blood. Mix the blood/liver, which has had vinegar added at the cleaning-out stage, with the remaining flour and gradually add some of the hot cooking liquid. Pour back into the pan and heat through to thicken. It should not boil. Add the port. Taste for seasoning. Serve in wide deep soup plates with a boiled mealy potato in the centre of the plate and Rowan Jelly on top.

*Bawd Bree*

**3-4 qt/3-4 L cold water**

**1 hare**

**Bundle of fresh herbs**

**4 sticks celery, chopped**

**3 carrots, diced**

**1 small piece turnip, diced**

**1 large onion, finely chopped**

**2 tablespoons flour**

**2 tablespoons butter or oil**

**3-4 tablespoons port**

**Salt and freshly ground black pepper**

# Rabbit

Rabbits were widely eaten in Scotland before myxomatosis. Today, good, well-flavoured rabbits are available and can be a better flavour than some modern chicken. They are best eaten fresh, though they can be hung. They should be skinned first (see instructions for Hare p.100).

## BUYING/COOKING

Look for soft ears and sharp teeth which indicate a young rabbit. They should be plump with a smooth fur. There is no close season. They can weigh from 1-3 lb (½-1½ kg)—2 small or 1 large for 4 servings.

Lowland Scots have always eaten more rabbit than Highlanders. The most popular method of cooking was with onions, though other traditional methods include: potted rabbit using the same method as for potted hough and including hough with the rabbit; roasted young rabbit; minced rabbit which was sometimes shaped into a meat roll with pork and onions; and rabbit made into soup and pies.

## ELSIE'S RABBIT WITH ONIONS

*Elsie's Rabbit with Onions*

1 rabbit, skinned, cleaned and jointed

Seasoned flour

Roast dripping

1 medium onion

Salt and pepper

**4 servings**

Rabbits were always making a nuisance of themselves on farms by eating the crops, which is why my father was sent out each morning—when working on a farm in an Angus glen during the 1920s—to collect the rabbits which had been caught in snares during the night. On his return for breakfast he had an armful of rabbits for the farmer's wife, Elsie, which constantly stretched her culinary imagination. This was a favourite Elsie way.

### To cook

Melt the dripping in a pan and brown the onions. Coat the rabbit with flour. Brown the rabbit well. Add seasoning and enough water to cover. Simmer gently for 1-1½ hours or until the rabbit is tender. Taste for seasoning and serve.

## HONEYED RABBIT

*Honeyed Rabbit*

*For the sauce*

3 tablespoons oil

1 medium onion, finely chopped

1½ lb/¾ kg tomatoes, skinned and chopped

4 tablespoons milk

4 tablespoons heather honey

1 clove of crushed garlic

*To finish the dish*

4 tablespoons oil

2 oz/50 g flour (½ c)

1 rabbit, cleaned and jointed

Salt and pepper

**3-4 servings**

Heather honey, tomatoes and a hint of garlic lift this rabbit stew out of the ordinary.

### Making the sauce

Heat the oil in a pan and add the onion, cook till soft without colouring then add the tomatoes, milk and honey and simmer to reduce. When it is a good, thick consistency, add the crushed garlic, salt and pepper to taste.

### Finishing the dish

Heat the oil in a pan and dip the rabbit joints into the tomato sauce (this helps to make more flour stick and gives a better crust) then into the flour. Brown the rabbit in the oil on all sides and then add the sauce. The liquid should almost cover the rabbit. Cover with a lid and simmer gently till tender, adding more stock or water if necessary. Taste for seasoning and sprinkle over plenty of chopped parsley before serving.

## RICH GAME STEW
### garnished with brambles* and choux pastry

**4 servings**

A 'low-and-slow' dish for old and tough game. At her Log Cabin Hotel, high on the grouse and venison moors of Perthshire, Elizabeth Sandell has many years of experience—'making delicious meals out of old boots. The secret,' she claims, 'is to give the said footwear a long soak in a well flavoured marinade of oil, wine, vinegar, chopped onions, celery, carrot, bay leaf, rosemary, garlic, fresh black peppers, salt and crushed juniper berries.' This aromatic marinade may be used for more than one marinating process. The choux pastry makes a good texture and flavour contrast to the finished dish but is optional. Serve with baked potatoes instead.

### To make the choux pastry (optional)

Pre-heat the oven to 400F/200C/Gas 6.

Bring the butter and water to boil in a pan. Draw off the heat and quickly tip in the sifted flour and seasoning. Stir vigorously till the mixture comes away from the sides of the pan. Beat the eggs in one at a time till the mixture is smooth and shiny. (This can also be done in a processor. Put the flour and seasoning into the bowl and switch on, adding the liquid in a steady stream through the feed tube until a smooth dough is formed. With the machine still on, drop in eggs one at a time.)

### To make the stew

Put the meat, marinade and stock into a pan and cook till the meat is tender. Strain off liquid and put the meat into a shallow gratin dish. Cover and keep warm while finishing the sauce. Add port and claret and reduce to a good consistency. Finally add enough of the jelly to give a slightly sweetish flavour. Some jellies are much sweeter than others so add gradually, tasting as you go. Season and pour over meat.

### Finishing the dish

Spoon the pastry round the edge of the dish, sprinkle browned crumbs

*Blackberries

### *Rich Game Stew*

*To make the choux pastry (optional)*

¼ pt/150 ml water (¾ c scant)

2 oz/50 g butter (½ stick)

2½ oz/65 g plain flour (½ c generous)

2 medium eggs

Salt and cayenne pepper

*To make the stew*

2 lb/1 kg game meat, cut in roughly 1 in (2 cm) squares

½ pt/300 ml strained marinade (1¼ c)

½ pt/300 ml game stock made with the carcasses (1¼ c) (see p.97)

2 tablespoons Redcurrant, Rowan or Crab-Apple Jelly

2 tablespoons port

2 tablespoons claret

Salt and pepper

103

over the stew and bake for about 20 minutes or until the pastry is crisp and well risen. Serve with a thick sprinkling of chopped parsley and some brambles.

(From Elizabeth Sandell, the Log Cabin Hotel in Kirkmichael, 1984.)

# Other Scottish Game

Sizes and seasons. All dates inclusive.

## DUCK

**MALLARD:** 2½-2¾ lb (1.1-1.3 kg), 2-3 servings. **Season**—below high-tide mark, 1st September to 20th February. Elsewhere—1st September to 31st January.

**TEAL:** 11-13 oz (300-370 g), 1 serving. **Season**—as for Mallard.

**WIDGEON:** 1½-2 lb (700-900 g), 2 servings. **Season**—as for Mallard.

## GOOSE

**PINK-FOOTED:** 6-7 lb (2.7-3.2 kg), 6 servings. **Season**—as for Mallard.

**GREYLAG:** 8-1p lb (3.7-5 kg), 6 servings. **Season**—as for Mallard.

**WOODPIGEON:** 1-1¼ lb (500-600 g), 1 serving. No close season.

**BLACK GAME:** 3-4 lb (1.4-1.8 kg), 3 servings. **Season**—20th August to 10th December.

**PTARMIGAN:** 1-1¼ lb (400-600 g), 1 serving. **Season** (Scotland only)—12th August to 10th December.

**CAPERCAILLIE:** 6-12 lb (2.7-5.5 kg), 1 serving. **Season**—1st October to 31st January.

**PARTRIDGE:** Cock 13-15 oz (350-450 g); Hen 12½-14½ oz (400 g), 1-2 servings. **Season**—1st September to 1st February.

**COMMON SNIPE:** 3½-4½ oz (100-130 g), 1-2 per person. **Season**—12th August to 31st January.

**WOODCOCK:** 8-14 oz (230-400 g), 1 serving. **Season**—1st September to 31st January.

# 5
# BEEF & LAMB

## Beef

Cattle ran wild like game in the forests and hills of Britain 700 years ago, give or take a century. Six wild bulls are mentioned as part of the feast given for George Neville when he was installed as Archbishop of York in 1466. But according to C. Ann Wilson in *Food and Drink in Britain*, 'by Elizabeth's reign (1558-1603) forest cattle had retreated from lowland Britain but were still to be found in the remote parts of Wales and Scotland.'

Once domesticated, they became an important part of the Highland economy in Scotland, with thousands sent every year to markets in the south along ancient drove roads, a trade which flourished until the '45 Rebellion. The Clearances, and then the introduction of steam ships and railways, put an end to this tradition.

Early in the nineteenth century, cattle were mostly replaced by sheep in the Highlands, but in the north-east some enterprising Scottish farmers, who knew a good thing when they saw it, began the process of moulding together the most valuable characteristics of the native black-polled breed. From the obscurity of the hills and glens of north-east Scotland, they succeeded in breeding Aberdeen Angus cattle which became the prime beef breed throughout the world.

Three men were principally responsible—Hugh Watson (1780-1865) of Keillor in Angus; William McCombie (1805-1880) of Tillyfour in Aberdeenshire and Sir George Macpherson Grant (1839-1907) of Ballindalloch in Banffshire. As they were keeping a sharp eye on utilitarian qualities while they built up their families of cattle, hardiness was very important. Also valued was the breed's ability to thrive on low-quality pasture and rough grazing, converting these simple rations quickly and effectively into high-quality, well-flavoured beef. Other plusses which they appreciated were the early maturing characteristics of the breed and also its well-marbled flesh and firm, white fat.

While previously cattle had been transported on the hoof for fattening

*Scotland's hill and upland farms provide ideal breeding grounds for beef cattle and sheep that come to maturity on the lush pastures of the Scottish lowlands.*
Scotch Quality Beef and Lamb Association

in the richer pastures of Norfolk and Suffolk, Watson changed this system and 'fixed' the new type of breed. The trade to London of prime beef in carcass (sending only the expensive cuts) developed alongside the success of the pioneering breeders. This new and more sophisticated method became the norm with the completion of the railway to London in 1850.

The new Aberdeen Angus breed's main rival was Amos Cruickshank's Scotch Shorthorn (established in Aberdeenshire the 1830s, though the breed originated in Yorkshire in the eighteenth century). It could be fattened more rapidly but did not milk so well and was less hardy than the Aberdeen Angus. The two were eventually crossed to become the source of most prime beef produced in Scotland. The Polled Cattle Herd Book was set up in 1862 and the Aberdeen Angus Cattle Society inaugurated in 1879.

Many changes have since occurred in the Angus breed. For most of the first fifty years of the twentieth century the demand was for a small, thick, heavy bull with its fat-marbled meat making a high ratio of fat to meat. This was reversed with entry to the EU when the fashion developed for a taller, leaner animal with a minimum of fat. Continental breeds were introduced with a leaner, fleshier carcass, initially the Charolais, but later the Simmental and Limousin. Though these Continental breeds are now well established in Scotland, the more recent trend of the '90s has been to reverse the ultra-lean approach, recognising that such meat lacks flavour and character.

Referring to this fashion for lean Continental beef, Jim Jack, Aberdeen Angus President (1994), said: 'This meat does not have the succulence and flavour that the consumer requires. Thus the aim now is to have meat that has marbling of fat through it, to give a product that is succulent and tasty.'

Similar comments came in 1995 from Sir Alistair Grant. Reporting to the Agricultural Scottish Affairs Committee as Chairman of the Safeway multiple, he suggested that something positive could be done to reverse the situation: 'The intermingling of French breeding stock, particularly Charolais, has produced a beef type which is not particularly Scottish. Over a long period we could attend to that, so that we produced a larger Scottish breed with a bit more fat and have the best of both worlds.' He had just bought his first Aberdeen Angus heifer.

The beef-breeding herd in Scotland is now largely composed of cross-bred animals. Of the pure native breeds, besides the Aberdeen Angus and the Beef Shorthorn, there are three other native breeds protected by breeding societies which hold the records of pedigree herds: the Galloway is of slower growth, but very hardy, its breeding society was established in 1877; the picturesque Highland cattle, also renowned for their hardiness, were established in 1884; and the Luing, established in 1966, is noted for producing good beef in the poor, wet conditions of the northwest.

## BUYING/CUTS OF BEEF

The late twentieth century will no doubt be remembered for the unsavoury facts which emerged about the degenerative disease in cattle, bovine spongiform encephalopathy (BSE), and its tragic effects on human health. Most breeders of prime beef in Scotland were not involved in the intensive systems which resorted to feeding sheep offal to cattle which may have caused the problem. Only a small percentage of cases were reported in Scotland compared with England and this had been reduced to a single case by 1999. Three-quarters of beef produced in Scotland is reared in an outdoors-extensive system. In what is known as beef-suckler herds, the calves are weaned naturally from their mothers and animals graze on pasture and silage, sometimes throughout the winter if the breed is a hardy one with a thick coat, such as the Galloway or Highland.

As more interest has been created about the origins of beef supplies and methods of production, some butchers have established, at the point of sale, more information about beef. The fashion for lean Continental breeds was largely supermarket-led. Fresh, pink, lean beef was a cheaper way of producing beef, reducing hanging times and allowing the meat to be sold with a much higher percentage of water than had previously been the case. Among the pioneers calling for a return to the quality of flavour found in fat-marbled native breeds, properly hung for 2-3 weeks, was butcher and beef farmer, Michael Gibson of Forres. In the 1980s when the craze for leaness was at its height, he was attempting to draw attention to high-quality, low-quantity, fat-marbled Highland beef. Others have followed, and many farmers now recognise that there is a market for well-hung, fat-marbled native breeds from extensive, and more environmentally friendly, systems of production. The only breed, so far, to have a registered certification mark is Aberdeen Angus, which guarantees that the breed mix has a minimum of 50% pure Aberdeen Angus, though usually it contains much more.

According to EU Regulation 820/97 which came into effect in 1997, retailers who give anything more than basic information on a beef label (i.e. cut, size, weight) must get prior approval and the information must be verified by an independent third party. This labelling scheme, however, is not compulsory and does not apply to over-the-counter selling by high street butchers who have always been happy, in my experience, to provide information about the source of their beef, the breeding and the hanging. These are the vital ingredients of quality on which their reputation depends.

Other schemes aimed at improving customer confidence about origins are the EU regulations set up in 1992 which protect regional names. Protected Designation of Origin (PDO) applies to products processed and prepared within a particular geographic area and with features and characteristics which are created because of it. Orkney Beef is the only PDO registered beef product, while Scotch Beef is the only Protected Geographical Indication (PGI), a designation for products produced solely within the geographical area.

## BOILED BEEF

This universal dish has many variations around the world, from the sophisticated Austrian Tafelspitz, made with sirloin and served with chive mayonnaise and apple purée mixed with grated horseradish, to the more ordinary English Boiled Beef and Carrots.

Combining soup and meat courses in one pot is central to the Scottish culinary tradition. A north-east farmer's daughter, Ethel McCurrach, recalls how on Sundays 'a 14 pint pot was used. That meant there was enough for Monday (Yavils)* and Tuesdays (Ley),* as well as half a turnip plus a few carrots as well as the beef.

'Now if a dumpling was needed for the dinner [12 noon] it was tied in a cloth and boiled in amongst the broth, if not a mealie pudding mixture was tied tightly in a cloth and boiled amongst the broth. All that was then needed to finish off a full three-course meal was a pot of boiled potatoes. Two pots for a three-course meal that would last three days—it would be a "pot man's" dream in a hotel kitchen today.'

In the north-east the meat was usually removed from the pot and served first while hot. It was sliced by the master of the house. Farm servants didn't often have knives or forks so they ate the meat with their fingers, taking pieces from the central platter. Then the broth was served into wooden bowls and they supped it with their hand-carved horn spoons.

### For boiling a whole piece of beef

#### 8-10 servings

Use a pot which will hold the beef and vegetables neatly. It is important not to have too large a pot with too much water since the flavour of both vegetables and meat will end up diluted in the liquid.

Place the meat in a very large pot, cover with cold water and bring to

*Refers to the farming system of 2nd and 3rd year corn rotation.

108

the boil. Remove the scum. Add onion, bay leaf and celery. Add salt, pepper and rosemary. Cover and simmer until the meat is just tender— approximately 1-2 hours depending on toughness of meat. Add carrots and turnips and cook for about 25 minutes till tender. Boil potatoes separately.

## To serve

Arrange the meat on a large ashet and carve in fairly thick slices. Surround with vegetables and pour a little of the broth on the meat to keep it well moistened. Give each person a cup of broth. Serve with Mustard (p.224), Apple chutney (p.223) or any other sharp pickles and some coarse salt.

## Dumplings

These may be added to the pot about 20 minutes before serving.

Mix together the flour, suet, baking powder, cold water and salt and pepper. Drop in spoonfuls on top of meat and vegetables, cover and simmer gently till they are well risen.

### For boiling pieces of beef

**8-10 servings**

This is Geordie Kelly's 'b'il't' beef'. He was the Scots/Irish cook on the *Clara*, a coal-carrying puffer sailing the Hebridean coasts in the 1920s. His recipe is described by Victor MacClure, who sat in the galley with him shelling peas and scrubbing carrots while gazing out to the islands of Colonsay and Mull, and learning the art of boiling beef.

' "Boiled" beef,' *Geordie said, 'is a misnomer. You only drop your meat into boilin' water to give it a skin that'll keep it sappy [moist]. If it was put into the pot in one piece like the Frenchies do it, you might need to give it five minutes real boilin'. But it's quite enough, when it's in bits like this, to bring it back to the boil for a jiffy. An' that's all the actual boilin' you ever give it. All it wants after that is as much heat as'll just keep the liquor saying "plup!" six to twelve times a minute. In the piece you would allow about twenty minutes for each pound-weight and twenty minutes over. You can hardly spoil the meat by simmering too long, except that in the piece it'll likely fall to bits when you try to carve it. But* simmering, *mind! If you* boil *meat—that's to say at the heat of water for makin' tea—you'll get somethin' as tough and tasteless as cahootchy [indiarubber]. An' nothin' in the world'll make it worth eatin' again.*

*'Of course,' Geordie went on, 'a certain amount o' the meat juice leaks out*

## Boiled Beef

4-5 lb beef brisket, nineholes, silverside or hough

Cold water to cover

1 onion stuck with cloves

1 bay leaf

1 stick celery, cut in four

Salt to taste

1 teaspoon freshly ground pepper

1 sprig rosemary

6 carrots

1 large turnip

1 leek

12 even-sized, floury potatoes, washed but unpeeled

## Dumplings

4 oz/125 g plain flour (1 c)

2 oz/50 g shredded suet

1 teaspoon baking powder

Cold water to mix

Salt and pepper

## Boiled Beef (Pieces)

4 lb/2 kg brisket or other
  boiling cut

4 pts/2 L boiling water

Bunch of parsley

Few peppercorns (my addi-
  tion—not Geordie's)

Bay leaf

Sprig of thyme

12 medium carrots, sliced

12 white turnips, sliced

4 lb/2 kg fresh peas (summer)

4 leeks (winter)

4 shallots, finely chopped

Salt and pepper

*Bit it's sorroo and grief if there's*
*no bilan' beef*
*An, ye canna hev broth, on 'e*
*Sunday.*
Donald Grant
*Broth on 'e Sunday*, 1961

*into the liquor. That's what makes the broth. An' when you come to put in the*
*vegetables, somethin' o' their juice gets into the meat, helpin' its flavour. But*
*the notion is to keep all the virtue you can in the beef, so you don't do*
*anything to encourage it to give its juices out. That's why you don't salt your*
*liquor until meat an' vegetables are nearly ready.'*
  Victor MacClure,
  *Good Appetite My Companion*, 1955.

Cut the meat up into portion-sized pieces and put into the water with
parsley, peppercorns, bay leaf and thyme. Bring to the boil and then
skim. Reduce the heat to a very gentle simmer. Cover and cook till
almost tender.

Add the carrots and turnips and simmer for half an hour.

Finally shell the peas or chop leeks finely and add with the shallots.
Taste and season. Simmer for five minutes and serve with Mealy Boiled
Potatoes (see p.165).

## SCOTCH BARLEY BROTH

This traditional broth occupies the high ground between soups on the
one hand and stews on the other. Meg Dods describes this and a variety
of other substantial Scottish soups as 'Soup and Stew or Mouthful Soups'.

Scots males, who normally find cooking something of a chore, will
turn their hand to a pot of broth and surprise everyone with their expertise. Such was auld Andra, an ex-Glasgow shipwright whose magnificent
Scotch Broth was something of a legend and the highlight of the week for
Madeleine Gibb when she was a teenage apprentice during the depres-
sion in the 1920s to Andra's dressmaker daughter. Monday they had
'stovies' made from the leftovers of the Sunday roast, Tuesday was 'cooheel'
but on Wednesday it was Andra's Special. Cooled and reheated overnight, the flavour developed and tasted even better on Thursday. Andra
was ever ready to reel off the recipe for the broth which was made in a
huge iron pot (probably holding 14 pts) over the kitchen range. The
procedure started at nine o'clock by filling the pot with cold water.

*'Intae this,' commanded the receipt, 'fling a sma' haunfie o' coorse saut.*
*Whan it biles pit in yer beef, a guid, fat, twa-pun piece. Then hauf-a-pun*
*o' weel-washed baurley and twa pun o' well-soakit peas.' About ten-thirty*
*Andra added 'wan guid swede turmut, fower carrots, eicht guid leeks and a*
*wee tait o' sugar.' Before departing for his 'bit dram' he added 'twa guid*
*haunfies o' choppit greens and eicht tautties'; and on his return—exuding the*

*rich and heady perfume of the Special, he stirred in another 'haunfie'—this
time of parsley which, with canny forethought, he had chopped before setting
forth.*

Madeline Gibb,
*Scotland's Magazine*, December 1960.

Earlier recipes from the more affluent nineteenth century have a much
higher proportion of beef and much less peas and barley but the basic
ingredients remain the same, as do the three basic stages.

## Cooking the meat/barley/peas

If possible, use about 1 lb/500 g of beef to 2 pts/1 L of cold water. The
cheapest cut is usual, something like nineholes (thick flank) or hough
(shin), though other cuts suitable for boiling, and larger or smaller pieces,
can be used. 1 oz/50 g barley and ½ oz/15 g split peas which have both
been steeped in hot water for a few hours or overnight with a small nut
of butter will give the broth a good lithing (thickening). All of this should
be put on to boil with a little salt and a bunch of sweet herbs for at least
an hour before the vegetables are added.

**Note:** Since it is difficult to know exactly the toughness or tenderness
of the meat I boil the meat till tender and then remove and keep warm.
If the vegetables are finely chopped they will not take long to cook,
though if some are to be served in larger pieces with the meat as a
vegetable then they must obviously be added sooner.

## Adding the vegetables

The ones which take longest to cook should be added first and the
additions so organised that all vegetables are just cooked through without
being overcooked when you are ready to serve the broth.

The proportions and the combinations are a matter of taste except
that almost everyone would agree that carrots and turnips (swedes), leek
or onion and parsley are essential. Only Mrs Cleland, writing in 1759,
varies widely from this when instead she uses 'four or five heads of celery
washed clean and cut small [this was to 12 pts of water] and a few
marigolds. Let this boil an hour. Take a cock or large fowl, clean picked
and washed, and put into the pot; boil it till the broth is quite good, then
season with salt, and send it to table, with the fowl in the middle.'

Potatoes were sometimes cooked in the broth, as in Andra's version,
or cooked separately but served with the broth.

Use a medium-sized carrot, a quarter of a medium-sized turnip and
two leeks or two medium onions to the 2 pts/1 L water. Peel and dice the
carrot and turnip and add first. Chop the leek and/or onion and add (leek

white only) when the carrot and turnips are about half cooked. Add a teaspoonful of sugar at this point.

### Finishing the broth

When all are tender, finish with a good handful of chopped parsley and the green of the leek, very finely chopped. Season well with salt and pepper and serve with the meat as a separate course or with the meat chopped finely or coarsely and added to the broth. It is often eaten with a large mealy potato making an island in the centre of the soup plate.

## MINCED COLLOPS
### (Mince and Tatties)

*Minced Collops*

2 tablespoons oil/fat for browning

1-2 onions, finely chopped

1 lb/500 g stewing steak, minced (2 c)

Salt and pepper

½ tablespoon vinegar (optional)

1 tablespoon medium oatmeal (optional)

**4 servings**

A popular, everyday Scottish dish, always eaten with potatoes and commonly known as 'Mince and Tatties'. Collops is a term for thin slices of meat of any kind, usually taken from the leg but with no bone. This version is based on a simple recipe given by Mrs Dalgairns in 1829, which depends for flavour on a very thorough browning of meat and onions. Scottish housewives use the best steak they can afford for mince and will often choose their steak first, then have the butcher mince it specially for them.

### To cook

Begin by melting the oil/fat in a pan and when it is quite hot add the onions. Cook slowly till a good, rich, dark golden-brown then add the mince. Break up with a fork and keep stirring while it is browning. This should be done slowly (takes about 10-15 minutes). After this, the meat is really cooked and simply needs moistening and seasoning before serving. Add about ½ pt/300 ml water or stock (1¼ c), boil up, add oatmeal, season, add vinegar and simmer for about 5-10 minutes. Usually served with creamed potatoes ('tatties'), and sometimes with triangles of hot toast. Also cooked with Dumplings (see p.109) or Bacon Dumplings.

    **Note:** For convenience, carrots and turnips are often cooked in mince which lengthens the cooking time once the liquid has been added but at the same time they bring additional flavour. They should be very thinly sliced to reduce cooking time.

# BACON DUMPLINGS

**4-6 servings**

These are richly flavoured dumplings of the kind dished up in high alpine restaurants where they provide much needed inner warmth.

Fry the bacon till lightly crisp, add the onion and continue cooking until soft. Add the bread and oil and toss in the pan until the bread is lightly crisp but not browned. Put the flour and parsley into a bowl and add the fried mixture. Add the milk and bring it together into a fairly stiff mixture. Taste for seasoning. Roll into balls about an inch and half in diameter. Press the mixture well so that they do not break up when cooking.

To cook: add to the mince about 10 minutes before serving. Return the lid to the pan and serve when they are cooked through.

## *Bacon Dumplings*

8 oz/250 g Ayrshire bacon, diced (see p.121)

1 finely chopped onion

8 oz/250 g day-old bread, diced

1-2 tablespoons oil

1 tablespoon parsley, finely chopped

2 tablespoons self-raising flour

3 tablespoons milk

salt and pepper

# BEEF OLIVES

**4 servings**

Rolls of thinly sliced beef or veal are stuffed to make this economical dish. Butchers in Scotland use a cut called Beef Ham to make their own sausage-stuffed beef olives. Although a name originally applied to Salted Beef, it now refers only to the very thin slice from some part of the leg of the animal—different butchers use different cuts but all cut it very thinly, sometimes on a machine.

Skirlie (see p.15) and Haggis (see p.134) make good stuffings. Since both are crumbly it is better to spread them over the meat and roll up swiss-roll-style. The one used here is a traditional, breadcrumb-based stuffing sharply flavoured with lemon and herbs.

## To cook

Mix all the stuffing ingredients together. Cut the steak into strips about 2 in (5 cm) wide. Place a spoonful of stuffing on each piece; roll up and skewer with cocktail stick, or tie with thread. Heat oil and brown onion then add olives and brown. Add water and seasoning and bring to the boil. Simmer gently till tender. Remove meat and reduce cooking liquor to a rich glaze. Serve with the olives.

## *Beef Olives*

*For the stuffing*

4 oz/125 g fresh breadcrumbs (2 c)

2 oz/50 g finely chopped suet (½ c)

1-2 tablespoons chopped parsley

1 tablespoon chopped lemon thyme

Grated rind of 1 lemon

Salt and pepper and 1 egg to bind together

1-2 tablespoons lemon juice

*For the olives*

1 lb/500 g rump steak, cut thinly, or Beef Ham

2 tablespoons oil

1 medium onion, finely chopped

¾ pt/400 ml water (2 c)

Salt and pepper

113

# CHARCOAL-GRILLED BEEFSTEAKS
## with whisky and shallot butter

**Serves 4**

*Lucky Laing…contrived to make her shop in the gloomy old Tolbooth a cosy little place, half tavern, half kitchen, whence issued pretty frequently the pleasant sounds of broiling beefsteaks, and the drawing of corks from bottles of ale and porter.*
    Marie W. Stuart,
    *Old Edinburgh Taverns*, 1952.

*Charcoal-Grilled Beefsteaks*

4 x 6-8 oz/200-250 g grilling
    steaks

Oil for brushing

*Whisky and Shallot Butter*

*Beat together*

4 oz/125g softened butter
    (1 stick)

1 tablespoon parsley, finely
    chopped

1 tablespoon shallot, finely
    chopped

2 tablespoons whisky

Salt and freshly milled pepper

Lucky Laing was a guidwife who had a basement tavern in the South Bridge about the beginning of the nineteenth century. Her *pièce de résistance* was a stew which she called 'Golli Gosperado' and which she conveniently placed beneath the iron gratings in the pavement so that the aroma wafted upwards and advertised the dish to the passers-by with enormously successful results. Unfortunately there is no record of her recipe.

The taste for simple, old-fashioned meat dishes served at steak bars is as much a part of our eating-out scene today as it was more than two hundred years ago. Beefsteaks were then, as they are now, one of the commonest restaurant dishes.

The Rules of the Beefsteak Club which was established in 1734 were—'Pound well the steak till all the fibres are broken. Don't spare the coal. Turn it frequently. Take care the fat is more done than the lean. Take care the juice is allowed now and then to fall in the dish. Butter the steak but do not season till dished.'

### To grill steaks

Brush steaks with oil and place over charcoal or cook under a very hot grill. Turn frequently, till required degree of doneness. When ready, spread the meat with the butter and serve.

# SPICED BEEF

### Dry Spicing

This is a method of preservation which adds a rich, mellow flavour to beef. Early methods simply involved burying the meat in dry salt in a stone trough during the winter months; spices were added but the proportion of salt was high and therefore it dominated the flavour of the meat. Today there is less need to use so much salt and more modified versions depend on subtle blends of spices making a rich and distinctive flavour in the meat.

## Cuts

It is not really worth spicing anything under 4 lb/2 kg since the whole point is to have enough to last for several weeks. A 6-10 lb/3-5 kg piece is best. The choice of cut really depends on how much you can afford. Prime cuts like a middle rib of roast carefully cooked make superb spiced beef, so do silverside, rump and 'salmon' cut, but equally successful are the cheaper brisket and nineholes.

There should be a good mixture of fat and lean. The fat is necessary to keep the meat moist during cooking, but also fat is a good absorber of flavour during the spicing process. The meat should have all bones removed and may be spiced rolled and tied, or unrolled. Penetration of the spices is quicker and more thorough in unrolled meat. Also, because the meat is flatter, more of it is sitting in the spicing liquor. It is important from this point of view to have a bowl or dish which fits the meat neatly. Pieces which are a fairly uniform shape like the salmon cut or silverside will not need rolling or tying before cooking but rib roast, brisket and nineholes will need some tying.

## Spicing

Put the meat into a fairly closely fitting dish and cover with the brown sugar. Cover well and leave for 2 days in a cool place, turning each day.

Pound all the spices and garlic together in a mortar. Experiment with spice combinations—I do not like using cloves since I think they dominate the more subtle juniper and coriander too much, though Meg Dods uses ½ oz/25 g in similar proportions. The spices may be ground coarsely in a grinder but they should not be finely powdered or it will be difficult to remove them from the outside surface of the meat at the end of the spicing, especially important if it is to be baked.

Mix spices with the salt and rub into the meat. Put on a cover, or foil, and rub and turn the meat every day. The length of time the meat should be left depends on how heavily or lightly spiced you like the meat. I left a 5 lb piece of silverside in the above mixture for a fortnight once and it was so strongly spiced no one would eat it. Nearly all old recipes recommend a month minimum—palates were more robust in those days. The pickling time also depends on the thickness of the meat—flat brisket will be quite well spiced in five to six days while a thick piece of rump will need about nine.

*Spiced Beef*

**A cut of beef 4-10 lb/2-5 kg**
**4 oz/125 g (1 c) brown sugar**
**1 oz/25 g allspice**
**1 oz/25 g juniper berries**
**1 oz/25 g black peppercorns**
**½ oz/15 g coriander seeds**
**½ grated nutmeg**
**2-3 crushed cloves of garlic**
**4 oz/125 g salt (½ c, scant)**

## Cooking

**For boiling**—(best for tougher cuts like brisket and nineholes) wipe off excess spice and put in a pot of boiling water, bring to the boil and skim well. Add **1 stick of celery**; an **onion stuck with a few cloves; 1 carrot; 1 small piece of turnip; bunch of parsley and thyme;** a **tablespoon peppercorns**. Bring back to the boil, skim and simmer very gently, allowing 30 minutes per lb/500 g plus 30 minutes or till tender.

**For braising**—Wipe off the excess spice. Melt **2 tablespoons oil** in a pan and add **2-3 chopped carrots, 1 small turnip** and **1 medium onion**, chopped, and sauté till lightly browned. Place the meat on top— cover with a skin of fat if necessary. Add enough water to cover the vegetables completely and come about halfway up the meat. Cover with a double layer of foil and then a tightly-fitting lid and bake at 300F/150C/Gas 2 for 30 minutes per lb/500 g plus 30 minutes or until tender.

## Pressing

Remove when cooked, wrap tightly in foil while still hot and put between two boards with a weight on top, leave overnight.

## Serving

It can be eaten hot, but the spice flavour is best appreciated when cold. Serve with Grated Boiled Beetroot mixed with a well-flavoured vinegar (I use the Japanese Red Umeboshi Plum Vinegar which has a unique effect on beetroot) and olive oil.

**As a sandwich**—spiced beef makes excellent sandwiches with a little mustard or chutney.

*We have one great advantage, that makes amends for many inconveniences, that is, wholesome and agreeable drink, I mean French Claret...*
Edward Burt (Chief Surveyor to General Wade during the making of roads through the Highlands)
*Letters from a Gentleman in the North of Scotland (1724-28)*

# BEEF
## cooked in claret

**6-8 servings**

With so much borrowing back and forward between Scotland and France, the use of French claret to cook Scottish beef seems an obvious combination. The cheapest cut of beef can be used with no loss of flavour, in fact the harder-working muscles like the leg have more flavour than other, less active ones.

Pre-heat the oven to 300F/150C/Gas 2.

## To cook

Heat the oil in a frying pan and brown the pieces of meat. Put into the casserole, add the garlic and sprinkle over flour. Leave uncovered in the oven to continue browning for 15 minutes, stirring from time to time. Add wine, season lightly, add herbs. Cover and simmer for 3 hours or until the meat is tender.

Meanwhile, cook the trimmings. Heat a frying pan and fry the bacon till lightly brown. Add the onions and cook uncovered for about 10 minutes. Then add the mushrooms, stir, cover and cook gently for another 10 minutes. Keep aside till serving.

Remove meat from the oven and stir in the trimmings. Heat through for five minutes and serve with chopped parsley and boiled potatoes.

## FORFAR BRIDIES

**Makes 4**

These convenient hand-held delicacies were made by itinerant sellers who mostly plied their trade at local fairs and markets. They may have taken their name from one such seller, Maggie Bridie of Glamis, though another story goes that because of their lucky horseshoe shape they were served at weddings and took their name from the bride.

Today they are a bakers' speciality, akin to a Cornish pasty turned on its side, and filled with steak. Forfar is an important centre of the beef trade in Angus and the first bridies I bought in Forfar were made by a local butcher who used the very best rump steak for filling—the pastry was crisp and slightly brittle rather than short and was well-flavoured with beef dripping.

Pre-heat the oven to 400F/200C/Gas 6.

### To make the pastry

Rub the fat into the flour, add salt and mix to a stiff dough with cold water. Divide into four and roll out into large ovals. Leave to rest.

### To prepare the meat

Beat out the steak with a meat bat or rolling pin and cut up roughly into ½ in (1 cm) pieces. Put the meat into a bowl with the onions and suet, season and divide into four. Cover half of each oval with the meat leaving about ½ in (1 cm) round the edge for sealing. Wet edges, fold over and seal. Crimp edge with fingers, make a hole in the top and bake on a greased baking sheet for about 45 minutes.

## *Beef Cooked in Claret*

*For the meat:*

**4 tablespoons oil**

**3 lb/1½ kg stewing steak, cut into 1½ in (4 cm) cubes**

**5 cloves garlic, crushed**

**2 tablespoons flour**

**1 bottle fruity young claret (Burgundy, Cotes-du-Rhone or Beaujolais)**

**Salt and freshly milled black pepper**

**1 teaspoon sugar**

**Bunch of fresh herbs**

*For the trimmings:*

**5 oz/150 g lean bacon**

**6-8 very small onions**

**14 oz/400 g button mushrooms, chopped**

## *Forfar Bridies*

*To make the pastry:*

**12 oz/400 g plain flour (3 c)**

**3 oz/100 g butter (¾ stick)**

**3 oz/100 g beef dripping**

**Water to mix**

**Salt**

*To prepare the meat*

**1 lb/500 g rump or topside**

**3 oz/75 g beef suet, finely chopped (¾ c)**

**2 medium onions, finely chopped**

**Salt and ground black pepper to taste**

# TRIPE SUPPERS

**6-8 servings**

*The frequenter of Douglas's, after ascending a few steps, found himself in a pretty large kitchen—a dark fiery Pandemonium, through which numerous ineffable ministers of flame were continually flying about, while beside the door sat the landlady, a large fat woman, in a towering head-dress and large flowered silk gown, who bowed to everyone passing. The House was noted for suppers of tripe, rizzard haddocks, mince collops and hashes which never cost more than sixpence a head.*

Robert Chambers,
*Traditions of Edinburgh*, 1868.

## *Tripe Suppers*

2 lb/1 kg prepared tripe cut into 2 in (5 cm) squares

2-3 medium onions, finely sliced

2½ lb/1¼ kg potatoes, sliced ¼ in (½ cm) thick

1 marrow bone/or knuckle of veal/or ham bone

*Seasoning*

3-4 bay leaves

2 teaspoons dried thyme (1 tablespoon fresh)

1 heaped tablespoon crushed garlic and salt

Even cheaper Tripe Suppers were provided for the poor at 'eating houses' in the industrial towns of the late nineteenth century. W. Anderson, writing in *The Poor of Edinburgh and Their Homes* (1867), describes how they were allowed 'as muckle as a man can eat' for a penny, and a plate of potatoes for another penny.

Tripe is a dish of strong character which arouses extremes of feeling in people, not just because it might be associated with poverty—you love it or hate it. This is a simple stew or hotpot of tripe, potatoes and onions which has the advantage of having everything cooked in one pot.

Use an 8-pt oven casserole.

Pre-heat the oven to 275F/140C/Gas 1.

## To cook

Place the meat bone in the base of the casserole. Arrange the tripe, onions and potato in layers with seasoning in between—finish with a layer of potato.

Press down well and pour in water to cover. Bring to the boil. Cover with a double layer of foil under a tightly-fitting lid and bake for 3-4 hours. Serve with lots of freshly chopped parsley.

# KIDNEY PUDDINGS

**4 servings**

While I am not a great fan of fiddling about with single-portion dishes, this is an exception, for the little individual puddings lose much of their charm if they are made into a large dumpling.

## To cook

Fry off bacon in a frying pan, then add the onion. Cook until soft and lightly browned. Add the kidney and cook for a few minutes. Then add the alcohol, stock or water and cook for about ten minutes. Season.

## To make the puddings

Mix the flour, suet and salt in a bowl and mix with water to a fairly stiff dough. Divide into four. Roll out into approximately 6-in rounds. Cut out a quarter to use as a lid. Flour four 6-in squares of cling film, back and front, and use to line four teacups. Fit the pastry into the cups leaving a little overhanging. Fill up with the kidney mixutre. Add some of the liquor, reserve the rest for a sauce to serve with the dumplings. Make the lids. Turn in overhanging flap, wet edges and fit on lid.

Place the cups in a deep baking tray with an inch of boiling water and cover with piece of greased foil. Seal round the edges and bake for 30 minutes. Turn out, remove cling film. Fry parsley till crisp, strain the sauce, season and serve with the dumplings and parsley.

From Ronnie Clydesdale's Ubiquitous Chip Restaurant in Glasgow, 1994.

### Kidney Puddings
*For the filling*

1 lb/500 g lambs' kidneys cored and diced

4 oz/125 g Ayrshire bacon, diced

1 large onion, finely chopped

4 fl oz/125 g Madeira, Malmsey or Amontillado sherry

1 pt/600 ml lamb stock or water

*For the pastry*

8 oz/250 g self-raising flour

4 oz/125 g beef suet, chopped or Atora

1 teaspoon salt

Cold water to mix

Few sprigs of parsley

# VEAL SWEETBREADS AND KIDNEYS

**4 servings**

On Monday 21st March 1737 the Murrays of Ochtertyre near Crieff had 'sweetbread and kidneys' for supper. Entirely appropriate, since that very day, according to the household accounts, they had 'killed an oxe' and for several days following they ate tripe in a variety of guises, which all goes to show a healthy Scots respect for innards even among the aristocracy. The theory that innards went to servants was not the case at Ochtertyre. According to the household accounts, servants fared very well, frequently eating beef and pig as well as 'puddings and hagas'.

If sweetbreads are not available use all kidneys and vice versa.

## To prepare both throat and heart sweetbreads

Wash well in running water for a few minutes and then leave them to soak for an hour with a tablespoon of salt. This removes traces of blood. Drain, rinse and put in enough cold water to cover. Add the lemon juice and a pinch of salt, bring to the boil and simmer until the sweetbreads become firm and white. This will only take a few minutes for lamb's sweetbreads; veal's will take about 10 minutes depending on size. Don't overcook. Drain them, reserving the cooking liquid for stock, and refresh under cold running water. Remove the skin and membranes, tubes and

### Veal Sweetbreads and Kidneys

1 lb/500 g veal (or lamb's) sweetbreads

8 oz/250 g veal (or lamb's) kidneys

Juice of half a lemon

Salt, freshly milled black pepper

119

hard bits, etc. For a firm texture, they may be pressed between two plates or boards with weights on top, and left overnight.

## To make the sauce

*For the sauce*

**4-5 tablespoons unsalted butter**

**2 tablespoons madeira**

**¾ pt/450 ml double cream (2 c)**

**1 teaspoon grated nutmeg**

**Salt, freshly milled black pepper**

Melt the butter in a pan. Slice the sweetbreads into 1 in (2½ cm) pieces. Skin and slice the kidneys in similar-sized pieces. Toss both in butter and cook quickly for about five minutes. Remove with a slotted spoon and keep hot. Add the madeira to the pan and boil for 2-3 minutes, mixing with the pan juices. Add the cream and nutmeg, and reduce for about ten minutes. Adjust seasoning and pour very hot over the sweetbreads.

## Serving

They can be served plainly on hot buttered toast or fried bread or with plain boiled rice.

Sometimes they are served in small pastry cases or vol-au-vent cases or on a bed of spinach. Lady Clark of Tillipronie served them with sorrel, the sharp, piquant sorrel making an excellent foil for sweetbreads.

Another easy and very effective way of serving is to put them between layers of puff pastry.

For the above quantities use 8 oz/250 g puff pastry. Pre-heat the oven to 350F/180C/Gas 4. Roll out the pastry to ¼ in (½ cm) thick and score lightly in a diamond pattern. With a sharp knife cut four rectangles 2 in x 3 in (6 cm x 8 cm). Brush with egg and bake for 20 minutes till risen and brown. Split open, remove any doughy bits in the middle and fill with cooked mixture. Replace lid and serve.

Serve with a White Burgundy.

## SWEETBREAD PIE

**8 servings**

Sweetbreads are a natural ingredient for pies and have been used for centuries in all kind of combinations highlighting their interesting flavour and texture. I like the subtle blend of pork, bacon, mushrooms and garlic in this pie which is originally from Jane Grigson's *Good Things*, 1971.

## Never Fail Pastry

This is a unique short crust pastry for all those who complain they are unsuccessful pastry-makers. It makes a light, crisp crust and is simple and quick to make—fat and boiling water beaten together (30 seconds); flour stirred in (10 seconds). It comes from Stella Atterbury's *It's Never*

*Too Late—An Original Cookery Book* (1963)—the story of how she learnt the hard way how to run a hotel when her husband retired. It is full of salutary stories of what not to do, but also includes some imaginative and inventive ideas for coping in the kitchen—this pastry is one of them and can be made in large quantities and stored for a few weeks.

## To make the pastry

Cut the butter and lard in small pieces into a bowl and pour on the boiling water. Whisk them together till the fat is all melted and mixed through—can also be done in a processor. It should make a thickish creamy mixture but this depends on how well the fat creams. It does not matter if the fat and water are still separated at the end of whisking. Now add the flour and salt and mix in, cover and place in refrigerator till hard—about an hour.

## For the filling

Prepare the veal sweetbreads as described on p.119.

Mince the pork or veal, pork fat and bacon finely together—the butcher will do this for you. Add the eggs and the flour.

Heat the oil in a pan and cook the mushrooms, onion and garlic together till soft.

Line a 3 pt/1½ L capacity loaf tin with the pastry, keeping enough aside for the lid.

Lay in a third of the pork mixture and put half of the mushroom mixture on top. Arrange half of the sweetbreads on top of this. Continue —pork/mushrooms/sweetbread—finishing with a layer of pork. Mound up nicely to support the pastry. Roll out lid, wet edges and cover. Decorate and brush with egg.

Bake 350F/180C/Gas 4 for 1 hour (protect the lid if necessary). Serve warm or cold.

**Note:** May be made as a meat loaf without pastry but cover with double layer of foil—leave off towards the end of the cooking to brown top. Cool and press under a light weight overnight.

**Note: Ayrshire Bacon.** The only native bacon cure, it depends on removing both skin and bones before wet salting. The back or cutlet part are not separated, so that once cured the whole piece is rolled up tightly with the fat side out to make the traditional round shape. Usually salted for two days then dried out for two to three weeks, it is unsmoked.

Bacon, however, which is described as 'Ayrshire-style' will have been produced differently. Though it will have the traditional round Ayrshire shape, the fat will have a waxy look and will be softer than the traditional

## Sweetbread Pie

*Never Fail Pastry*

2 oz/50 g butter (½ stick)

2 oz/50 g lard (½ stick)

2 fl oz/50 ml boiling water (¼ c)

6 oz/75 g plain flour, white or wholemeal or a mixture (1½ c)

½ teaspoon salt

*For the filling*

1 lb/500 g veal sweetbreads

¾ lb/350 g lean pork and/or veal

½ lb/250 g hard back pork fat

2 rashers unsmoked Ayrshire bacon (see note)

2 large eggs

1 heaped tablespoon flour

2 tablespoons oil

4 oz/125 g mushrooms, finely chopped (2 c)

2 tablespoons onion, finely chopped

1 clove garlic, crushed

cure. This is because the pigs are 'plotted' after killing. Plotting is a mass-production method which involves putting the carcass into boiling water to soften the skin. Then it is put into a tumble drier with friction pads which takes off the hair and finally it is blast-dried with a gas blower. This method will not have the same high quality of the original cure, which preserves the flavour and texture by chilling the carcass and removing the skin cold.

# POTTED HOUGH
## (Jellied Meat)

**4-6 servings**

A traditional economy food which was made with the tough parts of the animal, plus bones for flavour and setting gelatine properties.  It was originally a high tea dish, eaten with hot toast and sometimes pickled beetroot. A popular item in butchers' shops, it is made in varying sizes and with subtle differences in flavour from butcher to butcher. Made at home, it can be used as the basis for useful stock by adding a few extra bones: then the leftover jellied stock can be used for soup. Some butchers add salt-pickled beef.

## To cook

Place the ingredients in a large pan, cover with water and boil for 6 hours. Strain. Leave stock to get cold overnight and then remove the fat. Now chop up the meat very finely, put into a pan and cover with stock; you may not need all of it. It should make a good firm jelly when cold. Bring to the boil and simmer for a few minutes. Leave to cool and then season well. Pour into wetted moulds and serve with very hot toast and salad.

# POTTED TONGUE

Potted meats are an old tradition, originally high tea items, served with bread and butter and spicy pickles. Today, they can be served in smaller quantities at the beginning of a meal instead of the ubiquitous 'pâté', which was originally a French pie with pastry and not the soft meat paste which takes this name today.

## To cook

Pound the nutmeg, ground ginger, mace, thyme and garlic together in a mortar.

*Potted Hough*

1 lb/500 g hough (shin or beef)

Nap bone (put in more if making extra stock)

Blade of mace

3 or 4 whole cloves

Salt and pepper

*Potted Tongue*

Pinch of nutmeg, ground ginger, mace, thyme

Small garlic clove

8 oz/250 g cooked tongue

4 oz/125 g softened butter (1 stick)

Mix this spice mix together with the cooked tongue and the butter to make a smooth paste. This can be done with a pestle and mortar or in a food processor.

Pack into one large dish, preferably with a lid. Clarify butter (see pp.30-1), strain over tongue and leave to cool. It should make a layer about ¼ in (½ cm) thick. It will keep for several weeks in a cool place.

# OTHER TRADITIONAL BEEF PRODUCTS— LORNE SAUSAGE, SASSERMAET, SUET AND DRIPPING

## LORNE SAUSAGE

A square, sliced sausage which takes its name from the Music Hall comedian, Tommy Lorne, who frequently made jokes about the 'squeer' sausage and its use as a doormat. The square shape was developed to fit the sandwich made with a 'square loaf' (see p.213) which also often contained a fried egg. The sausage is made with minced beef and fat, plus a starchy binder, seasonings and water. This is then put into a Lorne tin, the surface pressed by hand and the tin inverted onto a tray. It is left to harden in the refrigerator before slicing.

## SASSERMAET

This is a Shetland version of a Lorne sausage. The variation depends on the alternative recipes which Shetlanders use. While the traditional version is made with beef and spices, there are also others made with pork. In its original form it was a crofter's preservation recipe. The meat was heavily spiced and packed into an earthenware crock. When it was required it was mixed with breadcrumbs and chopped onions, bound together with egg or milk. Among the spices used are black pepper, white pepper, ground cloves, allspice and cinnamon.

## SUET

This is the fat from the loin and kidney region in a beef carcass. Its primary use was as an ingredient in traditional boiled/steamed puddings. Those of the savoury variety were part of the staple diet as a starchy filler in the days before potatoes. It is still an essential ingredient for clootie dumpling, Christmas pudding and mincemeat. It is a creamy white, hard fat and may be sold by the butcher straight from the carcass, in which case it must have the sinewy membranes removed before chopping. Shredded suet is the ready-prepared product which is made from beef kidney suet.

## DRIPPING

This is the fat carefully collected in the roasting tray under meat during cooking. Butchers then pour it into clean pots and allow it to cool. Some sell it with a layer of the meat juices in the base of the pot underneath the dripping: this is sold as 'Stovie dripping'. It may be used as a spread on toast, or in sandwiches, especially those made with the roast meat which the dripping has come from. Also used for basting meat and roasting potatoes.

# Lamb

*Such a display of mutton broth...and Roasted jiggets of lamb.*
D.M. Moir
*Mansie Wauch*, 1828

Sheep and goats were the first wild animals gathered into herds by prehistoric man who saw the advantage of having milk and meat 'to hand'. Indigenous in their wild form to parts of the Near East, it was probably in Iraq, somewhere about 9000 BC, that domestication began. Since then, farmers and their herds have slowly moved westwards.

They reached Britain about 4000 BC when sheep and goats became established as valuable milk, meat and wool producers. In the Middle Ages the Border hills were well trodden by sheep who helped keep the English wool trade in business as well as providing milk for cheese (see p.225). Sheep and goats were also kept by Highlanders for meat, milk, cheese and wool, but in much smaller numbers compared with the Borders. Just a few sheep and goats were kept for domestic use and practically none were exported. The vast army of sheep, however, which came nibbling their way up strath and glen as a result of the mid-nineteenth-century Clearances were of value to their breeders principally as meat to satisfy the growing urban markets.

## BREEDS

While England can name some forty native breeds, Scottish sheep husbandry is mostly based on the native Blackface and North and South Country Cheviots with some local variants such as Shetland, Soay and North Ronaldsay. Much cross-breeding goes on to improve stock and give a good proportion of meat to bone as well as tender, well-flavoured flesh.

124

The Blackface or 'Blackies' are considered among the hardiest, surviving the worst snowstorms on open hills and still producing healthy lambs in the spring. They have a wild look which characterises their temperament as tough, courageous and determined animals, whose natural instincts keep them foraging for food in the most appalling conditions. They predominate on the vast areas of wild hill country. There are 2.5 million Blackies in the UK, representing 14 per cent of the sheep industry, and most are in Scotland.

The breed can be traced back to the twelfth century when they were mentioned by monks who exported their wool. But it was James IV of Scotland who began improving the breed, establishing a flock in the Ettrick Forrest in the sixteenth century. In the early nineteenth century they were taken, along with Cheviots, to the Highlands and by the end of the century had become the dominant breed. Such is the pursuit of excellence in the breed that a Blackie tup was sold at Perth in 1997 for a record £85,000.

'This small hill lamb is perhaps the finest quality in the world, giving a carcase free from superfluous fat and waste. The lightweight carcase satisfies a high demand by the housewife whether it be sold through Smithfield, a High Street butcher, the supermarkets or the continent.' *British Sheep* (The National Sheep Association 1982).

Another breed native to Scotland are the Cheviots, named after the Cheviot Hills which extend across the border between Scotland and England. Also hardy hill sheep, they are more often found on upland farms and grass-covered 'white' hills (as opposed to 'black' which are heather-covered). They produce a lightweight carcase, low in fat with a high percentage of well-flavoured lean meat and are one of the oldest breeds in Scotland. Described as South Country Cheviots, to distinguish them from the breed developed in the mid-eighteenth century, and described as the North Country Cheviots, their history goes back at least to the fourteenth century when they were bred for their wool by the monks of the Border Abbeys. To improve the wool quality, Merino sheep were introduced and the wool-manufacturing towns of Selkirk, Galashiels, Hawick and Langholm became famous for their woollen products.

It was in the Borders that the North Country Cheviots were first developed. Crossed with a variety of other breeds, besides the Merino sheep, they became known as 'Northies' when they were established in Caithness as a breed, displacing the people during the mid-nineteenth-century Clearances. Today the breed is still found mainly on the colder, more exposed, east side of Scotland from Shetland to the Borders. It is a tough breed which produces a large carcass with a high proportion of lean to fat.

English Leicesters, Suffolks, some of the Down breeds and continental breeds including Texels (from the island of Texel off the north-west coast of Holland) are used for crossing with the native Scottish breeds but usually there will be some Blackie in the cross to give hardiness.

Shetland sheep, which graze on rough grasslands, heather and seaweed on the Shetland shores, are one of the smallest British breeds, retaining many of the characteristics of wild sheep. They are hardy and self-reliant, surviving severe gales and winter blizzards. Because it is impossible to be more than three and a half miles from the sea anywhere on the islands, the air, activated by the strong winds, carries salt over all the pastures. This, combined with the heather and seaweed which they eat, gives the meat a unique, slightly gamey flavour which has been favourably compared with the much-praised French *Agneau de Pré-Salé*, which are the lambs fed on the salty grasses of the northern coastal region of France. Like the Shetland lamb, the *Pré-Salé* lamb is five to nine months old at the time of killing, but because of the poor-quality winter grazing, Shetland lamb is smaller in size. Despite this, the harsh environment has ensured that only the fittest lambs survive, making them well conditioned, hardy and vigorous.

Shetland sheep were also kept for their very fine, soft wool which was carded and spun in the crofthouses. This wool was not clipped but 'rooed'—pulled away by hand when the sheep started to lose its coat in summer, the finest wool coming from the neck. It was this neck wool which was used in the famous shawls which were so fine that they could pass through a wedding ring. Shetland lamb has never become widely known on the British mainland, partly due to distance and difficulties of transport. The scarcity of numbers has also been a limiting factor. The lambs are normally born from May onwards and do not become available until October or November.

Other native breeds, at present being preserved from extinction by the Rare Breeds Survival Trust, are the Boreray from the island of Boreray in the St Kilda group; also the Soay sheep from the St Kilda islands, and North Ronaldsay sheep from the Orkney island where they live entirely on a diet of seaweed on the shore. (A stone dyke round the whole island fences the sheep off the precious arable land, which is kept for other livestock, and the sheep's diet entirely of seaweed produces a uniquely flavoured meat and milk with a very high iodine content.)

Four breeds, the Soay, North Ronaldsay, Shetland and Castlemilk Moorit, are classed under the general heading of Scottish Primitive Breeds. Associated with the far north and west of Scotland, they are thought to be not that much different to breeds of Neolithic times. In the Hebrides and Shetland they have been influenced by breeds brought by the Vikings from Scandinavia. After a long period of decline, the primitive breeds are now being recognised for both their genetic and commercial factors. Studies indicate that the fatty acid composition of primitive sheep is different to commercial breeds, with a lower proportion of saturated fatty acids.

## AVAILABILITY/BUYING

Most lambing takes place on hill sheep farms during April, though some low-ground farms may start as early as February. A few low-ground farms produce early lambs from the end of December. Born and reared indoors in intensive systems, they are available in limited quantities for Easter, but because of high production costs they are expensive.

Flavour depends on breed, age, feeding and hanging. Lamb is at its best and most plentiful from July through to December, with most of the lamb from Scottish hill farms coming on the market from October on-wards. Killed before its first birthday it is still lamb but thereafter becomes hogget (year-old sheep).

In 1997 the Blackface Sheep Breeders Association ran a promotion with 60 butchers who agreed to label Blackface lamb during November when the lambs reached maturity. As they are grown to maturity slower than other faster-growing breeds, the selling point was the high-quality flavour. Lacking a large carcass size, by Continental standards, Blackies have a well-rounded muscle, a small amount of bone and, given their active lifestyle, not a high percentage of surplus fat. This was the first promotion which recognised a sheep breed at point of sale, and has been repeated since with many more butchers taking part.

Mutton has a good flavour. It was the meat used, before the Second World War, for traditional Scottish dishes based on long, slow, moist cooking. But it is difficult to buy now since butchers prefer to deal with the more uniform quality of lamb. Some admit that there is still a demand for the more flavourful mutton and, of course, it is theoretically available since not all sheep are killed before they reach their first birthday. Most mutton, however, is destined to end up in pies etc. A large amount of Scottish mutton is exported but a few butchers sell it. Halal butchers, who provide for the Muslim communities in Scotland, sell mutton.

All primitive breeds provide small joints of fine-flavoured meat. For optimum flavour they require a hanging time of at least seven days.

## To BOIL A GIGOT with Turnips
## Served with Caper Sauce

Only successful with well-matured mutton. Lamb is not robust enough to stand the long, slow cooking and will end up anaemic and tasteless.

*Mountain or wether mutton, from four to five years old, is by far the best... Simmer in an oval-shaped pot that will just hold it, letting the water come very slowly to the boil. Skim carefully. Boil sliced carrots and turnip with the mutton, and the younger and juicier they are the better they suit this joint. All meat ought to be well done, but a leg of mutton not overdone, to look plump and retain its juices. About two hours slow boiling will dress it.*

*Garnish with slices of carrot. Pour caper-sauce over the meat, and serve mashed turnip or cauliflower in a separate dish.*

Meg Dods,
*The Cook and Housewife's Manual*, 1826.

## ROAST RACK OF LAMB

*Roast Rack of Lamb*

**1 rack (8 chops) or 2 racks (8 chops each) of lamb**

**Herb and Breadcrumb stuffing for double rack (see p.113)**

**Salt and pepper**

**Oil for basting**

The advantage of roasting lamb chops in one piece on the bone is that they have a juicier, fuller flavour, since the bone on one side and the fat on the other prevent the meat juices running out. While a single rack is good for an everyday meal, a pair placed together with a stuffing in the centre (Guard of Honour) is good for a special occasion. Spring lamb is best (6-12 months) and the meat should be cooked medium rare for the best flavour.

For a single rack buy one with 8 uncut chops and ask the butcher to prepare—he should saw through the backbone but not remove it, since it protects the meat and can be removed before carving. He may trim the ends of the bones, but this is not essential.

For a double rack ask for two matching racks from the same animal if possible. The top 2-3 inches of the ribs need to be stripped to allow the two sides to interlace.

### For single rack

**4 servings**

Heat oil in oven, and when very hot, add meat. Turn meat in the oil and brown in a hot oven. For a medium-rare result cook for about 15 minutes at 450F/230C/Gas 8. This will obviously depend on the thickness of the chops. Allow another 5-10 minutes for well done. Leave to rest before carving. Follow the line of the rib bones and serve two chops per person.

Garnish with mint or watercress and serve with a green salad and Red-currant or Herb Jelly (see p.221).

## For double rack

### 8 servings

Place stuffing in the centre, interlace the rib bones, press well together and tie with string. Heat oil in roasting tin. Season meat and brown in a hot oven 450F/230C/Gas 8 for 15 minutes. Lower the heat 350F/180C/ Gas 4 and roast for another 20-25 minutes. Baste occasionally. Leave to rest for 10 minutes before carving. Carve by following the rib bones and cutting two chops together. Serve with the stuffing in the centre. Creamy Gratin Dauphinois (see p.241) is a good accompaniment to this with a green vegetable; or it may be garnished with mint and served with a green salad and redcurrant jelly for a lighter meal.

# GRILLED OR BARBECUED LEG OF LAMB

This is best barbecued over charcoal with some fresh rosemary thrown over the hot coals before and during the cooking. To make the piece of meat a uniform thickness so that it cooks evenly, the meat is boned out first. Your butcher may be willing to do this for you.

## To make the marinade

Mix all the marinade ingredients together.

## To bone out the meat

Begin by loosening the pelvic bone, following the contours of the bone. When you expose the ball-and-socket joint that connects the pelvic bone to the thighbone, cut through the tendons joining the bones. Make a straight cut down the length of the thighbone on the inside of the leg and again following the contours of the bone, loosen the flesh from the bone.

## Marinading the lamb

Flatten out the meat with a meat bat or rolling pin. It should be a fairly even thickness. Place in a dish which it will fit into neatly and add marinade. Leave for 12 hours or longer and turn once or twice.

## To cook the lamb

Grill or barbecue over a high heat for about 10-15 minutes depending on the degree of pinkness required. Keep turning and baste frequently with a little of the marinade to keep it moist. Make a gravy with some of the strained marinade and the pan juices. Serve with a green salad and baked potatoes.

*Grilled or Barbecued Leg of Lamb*

**1 leg of lamb**

*Marinade*

**¾ pt/450 ml dry red wine (2 c)**

**4 tablespoons olive oil**

**1 medium onion, finely sliced**

**1 carrot, thinly sliced**

**6 parsley stalks**

**2 bay leaves**

**A sprig of rosemary**

**1 clove garlic, crushed**

**1 teaspoon salt**

**Freshly ground black pepper**

Note: If your grill pan is not large enough to cope with a whole leg it can be roasted in a very hot oven—450F/230C/Gas 8 for 15 minutes per lb. Turn and baste once or twice during the cooking. Leave to rest for 10 minutes in a warm place before serving.

## BRAISED LAMB SHOULDER WITH CARROTS AND TURNIPS

*Braised Lamb Shoulder with Carrots and Turnips*

1 lamb shoulder (approx. 4-5 lb/2-2½ kg)

3 tablespoons olive oil

3 large carrots, peeled and sliced

½ medium turnip, peeled and sliced

2 large onions, finely chopped

¾ pt/450 ml white wine/water or stock (2 c)

Bouquet garni

**6-8 servings**

Pre-heat the oven to 325F/170C/Gas 3.

Heat oil in a large frying pan and brown meat all over. Place in large casserole just large enough to hold it. Add onions to pan and brown. Add some more oil if necessary, heat through and then add carrots and turnips. Toss in oil for 10-15 minutes.

Remove meat from casserole and place vegetables in base then meat on top. Season well. Add white wine or water to pan and boil up with pan juices. Pour over meat and add enough liquid to come just over halfway up. Cover and cook slowly for about 1½ hours till the meat is almost tender. To crisp the surface, remove the lid and turn up the oven to 450F/230C/Gas 8 and brown the surface. This should take about 15-20 minutes. Remove the meat, and the bones should slide out fairly easily. Cut the meat in wedges and serve with some of the vegetables. Taste the cooking liquid for seasoning and serve in a sauceboat or pour over meat when serving. Serve with baked potatoes.

## LAMB AND KIDNEY PIE

*Lamb and Kidney Pie*

2½ lb/1¼ kg stewing Scotch lamb

½ lb/250 g lamb's kidney

2 tablespoons flour

½ pt/300 ml stock or water (1¼ c)

6 oz/175 g cooked gammon (English: ham)

Salt and pepper

½ lb/250 g puff pastry

*For the marinade*

2 medium onions, finely sliced

3 tablespoons honey

1 lemon, zest and juice

2 tablespoons redcurrant jelly

**8-10 servings**

Tender lamb is marinated overnight in honey, redcurrant jelly and lemon juice to make a richly flavoured filling for this pie.

Pre-heat the oven to 400f/200C/Gas 6 for the first 20 minutes. Then turn down oven and cook for a further 80 minutes at 325F/170C/Gas 3.

Size of pie dish—2½ pt (1¼ L).

### To cook

Cut the lamb into dice and finely slice the kidney. Add to the marinade ingredients and leave overnight. Add flour, gammon, salt, pepper and stock. Mix well and place in pie dish. Cover with pastry and bake. Cover pastry if necessary towards the end of the cooking if it looks as though it is overcooking.

## SCOTCH PIES

Scottish bakers make these pies in large quantities, though no longer with mature mutton which was the original filling, but instead they use minced beef. They have also developed a wide range of variations, including some vegetarian fillings such as macaroni in a cheese sauce. The small, hand-held pies are made in special straight-sided moulds, usually about 3-3½ in (7.5-8.5 cm) in diameter by 1½ in (4 cm) deep. They are easily recognised by the rim of pastry which stands up above the lid making about ½ in (1 cm) space which can be filled with hot gravy, or beans and potatoes. They are best eaten hot—they are often sold hot by bakers and fish-and-chip shops. The meat-filled original variety are standard fare at football matches with a cup of hot Bovril. They were originally tavern food, an early form of 'fast food' for working people, and in the Candleriggs in Glasgow there still stands 'Grannie Black's' (now a pub and on a different site from the original), who made such good mutton pies that their fame spread far and wide. They cost twopence and were known as 'Tuppenny Struggles'.

Special pie moulds are necessary for their production, so that they have become a commercial product not normally made in the domestic kitchen.

# HOW TO USE A WHOLE SHEEP OR LAMB

These are Lady Clark's notes (*circa* 1893) which describe how to use up all the bits and pieces which are not part of the main meat carcass. Though there are few today faced with the prospect of dealing with this in a domestic situation, there are still lots of practical bits of advice on the use of offal.

'Heads are available, though not on display. Sometimes difficult to get if there is a circus in town since they are favourite food for lions and tigers. I suppose the same holds true if you live near a zoo.

'The blood makes black puddings, with sieved oatmeal, or groats, or rice...The head, trotters and breast of mutton, with some of the superfluous fat on this last cut off, make, with vegetables, the best broth, and afterwards all the meat is useful in other ways. The sheep's head, whole, is served with feet ('trotters') round as garnish, and with broth as sauce; or cut up in squares in dressed sauce as an entrée, vegetables in centre and fried brains as garnish; or can be boiled and turned out of a mould solid.

'The boiled breast of mutton used to boil with Sheep's Head, can afterwards be crumbled, with mixed herbs, and broiled or baked a nice brown, to eat hot. If for upstairs, serve a sharp sauce in a boat with chopped gherkins or capers in it.

'Kidneys can be sliced for breakfast, with bacon, or in an omelet, and the liver sliced and fried and served with bacon and fried potatoes.

'The sheep's heart is hard if roasted; it is better stuffed and braised— but must be eaten at once—it chills so immediately. A sheep's sweetbread is not worth cooking though in the lamb it is excellent. A lamb's head can be served upon a 'fugie', a mince of heart, sweetbread, liver etc. but no kidneys. Make it savoury.

'Much of the rest is used for Haggis. Any bits not otherwise wanted are very welcome additions to the scraps set aside for the keeper's dogs.'

# GRILLED FLANK (BREAST) OF LAMB
## with Tomato Sauce

*Grilled Flank of Lamb with Tomato Sauce*

Two pieces of flank (2 lb/1 kg)

4 oz/125 g fresh breadcrumbs (2 c)

Salt and pepper

Finely chopped herbs

2 eggs or melted butter

Tomato sauce

**4 servings**

Made from well-flavoured lamb, this succulent delicacy is moist and tender inside while crisp and crunchy on the outside. It has the advantage of using up the cheaper flank cut. Flank stuffed and rolled is also good roasted.

### To prepare the meat

Use two pieces of flank which have been simmered in some broth till tender, or poached on their own till tender with some vegetables. While still warm, remove the bones which should slip easily out of the meat. To make a good flat surface for grilling, put the meat between two boards overnight with a weight on top. The next day, cut each flank into small rectangles about the size of a small chop.

### Coating the pieces

Mix the breadcrumbs with salt, pepper and some finely chopped herbs. Dip the meat in beaten egg or some melted butter and then cover with breadcrumbs, pressing in well. Remove excess crumbs.

### Grilling

Place on a buttered baking tray; brush with butter and grill quickly under a hot grill for about 5 minutes each side. Baste with more butter if necessary. The purpose is simply to toast the coating and heat through the meat. Overcooking will dry out the meat and make it tough.

### Serving

Serve garnished with watercress and with a 'sharp' sauce. A well-flavoured tomato sauce is very good with this and can also be used for lamb chops, steaks or with meatballs.

## LAMB'S FRY

**4-6 servings**

Very thin strips of liver, heart, sweetbreads and kidneys are cooked very quickly to preserve flavour and texture—the heart may need a little longer.

### To cook

Heat the olive oil in a pan and add the lambs' hearts pared free of fat and tough vessels, split in half and cut lengthways into thin strips. Toss over a high heat for 2-3 minutes, reducing the heat if necessary.

Turn up the heat again and add the liver sliced and cut into thin strips, a kidney thinly sliced and the sweetbreads, thinly sliced (see p.119 for preparation). Sauté for one minute or until the liver and kidney have just changed colour.

Add 1 handful of chopped parsley mixed with the cloves of crushed garlic. Squeeze over some lemon juice and serve straight from the serving dish.

*Lamb's Fry*

**4 tablespoons olive oil**

**2 lambs' hearts**

**7 oz/200 g lambs' liver**

**4 oz/125 g sweetbreads**

**1 handful of chopped parsley**

**1-2 cloves crushed garlic**

**Lemon juice**

## HAGGIS

My first haggis-making exploits were as a student when the whole process took the best part of a day to complete. The raw sheep's pluck* was put into a large pot with the windpipe hanging over the side of the pot while the pluck cooked. The windpipe quietly disgorged blood and other impurities from the lungs into a jar on the cooker. It was not a job for the squeamish.

About ten years later, when I was working in a hotel which bought whole sheep, plucks started filling up the precious deep-freeze space and I had another go using my old recipe from *The Glasgow Cookery Book* (John Smith, Glasgow, Revised Edition, 1962). It is a standard-type recipe which is basically what most butchers work from, though no two will produce the same haggis. Variations are secret and have been developed over many years testing the Scottish palate for preferences. Haggis lovers have very definite ideas about the best qualities of haggis and a competition is held each year to find the best butcher's haggis.

*A sheep's pluck is the part of the animal which has been 'plucked' out of the belly and includes the liver, heart and lungs which are all joined together with the windpipe at one end.

133

## Qualities of a good Haggis

The flavour is a matter of taste, with some liking it spicy and 'hot' with plenty of pepper, while others prefer a milder flavour with more herbs than spices. Relative proportions of meat to oatmeal, suet and onions also depend on individual preferences, as does the type of offal used. Some butchers will use pig or ox liver because they say it is what their customers prefer. Heated debates occur about the authenticity of this variation. Many stick to the traditional sheep's liver—there are all kinds of permutations which make haggis eating something of an adventure. Whatever the source of the offal, there should be no tough gristly bits and the mixture should be moist and firm, rather than too dry and crumbly. Preferences vary from fine to coarse textured.

# TRADITIONAL METHOD

### Preparing the pluck and bag

Wash the stomach bag in cold water, scrape and clean well. Leave overnight in cold water. Wash the pluck and put it in a pan of boiling water. Let the windpipe lie over the side of the pot and have a small jar underneath to catch the drips. Simmer gently till all are tender—this depends on the age of animal but is usually between one and two hours. Place the cooked pluck in a large basin, cover with the liquid which it was boiled in and leave overnight.

### Making the Haggis (the next day)

Toast the oatmeal in the oven till thoroughly dried out but not browned. Cut off the windpipe, trim away all skin and black parts. Chop or mince the heart and lungs, grate the liver. Add the oatmeal, salt, pepper, herbs and about 1 pt/½ L (2½ c) of the liquid the pluck was boiled in. Mix well, fill the bag rather more than half full of the mixture. Press out the air, sew up and prick with a long needle. Place in boiling water; simmer for 3 hours, pricking again when it swells. The bag may be cut into several pieces to make smaller haggis in which case cook for only 1½-2 hours.

Serve hot with 'tatties'—creamed potatoes flavoured with nutmeg; 'neeps'—Mashed Turnip flavoured with ginger (see p.180) and a good blended whisky.

# OTHER WAYS OF SERVING

'Haggis meat, by those who cannot admire the natural shape,' says Meg Dods, 'may be poured out of the bag, and served in a deep dish. No dish

## Haggis

*(Quantities of suet, onions and oatmeal vary according to size of pluck)*

1 sheep's stomach bag and pluck

4 oz-1lb/125 g-500 g suet, finely chopped

4 medium onions, finely chopped

½ lb-2 lb/250 g-1 kg pinhead oatmeal, sometimes a mix of medium and pinhead

2-4 tablespoons salt

1 level teaspoon freshly ground black pepper

1 level teaspoon dried mixed herbs (2 for fresh)

heats up better.' It is also a very practical way of serving haggis to large numbers, provided it is well covered to prevent drying out. Knobs of butter dotted over the top surface are a good idea. Slices of haggis can be grilled, fried or wrapped in foil and baked in the oven with a bit of butter on top. The slices can be served as part of a Mixed Grill or for breakfast with bacon and egg. It is very good fried and served simply with fried onions or with an onion sauce lightly flavoured with whisky. I have had a slice of fried haggis served in a roll and described as a 'Haggisburger'. It was served with a whisky-flavoured chutney. It can also be used with mince in a Shepherd's Pie.

Provided you are careful about the dominating flavour it can be used as a stuffing. It should not be used with delicately flavoured meat like chicken unless it is a very mild haggis. Other ingredients can be added to the haggis such as nuts or cooked rice. Mixing in a little tomato sauce can work well.

An Edinburgh haggis manufacturer, Charles MacSween, has recently made a vegetarian haggis which is proving popular. It contains a variety of vegetables, spices, oatmeal and brown rice.

Perhaps the most unusual idea is that of serving cold haggis. Some years ago I met a chef whose local butcher made such a good haggis that he served a slice of it cold with hot toast as a starter course. It seemed that he used pork fat and meat rather than suet along with a delicate combination of herbs and spices with excellent results.

Variations in other recipes include adding the juice of a lemon or a little 'good vinegar'. Even flavouring with cayenne pepper. Quantities of oatmeal and suet vary a lot with up to 2 lb/1 kg oatmeal and 1 lb/500 g suet to a single pluck. Some are boiled for up to 6 hours. Meg Dods says that, 'A finer haggis may be made by parboiling and skinning sheep's tongues and kidneys, and substituting these minced, for most of the lights, and soaked bread or crisped crumbs for the toasted meal.' She also says that the parboiled minced meat from a sheep's head can be used for haggis.

## ORIGINS OF HAGGIS PUDDING

The ancient habit of gathering a selection of miscellaneous ingredients, and boiling them together in the stomach bag of an animal, is the origin of the haggis. The term 'pudding' meant stuffed stomach, and also the entrails of animals and men. Pudding Lane in London is thought to have derived its name, not from an association with edible puddings, but because the butchers of Eastcheap had their scalding-houses for hogs there, and their 'puddings', along with other debris, were taken down

135

Pudding Lane on their way to their dung-boats on the Thames.

Fifteenth-century recipes for puddings are closely connected with something called a 'Haggus' or 'Haggas' pudding. The general principle involved the use of the stomach bag with a filling of the cooked entrails plus some other ingredients including a sheep's paunch. Another recipe uses a calf's paunch and the entrails minced together with grated bread, yolks of eggs, cream, spices, dried fruits and herbs, served as a sweet with sugar and almonds.

Although the derivation is obscure, some etymologists believe that the term may have been transferred from the now obsolete name for a magpie: 'Haggiss' or 'Haggess'. It is thought that a medieval comparison may have been drawn between the magpie's habit of collecting and forming an accumulation of varied articles and the same general principle applied instead to ingredients for the pudding. This analogy may also apply to the pie. An early word for the magpie was 'maggot-pie' or 'Margaret-pie' or just 'pie'.

Whether the habits of the magpie had anything to do with it, a haggis pudding is clearly not an exclusive Scottish invention. Its Scottish tag came about as a result of Robert Burns' 'Address to a Haggis' which firstly strikes the celebratory note, dear to Scottish hearts. Then it honoured something of sense and worth, which Burns valued more than pure visual appeal. He made it a symbol for Scots: thriftily making the best use of plebeian ingredients. Yet at the same time the effect of his Address, and the subsequent Burns Supper phenomena, leaves Scots with a strong national food image. The poem, says James Kingsley, 'is an assertion of peasant virtue and strength, expressed in harsh violent diction and images of slaughter.'

# 6
# FRUIT, SWEETS, PUDDINGS & CAKES

*She put into the carriage a basket of excellent gooseberries, and some of the finest apricots I ever saw or tasted, which have grown out of doors; the season has been unusually favourable and her husband was fond of cultivating his garden.*

Robert Southey [at Inverness],
  *Journal of a Tour in Scotland in 1819.*

A colder, wetter climate than the rest of Britain, plus a lack of early gardening know-how, might appear to have put the Scots at a horticultural disadvantage, yet, as Southey noted, gardening expertise was not lacking and the climate not always hostile. Some parts, certainly, were better than others, and the terrain also varied considerably. But where the two combined favourably, there was a productive output. It was to these areas that Cistercian and Benedictine monks came in the eleventh and twelfth centuries, settling in the fertile Borders, the valleys of Strathmore and the Morayshire coast, and bringing both improved horticultural varieties and growing expertise. The range of fruits and vegetables grown by them, and subsequently in the gardens of the aristocratic houses of the land, was impressive. In the days before fresh fruits and vegetables started to be trucked around the world, the *Ochtertyre House Book of Accomps* (1737-1739) talks of asparagus, spinach, artichokes, French beans and cauliflower being grown in the house's kitchen-garden.

Such a range of vegetables, however, was unavailable to the mass of the population. Theirs was a narrower selection, with urban Lowlanders faring better than rural Highlanders in remote glens and isolated islands. The average eighteenth-century Scottish peasant depended on the limitations of the 'kail-yard' (garden) which provided kail, possibly cabbages or leeks, some bushes of gooseberries or blackcurrants and, by the end of the century, potatoes.

Scots consumption of vegetables in the past has always been a debatable issue. How many wild herbs they ate is not clear. But it should also be remembered that the traditional way of consuming vegetables was not as separate vegetables but in some form of broths. Then there was the erratic nature of eating vegetables, according to the seasons. Three platefuls of nettle broth in spring was regarded as an important tonic, as indeed it is. Medical herbalists today make good use of its high iron content in cases of anemia. Wild garlic was another popular springtime tonic which is still used to flavour cheese (see Hramsa, p.230).

Ever enterprising, the Scots have made good use also of wild fruits and berries: blaeberries, brambles, wild raspberries, rowans, sloes, rosehips, geans. These were used imaginatively to make conserves, jams and jellies, which were regarded as flavourings, not just to spread on bread, but to use as sauces with puddings, or even concocted into drinks such as the warming drink which Thomas Pennant was given when he visited the Macleods of Arnisdale in 1769.

'I shall never forget the hospitality of the house: before I could utter a denial, three glasses of rum, cordialised with jelly of bilberries, were poured into me by the irresistible hand of good Madam MacLeod.'

As one of the most eminent naturalists of the eighteenth century, his observations on the fruits eaten on Jura are also interesting—'Sloes are the only fruits of the island. An acid for punch is made of the berries of the mountain ash [rowan]: and a kind of spirit is also distilled from them.'

Everyone in Edinburgh in the eighteenth century was familiar with the street cry for apples and pears: 'Fine rosey-cheekit Carse o' Gowries— the tap o' the tree'. But today, neither apples nor pears are grown commercially in the Carse of Gowrie, or in any other part of Scotland for that matter, though there have been some attempts recently to revive the apple and pear orchard tradition.

Serious horticulture, to provide for growing markets, began in the eighteenth century and has been developing ever since. Now the Scottish horticultural industry grows crops successfully which use to advantage the cooler climate and the longer hours of summer daylight. Raspberries and peas are particularly successful, and Scotland is a major producer. They ripen more slowly, and therefore develop a better flavour, while the cooler weather means fewer pests and diseases and less use of pesticides.

In 1946, the Scottish Raspberry Investigation was set up at University College Dundee, transferring to Mylnefield Farm in the Carse of Gowrie in 1951 when the Scottish Crop Research Institute was established as a research station in the heart of berry-growing country. Over the years it has supported the industry and been instrumental in its success: pioneering new breeding varieties of many Scottish horticultural crops with a view to increasing yields, producing disease-resistant plants which will fit the special needs of the consumer while at the same time maintaining quality.

# Scottish Soft Fruits: Raspberries, Strawberries, Blackcurrants, Brambles (Blackberries), Red Currants and Blaeberries

## RASPBERRIES

It was a group of Scottish market gardeners in Angus in the early 1900s who decided to move out of traditional strawberry production and into raspberries. They formed a co-operative and in subsequent decades established the Scottish crop as the dominant British supply. On the fertile Tayside soils, once favoured by the farming monks of the Middle Ages, the raspberry matures slowly, producing a flavourful berry around the beginning of July. The quest for perfection in raspberry quality is everlasting. Among the experimental raspberry canes at Invergowrie, there is endless variety of size, colour, brightness, firmness and flavour; all to be considered in the search for a perfect raspberry.

Currently in production are Glen Clova, one of the oldest varieties (1969), Glen Moy and Glen Prosen (both released in 1981). While these three make up the bulk of the crop, other varieties include: Glencoe, a purple raspberry (1989), Glen Garry (1990), Glen Lyon (1991). There is also the autumn-fruiting variety, Autumn Bliss, which serves a niche market, while Magna, Ample and Rosa are the newest varieties of the 90s. Visual and taste differences between the main varieties are minimal. Clova is medium-sized, light- to medium-coloured fruit with a sweetish-sharp flavour. Prosen is medium-red coloured with a slightly sourer flavour but is a firmer, more easily transportable fruit, while Moy is a large berry, also medium-red coloured and generally regarded as the best flavoured of the three. Neither too sharp nor too sweet, its flavour is more rounded, but it is also the one with the shortest shelf-life. There are around 300 growers of which 183 have holdings of less than 50 hectares.

The Tayberry is the hybrid cross between the American blackberry and the European raspberry of the same type as the American Loganberry. The Tayberry has a strong personality, a rich, sweet, aromatic flavour and an exotic deep-purple colour. It is a firm berry which cooks well. Though not widely available for sale, it is  a very popular pick-your-own berry.

## STRAWBERRIES

While turn-of-the-century Tayside growers moved out of strawberries and into raspberries, strawberry growing continued to flourish in the smallholdings of the Clyde valley. Now the Clyde valley has turned to other crops and strawberry growing has been revived on the arable farms of Tayside, Fife and the North-East.

The most recent success has been the variety Elsanta. First developed for Dutch glasshouse growing and not for the outdoor Scottish summer, it has nevertheless proved its worth and now makes up 90 per cent of the Scottish crop. A large, orange-red berry, it has a deep pinkish-red flesh and when fully ripe is neither too soft nor too firm. It is a berry to be squashed when eating, when it releases its finely balanced flavours. Not too sweet, not too sharp, it is the gradual slow-ripening of the fruit in the long hours of summer daylight which develops the sugar content and gives the berries their superior taste.

'We sent our first consignment of Elsanta to France last week,' says William Halley of Scotfruit, Dundee distributors of Tayside soft fruits, 'and they have just multiplied the order by 10!'

Other large eating varieties are Pegasus, Symphony and Hapil (EM227) a large, soft, juicy berry with a short shelf-life which is only grown on Pick-Your-Owns. Cambridge Favourite and Tamella are the smaller-sized jam-making berries.

## BLACKCURRANTS, BLUEBERRIES, CHERRIES, BRAMBLES (BLACKBERRIES)

Blackcurrants are mostly grown for the juice market, but new, hardier varieties are being developed for growing in Scotland for the fresh market.

American high-bush blueberries have been made available to growers in Scotland by the Scottish Crop Research Institute and some growers have taken up the crop. They take a long time to establish, but when they do, they can remain cropping for fifty years. They are the same genus as the low-grown blaeberry and therefore like Scotland's acid soil. Their flavour, however, is less tangy. Their skins are slightly tougher than blackcurrants and they are not considered a good dessert berry, yet they add great character to fruit pies and are the most popular flavouring for American (blueberry) muffins. Currently they are imported from the US and South America, which is not an environmentally friendly use of fossil fuels when it has been proved that they grow successfully on native Scottish soil. There are currently only two growers who have taken up growing blueberries commercially. In the 1970s, my father began growing them in his domestic garden in Wester Ross and they have flourished now for the best part of twenty years. He has also grown successfully a variety of cherry: Stella. A number of experiments with cherries are also under way at the SCRI, though none are available commercially yet.

New varieties of brambles (blackberries) have been developed which ripen earlier and are available commercially in August.

## PICK-YOUR-OWN FRUIT, FARM SHOPS AND FARM STALLS

In all fruit-growing areas there are a variety of these outlets where you can not only obtain the freshest fruit, but also the best flavoured, which has been allowed to mature to full ripeness on the plant. It is also cheaper to buy it this way, provided the travelling distance is not too far.

The season usually begins in July, though the climate will always dictate when the fruit ripens. Some farms have early and late varieties which extends the season, but most soft fruit is finished by the end of August. Perthshire and Tayside are the areas with the greatest concentration of fruit farms.

Part of the service of a PYO is a full-time answering service throughout the season when state of the crop information is given, the varieties available and the weather conditions for picking. There is space to park and picnic and sometimes there are teas and home baking. Children are encouraged to pick.

Most PYOs also sell ready-picked fruit while other farms have shops selling soft fruit and other farm produce, which are worth seeking out.

## SOFT FRUIT AND CREAM

*It was quite a pantry; oatcakes, barley scones, flour scones, butter, honey, sweetmeats, cheese, and wine, and spiced whisky, all came out of the deep shelves of this agreeable recess, as did the great key of the dairy; this was often given to one of us to carry to old Mary the cook, with leave to see her skim and whip the fine rich cream, which Mrs Grant would afterwards pour on a whole pot of jam and give us for luncheon. This dish, under the name of 'bainne briste', or broken milk, is a great favourite wherever it has been introduced.*

Elizabeth Grant of Rothiemurchus
*Memoirs of a Highland Lady 1797-1827*

If the jam is lightly set, more in the style of a 'conserve' than a jam, this is an excellent way of combining fruit and cream. Such jewel-bright

141

colours and attractive shapes need no embellishments save the simple white background of cream. Its bland rich flavour highlights the natural sharpness of all these ready-to-eat fruits when they are ripe and full of fragrance.

Soft fruits have been linked with cream for centuries. In the fifteenth century the cream was made from almonds pounded and mixed with water: then the mixture was strained and the liquid used as cream. The recipe for 'Strawberye' which appears in the Harleian MS 279 (1420) also includes a formidable collection of flavourings which they added, with typical medieval passion for spicing—pepper, ginger, cinnamon, galyngale (from the root of the Cypress rush) and vinegar. No quantities are given, so we shall never know whether it was just a pinch or more which was added.

# Five ways of combining fruit with cream

**1. Fruit and Cream.** The simple fresh fruit, either singly or in a combination with cream, whipped or pouring as a garnish. Soured cream, crème fraîche, fromage frais and natural yoghurt can also be used in combinations.

**2. Fruit and Cream and Sauce.** Fruit plus cream with the addition of the juice of the berry or another berry for a sauce or a syrup sauce.

**3. Fruit Purée and Cream.** Consistency and texture will depend on the type of fruit and thickness of the cream.

**4. Fruit Purée and Cream—iced.** The answer for strawberries which are the only soft fruit which freezes badly whole.

**5. Fruit and Cream Cheese.** These two are combined in the classic Scottish dish of Cream-crowdie (Cranachan) though the cheesecake is another way of combining them, as is the French *Coeur à la Crème*, traditionally served with strawberries.

## 1. FRUIT AND CREAM

Presentation is one important factor, and the other is using fruit which is fully ripe and in its prime. White or glass dishes are the best foil for these brightly coloured fruits if to be served simply. Creating a fruit platter is another way of letting the fruit speak for itself.

# AN ASHET OF FRESH FRUIT
## or Fresh Fruit Platter

*At the end of meal a huge dish was put on the table, and on it an abstract design of prepared fruit, very bold and Matisse-like. We were each given a fork, to spear little pieces of this and that as we sat back and talked. It seemed to me the best possible way to end a meal with glory and without exhaustion for the cook.*

Jane Grigson,
*Observer Magazine*, December 1982.

This also makes an excellent centrepiece for a buffet table or is a good way of serving fruit at a simple family meal. Everyone helping themselves and leftovers used for fruit salad the next day.

Creating colour contrasts and textures is all part of the fun of presentation. It is first a question though, of what is fresh and ripe and secondly, what will make the most stunning effect.

Go to the shop or market first and look at the fruits; then start to create the picture. A whole pineapple not only provides an interesting green shape with its tufted top, and a soft yellow colour contrasting with the bright reds and blacks, but it also combines well flavourwise with raspberries and strawberries in particular. The same applies to melon of all kinds, and both these fruits can be cut into boat shapes. Leave the top on the pineapple and cut as for melon, loosening the fruit with a sharp knife close to the skin. Then cut the fruit into small, bite-sized wedges keeping the boat shape form, and place on the ashet.

Peaches combine well with soft fruits as do apricots, nectarines, greengages and plums—they should all be cut into bite-sized pieces. Apples and pears are a good texture contrast but should be chopped at the last minute to avoid discoloration. The same applies to bananas, unless you toss them in lemon juice. Grapes, cherries, and gooseberries are excellent as they are. I wouldn't bother removing stones for this kind of dish, unless it was for some sort of formal occasion. Oranges, tangerines and sweet grapefruit should be segmented either with or without the pith.

The odd exotic fruit, which is usually too expensive to use in quantity, can be added with great effect. Mangoes, fresh figs, kiwi fruit and passion fruit are the ones I've used most. Toasted nuts are also a good idea. I like to use hazelnuts with raspberries and almonds with strawberries. If you need some white colour then strips of fresh coconut are excellent.

## Assembling the fruits

This should be done in two stages. Work out the ones which you can safely arrange in advance without any drying out or discolouring. Have

143

some rough idea of how the finished platter is going to look and then prepare as much as possible in advance. It is not necessary to spend hours arranging patterns of fruit. Throw it together quickly; like a good water-colour painting it should not be 'over-worked'.

Serve with or without a jug of whipped cream and drink with a chilled sweet white wine or a light fruity Bordeaux.

# 2. FRUIT, CREAM AND SAUCE

## 'GOURMET' STRAWBERRIES

*'Gourmet' Strawberries*

1 lb/500 g strawberries, washed and hulled

Juice of 1 lemon

Sugar to taste

**4 servings**

The sauce is a simple purée of the fruit, sharpened with lemon. A good summer sweet which came from *Gourmet*, an American food magazine.

### To prepare

Take about a quarter of the strawberries and purée in the liquidiser or processor with lemon juice and sugar. Taste for sweetness. Put the strawberries in a bowl and sieve the purée on top. Chill for about half an hour before serving. Serve with or without cream.

**Note:** this works equally well with raspberries, or could for that matter be used with any other soft fruits. There is scope for experimentation by mixing the combinations rather than serving the fruit with its own fruit purée. I have often used strawberries with raspberry purée and vice versa. Of course the classic one is peaches with raspberry purée (Melba) but a very good combination which is often used is a red currant purée with strawberries and I have also served ripe blackcurrants and redcurrants in a raspberry purée.

## HOW ESCOFFIER SERVED STRAWBERRIES
### at the Carlton Hotel, London

*Soak some large strawberries in orange juice and Curaçao. Put them into a silver or glass dish and cover them with Chantilly cream.*

Auguste Escoffier,
*Ma Cuisine*, 1934.

**4 servings**

Known in classical cuisine as 'Strawberries Romanoff', this dish has had many interpretations but all have depended on Escoffier's original combination of strawberries and oranges.

## To prepare

Sprinkle the strawberries with sugar and leave overnight.

Add freshly squeezed orange juice and the orange-flavoured liqueur and leave to macerate for 1 hour.

Transfer to a serving dish. Whip the double cream and sweeten with 2 tablespoons vanilla sugar. Spread over berries and serve.

*Escoffier's Strawberries*

1 lb/500 g strawberries

¼ pt/150 ml (¾ c) freshly squeezed orange juice

5 tablespoons orange-flavoured liqueur

10 fl oz/300 ml double cream (1½ c)

2 tablespoons vanilla sugar

# BRANDIED FRUIT CUP

**8-10 servings**

This combination of dried and fresh fruits allows plenty of scope for variation according to season. It is a cross between a 'compote' and a fruit salad but will keep well for a few days, so is worth making up in quantity.

## To prepare the dried fruit

Place the dried apricots and mixed dried fruit in a saucepan with water to cover and simmer till tender—cool and cut up into pieces.

Add the rest of the fruit and combine in a large bowl; add the lemon juice and sugar and cognac to taste. Leave overnight for flavours to develop and blend together.

Serve slightly chilled with Almond Biscuits (see p.211).

*Brandied Fruit Cup*

5 oz/150 g dried apricots (1 c)

12 oz/350 g mixed dried fruit (2 c)

1 lb/500 g fresh cherries

1 grapefruit, segmented

4 oz/125 g preserved kum-quats

1 lb/500 g figs in syrup

3 bananas, sliced

Strawberries, raspberries or any other soft fruits in season

Juice of 1 lemon

Sugar to taste

Cognac—a few tablespoons

# RASPBERRY VINEGAR

Recipes for fruit vinegars are common in eighteenth-century cookery books. Mrs Dalgairns (*circa* 1829) uses a pint of vinegar to a quart of raspberries. It is left for three days, stirred daily, then strained. A pound of sugar is used to every pint of juice, then it is boiled for ten minutes, cooled and bottled with one glass of brandy added to every quart of vinegar.

It was used mostly as a refreshing drink diluted in cold water, though it was also used diluted with warm water for sore throats. In Yorkshire it is served with Yorkshire pudding as a sweet. It can give a lift to any vinaigrette or mayonnaise and a tablespoon can be used most effectively when finishing rich sauces for meat and game when a sweet-sour balance is required.

# USING WINE AS A SAUCE
## with soft fruits

The fruit is usually prepared just before serving, piled into a wine glass and the wine poured over when ready to eat. If left for some time the fruit tends to disintegrate and the flavours can lose their identity.

## Choosing the right wine

This is a matter of knowing your wine and not letting either fruit or wine dominate. Too much sugar in the fruit will obscure the flavour of the wine. There is a tradition in Bordeaux of pouring a fine old claret, which has begun to decline, over lightly crushed strawberries which gives the wine a momentary sparkle of life. A sweet Sauterne is good with raspberries.

## Marinated Strawberries and Raspberries

*Fruit marinade*

½ lb/250 g strawberries

½ lb/250 g raspberries

1 mango (optional)

4 tablespoons freshly squeezed orange juice or kirsch

Sugar to taste

*Sauce*

3 egg yolks

3 tablespoons sugar

1½ tablespoons kirsch

1 teaspoon lemon juice

1 teaspoon grated lemon rind

4 fl oz/125 ml whipped double cream (½ c)

# MARINATED STRAWBERRIES AND RASPBERRIES
## with Whipkull

**Serves 4**

Whipkull is a Shetland speciality which was originally eaten with thin, crisp, butter shortbread for Yule breakfast (see p.248). Eggs and sugar are beaten over heat till thick and creamy, then flavoured with rum. This version uses a little cream, which is not traditional.

## To marinade the fruit

Slice the strawberries and cut up the mango into small dice. Leave the raspberries whole. Put into an ovenproof dish and sprinkle with orange juice or kirsch and sugar. Cover and leave in a cool place for a few hours.

## To make the sauce

Beat the eggs and sugar together over hot water till they are thick and creamy, then beat in flavourings and finally fold in the cream. Pour over the marinated fruit and serve immediately.

# 3. FRUIT PURÉE AND CREAM

Pure fruit purée, mixed with whipped double cream, sounds simple enough but there are many variations. The degree of puréeing is a matter of taste but it is generally agreed that uniformity leads to boredom, and mashing the fruit, rather than reducing to a fine pulp in a food processor, provides a more interesting texture. Some of the fruit can even be left whole. Also, for the same reasons, the cream need not be thoroughly mixed in, but can create a marbled effect if it is only partially mixed through the fruit.

## WHIPPED FRUIT PUDDING

**4 servings**

To begin with, a thickened fruit syrup is made and then the crushed fruit and cream or yoghurt is mixed through. It is a good way of 'stretching' the fruit if in short supply, with no real loss of flavour. It is similar in method to a Russian 'Kissel'.

Maple syrup with strawberries gives this dish a special taste and fragrance. But don't just stick to these flavours—mix and match your favourite fruits and juices.

### To make the syrup

Heat the juice and then blend the potato flour or arrowroot with a little of the hot juice. Return to the pan and bring to the boil to thicken, stirring all the time. Pour into a bowl and whip with a wire whisk, or beater, till light and fluffy. Leave to cool.

Add lemon juice, berries, cream, maple syrup, cinnamon and nutmeg.

### Finishing the dish

Mash up the fruit roughly, leaving some berries whole, and fold in with the cream or equivalent. Chill. Serve with whole berries for garnish and/or chopped toasted nuts.

*Whipped Fruit Pudding*

¾ pt/450 ml freshly squeezed orange juice (2 c, scant)

Juice from ½ lemon

1 oz/50 g potato flour or arrowroot (1 tablespoon)

3 tablespoons maple syrup or 2 tablespoons honey

½ lb/250 g raspberries and strawberries

¼ pt/150 ml whipped double cream or natural yoghurt or soured cream or any mixture of all three (¾ c)

Pinch of cinnamon and nutmeg

## 4. FRUIT PURÉE WITH CREAM—ICED

Ice-cream making in Scotland has been dominated by Italians and their Scottish descendants for at least a century. Their 'real' ice-cream cafés are a welcome haven for weary shoppers and the cheerful, friendly Italian service an added bonus. Recipes are jealously guarded secrets and annual awards are given for the best ice-cream. Needless to say Italian ice-cream makers dominate the event.

The classic Scottish way of eating an ice-cream cone is with a topping of raspberry syrup. Of uncertain origins, this is known as a MacCallum, and one legend claims that is was made by a Glasgow 'Tally' for a customer, MacCallum, a supporter of Clyde Football Club, whose colours are red and white.

Ice-cream became a 'street food' for the ordinary people around the mid-nineteenth century, though it had been eaten by the wealthy classes for much longer. According to Henry Mayhew, writing in *London Labour and the London Poor* (1850), the initial reception was not all favourable. People who tried it complained that it gave them the 'shivers' and he forecast an uncertain future for the trade.

# A RICH ICE-CREAM
## suitable for moulding

*A Rich Ice Cream*

3 egg yolks

3 tablespoons icing sugar

2-3 teaspoons lemon juice

¼ pt/150 ml whipping cream, whipped (¾ c)

½ lb/250 g strawberries or raspberries or any other fresh fruit in season

This is the simplest way of making ice-cream at home in the absence of any special ice-cream-making equipment. Described by ice-cream makers as a 'parfait', such mixtures which have a high proportion of egg yolks and cream do not crystallise as they freeze and so it is not necessary to have an ice-cream churn. It is not even necessary to stir occasionally while they are freezing—all you need in the way of equipment is three clean bowls. The mixture can be set in a special mould and turned out for serving. To remove from the mould simply run briefly under some hot water to loosen, about half an hour before serving.

## Quantities, flavours

It is better not to make up in very large quantities since some of the delicate flavouring will be lost if kept frozen for any length of time. I would say about one month maximum. Some flavours are more robust than others. Bear in mind also that the frozen flavour will be less strong than unfrozen so flavour strongly rather than mildly.

## To prepare

Put the eggs and sugar over hot water and beat till thick and creamy. Press the fruit through a sieve to make the purée or purée in the liquidiser or food processor. With fruits like strawberries and raspberries you will also have to sieve after liquidising to remove the pips. Add the lemon juice. Mix the egg and sugar with the purée, folding in lightly and then fold in the cream. Taste for flavour and pour into a plastic container or mould and freeze.

## Serving

Never serve too cold or too hard. Ice-cream should be allowed to soften slightly for about 30 minutes at room temperature which will greatly improve the texture and also the flavour.

## ETTRICKSHAWS HOME-MADE ICE-CREAM

Mix 1 lb/500 g each of fruit pulp and sugar to every pint of whipped double cream. Add a 'generous measure of any complementary liqueur' and freeze. Serve with a homemade cinnamon biscuit.

From Peter Slaney, Ettrickshaws Country House Hotel in Selkirkshire.

## CLEAR SHARP-FLAVOURED WATER ICE
### (Sorbet)

Uncomplicated mixtures of fruit purée and sugar syrup give the kind of clean, penetrating flavours which were used in meals of many courses somewhere about the middle to 'refresh the palate'; Queen Victoria particularly liked a rum-flavoured one. For eating styles today, they are possibly better suited to the end of a meal, garnished with some of the fresh fruit they have been made from—though I have also seen on menus recently herb-flavoured ones such as mint and fennel served at the beginning of the meal.

### Making the syrup

Dissolve the sugar in the water, bring to the boil and simmer for about five minutes. Cool and add the orange and lemon juice.

### Preparing the fruit

Pass the fruit through a sieve or purée in the liquidiser or processor and then sieve.

### Making the water ice

Mix the purée and syrup together and pour into a plastic container with a lid. The shallower it is, the quicker it will freeze. Put into the deep-freeze and remove every half-hour or so to stir in the crystals which have formed, giving it a beat to prevent large crystals forming. When it is uniformly solid but not too hard, it can be beaten into one stiffly beaten egg white to give it more volume and a lighter texture. Beat the egg white in the bowl first, and then gradually add spoonfuls of the water ice. It must not be too hard or it will be difficult to mix in. Refreeze. Like all ices these water ices should not be kept for too long in the freezer since their flavour will begin to fade after a month or so.

*Clear Sharp-flavoured Water Ice*

8 oz/250 g granulated sugar (1¼ c)

½ pt/300 ml water (1¼ c)

Juice of 1 lemon

Juice of 1 orange

1 lb/500 g raspberries, strawberries or any other soft fruit

1 stiffly beaten egg white

149

*Peach Highland Cream*

**4 fresh peaches**

**¼ pt/150 ml water (¾ c)**

**2-3 tablespoons sugar**

**2-3 tablespoons whisky**

**4 tablespoons raspberry sorbet**

**3 egg yolks**

# PEACH HIGHLAND CREAM

**4 servings**

This is one of many dishes created by Chef Paul Rogerson while cooking in several British Transport Hotels in Scotland during the 1980s. Though born in Yorkshire, he had a fine sensitivity for Scottish raw materials, and the creative flair and ability to transmit his enthusiasm into the finished dish, compiling imaginative menus which he liked to call a 'modern taste of Scotland.'

## To prepare

Put the peaches briefly into boiling water to loosen the skins, peel. Put the water, sugar and whisky into a pan and boil up for 5-10 minutes. Poach the peaches very lightly in the syrup—they should be only slightly softened. Remove and leave to cool in the syrup. When cool remove peaches from the syrup, halve them and take out the stones. Fill the centres with raspberry sorbet and put back together again.

To make the sauce beat the egg yolks over hot water till thick. Reduce the syrup to about 3 tablespoons and add to the egg yolks. Beat till fairly thick and half fill four wine goblets. Place the peach on top of the sauce and decorate with some fresh raspberries. Serve slightly chilled with a thin, crisp shortbread.

# 5. FRUIT, CREAM AND CHEESE

Fresh fruit with a complementary cheese is one of the easiest ways of ending a meal. Soft fruits with a soft cheese are ideal.

# CRANACHAN
## (Cream-Crowdie)

Unique Scottish flavours—whisky, heather honey and oatmeal—combine with cream and soft fruits in this versatile tradition.

The best way to make and eat this is in the traditional way; mixing your own, to your own taste, as you sit round a table with family or friends. The toasted oatmeal doesn't lose its 'bite' when mixed and eaten immediately, though some do prefer it softened, as it is when the mixture is made up some time in advance.

The ritual eating was originally a celebration of 'harvest home' when brambles and blaeberries would most likely have been used. (For origins of crowdie see pp.225-6.)

Set on the table the following:

A bowl of **cream**—freshly whipped double cream (this was the traditional mixture but it may be varied according to taste, with soured cream, fromage frais, crème fraîche or natural yoghurt used if preferred).

A bowl of **pinhead (coarse) or medium oatmeal** which has been toasted slowly and gently in the oven. This drives off excess moisture, concentrates and greatly improves the flavour.

A bowl of **fresh soft fruits**—either a single fruit, or combination, but must be soft and fresh. Picking the fruit is traditionally done by children and they are sent out to collect a bowlful.

A jar of **heather honey** to sweeten, though sugar may also be used.

A bottle of **whisky**.

Give each person a bowl and spoon (in old Scots households the bowls would have been wooden and the spoons hand-carved horn). The ingredients are then passed round the table and each person creates their own mixture, lubricating it with generous tots of whisky.

# OTHER SCOTTISH CREAM SWEETS

## TRIFLE

I always think of trifle as something akin to the court jester. The foolish part of the meal, the light, passing triviality which comes at the end, adding the essential element of fun and enjoyment. Highly decorated trifles were the centrepiece of the table in the days when everything was laid out in advance. Hot and cold dishes, sweets and savoury dishes decorated upper-class tables and the diners sat round the table in sit-down buffet-style, with dishes being passed and removed throughout the meal in the days before a formal structure of courses became the norm.

A trifle is a difficult dish to define, since it lends itself to so much improvisation—you make of it what you fancy. Alistair Little, of Little's Restaurant in London, argues that a trifle can be presented with the components in separate piles on the same plate. A convenient method if you are running a restaurant and you must cook-to-order to avoid leftovers. But looking back through eighteenth and nineteenth-century recipes, it seems that while the contents vary enormously, the basic structure has remained fairly constant.

There is a first layer of sponge and/or biscuits. The sponge is some-

*That most wonderful object of domestic art called trifle...with its charming confusion of cream and cake and almonds and jam and jelly and wine and cinnamon and froth.*
Oliver W. Holmes
*Elsie Venner*, 1861

times stuck with flaked almonds or they are strewn on top of it. The biscuits always contain almonds (macaroons or ratafias) and the whole is always thoroughly soaked in some kind of wine or spirit. White wine is popular, also sherry and Madeira. Brandy and rum are the most common spirits.

On top of this there is always a layer of jam, most frequently raspberry but also marmalade on occasion.

The third layer is a rich, thick custard, thickened with lots of eggs: in earlier days they thought nothing of adding eight eggs to a pint of milk or cream. The thickness varies, but is usually between one and two inches and it is hardly ever flavoured, the bland richness acting as a foil for the highly flavoured bottom layer.

On top of the custard is the cream layer, which has several variations. Sometimes it is left plain, only sweetened and with a hint of lemon zest. Or the cream has beaten egg whites added. Mostly, though, it is described as a 'whipped syllabub' and the variations are endless. Syllabubs developed in the sixteenth century as a sweet drink made originally by milking the cow on top of some wine. The object was to produce a frothy head to a drink which was drunk from a special syllabub pot. The liquid was drunk from the spout first, then the froth eaten with a spoon. In the eighteenth century they were served in special syllabub glasses showing the two layers of cream and liquid.

Flavourings which I've come across include:

**White wine with lemon zest**
**Port with nutmeg**
**Brandy, sherry or Madeira, nutmeg and lemon**
**Nutmeg, beer, cider and currants (farmhouse syllabub)**
**Rosemary, nutmeg, lemon juice and zest, white wine and a red fruit juice or thin fruit purée**
**Nutmeg, strong beer and brandy**
**Nutmeg, lemon juice, rum and brandy**

Lemons and nutmeg keep appearing and they are particularly good in cream. The alcohol content is a matter of taste, but sherry and brandy are good combinations and the ones that I use most, though there is something to be said for a good white dessert wine which gives a more gentle result. This is better if there is a lot of flavouring in the bottom layer and you want to make a contrast.

You are instructed to make the dish 'high and handsome'. To 'garnish with a few sprigs of light flowers of fine colours...or a sprinkling of Harlequin comfits*. This last we think vulgar, but it is in frequent use,' says Meg Dods (1826).

*More commonly known as 'hundreds and thousands'.

# TO MAKE A TRIFLE

**8 servings**

## Layer 1, the base + layer 2, jam

Put cake in the bottom, crumble biscuits on top, scatter with flaked almonds and soak everything in the chosen alcohol (Whisky may also be used though I prefer not to use it in Trifle. The Scottish sweet liqueurs are good). Cover with a layer of raspberry jam. Leave for at least an hour.

## Layer 3, the custard

Put the cream in a pan and heat till almost boiling. Blend together the egg yolks, sugar and cornflour. Pour the hot cream over, stirring well. Strain and return to the pan. Cook very gently stirring all the time till it thickens. This can be done in a double boiler. Leave till almost cold; add a few drops of vanilla essence before pouring over the first layer.

## Layer 4, the cream or syllabub

Use Syllabub recipe on p.156, or ¾ pt/450 ml whipping cream (2 c) whipped stiffly and flavoured with some lemon zest.

Decorate with fresh flowers or crystallised violets and toasted almonds.

For a **CHILDREN'S TRIFLE** omit all the alcohol and use fruit juice instead. Use fancy sweets to decorate on top along with some well-washed flowers which they can eat, such as nasturtiums, rose petals, primroses, violets, mimosa, lilacs, cowslips; fruit or herb flowers such as borage are very good. To crystallise them for longer-keeping, pick the flowers on a dry day, remove all stems and green. Wash and dry thoroughly. Paint each flower with lightly beaten egg white, then hold with tweezers and dip in caster sugar till thoroughly coated. Place on baking sheet and dry off in a warm airy place. When dry place between sheets of greaseproof paper in an airtight tin.

*Trifle*

*Layers 1 and 2*

**8 oz/250 g left-over sponge cake**

**4 oz/150 g almond biscuits (see p.226)**

**1 tablespoon flaked almonds**

**10 fl oz/300 ml wine/brandy/ sherry/madeira/port (1¼ c)**

*Layer 3, custard*

**½ pt/300 ml single cream or milk (1¼ c)**

**3 large egg yolks**

**1 tablespoon caster sugar**

**1 teaspoon cornflour**

**Vanilla essence**

153

# CALEDONIAN CREAM

*Caledonian Cream*

4 oz/125 g cream cheese (½ c)

4 fl oz/125 ml double cream (½ c)

1 tablespoon thick bitter Chip Marmalade (see p.219)

2 tablespoons brandy (or rum)

2 teaspoons lemon juice

Sugar to taste

4 oranges

**4 servings**

Mrs Dalgairns (*circa* 1829) pours her Caledonian cream into a 'shape with holes with thin muslin in', she mixes **1 tablespoon orange marmalade** (minced) with **1 glass brandy**, **sugar** to taste and the **juice of 1 lemon** to **2 pints of cream**. This is not perhaps the best method, since some of the brandy and lemon flavour will inevitably be lost in draining, which I have omitted.

The following recipe is simple and quick. Using cream cheese with a bitter Seville marmalade gives a sharp flavour to the cream mixture which goes on top of sweet oranges. Fresh cream may be used instead of the cheese, and with a less bitter marmalade it will make a sweeter result.

## For the cream

Blend the cream cheese, cream, marmalade, brandy or rum, lemon juice and sugar all together in a liquidiser or processor till smooth.

## Finishing the dish

Fill four long-stemmed glasses firstly with the oranges which have been segmented free of pith, sprinkle with some brandy (about 1 teaspoon each—optional) then pile the cream on top. Serve garnished with a few strands of orange zest which have first been boiled in water for a few minutes to remove some of the bitterness. Serve slightly chilled.

# BISCUITS AND CREAM

*Biscuits and Cream*

A packet of biscuits

1 x 10 fl oz/300 ml carton of whipping or double cream

Jam

Vanilla essence

**4 servings**

Unbelievably simple to make—layers of biscuits and cream are stuck together in a log shape and the whole is then covered in cream. Then it is left for a few hours while the biscuits soften and the cream absorbs the flavours with delectable results. A dish which very young children can make, it's dedicated to mothers and the many hours they spend keeping children happy in the kitchen.

All it requires is a packet of biscuits (homemade ones if you happen to have them), whipping or double cream, some well-flavoured jam and a little vanilla essence.

## To make

Whip the cream stiffly and flavour with essence, spread the biscuits first with jam and then cream. Sandwich them together standing them on their ends so that a kind of log shape is formed. The cream should make it all stick together quite easily. Finish by spreading the cream on the top and sides of the log; decorate with some fresh fruit or grated chocolate and leave to soften for at least 2-3 hours.

Use a thin shortbread biscuit and blackcurrant jam, sometimes raspberry. Ginger snaps should be flavoured with a cream which has some crystallised ginger added.

## RHUBARB CUSTARD TART

**4 servings**

Rhubarb was very popular in eighteenth-century Scotland when there was a craze for growing rhubarb plantations. Considered a cure for many ills, it continues to be consumed with enthusiasm.

At one time it was common to pour custard through the hole in the centre of a fruit pie halfway through the cooking. The custard was known as a 'caudle'. This is the same idea, though there is no top to the pie. The custard is cooked till set and risen.

### To prepare

Line a 9-in (22 cm) flan with short pastry (see p.120) and fill with neat rows of tightly packed fruit about ½ in (1 cm) thick. This takes about 1 lb/500 g rhubarb. Bake at 400F/200C/Gas 6 till the fruit is almost soft.

Mix the eggs, cream and sugar to make the custard, pour over fruit and finish baking. When cool, sprinkle with icing sugar and serve warm or cold.

*Rhubarb Custard Tart*

1 lb/500 g rhubarb

12 oz/375 g short pastry

2 eggs

2 fl oz/50 ml double cream (¼ c)

Sugar to taste

## RHUBARB AND BANANAS

**4 servings**

Layers of cooked rhubarb and sliced bananas contrast with each other both in texture and flavour in this quick-and-easy sweet.

### To prepare

Cut up the rhubarb and place in a baking dish, cover with orange juice and zest and sprinkle over sugar. Bake till just soft. Leave to cool then arrange in a glass dish with layers of finely sliced bananas ending with a layer of rhubarb. Sprinkle with some freshly ground cinnamon and serve.

*Rhubarb and Bananas*

1 lb/500 g rhubarb

1 orange

2-3 tablespoons brown sugar

3 bananas

Pinch of cinnamon

## SYLLABUB
### A richly flavoured cream

**6-8 servings**

Excellent with a crisp, buttery shortbread but can also be served with fresh fruits or used in trifle.

*Syllabub*

7 oz/200 g caster sugar (1 c)

2 lemons, grated zest and juice

1 cinnamon stick

8 tablespoons dry sherry

8 tablespoons brandy

1 pt/600 ml double cream (2½ c)

### To prepare

Place the lemons, sugar and cinnamon in a pan, dissolve the sugar and simmer gently for a few minutes to concentrate flavours.

Add the sherry and brandy, warm through and decant into a jug.

Add the cream and whip. Serve warm with a rich, crisp shortbread.

## BUTTERSCOTCH SAUCE

A good 'store sauce'—one of its most useful functions is as part of a sundae.

*Butterscotch Sauce*

3 oz/75 g butter (¾ stick)

2 tablespoons syrup

5 oz/150 g moist brown sugar

2 fl oz/50 ml water (¼ c)

1 tablespoon plain flour

¼ pt/125 ml milk (¾ c)

### To prepare

Place the butter, syrup, sugar and water in a pan and stir till the sugar is dissolved, then boil for 3 minutes without stirring. Sieve flour and stir in. Gradually add milk and continue stirring till it thickens. Leave to cool, cover and store. It will keep in a cool place for at least 2-3 weeks.

# Some Other Ways with Scottish Soft Fruits

## BLACKCURRANT AND APPLE PUDDING
### New England Blueberry Slump

**4 servings**

A popular American dessert which is a stew of fruits topped with squares of very plain scone dough which absorbs the fruit flavours and juices—Louisa May Alcott named her house Apple Slump. Any variety of fruits in season can be used: a mixture of half blackcurrants and half apple is very good, so also are Tayberries. Quick and easy to make, it is a 'good fun' pudding for children to make.

## To prepare

Put the fruit, sugar and water into a large frying-pan and simmer very gently till heated through and just beginning to run with juice.

## To make the scone mix

Put the flour and baking powder into a bowl, rub in the butter and add enough milk to make a stiff paste. Roll out the mixture about ½ in thick and cut up into 1 in (2½ cm) squares.

Lay on top of the fruit, cover and simmer very gently for about 15 minutes. The scone will be well risen on top and soaked in fruit juices underneath. Serve hot with cream.

# A RICH STRAWBERRY TART

**6-8 servings**

Sandwiched between a crisp pastry base and a layer of fresh strawberries covered in a jammy glaze, is a remarkable layer of creamy filling which gives this flan its special character. The filling ingredients are for an 8-in flan, though more empty flan shells can be made at the same time and kept in a sealed tin for future use. Double the filling quantities for a 12-14-in flan which will serve approximately twelve portions.

Preheat the oven to 350F/180C/Gas 4.

## To make the pastry

To line 3 x 7-in, 2 x 8-in or 1 x 12-14-in flan tins.

Put the flour, butter, lard sugar and egg into a food processor and blend until it comes into a firm ball. Remove and knead for a few minutes. If it is too dry add a tablespoon of water. It should be firm and pliable. Chill for 30 minutes before use.

Grease flan tins and roll out pastry to fit. Line tins. Press in a sheet of foil to prevent the pastry rising and bake blind removing the foil after 20 minutes when the pastry has set.

Bake till an even golden brown. Leave to cool.

## To make the filling

Put the sugar and eggs into a bowl and beat with a whisk. Whisk in the flour and then gradually whisk in the boiling milk. Put into a pan over a moderate heat and cook until it has thickened. Stir in 1 tablespoon kirsch or cognac. Put a few pieces of softened butter on top and leave to cool. This can be stored in the fridge for about a week.

### *Blackcurrant and Apple Pudding*

1 lb/500 g blackcurrants and apples or other combinations

4 tablespoons sugar

2 tablespoons water

*Scone mix*

5 oz/150 g plain flour (1 c generous)

1½ teaspoons baking powder

1½ oz/40 g butter

Milk to mix

### *A Rich Strawberry Tart*

*Pastry*

9 oz/275 g extra-fine plain flour

4 oz/125 g butter

1 oz/50 g lard

2 tablespoons sugar

1 egg

*Filling*

2 oz/50 g granulated sugar

2 egg yolks

1 tablespoon plain flour

10 fl oz/300 ml boiling milk

2 tablespoons kirsch or cognac

8 oz/250 g large ripe hulled strawberries

5 fl oz/150 ml redcurrant jelly

## To assemble tart

Put a layer of the filling in the base and cover with the strawberries. Melt the jam in a pan and add the other tablespoon of kirsch or cognac. Pour over the strawberries.

# HAZELNUT MERINGUE CAKE
## with fresh raspberries and cream

### 4-6 servings

*Hazelnut Meringue Cake*

*For the meringue*

**8 oz/250 g hazelnuts (1½ c)**

**4 egg whites**

**8 oz/250 g caster sugar (1¼ c)**

**8 oz/250 g raspberries (2 c)**

*For the filling*

**10 fl oz/300 ml whipping cream, stiffly whipped**

The top should be crisp, the centre soft and moist, slightly chewy—the flavour heavy with hazelnuts. Two layers of chewy hazelnut meringue are sandwiched with a thick layer of whipped cream and an equally thick layer of raspberries. It should be made up a few hours before eating so that the raspberry juice seeps through into the bottom layer of meringue. The nuts can be either finely or coarsely ground, the latter giving a crunchier texture.

This is a good cook-ahead-and-stop-worrying cake since the meringues will keep for several weeks if they are tightly, but carefully, wrapped in foil and kept in an airtight tin.

Line 2 x 8-in (20 cm) sandwich tins.

Pre-heat the oven to 350F/180C/Gas 4.

### To prepare

Toast the hazelnuts in a cool oven for about 10 minutes then cool. Grind them till fairly fine. (This is a matter of taste.) Whisk the egg whites till well bulked up but not too stiff and then add the sugar a tablespoon at a time, beating well. Finally fold in the ground hazelnuts and pour into the prepared tins. Bake for 20 minutes till the meringue is set but not dried out. Remove from the tins and leave to cool.

Assembling the cake: spread the cream thickly on one half, cover with raspberries and place the other half on top. Dust thickly with icing sugar and leave for an hour at least before serving.

# LEMON PUDDING OR TART

### 6-8 servings

This is the forerunner of the Lemon Meringue Pie. Instead of separating the eggs and making a meringue top, whole eggs are added to the filling which is rich, sharp and creamy.

Pre-heat the oven to 350F/180C/Gas 4.
Use an 8-in (20 cm) flan tin.

## To make the pastry

Sift the flour onto a board, add sugar, rub in butter and then make a well in the centre. Drop in the egg yolk and put the tips of your fingers into it and start working in the flour gradually, keeping the mixture in one lump until all the flour is worked in. It should be smooth, firm but pliable. Or blend together in a processor. Roll out to fit tin.

## To make the filling

Put the butter into the oven for a few minutes to soften. Put the eggs and sugar into a bowl and beat for a few minutes; it is not necessary to beat in air so they should not be too frothy. Now beat in the softened butter gradually, then the juice and zest of the lemons.

Pour into the pastry and bake in a moderate oven for about 30 minutes or until the filling is set and lightly brown on top. Eat warm or cold with whipped cream.

### *Lemon Pudding*

*For the filling*

**5 eggs**

**6 oz/200 g caster sugar (1 c)**

**4 oz/100 g butter (1 stick)**

**3 lemons, zest and juice**

*For the pastry*

**4 oz/125 g flour (1 c)**

**2½ oz/65 g butter (⅓ cup)**

**1 tablespoon caster sugar**

**1 egg yolk**

# 7

# VEGETABLES, SOUPS & OTHER DISHES

## Potatoes

*...We were conducted...into a room where about twenty Scotch Drovers [i.e. cattle drivers] were regaling themselves with whisky and potatoes.*
   Robert Chambers,
   *Walks in Edinburgh*, 1825.

Suiting their needs for a starchy filler, the drovers' potatoes were a newcomer vegetable to Scotland, only fully established a few decades, when they sat down to them with their whisky in an Edinburgh tavern. Yet potatoes had arrived in Europe three centuries earlier, when conquering Spaniards brought back primitive varieties from South America.

'Papas' were one of the native staple crops amid the icy, windswept high peaks of the Andes where the ingenious Incas are thought to have built their formidable empire largely as a result of their discovery of how to 'freeze-dry' a potato. The freeze-dried version, which was known as a chuno, was stored in warehouses in times of plenty so that surplus supplies provided the Incas with the power to control and conquer others when food became scarce. Chunos are still to be found in the street markets of Peru and Bolivia. On first sight, they look like little grey pebbles, but they must be steeped in water for a few hours when they will soften. Then they are boiled and eaten, well flavoured with mountain herbs and other local flavourings.

   The first written reports of potatoes by Europeans date from 1537, when Cieze de Leon joined an expedition to what is now Colombia, while in the 1560s another Spaniard, Juan de Castellonos, described the potato as something like a truffle, about the size of an egg, round or elongated, and white, purple or yellow in colour—'floury roots of good flavour, a

160

delicacy to the Indians and a dainty dish even for the Spaniards'.

At first they were considered a novelty in Europe, but during the Napoleonic wars the authorities, like the Incas in Peru, recognised their potential as a valuable food reserve in difficult times, and potatoes began to take on the role of a major staple food.

There was a gradual, if reluctant, acceptance of the potato in Scotland as their cultivation was encouraged. By the late eighteenth century they had become more accepted since they were a welcome addition to scant food supplies in areas where there was an impoverished smallholding peasantry, poor communications and lack of monetary resources. Their ability to flourish in difficult conditions was an important factor in their development as a staple crop in both Scotland and Ireland. They arrived at a crucial time in the history of both countries as a vital saviour from a widespread and increasing deterioration, cultural, social and economic, in the life of the people.

J. Walker describes the early difficulties in his *Economic History of the Hebrides and Highlands* (1808)—'Typical of the suspicion with which new methods were viewed was the attitude to the introduction of potatoes: in 1743 the Chief Clanranald brought a small quantity for the first time to South Uist, but the farmers suffered imprisonment before they would submit to planting them. When autumn came they brought the obnoxious roots to the Chief's door, protesting that he might force them to plant them, but not to eat them. Hunger was, however, a more effectual argument and within twenty years many Highlanders were subsisting on potatoes for nine months of the year.'

While in Ireland there was more or less a universal dependence on potatoes, regional differences of climate and custom in Scotland meant that some parts depended on the potato more than others. In the Highlands and Islands, coinciding with the period of the Clearances, it became an important staple item of diet. Its advantage was that it grew underground and was therefore less susceptible to the vagaries of weather than oats and barley. Also it produced more food per acre and combined well—not just with whisky—but also with other staples such as milk and fish. Elizabeth Edmondston writing in *Sketches and Tales of The Shetland Isles* (1856) says that—'Fish with oat bread or potatoes…without any accompaniment at all, forms the three daily meals of the Shetland cottager'. Though Lowlanders also grew potatoes for human consumption they had other alternatives and also used potatoes for feeding horses, cows, poultry and pigs.

But despite these variations, the Scots (and the Irish) had a very high appreciation of the value of potatoes as 'meat' with farm carts trundling through the city streets selling 'mealie tatties'. The dry, floury, boiled potatoes had become the favourite in both Ireland and Scotland.

Distinguished from the varieties preferred in England, which were a wetter, more waxy-textured potato, the Scottish and Irish potato had a very high dry-matter content giving it a low water content and more concentrated flavour. When tragedy struck in Ireland in 1845/46 with the potato crop ruined with blight, breeders set about developing new varieties which would be blight-free, sourcing new potato cultivars from South America.

A Scottish breeder of this period, William Paterson of Dundee, began by gathering stocks from abroad which were not affected with the virus. He raised several distinct varieties, including Victoria (1863), which was an important variety of the period.

In 1901, a Lamlash shopkeeper on the Isle of Arran, Donald McKelvie, was given some potatoes from a friend and in a few plots on the island he began to breed potatoes, becoming one of the best known breeders of his day. In 1925 he was awarded an MBE for his services to potato breeding. McKelvie's contribution to the development of potato variety was particularly important, since his varieties have been used for future development. Arran Victory is still popular with specialist breeders, and one of the most widely grown modern varieties, Maris Piper, was bred from McKelvie's Arran Cairn.

In *A Book of Arran Verse* (1930) he is celebrated:

> Donald o' tattie fame
> —Health to McKelvie!
> Long shall we praise his name
> Whilst Arranmen delve ye.
> 'Arran Chief', 'Arran Rose',
> 'Comrade' and 'Ally',
> Yea where the 'Consul' grows—
> Health to McKelvie!

## THE DEVELOPMENT OF TRADITIONAL POTATO VARIETIES

*Old traditional varieties such as Arran Pilot, Craig's Royal and Epicure have given way to Pentland Javelin, Estima, Wilja, Maris Peer and Maris Bard. Similarly, traditonal maincrop varieties such as Majestic, King Edward and Redskin have been largely displaced by Desiree, Maris Piper, the Pentland varieties (particularly Pentland Crown) and Record, although King Edward has retained a place of some importance.*

N.A. Young, *The European Potato Industry*, 1981.

These changes in potato varieties were largely to do with improving yields and reducing disease. In the process this often produced a potato with less dry matter which usually meant less flavour. For the first half of the twentieth century, the major flavourful, floury potatoes were Golden Wonder, Kerr's Pink, Majestic and King Edward, which accounted for 75 per cent of the potato acreage in Scotland. By the end of the century, however, they were down to 5-10 per cent. Now they are described as Scottish Quality Varieties, joining a niche sector along with 'early', 'salad' and 'baking' potatoes.

Campaigning for over thirty years for the preservation of some of the quality in the old varieties, the late Donald MacLean, Chairman of the National Vegetable Society, wrote in the *Scots Magazine* in October 1978: 'This autumn I will be harvesting small amounts of over 200 varieties and disposing of them all over the UK to appreciative gourmets and enthusiasts, thus in small measure, keeping alive my kind of dodos and dinosaurs.'

He felt that there should be a wider choice of potato at the point of sale, considering the rich history of potato growing in Scotland. He also campaigned for better labelling so that varieties would be clearly labelled and individual quality judged more easily. There were many old varieties which he felt were worth keeping and it is thanks to him, and others, that the revival of interest in old potato varieties has developed.

The potatoes which MacLean thought worth preserving included the dry and mealy **DUKE OF YORK**, a low-yielding potato which was first raised in Aberdeenshire by W. Sim in 1891. But due largely to low yields, compared with its rivals, it fought a losing battle and was for years only grown by specialist allotment holders or people like MacLean. Now it is being revived as a commercial crop with the 'specialist' potato tag. It is a yellow-fleshed potato with an outstanding flavour which is at its best when young. As maturity is reached the flavour is less intense and it becomes difficult to boil without breaking down into soup. When mature, it is best baked.

**KING EDWARD** is a floury, maincrop potato which was the UK's most popular potato for the first half of the century. It was raised in 1902 by an unknown gardener in Northumberland and first named 'Fellside Hero' It has a pale-yellow flesh and aromatic flavour. It is at its best roasted or baked. It was abandoned by many growers because it is not an easy potato to grow, requiring good irrigation and a strong soil with plenty of organic matter. It does not do well on heavy, acidic or sandy soils.

In 1906 John Brown near Arbroath raised the **GOLDEN WONDER**, a late maincrop potato with a good flavour and an unusually thick, brown, rough skin. It has a very high dry matter content which has made it the premium floury/mealy tattie in Scotland and Ireland.

Vying for premier position in the floury market with Golden Wonder is **KERR'S PINK,** which was raised by J. Henry of Banff and first named Henry's Seedling when it won a Gold Medal in 1916. Henry sold all the seed to a Mr Kerr who renamed it and launched it on the market in 1917. For the next fifty years it remained among the top ten varieties in the UK. Easier to grow than King Edward and a bigger cropper than Golden Wonder, it continues to dominate the acreage of floury potatoes in Ireland. Though traditionally a maincrop potato, many Irish growers harvest the crop early and sell it as an early potato.

The Scottish Plant Breeding Institute at Pentlandfield near Edinburgh produced the floury **PENTLAND** varieties: Pentland Crown (1958); Pentland Dell (1960); Pentland Squire (1970).

**Floury and/or Dry**—Arran Consul; Arran Victory; Catriona; Di Vernon; Duke of York; Dunbar Rover; Dunbar Standard; Edzell Blue; Epicure; Golden Wonder; Kerr's Pink; King Edward; Maris Piper; Record; Red Craigs Royal.

**Waxy and/or Moist**—Arran Comet; Arran Pilot; Bintje; Colomo; Craigs Alliance; Desirée; Dr McIntosh; Estima; Home Guard; Irish Peace; Jersey Royal; Majestic; Maris Bard; Maris Peer; Pentland Crown; Pentland Hawk; Pentland Javelin; Royal Kidney; Foremost; Ulster Sceptre; Vanessa; Wilja.

# EARLIES

*In a parking space at the side of the A77 a few miles north of Girvan there is a white van with a sign: AYRSHIRE EPICURES. A row of cars are parked beside it and the queue at the van is for a bag of the season's first earlies lifted that day.*

*The Herald Magazine,* June 1997.

While there are many other varieties of early potato grown along this fertile coastal strip, it is the Epicure which is rated the best by the Ayrshire people. Simply boiled and eaten with butter, they are regarded 'a dinner' and local butchers report a loss of sales for the few weeks of the earlies when everyone eats potatoes instead of meat. Their quality is elusive since they lose their bloom very quickly and should, literally, be eaten within hours of lifting. The season on the West Coast always starts a few weeks earlier than the East.

### Buying/storing

Earlies are available from the end of May through June while Second

Earlies start in July and go through into the end of August. The Maincrop starts lifting in September. All sacks of potatoes sold to the market must bear the variety name and the retailer must display the name of the variety.

Keep in a cool, dark place: warmth makes them sprout, damp encourages storage diseases, and light turns them an unhealthy green. Polythene bags will cause problems since the potatoes can't breathe properly and condensation accumulates in the bag.

## MEALY TATTIES

Sold from farm carts, these had been simply boiled in salted water. Use a floury potato (see p.164) and dry off well after cooking. First boil the potatoes slowly in their skins. This takes longer for floury potatoes and care should be taken that they do not burst or they will 'easily go into the bree'. Drain well. For really well-dried Scottish potatoes take the pot to an open door and, holding the handle of the pot in one hand and the lid in the other, lift one side of the lid up and down quickly, sending out billows of steam; this way the heat is kept in and the moisture driven out. It should only take a few minutes. Put a folded cloth on top of the potatoes and cover with the lid to keep warm. In the days of the kitchen range these dried out potatoes would sit in the corner quietly continuing to steam with the cloth absorbing the moisture till they were required.

## STOVIES

Perhaps this old Scottish method of cooking potatoes was influenced by early and close ties with France, certainly it makes the same use of the thinly sliced potatoes, cooked slowly, as in the French *Gratin Dauphinois* (see p.241).

There is some confusion about the origin of the word 'stovie' and it has been claimed by F. Marian McNeill (*The Scots Kitchen*, 1929) that it comes from the French verb '*étuvé*' (meaning stewed). But it seems that 'to stove' is a genuine Scottish and North of England verb which comes from the use of the word 'stove' to define 'a closed box or vessel of earthenware, porcelain, or (now more usually) of metal, portable or fixed to contain burning fuel' (*OED*). It was originally applied to the idea of 'sweating'. Gervase Markham in 1631 talks about letting a bird 'stove and sweate [*sic*] till evening' while later recipes show that it becomes more associated with stewing, but remaining almost a cross between sweating and stewing—as in stovies.

165

## *Stovies*

2 oz/50 g fat

3 medium onions, finely
   sliced

4 large floury potatoes

Water, stock or gravy

Leftover meat

Salt

Nutmeg or allspice or black
   pepper

2-3 tablespoons chopped
   parsley, chives or coriander

## To make Stovies

### 4-6 servings

Melt fat in a heavy pan with a tight-fitting lid. The type of fat depends on taste and availability but good dripping from meat or bacon gives a better flavour, as does butter. Oil, though not traditional, may also be used.

Slice onions, and when the fat is hot, add to the pan. Reduce the heat and cook gently while preparing the potatoes. Peel and slice. They may be unevenly sliced, so that the thin ones reduce to a mush while the thick ones stay whole when cooked. Add to the pan and stir well coating all sides with fat.

Place a lid on the pan and leave for about 10 minutes, stirring when necessary to prevent sticking. The heat must be at its lowest possible. Add a little water, stock or gravy from a roast. If you like stovies fairly dry, add only about 2-3 tablespoons, while if you like them wet add more. Cover again with the lid and cook till potatoes are soft, stirring occasionally.

Add cooked meat or fish at this point and only just heat through. Taste for seasoning and add spices if you wish. Nutmeg was a favourite with potatoes but allspice was also used. A grinding of black pepper is certainly a good idea. Some people like stovies with brown bits through them and for this you must reduce much of the cooking liquid and fry the potatoes slightly, mixing in the browned bits in the style of American 'Hash Browns'. Before serving, sprinkle with a handful of finely chopped parsley, chives or coriander.

## *Stovies in the Oven with Bacon*

4 large floury potatoes, peeled
   and finely sliced

4 medium onions, finely
   chopped

8 oz/250 g smoked streaky
   bacon, finely diced

2 tablespoons chopped parsley

2 oz/50 g plain flour

1 pt/300 ml milk

2 oz/50 g butter, melted

Salt, pepper and nutmeg

## STOVIES IN THE OVEN WITH BACON

### 4-6 servings

This is a stovies variation which makes a casserole dish requiring no attention while cooking. Milk is used instead of water or stock but the end result is the same thick, filling, good-flavoured potato mixture. Some cream can be added for a richer dish.

Pre-heat the oven to 400F/200C/Gas 6

### To cook

Fill the dish with layers of potatoes, onions, bacon and chopped parsley, sprinkling each layer with a little flour. Finish with a layer of potatoes. Pour in the milk and then pour the butter over the top layer of potatoes so that they are all covered with butter. Cover and bake for about an hour. Remove the lid and continue the cooking till the top potatoes are well-browned. This should take about 20-30 minutes.

# CHAPPIT TATTIES

Irish Champ: *Two stones or more of potatoes were peeled and boiled for the dinner. Then the man of the house was summoned when all was ready, and while he pounded this enormous potful of potatoes with a sturdy wooden beetle (potato masher) his wife added the potful of milk and nettles, or scallions, or chives or parsley, and he beetled till it was smooth as butter and not a lump anywhere. Everyone got a large bowlful, made a hole in the centre, and into this put a large lump of butter. Then the champ was eaten from the outside with a spoon or fork, dipping it into the melting butter in the centre. All was washed down with new milk or freshly churned buttermilk.*

Florence Irwin in *The Cookin' Woman* (1949).

With much Celtic interchange between the two countries, it's not surprising that the Scots also make this dish so much loved in Ireland.

**4 servings**

There are three methods—either the greens are cooked in milk till soft and then added to the potatoes or they are added to the heated milk just before serving rather than cooked or they are simply added to the potatoes raw.

Whatever method is preferred, the mixture must be thoroughly beaten over heat till smooth. Serve very hot in heated plates with butter 'Irish style', if you like.

*Chappit Tatties*

**2 lb/1 kg floury potatoes— cooked, steamed dry, peeled and mashed**

**½ pt/300 ml hot milk (1¼ c)**

**4 oz/125 g butter (1 stick)**

**Pepper and salt**

*With either*

**1 cup, chopped or minced nettle tops or**

**½ cup chopped chives or**

**6 finely chopped spring onions or**

**2 large tablespoons chopped parsley or**

**1 cup fresh peas**

# OATMEALED POTATOES

**4-6 servings**

This is best with new potatoes. Boil or steam **2 lb/1 kg floury potatoes** and while they are cooking toast **2 tablespoons pinhead oatmeal** slowly in the oven. Drain the potatoes, toss in **1 tablespoon butter** and then coat with the toasted oatmeal. Sprinkle with chopped parsley, chives or chervil and serve.

# DRIPPING POTATOES

*Wash the potatoes and peel them very thin; boil them 10 minutes with a little salt, and then put them in a Yorkshire-pudding tin under the joint which is roasting before an open fire, to catch the gravy; when enough moistened, put them into the oven, still in the tin, turn the potatoes often, and baste them with a little dripping, till crisp and brown. Serve very hot, but not round the joint, or they will become sodden. Potatoes done in this way are mealy inside and crisp on the outside.*

*The Cookery Book of Lady Clark of Tillypronie* 1909.

These are the best roast potatoes, absorbing as they do all the dripping flavour from the meat. In the days when all roasts were cooked on a spit, cooking things under the roasting joint was a well-developed art, to which Yorkshire pudding owes its existence.

## FRIED POTATO CAKE

*Fried Potato Cake*

4 large cooked potatoes, peeled

Salt and pepper

4 oz/125 g smoked streaky bacon, finely diced

2 tablespoons oil

5 oz/150 g Dunlop or Scottish cheddar, grated

**4 servings**

A good dish for leftover potatoes.

Grate the potatoes into a bowl, season. Put the bacon into a hot frying pan and cook till lightly crisp. Add a tablespoon of oil and pour into the potatoes. Mix well. Put another tablespoon of oil into the hot pan and add the mixture. Spread flat and cook for about 10 minutes when it should be lightly browned underneath. Put a plate on top. Invert and put another tablespoon of oil into the pan. Return the potato cake, cover the top with cheese and put on a lid. Cook for about 5 minutes until the cheese has melted.

## TATTIE SCONES

*Tattie Scones*

½ lb/250 kg mashed, floury maincrop potatoes

1 oz/50 g melted butter (¼ stick)

2 oz/50 g flour (½ c)

Salt

These thin, triangular, unleavened scones have a dark-brown, mottled surface and should be so thin that they 'wiggle' when you hold one corner and give them a shake. They are traditionally eaten for high tea, spread with jam or butter and rolled up into a stick-of-rock shape. May also be fried with bacon for breakfast.

**To cook**

Add the butter and salt to the potatoes and work in as much flour as the mixture will take without becoming dry.

Roll out very thinly, cut into rounds and quarters—prick with a fork and cook on a hot girdle about 3 minutes on each side. Wrap in a towel till required.

## POTATO SOUP

**4-6 servings**

A hearty soup which makes a main meal dish with crusty bread and cheese. Potatoes combine well with all the onion family and are also good with many herbs. Coriander is good in this soup.

## To cook

Chop the vegetables into roughly even sized pieces. Begin by melting the butter and sautéing the onion till yellow and soft. Then add the other vegetables and continue sautéing with the lid on over a low heat for 5-10 minutes.

Add the cups of water or stock and season with salt and pepper and bay leaf. Cook till vegetables are tender.

## Serving

When ready to serve add the milk.

Garnish with fresh coriander, finely chopped. Season and serve.

## POTATOES AND HARD BOILED EGGS

**4-6 servings**

Lady Grisell Baillie notes in her *Household Book* (1692-1733) that 60 dozen eggs were used in one month. They were eaten frequently for supper with peas, with spinach and with mushrooms but most often with potatoes and sometimes ham.

The idea of finishing the dish with a sharp butter sauce comes from Richard Olney's *Simple French Cooking* (1974).

## To cook

Put a layer of potatoes in an earthenware gratin dish. Quarter the eggs and put on top.

Cook shallots in butter till soft and yellow, and add parsley, salt and pepper and wine vinegar. Pour the contents evenly over the potatoes and eggs and serve hot.

# Leeks

Leeks are thought to have been introduced to Britain by the Romans. Scots have made good use of them in soups and stews and particularly in the classic combination with chicken: Cock-a-Leekie. A variety of the Common Long Winter Leek, raised on the fertile soils of East Lothian, had a longer, thicker stem and broader leaves. It was described as the Musselburgh Leek (*Poireau de Musselbourgh*) by William Robinson in

*Potato Soup*

1 medium onion or leek, finely chopped

3 stalks celery, finely chopped

3 medium-sized floury potatoes, peeled and diced

2 oz/50 g butter (¼ stick) or 2 tablespoons oil

Salt and pepper

3 cups water or stock

Bay leaf

1 cup milk

2 tablespoons fresh coriander

*Potatoes and Hard Boiled Eggs*

2 lb/1 kg cooked new potatoes

4 hard-boiled eggs

*For the sauce*

2 tablespoons finely chopped shallots

4 oz/125 g butter

Handful of chopped parsley

Salt and pepper

2-3 tablespoons wine vinegar

*The Vegetable Garden* (1885) when he says that the 'fine qualities of this vegetable are much better known to the Welsh, Scotch and French than to the English or Irish'.

The regions of Fife and Lothian with their fertile soils continue to be important for leek growing. Small to medium sized leeks have the sweetest flavour. The hardy, winter-growing Musselburgh Leek is no longer grown commercially though it continues to be grown in domestic gardens.

Their use as a vegetable in their own right, rather than a flavouring for soups, has been encouraged by the fact that they are no longer only a winter vegetable but are grown year-round. Scots have always liked a longer green leaf 'green flag' and shorter 'blanch', since this gives a better colour and flavour to soups. A supply of young tender leeks means they can be used as a salad vegetable with vinaigrette.

## BUYING

Very large leeks have a coarser flavour than young thin ones. They can be useful in richly flavoured soups and stews but for serving on their own as a vegetable or for salads use the young tender ones. Both winter and summer leeks should be lifted before they 'shoot', i.e. start forming the flower head making a hard woody stalk in the centre which should be removed before use.

## PREPARING

Most of the grit is usually in the top half of the leeks, so if you want to use the bottom white half whole then it is usually quite safe to cut off just below the green and wash only the outer leaves. Trim off root and any wilted green leaves. All of the green ought to be useable unless the leeks are mature, in which case the tops will be too coarse and should be removed. If using the whole leek for soups, slit from the base to the tips, then make another slit at right angles which then opens up the leeks for easy washing and chopping. Leave to soak for a few minutes, if they are very earthy, to loosen the soil.

## COCK-A-LEEKIE

**8-10 servings**

Essential elements of this classic Scottish soup are chicken, leeks and a good beef stock. Prunes add interest to the flavour and colour contrast of the finished soup, but their addition or omission continues to arouse heated debate. Meg Dods infers that the prunes were only added when the leeks were old and bitter. But since people are so divided on the subject my solution is to cook them separately in some of the stock then stone them and serve them in a separate dish with the soup, thus keeping everybody happy. Raisins were also used in the past and prune-haters may accept these more readily.

Many of the early recipes talk about serving the whole chicken in the soup tureen when, presumably, it must then have been jointed at table since there are references to whole joints being served in the broth. (In Peru all soup served today still comes in this style, with an island of large chunks of vegetables and meat in the centre of the plate.) The chicken would have been removed to an ashet and carved as the soup was ladled into plates. Grisell Baillie describes her Cock-a-Leekie as 'Chicken soup with chickens in it' which nicely describes the Scots' liking for soup/ stews or 'mouthful' soups, as Meg Dods calls them, 'with plenty in them'.

The system was to sup the broth first then eat the joint with a knife and fork. Scottish soup plates are large and wide for this purpose. Some other more refined recipes use only slices from the breast in serving.

### To make the stock

Put the bones/beef in a pan with the cold water and herbs and bring to the boil, skim, turn down the heat, cover and simmer for about 1 hour. Now add the chicken and simmer gently till the chicken is just tender. This will depend on the age of the bird. Strain and leave to cool. Remove any excess fat. Cut up the chicken into small or large pieces for returning to the broth when ready.

### Finishing the broth

Melt the fat in a large pan and add the onions. Cook till soft and yellow. Meanwhile clean the leeks and chop finely. Add to the onions, stir well, cover and leave to sweat for about five minutes stirring occasionally. The leeks should be really soft now. Add the strained stock and the chicken meat and bring to the boil. Simmer for a few minutes to heat everything through. Taste for seasoning, add prunes and parsley and serve.

## Cock-a-leekie

6 pts/3 L water

2 lb/1 kg knuckle of veal, hough (shin) bone or piece of boiling beef

1 boiling fowl or roast chicken carcass

Bundle of fresh herbs

2 lb/1 kg leeks

2 medium onions, finely chopped

Salt and pepper

4 oz/125 g cooked, stoned prunes

2 tablespoons chopped parsley

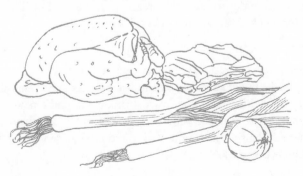

171

# SAUTEÉD CHICKEN AND LEEKS
## with Skirlie

*Sauteed Chicken and Leeks*

**1 x 3 lb/1½ kg chicken**

**3 oz/75 g butter (¾ stick) or 4 fl oz oil**

**Salt, freshly ground black pepper**

**¼ pt/150 m water, stock or dry white wine (¾ c)**

**3 leeks + 1 oz/50 g butter (¼ stick)**

**Handful of chopped parsley**

**4 servings**

The chicken and leeks combination seems to me worth developing and this simple method of cooking preserves the natural flavour of both. Skirlie (see p.15) is a good accompaniment to all birds.

Chicken joints, ready prepared, may be used for this dish or you can joint a whole chicken yourself. This has the advantage of giving you the backbone and the giblets for stock as well as the added satisfaction of making your own neat joints. There are various ways of jointing a chicken for different purposes. It can be cut off the bone into quarters (2 legs, 2 single breasts), into five pieces (2 legs, 2 wings, 1 breast), or into 7 pieces if it is large enough (divide the legs into two giving 4 legs, the 2 wings, 1 breast). The following method is for the larger chicken giving 7 pieces.

## To joint a chicken

Begin by cutting off the leg at the ball and socket joint. First locate the joint with your fingers and then cut through the connecting skin and flesh. Bend the leg back away from the body until the ball is visible and cut round the sinew to remove the ball from the socket, then cut through the rest of the flesh. Repeat on the other leg. Separate thighs from drumsticks at the joint.

Next remove the wings—with the chicken on its side hold onto the wing, pull back and find the ball and socket joint with your knife. Cut through to loosen socket joint only. Cut along through about half of the breast so that this part of the white meat is still attached to the wing. Then holding the chicken firmly, pull the wing piece out. Repeat with the other side.

To separate the breasts, sit the chicken on end with the neck on the board and, holding on to the back, cut through the entire length of the bird with a heavy, sharp knife; this means cutting through the ribs and straight down to the wing joint. Bend the back and then cut through the bones at the shoulder to sever the breast from the carcass. The back may be used for stock. You will now have 7 joints.

## Cooking the chicken

Melt the butter/oil in a large, heavy pan which has a tight-fitting lid. When hot, add the chicken pieces and brown over a medium heat, turning as they brown. Lower the heat, sprinkle the chicken with salt and pepper, cover the pan and simmer gently for 5-8 minutes. Turn the pieces and add half of the liquid. Cover and cook for another 10 minutes till the chicken is cooked.

## Finishing the dish

Remove the chicken pieces to the serving dish and keep warm. Add the rest of the liquid to the pan and turn up the heat. Stir the juices with a wooden spoon, scraping the browned bits from the bottom of the pan. Boil until reduced by half and a good consistency. Taste for seasoning. Pour over the chicken; sprinkle with parsley.

## Cooking the leeks

Melt butter in a pan and add the leeks, toss over a gentle heat till they are soft—it will only take a few minutes. Season and serve with Skirlie (see p.32).

# LEEK SALAD

**4 servings**

A dish for small, slender young leeks which have a delicate flavour. They may also be added to other raw salads with great effect. Allow about two leeks per person depending on size.

## To prepare

Put the dressing ingredients into a screw-top jar and shake well. Taste for seasoning. Clean leeks in the usual way and then chop into 1 in slices. Put in salad bowl and toss in the dressing. Good with cooked ham, spiced beef, mutton, ham or pickled tongue.

# LEEK AND BACON PIE

**4-6 servings**

A one-meal-in-a-dish pie in which any selection of cooked vegetables are arranged in a pie dish with a bacon and leek sauce. The top is finished with crisp crumbs and cheese. It could also be made in a shallow gratin dish.

## To make the sauce

Melt half the butter in a pan and add the bacon. Cook for a few minutes and then add the rest of the butter. Stir in the flour, cook for a few minutes, and then add chicken or vegetable stock. Simmer till thickened, then add finely chopped leeks.

## To assemble the dish

Peel and mash the sweet potato, spread in the base of the gratin dish,

*Leek Salad*

4-5 tablespoons oil

1 tablespoon vinegar/lemon juice

Freshly ground sea salt and black pepper

Pinch of sugar

Handful of chopped parsley

8 young leeks

*Leek and Bacon Pie*

*Sauce*

2 oz/50 g butter (½ stick)

½ lb/250 g chopped bacon

2 oz/50 g flour (½ c)

1 pt/500 ml chicken/vegetable stock (2½ c)

2 finely chopped leeks

*To assemble the dish*

3 medium potatoes—cooked

1 large sweet potato—cooked

4-5 medium carrots—cooked

173

cover with a layer of carrots and then sliced potatoes. Pour over leek and bacon mixture. Cover with a mixture of grated cheese and breadcrumbs and grill till crisp and brown on top, or brown in the oven.

## ROASTED LEEKS

*Roasted Leeks*

8 young leeks

2-3 tablespoons olive oil

Sea salt

4 servings

Preheat the oven to 500F/250C/Gas 9.

Remove any wilted outer leaves and the root end. Slit open to just below the green stalk and wash well. Cut into two inch pieces. Oil a large gratin dish and make a single layer of leeks. Cover with remaining oil and sprinkle with salt. Roast for about 10 minutes. Remove and turn. Roast for another 10 minutes when they should be soft and lightly browned. Serve hot with cheese and bread.

## LEEKS SERVED COLD WITH VINAIGRETTE AND HARD-BOILED EGGS

Put **1 tablespoon of balsamic vinegar** in a bowl and add about **4-5 tablespoons extra virgin olive oil**. Season with **Dijon mustard, salt** and **freshly ground black pepper**. Add **2 tablespoons chopped parsley**. Pour over the roasted leeks while still warm. Leave to marinate overnight.

To serve: chop **two hard-boiled eggs** finely and sprinkle on top. Finish with a tablespoon of **finely chopped parsley**.

# Carrots

Though carrots were first cultivated in the eastern Mediterranean, the Dutch are credited with developing the bright orange carrot in the seventeenth century. Modern breeding has concentrated on reducing the proportion of the root which forms the tougher core; also on developing more sweetness and on making the shape more uniform and the crop heavier.

Their principal use in Scotland has been in broths and stews, though their sweetness was much appreciated by the nineteenth-century cooks who made delicious soufflé-type puddings with them. Their sweet, moist qualities also made them useful additions to a Clootie Dumpling, while

Americans have celebrated them for the same reasons by popularising the Carrot Cake.

# BUYING

Young spring carrots are sold in bunches, usually with foliage attached. They should be about the thickness of a man's thumb. Maincrop varieties are sold trimmed and loose and should be tender with no woody core. Unless the carrots are organically grown, Government advice is to remove the tops and tails and peel off the skins, since higher than recommended levels of pesticides have been found in these parts of some commercially grown carrots.

# CARROT OR TURNIP SOUP

**6-8 servings**

The Scots have a reputation as skilled soup makers. It is a tradition not confined to traditional classic varieties but a constantly developing feature. This is from a collection of ideas for soups by Mollie Katzen, who cooked in the Mosewood Restaurant in Ithaca, New York. All her soups have an adventurous spirit to them, as she constantly refines and improves them.

## Cooking the vegetables

Put the vegetables in a pan with the water or stock and salt, bring to the boil, cover and simmer for 12-15 minutes. Leave to cool to room temperature.

## Cooking the onions and nuts

Sauté the onions, garlic and nuts in butter with a little salt till the onions are soft and yellow.

## Finishing the soup

Purée everything together in a blender till smooth. Return the purée to a pan and whisk in ONE of the following:
  **1 cup milk**
  **1 cup yoghurt or buttermilk plus a little honey**
  **1 cup double cream**
  **1 cup sour cream**
  Heat very slowly.
  Seasoning combinations to choose from:

**1.** 2 pinches nutmeg; ½ teaspoon dried mint; dash of cinnamon (this is good with carrots—the Turks and Persians combine carrots with rice in

*Carrot or Turnip Soup*

**2 lb/1 kg carrots or turnips (swedes)**

**1½ pt/850 ml water or stock (3¾ c)**

**1½ teaspoons salt**

**2 medium onions, finely chopped**

**1-2 small cloves garlic, crushed**

**2 oz/50 g whole cashews or almonds (½ cup)**

**3-4 tablespoons butter or oil**

175

a sweet cinnamon-flavoured pilau which they eat with lamb).

2. ½–1 teaspoon each—thyme, marjoram, basil.

3. 1 teaspoon fresh-grated ginger root, sautéed in butter plus a dash of sherry added just before serving (this is best with the turnip version. Bashed Neeps in Scotland are traditionally flavoured with ginger).

Garnish with grated apple or toasted nuts or yoghurt or sour cream.

## CARROT AND BACON SOUP

*Carrot and Bacon Soup*

1 medium onion, coarsely chopped

3 oz/75 g streaky bacon, coarsely chopped

2 tablespoons extra virgin olive oil

1 lb/500 g carrots, peeled and chopped

8 fl oz/250 ml water

Salt and pepper

Milk

**4-6 servings**

An almost instant soup which is made with the microwave and processor for a natural, fresh-tasting flavour. Best made with fairly young carrots, but other vegetables can be used following the basic method.

Put the bacon, onion and olive oil into a bowl. Cover with cling film and microwave on high for 6 minutes. Remove and add the carrots and water. Cover again and microwave for 10 minutes or until the carrots are soft. Put into food processor and blend until smooth. Add milk to required consistency. Reheat. Season and serve.

## CARROT PUDDINGS

Carrots have been used as the basis for puddings for many centuries, not just for their carrot flavour, but for the moist sweetness which they impart. Mrs MacIver's recipe (1773) has something of the 'Genoese sponge' concept about it. It is rich, moist and full of subtle flavour—it is also expensive by today's standards, though eggs in the eighteenth century were so cheap and plentiful that 'Beat 10 eggs...' was commonplace.

## A RICH MOIST CARROT CAKE

**8-10 portions**

Carrot cakes today are popular and vary in type and contents from really dark, spicy fruit cakes to much lighter sponges, but none appear to use cooked carrots.

## To make

This one is best made in a loaf tin. The icing may be omitted and the cake served instead as a pudding with an Orange Sauce.

Pre-heat the oven to 350F/180C/Gas 4.

Use 2 x 1 lb/500 g loaf tins or 1 x 2 lb/1 kg loaf tin or 9 in (22 cm) round cake tin.

Sift the dry ingredients together then add walnuts and carrots. Mix well. Add oil/butter and then mix in the eggs. Pour into tins and bake for about 1 hour.

## Icing

Beat the icing sugar, cream cheese, vanilla essence and butter together till fluffy. Ice top and sides of cake.

## Orange sauce

Put **3 tablespoons Brandy Marmalade** (see p.220) in the liquidiser or processor with **4 tablespoons of water** and puree till the orange chips are fine. Put into a pan and reduce till a thin syrupy consistency.

From Thelma MacBeth, Wood'n Spoon Restaurant, Kingussie, 1984.

# GLAZED CARROTS

4 servings

Because of their natural sweetness, carrots are ideal for this method of cooking vegetables. The slow cooking with butter and sugar gives them an attractive syrupy coating. Turnips, parsnips and beetroot are also good cooked in the same way. Beetroots should be cooked till soft first.

Slice larger, older carrots into even sized pieces and leave new carrots whole. Put into the pan with butter, sugar, salt and enough water to come halfway up the carrots. Cover and simmer till the carrots are almost cooked—this will depend on age and also whether you like vegetables well cooked or with a 'bite' left in them. There should not be too much liquid left now. Remove the lid and boil hard to evaporate, gently shaking the pan to prevent the vegetables from sticking. Take the pan off the heat and finish with a knob of butter, shaking the pan well to coat all the carrots. Taste for seasoning and sprinkle with freshly chopped parsley and a few drops of lemon juice before serving.

*Rich Moist Carrot Cake*

8 oz/250 g wholemeal flour (2 c)

8 oz/250 g brown sugar (2 c)

4 teaspoons baking powder

2 tablespoons cinnamon

1 teaspoon salt

½ cup oil or melted butter

4 eggs, beaten

½ cup chopped walnuts

1 oz/400 g grated carrot (3 c)

(Grated zest of 1 orange—my addition)

*Icing*

½ lb/250 g icing sugar (2 c)

3 oz/75 g cream cheese (½ c scant)

1 teaspoon vanilla essence

3 oz/75 g butter (¾ c)

*Glazed Carrots*

1 lb/500 g carrots

1 oz/25 g butter (¼ stick)

1 tablespoon brown sugar

Salt

Cold water

1 teaspoon lemon juice

# Cabbage and related vegetables: Turnips, Kale and Sprouting Broccoli

In the thousands of years since wild cabbage was first cultivated, it has developed into several distinct vegetables. In addition to turnips, kale and broccoli, there is cauliflower, Brussels sprouts and kohlrabi, not to mention many different forms of the Chinese cabbage and oil-seed rape. The earliest records of cultivated cabbages date from around 600 BC when kale is mentioned in early Greek literature.

Modern cabbages are thought to have originated in Germany where both red and white cabbages were grown by 1150. At present they are divided into eight main types: Spring, which have fresh loose leafy heads; Summer, which have either pointed or rounded hearts; Autumn, which are harvested in September; Winter white, which are large cabbages grown for storage as solid white heads; Savoy, which have crinkly, often bluish leaves; Savoy hybrids, which are crosses between Savoy and white cabbages: being denser than Savoys they will often stand in good condition in the ground until March; January King cultivators, hardy varieties which stand throughout the winter, and particularly handsome cabbages with slightly crinkly and purplish leaves; and Red, which are harvested in October/November and can be stored through the winter.

The people of the Orkney and Shetland Isles share with Scandinavians an extensive use of cabbage in their diet in preference to other vegetables. Combined with fish, it became a staple item of diet and, unlike other parts of the country, it was also pickled in barrels for winter use, as they do in Eastern Europe. The chopped cabbage was packed into wooden barrels with layers of animal fat, oatmeal, salt and spices. Weighted down, it was used as required to make broth.

## *Rumbledethumps*

1 lb/500 g cooked potatoes

1 lb/500 g cooked cabbage

2 oz/50 g butter (½ stick)

1 medium onion, finely chopped

2 oz/50 g grated Scottish cheddar (½ c)

Chopped chives

## RUMBLEDETHUMPS

**4 servings**

The curious name of this dish comes from the old Scots word for 'mixed together', rumbled, and 'bashed together'—thumped. Eaten as a main course, meatless dish, it can also be served as a vegetable with meat.

Melt the butter in a large pan and add the onion. Cook gently for 5 minutes without browning. Add potatoes, chives and cabbage and mix together. Season well and put into a pie dish. Cover with cheese and brown under the grill or in the oven.

## RED CABBAGE WITH APPLES

**4-6 servings**

An aromatic combination which depends for its depth of flavour on some good-flavoured fat bacon (a piece of speck if possible): it is a dish which goes well with roasts of mature-flavoured game.

### To cook

Heat the lard or fat and cook the onions until soft but not brown. Add the cabbage, vinegar, cloves, bay leaf and lemon. Sprinkle the sugar on top and add water to almost cover. Push a piece of fat bacon into the centre. Cover and simmer gently for 3-4 hours. Add the apples near the end of the cooking and cook until they are just soft.

# Scottish Turnips

*Our club [The Cleikum] put a little powdered gineger [sic] to their mashed turnips, which were studiously chosen of the yellow, sweet, juicy sort, for which Scotland is celebrated...*

> Meg Dods,
> *The Cook and Housewife's Manual*, 1826

This yellow variety, which Meg Dods was referring to, is the same variety which accompanies Haggis and mixes so well with Orkney Clapshot. It is a variety of *Brassica campestris*, which is known as a Swedish turnip, swede or Rutabaga—*Brassica napus*. It came from Sweden to Scotland in the late eighteenth century and is known in England as a swede.

*Brassica rapa*, the white-fleshed, cultivated turnip, is the plant from which many other turnips, oil seed rape and many varieties of Chinese cabbage have been developed. It is related to the ordinary cabbage, which it was originally crossed with to form the swede. It is likely that swedes first appeared in medieval gardens where turnips and varieties of cabbage were growing together.

## BUYING/PREPARING

Much hardier than the cultivated turnip, Scottish turnips are at their best throughout the winter when their flesh is less watery. Available

*Red Cabbage with Apples*

2 oz/50 g lard

2 medium onions

1 medium sized red cabbage

4 tablespoons red wine vinegar

1 level teaspoon ground cloves

Bay leaf

Zest of 2 lemons

2 tablespoons soft brown sugar

Water

Piece of fat bacon

12 oz/375 g cooking apples, peeled, cored and sliced

August to April. Smaller ones have less of a woody outer layer, all of which must be removed before cooking: they also have a milder flavour.

## MASHED TURNIP
### Often described with Haggis as Bashed Neeps

*Mashed Turnip*

1 lb/500 g turnip

Cold water to cover

Salt and white pepper

2 tablespoons butter

1 teaspoon grated ginger root
   or ground ginger to taste

Handful of chopped chives for
   garnish

**4 servings**

Remove the hard, woody outer skin of the turnip. It is essential that all is removed since it will not soften with cooking and bits left in are unpleasant. Put into a pan with water and boil till soft. Drain, dry off in the pan over a gentle heat for a few minutes, stirring to drive off excess moisture. Add the butter and grated ginger root. Stir for another few minutes then mash thoroughly with a fork or potato masher. Beat well till smooth. Taste for seasoning and serve.

Garnish with a handful of chopped chives.

### Variation

To make Orkney Clapshot, which is often served with Haggis, mix the above mixture with an equal quantity of Creamed Potatoes—beat well till smooth. This mixture can be put in a pie or gratin dish, thickly covered with grated cheddar cheese and baked in the oven, or under the grill, until browned.

# Kale

*The old fashioned easy way of asking a friend to dinner was to ask him if he would take his kale with the family.*
   Dean Ramsay,
   *Reminiscences of Scottish Life and Character*, 1858.

Ramsay did not mean that they were necessarily going to eat kale for dinner. But so ubiquitous had it become in the Scottish diet that the term kale meant 'your dinner'. While Scots referred to it as 'Kail', the northern English referred to it as 'Cale'. It is also known as 'Borecole', from the Dutch 'Boerenckool' meaning 'Peasants' cabbage'.

Kale applies to various forms of non-heading brassicas. Most have a tall, thick stem, curled leaves and are very hardy. They are thought to have been the earliest type of cultivated cabbage and are closest to the wild forms. Kale's success in Scotland was largely due to its hardiness and, in particular, its resistance to frost. Its flavour improves after the first frost of winter. It also has the advantage of providing a good source of green, iron and vitamin-rich, vegetable throughout the winter.

# BUYING/PREPARING

Limited supplies are available commercially from November through to May. The young leaves from the top of the plant are the best. Young kale is good raw in a salad finely chopped. The thicker, coarse, woody stems should be removed.

## BUTTERED KALE
### with oatmeal

**4 servings**

Fresh young kale tops can be treated as for spinach though kale has a stronger, spicier taste and more robust texture. The best method is to stir-fry though most early recipes advise boiling. Lady Clark of Tillypronie adds a tablespoon of cream to kale as well as two tablespoons of stock before serving. This is then reduced to a 'proper consistency', she says, and eaten with 'brown meat'. The Scots, she says 'add a dust of oatmeal, or eat kale with a spoon and a piece of oatcake with it'.

### To cook

Melt the butter in a pan with a good heavy base. Add the kale and stir for a few minutes until it has reduced and is cooked. It should be soft and buttery. Season well and serve. Sprinkle the toasted oatmeal on top.

## KALE AND CROWDIE PIE

**6-8 servings**

The pale-green filling mixture for this flan is topped with some soured cream then dusted with paprika. Swirled with a fork, it makes a colourful pattern on top and is also a good blend of flavours. The filling may also be used for stuffing pancakes.

Pre-heat the oven to 375F/190C/Gas 5.

### To cook

Melt the butter in a pan and sauté the kale till soft as in the previous recipe. Season with salt and black pepper. Mix with eggs, flour, cheese and nutmeg. Spread into the base of a flan shell. Cover with the soured cream, dust the top with paprika and swirl a design on top. Bake for 40-45 minutes.

*Buttered Kale with Oatmeal*

1 lb/500 g kale tops, finely chopped or ground finely in a food processor

2 oz/50 g butter (½ stick)

Salt and freshly ground black pepper

1 tablespoon toasted pinhead oatmeal

*Kale and Crowdie Pie*

1 lb/500 g crowdie cheese (2 c)

3 beaten eggs

½ lb/250 g kale or spinach, chopped or ground finely in food processor

1 small onion, finely chopped

1 tablespoon butter

3 tablespoons flour

½ teaspoon grated nutmeg

8 fl oz/250 ml soured cream (1 c)

Salt and freshly ground black pepper

Paprika for dusting top

9-in flan shell, baked blind (p.55)

181

## GREEN KALE SOUP WITH BACON

*Green Kale Soup with Bacon*

*For the stock*

1 lb/500g unsmoked ham

3 medium potatoes

4 medium carrots

3 pts/1.8 L water

*To make up the soup*

8 oz/250 g kale or spinach

2 leeks

**6-8 servings**

### For the stock

Put the ham,* potatoes, carrots and water into a pan, cover and cook till the meat is tender, then remove.

### To make up the soup

Remove the coarse stalks from the kale or spinach, wash and chop finely. Trim and clean the leeks, chop finely. Mash the potatoes and carrots or liquidise. Add the leeks and kale and bring to the boil then simmer till tender. Chop up the meat and add to the soup or serve separately. Taste for seasoning.

# Broccoli, Calabrese

A recent addition to Scotland's commercial vegetables, producers are researching new varieties and growing methods for broccoli which came from Italy to northern Europe where it was first known as Italian asparagus. Its name comes from the Italian 'brocco' meaning 'shoot'. The types grown are: **green**, which matures during the summer; **romanesco**, which matures later and has a very handsome head consisting of numerous yellowish-green conical groups of buds arranged in spirals; and **sprouting broccoli**, which is an outwintering annual, or perennial, ready in early spring and usually white or purple. Calabrese is the name of the region in Italy where it has been grown since the Middle Ages.

## CREAMY BROCCOLI SALAD

**4 servings**

This salad comes from Mollie Katzen's second book *The Enchanted Broccoli Forest...and Other Timeless Delicacies* (1982) and is written in the same spirit of adventure as her previous *Mosewood Cookbook*.

*The use of the term Ham in Scotland loosely refers to any kind of bacon and not merely the cured leg joint and the cooked meat from it which is the usual English interpretation of the word. In Scotland this is usually called Cooked Ham or Gammon.

## To prepare the broccoli

Cut off the bottom few inches of the broccoli stalks and discard if they look tough and woody (crunch a bit off the end if you are not sure), otherwise keep for Stir-fried Vegetables (see p.253).

Young broccoli should have a tender outer skin on the stalks but older specimens may need to have their tough outer skin peeled off with a potato peeler. Divide the broccoli up into manageable-sized spears. Steam till just tender and bright green. Drain.

## Finishing the dish

Combine the lemon juice with mayonnaise, yoghurt or sour cream, tarragon and shallots and season well with salt and pepper. Toss the broccoli in this till well mixed. Cover and chill.

*Creamy Broccoli Salad*

1 lb/500 g fresh green romanesco or sprouting broccoli shoots

1 lemon, juice of

2 fl oz/75 ml mayonnaise (¼ c)

2 fl oz/75 ml yoghurt or sour cream or a combination (¼ c)

¼ teaspoon salt

Sprig of tarragon

2 finely chopped shallots

Lots of freshly ground black pepper

# Peas

Pea seeds have been found in deposits from neolithic settlements in Jericho while other early evidence of cultivation comes from the ruins of Troy where a jar was found containing 440 lbs of peas.

They have been grown in southern Europe and the Near East for thousands of years, eaten either as fresh green peas when immature, or as dried peas for making into soup. Mangetout, sugar peas or snow peas do not have the stiff parchment-like walls on their pods, so are edible whole.

Peas were probably first cultivated in Turkey. At present there are several major groups of pea types: pod peas, which are for dried peas; pod peas for garden peas or petit pois; mangetout peas with flat pods; mangetout peas with swollen pods.

Peas must be picked and eaten young. A crop can come to ripeness in a matter of hours and must be picked and used quickly to preserve the sweet, fresh flavour.

## BUTTERED PEAS WITH MINT

Toss **1 lb/500 g of fresh young peas** in **1 tablespoon melted butter** and **1 tablespoon stock or water**, keeping them moving all the time. Finish with **chopped mint**, a **pinch of sugar** and **salt and pepper** to taste.

*Purée of Green Peas*

1 lb/500 g buttered peas with mint

2 fl oz/50 ml double cream (¼ c)

1 egg

Salt and white pepper

Grated nutmeg

# PURÉE OF GREEN PEAS
## baked in a mould

**4 servings**

Pre-heat the oven to 350F/180C/Gas 4.

Prepare the mould—brush well with melted butter. Purée the Buttered Peas (see previous recipe) with the cream and egg. Taste for seasoning and add a little grated nutmeg. Pour into the mould and place in a tray of water coming halfway up the dish. Place in the oven and poach for 20-25 minutes until just set.

**Note:** Purées of other vegetables may be used either singly or in combinations making colour and flavour contrasts, with alternating layers of different vegetables.

# Mixed Vegetable Dishes

## HOTCH POTCH
### Spring Vegetable Soup

*Hotch Potch*

*For the stock*

2 lb/1 kg neck of lamb

6 pt/3 L water

1 onion stuck with a few cloves

Bay leaf

Bundle of fresh herbs

*Added vegetables*

4 oz/125 g fresh green peas

4 oz/125 g fresh broad beans

3 oz/75 g spring onions, finely chopped

¼ medium turnip, diced

2-3 young carrots, diced

½ medium cauliflower, broken into small sprigs

½ lettuce, finely chopped

Salt and pepper

Chopped chives for garnish

**8-10 servings**

*That's Hotch-Potch—and that's cocky-leeky—the twa best soups in natur. Broon soup's moss-water—and white soup's like scauded [scalded] milk wi' worms in't. But see, sirs, hoo the ladle stauns o' itsel in the potch....*

The Ettrick Shepherd,
*Noctes Ambrosianae*, 1822-1835.

The Shepherd's enthusiasm for Hotch Potch led him into another eulogy when he describes it as 'an emblem o' the haill vegetable and animal creation.' Its virtue lies in the freshness and variety of the young spring vegetables and the universal liking in Scotland for a soup which has as much in it as possible.

### Making the stock

Put the lamb into cold water and bring to the boil, skim. Add an onion stuck with cloves and bay leaf and bundle of fresh herbs and simmer till the meat is tender. Strain, leave to cool, remove excess fat and take the meat off the bone. Chop it up finely.

### To finish the soup

Melt the butter in a pan and add cauliflower, carrots and turnip. Toss for about five minutes, cover and sweat for five minutes without colouring. Now add the peas, beans and spring onions. Toss for a few minutes. Add

184

the strained stock, bring to the boil and simmer very gently till the vegetables are just tender. They will lose their fresh flavour if over-cooked. Finally, just before serving, taste for seasoning and add meat, lettuce and chives.

# LENTIL SOUP

**6-8 servings**

This basic lentil soup is finished with tomatoes, lemon juice, vinegar and molasses which deepens the flavour, though they may be omitted for a simpler, more traditional version. Both are good with grated mature cheddar on top.

## To cook

Put the lentils in the water or stock (or use a ham bone with water) and salt, and simmer covered for 3-4 hours.

Sauté the onion, celery or fennel, carrots, potato and turnip in the butter for 10 minutes.

Add to the lentil stock and simmer till all are just tender.

## Finishing the soup

As an option for finishing the soup, add the chopped tomatoes, lemon juice, cider vinegar, molasses and black pepper to the soup about 30 minutes before serving. Thyme, oregano or basil can also be added. Taste for seasoning and adjust consistency if necessary.

### Lentil Soup

8 oz/250 g red lentils (3 c)

3½ pt/2 L water or stock (or use a ham bone with water)

2 tablespoons salt

2 oz/50 g butter (½ stick)

1 medium onion, finely chopped

2-3 stalks of celery or fennel, finely chopped

2 medium carrots, finely chopped

3-4 sliced potatoes

¼ of a medium turnip, sliced

*Finishing the soup—optional*

3-4 chopped tomatoes

2 tablespoons lemon juice

1 tablespoon apple cider vinegar

1½ tablespoons molasses

Black pepper

*Optional*—thyme, oregano or basil

# 8
# SUGAR & SPICE & BAKING, SCOTTISH SWEETIES & PRESERVES

*Besides such homely sweets as gundy, glessie, cheugh jeans and black man, there were bottles of 'boilings' (Scotch Mixtures) that glittered like rubies, emeralds, topazes and all the jewels of the Orient, and tasted of all the fruits of the orchard and spices of the Indies.*
  F. Marian McNeill,
  *The Scots Kitchen,* 1929.

With such temptations it's not surprising that Scots have a sweet tooth. Sweetie boiling, it seems, was a national pastime in the days before television, and the Scots liking for sweet things continues. It also seems that they consume more biscuits, but fewer cakes and pastries, than the rest of the UK, which may have something to do with the fact that the oven came late to Scotland and the people were more used to crisp, hard oatcakes baked on girdles than soft cakes and crisp pastries. But the sugary sweet tooth is of fairly recent origins. Before the eighteenth century it was honey which sweetened foods, though the rich also had access to expensive sugar loaves made from Arabian sugar cane, pressed to extract the syrup, then boiled to evaporate most of the moisture and finally poured into long conical moulds to harden. A loaf could weigh anything from 3 to 14 pounds and the sugar was chipped off, when required, with pincers.

When sugar was first carried to the West it was regarded, along with spices, as an important medicine valued for its warming qualities. The health benefits of sugar were based on a medieval concept of pathology, similar to ancient Chinese beliefs, which taught that those in a physical state of cold (yin) required the heating (yang) power of a warming dose of

186

medicinal sugar or other such 'heating' food. Apothecaries made and sold humbugs, toffees, tablets, lozenges and liquorice to relieve the symptoms of coughs, colds and other ailments. Though it is not considered a medicinal sweet today, tablet originated as a small, flat disc containing some natural health-giving substance flavoured with sugar. There was also the use of sugar as a convenient sweetener of bitter medicinal potions. Spices were also valued for their healing qualities and ability to add a special zest to food.

Around the middle of the seventeenth century, Britain began to acquire sugar-cane-producing colonies in the New World, and the sugar trade across the Atlantic developed. While the rich indulged in sugar fantasies for table decoration, the poor didn't see much of it until sugar became cheap towards the end of the nineteenth century. Meanwhile, honey continued as the popular sweetener, and the Scots were enthusiastic beekeepers. Their practice of taking the bees to the heather in the summer produced a useful supply of specially flavoured honey.

Sugar, however, was gaining a hold, getting cheaper all the time as imports increased. The world's first sugar-beet factory was built in Silesia in 1801-2, which led the way eventually to an enormous increase in consumption by the mass of the population. The tea-drinking habit was also spreading, and by the end of the nineteenth century the two had become inseparable companions. Hot, sugary tea fulfilled the need for a stimulating drink which lifted spirits and blood sugar levels for a short time, but did little to satisfy long-term nutritional needs.

Sugar's healing value had become debased as consumption had increased, so that it was no longer regarded as a useful warmer and the damage to health of excessive consumption became clear.

Spices, on the other hand, never became debased in this way and have retained their original allure. Their history is a rich tapestry of Arab monopoly, Italian intrigue and dangerous journeying across the globe. The spice trade developed in the first century AD, but British enthusiasm took off after Crusaders returned from the 'holy wars' in the eleventh, twelfth and thirteenth centuries with supplies of spices, dates, figs, almonds, sherbets and sweetmeats. From then on spices transformed simple British tastes, adding interest and variety which was further encouraged when Britain added India to her Empire.

But it does seem that tastes and palates for spices have changed over the centuries. We no longer sprinkle a layer of pepper over sweet custards, or can afford to add saffron in the quantities used by mediaeval cooks to enliven foods with its colour and enticing aroma. Their use as a medicine, however, continues, with spices like ginger used in potions prescribed in Chinese medicine. Yet despite changes in use, some early sugar and spice innovations continue in popularity such as marzipan, gingerbread, mincemeat, plum puddings and black bun. Except for gingerbread, which we now eat at any time of the year, the others are all festive foods reflecting their early restricted use to festivals and holidays only.

# SUGAR

Granulated white sugar is refined from cane or beet and is the most commonly used sugar, consisting of 100 per cent pure sucrose. Caster, which is finer, and icing, finer still, are also both 100 per cent pure sucrose.

Brown sugars may be made in two ways. Either they are made from highly processed white beet sugar, which has had all its trace elements removed, and mixed with a small proportion of cane molasses. Or they can be made by halting the refining process, in which case they should be described as 'unrefined' on the label.

These will come from ex-colonial countries such as Mauritius, Barbados and Guyana where entire communities depend on sugar for jobs, not just in its harvesting but also in its refining. These sugars have a better, fudgier flavour and produce a more interesting end result. They also contain trace elements and vitamins, occurring naturally in sugar cane, but lost by refining. They are now available in various grades from 'golden' (equivalent to white granulated but a golden colour); to 'soft brown' which is akin to caster sugar.

Muscovado has less molasses removed and demerara is a larger crystal than granulated. Black treacle is a more refined form of pure cane molasses.

# SPICES

India leads the export league in spices (mostly pepper, cardamom, chillies, ginger, turmeric and cumin) followed by Indonesia (pepper, nutmeg, mace, cassia, ginger, cardamom, vanilla), Madagascar (vanilla, cloves) and Malaysia (pepper, ginger). More than 80 per cent of spices are from developing countries, and production and export are an important element of their agricultural economy.

Differences in quality depend on the climate, the soil and how the peasants have grown the crop. Though ginger is grown throughout the spice world, Jamaican ginger is widely regarded as the best. It is also the most expensive. Grown in small quantities, it is the specially good growing conditions, plus the rich soils, which have increased the level of essential oil in their ginger giving it a deep-yellow colour. Most is made into ginger oil and none is now sold as ground ginger in the UK.

Other differences in quality depend on the methods of production, distribution and storing. Ginger can lose its pungency if it has been treated to remove some of its oils before grinding. Cinnamon and cloves are the other spices most likely to have had some oil extracted. It is surprising the differences in pungency between brands. Top spice buyers will laboratory-test spices before buying to check the oil content. They also prefer to buy whole, rather than ground.

Exposure to light, warmth and air will also deplete spicy pungency. Ultraviolet light dries out the oil and lightens the colour of the spice. Those sitting on shelves in clear glass jars for too long will eventually lose their potency. To test the quality of a spice, buyers judge first the aroma. Then, if it's ground, they will put a pinch in the palm of the hand and rub gently with the thumb to release the full aroma.

The best and cheapest way to buy spices is from small companies where the turnover is low. This means that they will buy in small quantities and the spices will be sold faster and will therefore be fresher. Buying from small mail-order companies, such as Fox's Spices in Stratford-upon-Avon, can result in a saving of 30-50 per cent compared with the prices of the larger market leaders, who have higher overheads and large advertising budgets to finance.

## HONEY

Honey from a single type of blossom is the most expensive but has the best flavour. Highly blended honeys have nondescript flavours and some may contain amounts of ordinary sugar. These often taste sickly-sweet whereas pure honey will have greater depth of flavour. Scottish heather honey comes from bees which have been taken to the heather-clad hills during the summer months and this gives the honey its strongly aromatic flavour and dark colour.

Honey does not deteriorate if stored for 1-2 years at around room temperature. It does not like the cold, however, and must be kept away from strong smells. Viscosity varies according to the amount of water in the honey. If it is too runny, it has too much water and is not a good buy. It will also be lacking in flavour. Of the heather honeys, pure ling is the only one which is thixotropic, setting like a jelly. Honey that has crystallised and set should be put in a bowl of warm water (not hotter than 50C) to melt. It contains extra ingredients (traces of minerals, iron, calcium, magnesium, phosphorous, vitamins C, B, B2, B5, B6, nicotinic acid and other residues including enzymes, gums and resins) some of which will be destroyed if the honey is heated above 50C.

# SCOTTISH BAKING

# Shortbread

*If every Frenchwoman is born with a wooden spoon in her hand, every Scotswoman is born with a rolling-pin under her arm. There may be a divergence of opinion as to her skill in cooking, but it is certain that she has developed a remarkable technique in baking—not only in bannocks, scones and oatcakes, but also in the finer manipulations of wheat—in cakes, pastry and shortbread.*

F. Marian McNeill
*The Scots Kitchen,* 1929

Six, four, two we were taught at school: six ounces of flour, four of butter and two of sugar. It was our first shortbread lesson and the recipe has never been forgotten. The method, also, remains vivid. The lump of butter was put in the middle of the wooden pastry board, with its pile of sugar beside it. The flour was sifted onto the top right-hand corner. Then sugar was kneaded into butter with clean hands, before flour was worked in and the mound began to change in size and texture. We learnt to judge the consistency: pliable, without being too soft; firm, but not too crumbly.

Feeling the 'life' of dough is something which bakers will tell you only an experienced hand can judge. No recipe is a foolproof guide, especially when using things like flour and butter which both have varying degrees of absorbency depending on their moisture content. This delicate balance between the right and wrong consistency is so crucial to the finished result, that I'm glad we were encouraged to get our hands into things at an age when habits are formed.

## ORIGIN OF SHORTBREAD

'Short' has been used for at least five centuries to describe anything which is crisp and easily crumbled. In medieval times they ate 'shortpaste' in Lent. Later the word was prefixed to both cake and bread, which goes back to the confusion which arose when they called a piece of a 'loaf' a 'cake of bread' (see p.5). By the early nineteenth century the Scots were commonly referring to it as short 'bread' rather than short 'cake' though it would have been more logical to have kept continuity with the oat 'cake' and the pan 'cake'. However, by deviating from the rest of Britain and America, the Scots have produced a more distinctive item. Not a common biscuit, it is classed (for tax purposes) as an item of flour confectionery. A status which the Scottish Association of Master Bakers fought to preserve when EU bureaucrats thought to name it just another biscuit.

## FLOUR

A soft, white flour with a low gluten content is best. If a strong flour is used, the dough will be tough and the baked shortbread too hard. A soft fine wholemeal may be used in a mixture with white but it does have a stronger flavour and the butter taste may not come through so well. Some use a little rice flour for a crunchier result, while others claim that a little cornflour improves the shortbread. A little of both is also used.

# BUTTER

This is the main flavouring and shortening agent which gives distinction to shortbread—the finished result will be judged by the quality of the butter used. It should have a low water content.

# SUGAR

Caster sugar gives the best result, though some icing sugar may be used for a finer result. Brown sugars tend to dominate flavourwise and spoil the natural flavour of the butter.

## SHORTBREAD

Pre-heat the oven to 300F/150C/Gas 2.
    Prepare a greased baking tray.

*Shortbread*
**6 oz/150 g plain flour (1½ c)**
**4 oz/100 g butter (1 stick)**
**2 oz/50g sugar (⅓ c)**

### Kneading the dough

Put the sugar and butter on the board and knead together. Sift the flour into a corner and start working in gradually till the dough is still soft and pliable and not too firm. Add more flour if you think it can take it without the dough breaking up.

### Shaping the dough

Roll out into a round or cut into fingers or fancy shapes. The thickness is a matter of taste but thicker will take longer to bake. The above quantity may be pressed into a Swiss roll tin (7 in x 11 in—17 cm x 27 cm) and then cut into fingers. (Makes 20 biscuits.) If using a special shortbread mould, flour it well then knock out excess flour and press in the dough. Level off with a rolling-pin and knock out the round. It can also be rolled in either granulated sugar or demerara sugar into a cylinder shape and then put in the refrigerator before slicing into round biscuits.

    Before baking, shortbread of all shapes or sizes should be pricked all over with a fork (docked) to let the steam escape evenly and avoid it distorting the shape.

### Baking

Shortbread should be baked slowly to develop the rich butter taste. It should be evenly baked to a light-golden colour throughout the whole biscuit. If the temperature is too low it will have an undesirable greyish colour inside while if it is too high then it will have a 'bone' in the centre. Place in the bottom half of the oven: thick shortbread can take up to an hour. About five minutes before it is ready, remove from the oven and dust lightly with caster sugar. The sugar will stick to the hot surface much better if done at this stage, though it is not essential that it should be dusted with sugar at all.

# RICH SHORTBREAD

## Shapes

Oval and oblong shapes are described in early recipes with some variations. Mrs MacIver (1773) shaped hers into an oval then cut through the middle and plaited it at the ends. Some other ovals are cut in two 'the narrow way, so as to have two cakes somewhat the shape of a Saxon arch'.—Meg Dods (1826). Others divide it into squares or oblongs but all seem to agree that the thickness should be one inch.

## Use of melted butter

Mrs MacIver uses three pounds of boiling butter to four pounds flour as well as 'a mutchkin of good yest'. Most early methods use melted butter and this seems to have been used well into the twentieth century. Which makes a mockery of all those recipes which warn you about putting your warm hands into the shortbread in case you 'oil' it. Janet Murray in *Traditional Recipes from Scotland* (BBC, 1964) refers to a listener who was reminded of this method when she gave a recipe for a rich shortbread strongly flavoured with caraway and using melted butter.

## Rich Shortbread for festive occasions and as a present

This was a thick round of shortbread with ground or chopped almonds added to the mixture as well as caraway seeds, decorated on top with crystallised lemon and orange peel and sometimes caraway comfits. It was so thick that recipes advise putting a band of paper round the outside, as well as sitting it on several layers of paper while baking, so that it does not brown too quickly round the edges and on the base. This special shortbread was baked for New Year celebrations and in some areas it was known as a Pitcaithly Bannock. Even in the 1820s Scots were sending it as a present from Scotland. Meg Dods put in more almonds and butter to make a very rich Scotch Shortbread 'for sending as a holiday present to England'.

## RICH SHORTBREAD
### Pitcaithly Bannock

This thick, golden round of festive shortbread is traditionally flavoured with almonds, caraway and crystallised orange and lemon peel, which decorates the top. I prefer to flavour only with almonds and press about eight whole blanched ones onto the top surface before baking in the same style as a Dundee cake.

### To bake

Make up a double quantity of the basic mix and add the blanched almonds and caraway seeds.

Decorate the top with either the orange/lemon peel or blanched almonds.

Shape into a 1-inch-thick round or rectangle. Protect the edge with a strip of greaseproof paper and bake as for the basic mix.

*Rich Shortbread*

**Double quantity basic mix**

**2 oz/50 g blanched almonds, finely chopped**

**1 tablespoon caraway seeds**

*Decoration*

**1 oz candied orange or lemon peel**

*or*

**8 blanched almonds**

# Scones

Scones belong to the British family of small tea-cakes, though their Scottish pedigree goes back at least to the eighteenth century when Robert Burns rightly described them as 'souple [soft] scones, the wale [choicest] of food'. How they got their name is difficult to say. The *SND* suggests that the word may be a shortened version of the Dutch 'schoonbrot' meaning fine bread, while Chambers *Dictionary* suggests that the word is from the Gaelic 'sgonn', a shapeless mass. There is no confusion, however, about its pronunciation, at least in Scotland, where it is universally spoken of as a 'skawn' as in gone. The English pronounce it in some regions as the Scots do, while others pronounce the word to rhyme with own.

### When to eat

They should not be limited to afternoon teatime. Savoury ones make good accompaniments to soups; they are also good at the end of a meal with cheese. They are so incredibly quick and easy to make that it is possible to make them for breakfast/brunch.

### The secret of a good scone

The dough should be as wet as you can handle. The mixing should be done quickly and lightly. There should be the minimum of handling and they should be baked until they are just risen and dried out. The outer surface should be very crisp: the inner very soft.

*We lay upon the bare top of a rock like scones upon a girdle.*
Robert Louis Stevenson
*Kidnapped*, 1886

193

### Ingredients

Scots traditionally make scones with buttermilk and bicarbonate of soda—known as soda scones. There is a subtle difference in the result which is softer, lighter, moister and with a sharper flavour than scones made with fresh milk and baking powder. If buttermilk is not available then sour milk may be used or fresh milk can be soured by adding about 2 teaspoons of lemon juice.

### Mixing and shaping

'Deftly mixed' is probably as good a description as any of the technique which depends on light, quick handling for a perfect result. The flour should be well sifted and all the buttermilk poured into a well in the centre. Stir with a fork, gradually bringing in the flour; if the mixture is too dry and 'ragged' looking, the scones will not be light. The mixing should be done with as little 'working' as possible and it should be a soft, elastic consistency, sticky unless well floured. It should be handled as little as possible and for this reason it is not rolled out but lifted in well-floured hands and placed on either girdle or baking tray. Then it is well floured on top and lightly pressed down into a rough round shape (a bannock) for the girdle ½ in (1½ cm) thick, and for the oven 1¼ in (3½ cm), and only at this point is it divided into scones. Chambers *Scots Dictionary* has the right description: a 'shapeless mass'. If liked, they may be separate or touching; if the latter they will take longer to cook but can be broken after baking.

### Baking

All scones may be baked either on a girdle in the traditional way or in the oven. There will be differences in shape and texture. Those baked on the girdle will have smooth, flat top and bottom surfaces while the oven ones will be rough on top. The oven ones are more likely to be drier while girdle scones will be moister.

The girdle-baking technique allows more control over the baking since you can watch them as they cook and learn to judge when they should be turned and, more importantly, when they are ready. The girdle should not be too hot to begin with or the scones will brown too quickly. Cook slowly, till risen, and till there is a white skin on top. This usually takes about five or six minutes. The heat should have penetrated to the top, and the centre should be well set before turning. Increase the heat if necessary till brown underneath then turn and brown on the other side. It should take about 15 minutes altogether. Open up a little at the edge to check they are quite dry. Wrap in a towel to keep them soft. It is more difficult to judge when they are in the oven but they will take a shorter time than you imagine. Overcooked or undercooked, they lose their softness and lightness.

# TYPES OF SCONES

## SODA SCONES
### made with buttermilk

The Irish have perfected the art of making these simplest of scones and call them 'bread'. The word scone they use for the sweet variety. No additional flavouring should be added. Try baking them, as the Irish do, in a pot. Originally the iron pot was buried in the burning peats to make a 'pot oven', but a heavy-based enamel, or other similar pot which will go in the oven, will do just as well. I use a chicken brick with good results since the steam which develops inside prevents a crust forming too quickly, allowing full 'oven spring' and enabling the loaf to swell to its maximum size before the top sets. Buttermilk scones (bread) made in this way are much lighter and better risen. It is not necessary to remove the lid half way through as some recipes tell you; it browns well with the lid on. Chinese steamed bread also makes use of this practice.

Pre-heat the oven to 450F/230C/Gas 8.

### To bake

Prepare either a moderately hot girdle, greased and floured, a baking tray, greased and floured or a 7-in (18-cm) round pot or chicken brick, greased and floured.

Sift the flour, bicarbonate of soda and salt into a bowl, make a well in the centre and add the buttermilk. Mix with a fork till it is a soft, elastic consistency. Add more milk if it is too dry. Dust the surface with flour and drop in spoonfuls on a baking tray or a hot girdle or put the whole mixture into a pot or brick. Cook till risen and dry. Bake girdle scones on both sides. Wrap in towel when cooked. Serve warm.

## SWEET MILK SCONES—BASIC DOUGH

### Makes 8 scones

These scones will be drier and less spongy than those made with buttermilk but their firmer texture means additional ingredients can be added. The absorbency of the flour will dictate the exact amount of liquid required for the right consistency, so add more if necessary. Wholemeal flour will absorb more than white.

*Soda Scones*

8 oz/250 g plain flour (2 c)

1 teaspoon bicarbonate of soda

½ teaspoon salt

8 fl oz/250 ml buttermilk or sweet milk soured with the juice of a lemon (1 c)

195

*Sweet Milk Scones*

8 oz/250 g plain flour (2 c)

Raising agent, either

(a) 1 teaspoon bicarbonate of soda and 2 teaspoons cream of tartar, or

(b) 2 teaspoons baking powder, or

(c) use self-raising flour

2 oz/50 g butter (½ stick)— this can be varied according to taste or even oil used instead

5 fl oz/150 ml fresh milk (¾ c)

Salt to taste

Pre-heat the oven to 450F/230C/Gas 8.

### To bake

Sift all the dry ingredients into a bowl and rub in the butter. This can be done in the processor, but the mixing should be done by hand, so it seems hardly worth it unless you are in a desperate hurry to get the scones into the oven. Pour the milk into the centre and mix to a soft, elastic dough, slightly stiffer and more manageable than for soda scones. Knead lightly on a floured surface till smooth and press out with your hands or roll out. Cut into shapes, flour or brush with egg on top and bake. Wrap in towel when ready to keep soft and warm. Serve warm.

## SULTANA SCONES

Use an **80 per cent wholemeal self-raising flour**. Add **1 tablespoon raw brown sugar** and **3 oz/75 g sultanas (½ c)**.

## TREACLE SCONES
### with walnuts or pecans

Mix **2 tablespoons treacle or molasses** to the milk before mixing; **20 oz/50 g chopped walnuts or pecans (½ c)**.

## HONEY SCONES
### with orange and lemon

Substitute **fresh orange juice** for **2 fl oz/50 ml of the sweet milk (¼ cup)**. Add **2 tablespoons honey** and the **grated zest of a lemon** and **1 tablespoon chopped walnuts**.

## CREAM SCONES
### with raspberry jam

Sift **4 oz/125 g self-raising cake flour** and **4 oz/125 g fine plain flour** together with **1 teaspoon bicarbonate of soda**. Add **1 egg, 2 tablespoons oil** and **7 fl oz/200 ml carton of soured cream**. Mix with a fork to a light dough and divide into six. Flour well and bake at 450F/230C/Gas 8 for 20 minutes. Serve warm with **raspberry jam** (see p.220).

## FRESH FRUIT SCONES

Use soft fruits—raspberries are very good—add about **4 oz/125 g** to the basic mix. Add **sugar** to taste. Serve with **fresh cream**. For an Apple or Rhubarb Scone: Add to the basic mix **1 egg**; another **2 oz (50 g) butter**; **3 tablespoons sugar** and **1 lb/500 g peeled, cored and roughly chopped cooking apple or chopped rhubarb**. Spread in a greased baking tin 11 in x 7 in (27 cm x 17 cm). Sprinkle with a layer of granulated sugar and bake.

## HERB SCONES
### for serving with cheese

Add **2 teaspoons fresh herbs** to the basic mix.

## CHEESE SCONES
### for serving with soup

Add **5 oz/150 g grated Scottish cheddar cheese (1 c generous)** and a **large pinch of cayenne pepper** sifted in with the flour. Season well with salt. Brush with **egg** and sprinkle cheese on top.

## ONION SCONES

Melt **2 tablespoons bacon fat** in a pan, add **1 small onion, finely chopped** and cook till soft but not browned. Leave to cool. Add most of it to the dough but keep back some to put on top after brushing with **egg**. For Cheese and Onion Scones add the onion mix to the cheese scones and put both onion and cheese on top. For Cheese and Onion with Herbs combine last three variations. Chives are particularly good.

# Scottish Pancakes and Crumpets

The word 'cake' was originally applied to a small regularly shaped item which was eaten as bread and known as a 'kaak of bread' (see origins of oatcake p.5). The sweetening part came later, as did the change in size to the large sweetened and flavoured items we call cakes today. The Scottish 'pan-cake' is a throw-back to the original meaning, as is the Yorkshire 'tea-cake'.

197

## Scottish Pancakes and Crumpets

8 oz/250 g plain flour (2 c)

Raising agent, either

(a) 1 teaspoon bicarbonate of soda and 2 teaspoons cream of tartar with fresh milk, or

(b) 1 teaspoon bicarbonate of soda with buttermilk, or

(c) 2 teaspoons baking powder with fresh milk, or

(d) self-raising flour and fresh milk

1 tablespoon syrup, honey or sugar

1 large egg

8 fl oz/250 ml liquid (1 c) for pancakes

12 fl oz/375 ml liquid (1½ c) for crumpets

In the late seventeenth century there emerged another type of cake—the crumpet. This got its name 'crompid cake' from the fact that it curled up or bent into a curve when baked, the verb to 'crump' or 'crimp' meaning to curl. The original crumpet was baked very thinly and cooked on a girdle, which is why it curled. English crumpets are quite different affairs now. The Scottish crumpet is still thin, but not baked hard enough any more so that it will curl naturally, though it is usually rolled up into a curl when eaten.

The same mixture can be used for both pancakes and crumpets; the difference is in the consistency, with crumpets mixed to a much thinner consistency.

Pre-heat the girdle till moderately hot and grease very lightly.

### Mixing the ingredients

Sift the dry ingredients into a bowl. Mix the honey and egg with the milk and pour into a well in the centre of the flour. Mix till smooth but do not beat.

### Size

Drop spoonfuls onto the heated, greased girdle. Pancakes should spread up to about 3 in (7 cm) while crumpets are much larger, about double the size of pancakes.

### Firing

Turn when the heat has penetrated to the top surface and it is beginning to bubble. They should be lightly brown underneath and should only take 1-2 minutes on each side.

Wrap in a towel immediately they are cooked and serve warm.

# Scottish Cookies

*I want a plain ham-and-egg tea…and some cookies and cakes.*
R.M. Williamson in *Scotland, Readings etc.*
Edited T.W. Paterson, 1929

A cookie is a plain, round, yeasted, sweet bun. It is very light in texture with a dark-golden, shiny top. Split, filled with whipped cream and dusted on top with icing sugar, it is known as a Cream Cookie: with an iced top only it is known as an Iced Cookie. These three types are the most common ones available in high street bakers' shops in Scotland. Spice and fruit may also be added, with the appropriate descriptive epithet.

The name was probably adopted from the Dutch 'koekje' which is actually the diminutive of 'koek'—cake. With the development of English supermarket chains in Scotland, the Scottish cookie is in danger of extinction, since they refer to this item as a Devon Split.

Even more confusingly, the same item in America is called a 'biscuit'. A 'cookie shine' is the Scottish equivalent of the English 'bun fight'. 'From the frequent appearance of these [cookies] at tea-parties the latter are irreverently spoken of as cookie shines.'

# PLAIN COOKIES

**Makes 25-30**

Pre-heat the oven to 425F/220C/Gas 7. Prepare 2 large greased baking trays.

## Mixing and kneading the dough

Begin by warming both the milk and flour separately to blood heat. Yeast will work much more efficiently if everything is warm. Blend the fresh yeast with a little of the milk or dissolve the dried yeast in some and leave until it begins to froth up.

Make a well in the centre of the flour and add most of the milk, yeast (Easy Bake), salt, butter and eggs. (Keep back some of the egg for glazing.) Bring together with your hands till it is a soft, sticky dough, adding more milk if necessary. If it is too wet, add more flour. So many recipes tell you to knead the dough for so many minutes that it is confusing, and really what you must do is knead it until it is the right consistency, and the time it takes to reach this stage varies. It should be transformed during the kneading process from a soft, sticky mess to a smooth, silky rounded ball which comes away from your fingers easily. If the gluten content of the flour is poor, achieving this result is impossible. Always use a strong flour.

## Rising

Cover the bowl with a wet towel (dough likes a damp, steamy atmosphere for rising) and leave in a warm place till it has almost doubled in size.

## Knocking back and shaping the dough

Knock all the air out of the dough, give it another knead to redistribute the yeast and shape the dough into 25-30 small round buns about 2 in (5 cm) in diameter.

## Proving

This is aptly described—to prove that the yeast is still working. Place in a warm place again, cover with a sheet of very lightly greased cling film

*Plain Cookies*

1½ lb/750 g strong plain flour (6 c)

½ pt/300 ml milk (1¼ c)

1 oz/50 g fresh yeast, 1 tablespoon dried yeast or 1 pkt Easy Bake

1 teaspoon salt

4 tablespoons sugar

4 oz/125 g butter, softened (1 stick)

2 large eggs

and leave till the buns have doubled in size. Brush with an egg and milk glaze and bake for 10-15 minutes.

## CREAM COOKIES

Split when cold and fill with whipped cream. Dust on top with icing sugar.

## ICED COOKIES

Make up a fairly stiff water icing, colour and coat the top of the cookie.

## CURRANT COOKIES

Add **4 oz/125 g currants (1 c, scant)** to the dough.

## JAMES BURGESS' SPICED COOKIES

*James Burgess' Spiced Cookies*

*For the starter*

12 oz/350 ml tepid water

1 oz/25 g fresh yeast

1 tablespoon sugar

1 oz/25 g dried milk powder

3 oz/75 g strong white flour

*For the spice mix*

½ oz/15 g nutmeg (about 4 small, 3 large)

½ oz/15 g allspice (3 teaspoons)

¼ oz/7 g cinnamon bark (6-in/15-cm stick)

¼ oz/7 g whole cloves (2 teaspoons, scant)

¼ oz/7 g dried ginger root (about 2 in/5 cm piece)

*For the cookies*

1 oz/25 g spice mix

1 lb 5 oz/650 g strong white flour

3 oz/75 g solid vegetable fat

2 oz/50 g sugar

8 oz/250 g dried mixed fruit

A basic spiced bun mix which is made in 'the pastry' at One Devonshire Gardens in Glasgow by Jimmy Burgess, who brought his baking skills to the hotel industry when he left High Street craft baking to become hotel *pâtissier* and a legend for his fine bread, rolls and pastries.

Preheat the oven to 400F/200C/Gas 6.

### To make the starter

Mix everything together and leave in a warm place until the top is frothing and bubbling.

### To make the spice mix

Blend the spices together in a coffee grinder. Grind till fine. They will not be quite as fine as the commercial variety but this does not matter for baking. Store in an airtight jar, label with the date and keep in a cool place and use within the month.

### To make the dough

Put the flour into a bowl and add the fat. Rub in and add the egg with the sugar, dried fruit, starter and spice mix. Mix together and add more tepid water to make a softish dough. Knead until it becomes silky and pliable but does not stick to your hands. Put in a warm place to prove until double in size. Knock back and shape into round buns. Put on a greased tray. Mark with a cross using a very sharp knife or put on a pastry cross for hot cross buns. Brush with egg and bake for 20-30 minutes. Serve warm.

200

## A SPECIAL YEAST CAKE

This rich yeast cake, with its delicious sticky top, is a good New Year alternative to Black Bun. It comes from Neil Rieley, a retired Glasgow grocer, who bakes for a hobby in a remote Highland glen, firing his bread in a wood-burning stove since his nearest baker is fifty miles away. His deep freeze stands in the porch at the back door, and as visitors leave they are presented with a homemade loaf from his week's baking. While domestic breadmaking satisfies a practical need in these areas, more hotels are also realising the advantages of freshly baked bread and rolls as a positive attraction for customers.

### Enriched White Bread Dough

Use same dough as for Cookies (see p.199) and follow the basic method for making the dough. When ready for shaping make up the sticky top as follows:

### Sticky top

Pre-heat the oven to 425F/220C/Gas 7.

Grease and line a 7 in cake tin (25 cm).

Melt butter, sugar and syrup together and bring to the boil. Remove from the heat and pour into the base of the tin.

Sprinkle over half the currants.

Shape the dough into about 20 to 30 small balls. Arrange the balls in the tin in loose layers sprinkling with rest of the currants. Cover with oiled cling film and leave to rise in a warm place. Bake for ¾-1 hour. Turn upside down onto a plate.

*Special Yeast Cake*

**Dough as for Cookies (see p.199)**

*Sticky top*

**1 oz/25 g butter (¼ stick)**

**1 oz/25 g brown sugar**

**1 tablespoon golden syrup**

**3 tablespoons currants**

## WHITE FLOURY BAPS

Lady Clark of Tillypronie (1909) says that ' "Baps" are mixed very slack—water, flour, salt, yeast. (Neither butter, eggs, nor milk.) They are well dusted with flour, and eaten fresh as soon as baked.'

The etymology of the word is unknown but it seems that they were always breakfast rolls made from a very plain bread dough, and the shapes and sizes varied greatly from one part of the country to another, possibly even from one household to another. 'Are ye for your burial baps round or square?' says Mrs Lion in *Reminiscences of Scottish Life and Character* by Dean Ramsay (1870).

Whatever size or shape, they are distinguished by their fresh, soft, white, floury qualities. Most bakers today make them round and call them white or floury morning rolls. The thick floury coating prevents an

*He grew, the great Macguldroch grew,*
*On butter'd baps and ale.*
R. Couper
*Poems, 1804*

early crust forming (see p.195) and allows them to rise well.

Makes about 10 'man-sized' baps.

Pre-heat the oven to 425F/220C/Gas 7. Grease a baking tray.

## *White Floury Baps*

1lb/500 g strong white flour (5 cups)

2 oz/50 g lard (¼ cup)

2 teaspoons salt

1 oz/25 g fresh yeast, 1 table-spoon dried or 1 pkt Easy Bake

1 teaspoon sugar

10 fl oz/300 ml water and milk, warmed (1¼ c, scant)

## Making the dough

Sift the flour into a bowl, add salt and put to warm. Meanwhile cream yeast and sugar together and then mix with the milk and water. Add the dried yeast to the milk/water and dissolve it. Mix in the Easy Bake to the dry ingredients. Rub the lard into the flour, add the liquid and knead together till smooth and pliable. Leave to rise till doubled in size—about an hour. Knock back, knead and then shape into baps.

## Size

The size of oval baps is usually about 4 in (10 cm) long by about 3 in (7 cm) wide at this stage before rising. Round ones are about 4 in (10 cm) diameter. Once shaped, they are brushed with milk, dusted with flour and set in a warm place to prove. When they have risen, dust again lightly with flour and bake for 15 minutes. Dust again lightly with flour, cool and eat warm.

*An had I but one penny in the whole world,*
*Thou shouldst have it to buy gingerbread.*
William Shakespeare
*Love's Labour's Lost*

# GINGERBREAD

Gingerbread began its life as an enormously popular 'fun' biscuit sold at annual fairs. The gingerbread booth was a colourful affair with ornamental gingerbread in the form of 'crowns, kings and queens, cocks, etc.', dazzlingly resplendent with pseudo gold leaf' and brightly decorated with coloured satin ribbons.

It wasn't the kind of soft gingerbread we make today, but a much harder biscuit and therefore more easily shaped. In fact the mixture was not even cooked. Honey was mixed with grated bread, according to a recipe of 1430, till the mixture was stiff, then it was flavoured with cinnamon and pepper, coloured with red and yellow, shaped, stuck with cloves and allowed to dry out. Novel shapes included the inevitable gingerbread men as well as letters and numbers which were used to teach children to read and count.

Robbie Salmond was an eccentric itinerant gingerbread seller, according to J.H. Jamieson in his article on 'Street Traders and their Cries' in the *Book of the Old Edinburgh Club* (1909). At the Hallow Fair in Edinburgh he was to be found 'encouraging' his customers by occasionally tossing his gingerbread into the crowd and calling out—'Bullock's blood and sawdust—Feed the ravens, Feed the ravens.'

Another Edinburgh reference to gingerbread appears in Robert Chambers' *Traditions of Edinburgh* (1868) when he refers to the shop and 'tavern' run by Mrs Flockhart in the Potterrow. Her nickname was 'Lucky Fykie'* and, in a fifteen-feet-square room, she had a shop selling a variety of miscellaneous items; a living area; a tiny closet (side room); and adjoining this a small room described as a 'hotel'. 'Each forenoon was this place…put into the neatest order; at the same time three bottles, severally containing brandy, rum, and whisky, were placed on a bunker-seat in the window of the "hotel", flanked by a few glasses and a salver of gingerbread biscuits. About noon any one watching the place from an opposite window would have observed an elderly gentleman entering the humble shop, where he saluted the lady with a "Hoo d'ye do, mem?" and then passed into the side space to indulge himself with a glass from one or other of the bottles. After him came another, who went through the same ceremonial; after him another again; and so on. Strange to say, these were men of importance in society—some of them lawyers in good employment, some bankers, and so forth…On special occasions Lucky could furnish forth a soss—that is, stew—which the votary might partake of upon a clean napkin in the closet, a place which only admitted of one chair being placed on it.'

# DARK GINGERBREAD

This remarkable gingerbread is heavy with spices and treacle. So much so that it is likely to sink in the middle—a sign of success, rather than failure.

Use a 9-in (23-cm) square tin, lined.

Pre-heat the oven to 350F/180C/Gas 4.

## Mixing the dough

Sour the milk if necessary and sift the flour. Put the butter, sugar and treacle into a large saucepan which will hold the finished mixture. Warm slightly so that the butter begins to melt. Remove from the heat and beat in the eggs. Sift the soda and spices into the flour and add to the pan. Mix all together. Add the raisins and ginger and finally the milk to make a thin consistency. Pour into the tin and scatter over the flaked almonds. Bake for about 1 hour till springy when touched.

*Lucky = guidwife, Fykie = fussy, fastidious

*Dark Gingerbread*

8 fl oz/250 ml buttermilk or fresh milk soured with the juice of a lemon

6 oz/175 g plain or self-raising flour (1½ c)

6 oz/175 g butter

6 oz/175 g soft brown sugar

6 oz/175 g treacle

2 eggs

1 teaspoon bicarbonate of soda

1 tablespoon ground ginger

1 tablespoon ground cinnamon

1 teaspoon allspice

4 oz/125 g raisins

2 oz/50 g stem ginger, chopped

1 oz/25 g flaked almonds

# BLACK BUN

Also known as 'Rich Bun' or a 'Scotch Christmas Bun' or 'Scotch Bun'.

It originated in bakers' shops in the days when they were only allowed to make cakes for special holidays. A lump of the bread dough was set aside and fruit and spices worked in. Selkirk Bannocks originated in this way but the Rich Bun was, as the name implies, a much richer and spicier affair. So much so that it was originally enclosed in a thin casing of plain bread dough. This was later converted to pastry and the bread dough abandoned, making a heavier texture. This recipe is for the bread-dough method which has a lighter, more open texture.

## *Black Bun*

*For the dough*

2 lb/1 kg strong plain white flour (8 c)

¾ lb/350 g butter (3 sticks)

1 oz/25 g fresh yeast or 1 tablespoon dried, or 1 pkt Easy Bake

¾ pt/450 ml warm water (2 c, scant)

½ teaspoon salt

*Fruit and Spice Mix*

1½ lb/¾ kg stoned raisins

1½ lb/¾ kg currants

4 oz/125 g flaked almonds (1 c)

8 oz/250 g mixed peel (2 c)

2 teaspoons ground cloves

1 oz/25 g freshly ground cinnamon

½ oz/15 g ground ginger

3-4 tablespoons rum

1 egg yolk plus 1 teaspoon water for glaze

## For the dough

Cream the yeast and add water. Mix the dried yeast with the water to reconstitute. Add the Easy Bake with the dry ingredients. Sieve the flour and salt and rub in the butter. Mix in the yeast mixture and water and knead to smooth pliable dough adding more warm water if necessary. Cover and set to rise in a warm place till doubled in size.

## Fruit and Spice Mix

Many permutations exist and it is worthwhile experimenting with flavours. Rum or brandy were used in old recipes. With rum I use more cinnamon; with brandy more allspice. Freshly ground spices will give a better flavour.

Pre-heat the oven to 350F/180C/Gas 4.

Line a 12-in round cake tin with greaseproof paper.

Knock down the dough. Divide into ⅓ and ⅔ pieces. Mix fruit spices well together and then sprinkle rum or brandy over fruit; mix thoroughly. Now work fruit and spices into larger piece of dough. This is done most easily on a flat surface rather than in a bowl since you really have to knead the fruit in; not difficult, since the fruit sticks easily to the dough.

When well mixed in, roll out the smaller piece to a large round a few inches larger than the bun. Place the bun in the centre and bring up the sides to meet in the centre at the top. Bring all the edges together and mould evenly round the bun.

Turn over on the join and put into a lined cake tin. Leave to prove in a warm place for 30 minutes when it should have risen by about a third. Prick all over with a long skewer right through to the bottom of the bun, brush with glaze and bake for about 2 hours. Cover the top if it is browning too much.

# SELKIRK BANNOCK

This rich yeasted bannock is shaped like a round cob loaf, generously filled with sultanas and raisins, and sold in bakers' shops in the Borders in small and large sizes. When Queen Victoria visited Sir Walter Scott's granddaughter at Abbotsford she is said to have refused all else with her tea but a slice of the Bannock.

Pre-heat the oven to 425F/220C/Gas 7: bake for 15-20 minutes. Reduce to 375F/190C/Gas 5: bake for 20-30 minutes.

## To make the dough

Sift the flour into a bowl and warm slightly. Meanwhile, either cream the fresh yeast, or reconstitute the dried yeast with a little of the measured milk. Mix the Easy Bake into the dry ingredients. Melt the butter and lard and add to the milk; add the sugar and stir to dissolve. Leave to cool until just lukewarm. Make a well in the centre of the flour and add the milk and yeast. Mix to a fairly soft but not sticky dough. Add more milk or flour as necessary. Knead till smooth and silky and till it comes away easily from your hands. Return to the bowl, cover with a damp cloth and leave to rise till double in size.

## Knocking down/Adding fruit

Turn out the dough onto a floured surface and knead in the fruit. Shape into four small or two large buns. Place on a greased baking tray, cover with some lightly oiled cling film, and leave in a warm place till they have doubled in size. Brush with egg glaze and put in a hot oven for 15-20 minutes then reduce the heat and bake for another 20-30 minutes. Test by sounding one with your knuckles on the base; it should sound hollow. (Large ones will take longer.)

# FRENCH TOASTS WITH RUM

**6 toasts**

Beat the eggs, milk, sugar and rum. Soak the bread. Heat the oil and butter and fry the bread on both sides. Sprinkle with cinnamon sugar and serve.

*Selkirk Bannock*

2 lb/1 kg strong plain flour

1 oz/50 g fresh yeast or 1 tablespoon dried or 1 pkt Easy Bake

4 oz/125 g butter (1 stick)

4 oz/125 g lard

¾ pt/450 ml milk (2 c, scant)

8 oz/250 g sugar (1¼ c)

1 lb/500 g sultanas or raisins or a mixture of the two

1 teaspoon salt

1 egg yolk plus 1 teaspoon water for glazing

*French Toasts with Rum*

6 slices of week-old rich bread such as Selkirk Bannock

3 eggs, beaten

1 cup milk

1 oz/25 g sugar

4 fl oz/125 ml rum

2 oz/50 g butter

2 tablespoons oil

1 tablespoon sugar, mixed with 1 teaspoon cinnamon

*Ecclefechan Butter Tart*

2 oz/50 g melted butter

3 oz/75 g soft brown sugar

1 egg

1 desertspoon apple cider
vinegar

4 oz/125 g mixed dried fruits

1 oz/50 g chopped walnuts

*A Rich Almond Tart*

4 oz/125g ground almonds

1 oz/25 g butter, softened

2 medium eggs

2 oz/50 g caster sugar

2 tablespoons brandy

3 oz/75 g whipping cream

Dusting of freshly ground
cinnamon for the top

## ECCLEFECHAN BUTTER TART

Prepare an 8-in flan, lined with pastry (see p.55).

Preheat the oven to 350F/180C/Gas 4.

Mix all the ingredients together and pour into the lined tin. Bake for 30 minutes and serve hot or cold with whipped cream.

## A RICH ALMOND TART
### (Mrs McLintock, 1736)

Preheat the oven to 350F/180C/Gas 4.

Mix all the ingredients in a bowl and mix until smooth. Pour into the lined flan tin and dust the top with the cinnamon. Bake for 30 minutes until risen and firm and serve hot or cold with cream.

# Easy-to-make Rich Cakes

These are a late-twentieth-century development, which are made using very quick and easy-mix methods, abandoning the old and more time-consuming method of creaming butter and sugar. This breakthrough for home bakers has been made possible by the recent availability of special cake flours, once only available to professional bakers.

They are variously described as 'ideal for cakes and scones', 'light', 'supreme sponge', and 'extra fine'. What they all achieve is a higher rise and finer texture than standard plain or self-raising flour.

The main reason for their success is a very high starch content, which is required to emulsify the butter and eggs and make a tender crumb. They are low in gluten which toughens a cake. They have also been well sifted and aerated, so that they are much easier and quicker to sieve and mix in than standard flours. The reason for their easy mixing and smooth finished texture is that they have been selected from the finest grade of flour particles which are finer and more even than other flours. They may have been heat-treated to modify the gluten content.

Self-raising (SR) or plain? Always self-raising for quick-and-easy cakes, but do not use SR flour which has been stored too long or the raising qualities may be less efficient. Where there is a high percentage of eggs and the beating incorporates a lot of air, as in the Dundee cake, fine plain cake flour gives a finer texture while SR makes it more open. This is a matter of taste.

# SECRETS OF SUCCESSFUL CAKE BAKING

This depends on getting the correct balance of strengthening and tenderising ingredients.

While flour and eggs contain the proteins which strengthen the cake, sugar, butter and liquids soften and tenderise it. If the proportion of flour and eggs is too high, the cake texture will be too dry and tough, if it is too low, the cake will not hold its shape, collapsing in the oven or as it cools. Because this balance is easily disturbed, it is important in cakemaking to follow recipes precisely.

# BASIC EASY-CREAM METHOD

Put the cake flour and caster sugar into a bowl and mix with an electric beater for 60 seconds. This brings the flour and sugar particles together more intimately so that the sugar crystals puncture the flour particles allowing more liquid to be absorbed more quickly.

Add three-quarters of the eggs/liquid along with the butter which has been softened and beat for about 60 seconds until it comes creamy and light. This is when the strength of the cake is developed. Add the remaining liquid and beat in. This method also works with spreadable margarine, though the finished flavour lacks the depth of butteriness. Margarine may also contain a higher percentage of water than pure butter, which will disturb the balance and may cause a sinking cake.

## DUNDEE CAKE

Whole almonds cover the surface of this cake before it is baked, roasting gently to a golden brown during the baking, giving the cake its distinctive appearance, while also dispensing with the need for icings. The flavourings are sultanas and candied orange peel. This is the cake that was first made in Keillers marmalade and confectionery factory in the late nineteenth century as the seasons changed and production lines turned from marmalades and jams to festive baking. Using the Seville orange peel from the marmalade process, and employing all their high-quality principles of production they made this outstanding cake which eventually took on the name of the town. While its fame spread, commercial bakers elsewhere changed and altered the Keiller original. Currant, raisins, cherries,

## *Dundee Cake*

10 oz/300 g plain or SR cake flour (see note on flours)

8 oz/250 g caster sugar

8 oz/250 g butter

5 eggs, large

3 tablespoons milk

1 lb/500 g sultanas

2 oz/50 g orange peel

2 oz/50 g whole blanched almonds for the top (½ c)

lemon peel and flaked, instead of whole almonds, were put on top of 'Dundee' cakes around the country. Then the Keiller family lost control of the company and today it no longer exists. But the unique cake which they invented lives on. This is it in its original form as Dundonians of the Keiller era remember it.

Pre-heat the oven to 350F/180C/Gas 4.

Use a 7-in (18-cm) round cake tin, lined.

### To bake

Follow the Easy-Cream method (see p.207): flour beaten with sugar, then butter, three-quarters of the eggs added with the butter. Beat till creamy. Add remaining eggs/milk. Finally mix in the sultanas and orange peel. It shoud be a soft, dropping consistency. Turn into a lined tin. Level the top and cover with whole almonds. Bake till lightly browned on top and until a skewer inserted into the centre of the cake comes out cleanly. About 1-1½ hours.

## 'A CAKE WITH APPLES IN IT'

This was made in the autumn to use up excess fruit: clearly a very popular cake, it was mentioned frequently in Grisell Baillie's *Household Book (1692-1733)*. Perhaps they also used other fruits in season. Pears and plums would work equally well in a cake mixture. For another version made with a scone mix, see Apple Scone (p.197).

The apples are the decoration in this cake. They are cut so that they fan open during cooking giving a pleasing effect on top. This is a simple apples-and-sponge combination, as in the classic Eve's Pudding.

Pre-heat the oven to 350F/180C/Gas 4.

Use a 9/10-in (23/25-cm) cake tin, greased and lined.

### Making the sponge and Finishing

Follow the Basic Easy-Cream Method (see p.207): flour beaten with sugar for 60 seconds. Then butter and three-quarters of the eggs/liquid added. Beat for 60 seconds. Add remaining liquid and beat for another 60 seconds. Pour into the tin, level the top.

## *'A Cake with Apples in It'*

*Easy-Cream Sponge Cake mix*

7 oz/200g SR cake flour (1¾ c)

6 oz/175 g caster sugar (1 c)

6 oz/175 g butter (1½ sticks)

3 large eggs, beaten with 1 tablespoon milk

*Flavourings*

4-5 well-flavoured eating apples

1 tablespoon melted butter for brushing

1 tablespoon caster sugar mixed with 1 heaped teaspoon ground cinnamon

### Preparing the apples

Peel and cut in half. Scoop out the core then turn onto cut side and make about 4-5 incisions, almost, but not quite, through the apple, cutting from north to south pole rather than round the equator.

Lay apples on top of sponge. Do not press in. Brush liberally with the melted butter and coat the whole surface with cinnamon sugar. Bake for

¾-1 hour. Serve warm as a pudding, then use later as a cake.

It will keep for a few days.

## MINCEMEAT SANDWICH CAKE

A sandwich cake of contrasting textures—velvety sponge base, mincemeat middle and crunchy oat top—its charm lies, not just in its flavours and textures, but also in the fact that it needs no fancy adornment save a dust of icing sugar.

Pre-heat the oven to 350F/150C/Gas 4.

Line an 8/9-in (20/23-cm) cake tin with removable base.

Make the sponge and put into the tin. Level the top and spread on mincemeat. Put all the ingredients for the topping into the food processor and pulse until it forms fine crumbs. Sprinkle on top of the mincemeat. Bake for 1 hour or until a skewer comes out clean.

Remove the sides of the cake tin, dust with icing sugar, and serve hot or cold with whipped cream.

## MAPLE SYRUP CAKE

A simple, but stunning, flavour combination which is something akin to an old-fashioned steamed pudding as the cake is turned out upside-down needing no other adornment save the syrupy topping. I have tried it with golden syrup, but to my mind this makes it too sweet. Also, the depth of flavour which you get from maple syrup is lost. It can be served for breakfast with crisp, fried bacon.

Pre-heat the oven to 350F/180C/Gas 4.

Prepare a 7/8-in (19/20-cm) round soufflé or earthenware ovenproof dish, greased.

### To bake

Put the maple syrup into a pan and heat to just below boiling. Keep warm. Make Easy-Cream Sponge (see p.207): flour and sugar beaten for 60 seconds. Then add butter and three-quarters of the liquid, beat for 60 seconds. Finally beat in the remaining liquid, beat for 60 seconds.

Pour hot maple syrup into the dish. Cover evenly with spoonfuls of the cake mixture. Bake for 45-50 minutes or until a skewer inserted in the centre comes out clean. Remove from the oven and invert onto a serving dish. If some of the syrup has stuck to the base, scrape off and spread on top of cake. Serve warm.

*Mincemeat Sandwich Cake*

**Easy-Cream Sponge Cake mix from 'A Cake with Apples in It' (see p.208)**

**Mincemeat layer**

**412g jar mincemeat**

**Crunchy oat top**

**3 oz/75 g soft brown sugar**

**4 oz/125 g buttered oats (see p.22) or use a 'crunchy' oat cereal**

**3 teaspoons freshly ground cinnamon**

**2 oz/50 g fine plain flour**

**2 oz/50 g butter, chopped roughly**

**Icing sugar for dusting**

*Maple Syrup Cake*

**8 fl oz/250 ml maple syrup**

**4 oz/125 g SR cake flour**

**4 oz/125 g caster sugar**

**4 oz/125g butter, softened**

**2 medium eggs beaten with 2 tablespoons milk**

## CHOCOLATE DROP CAKE

*Chocolate Drop Cake*

1 oz/25 g cocoa powder

4 tablespoons boiling water

3 eggs

4 oz/125 g SR cake flour

5 oz/150 g caster sugar

5 oz/150 g butter, softened

1 x 175 g pkt white chocolate drops

2 teaspoons vanilla extract

This is made in a loaf tin and has a deeply chocolate flavour; it is speckled with white chocolate drops, so that there is no need for icings etc. Mixing cocoa powder with hot water releases more of the chocolate flavour which will depend, of course, on the quality of cocoa powder. Some are better than others since cocoa beans are not born equal. Usually, but not always, the most expensive are the best. Experiment to compare the quality of chocolate flavour.

Pre-heat the oven to 350F/180C/Gas 4.

Line or grease and flour a 1 lb (500 g) loaf tin.

### To bake

Add the boiling water to the cocoa powder and mix until smooth. Beat in the eggs. Follow the Easy-Cream Method (see p.207): flour and sugar beaten for 60 seconds. Then butter and three-quarters of the eggs/chocolate mix added, beat for 60 seconds. Add remainder and beat another 60 seconds. Mix in the chocolate drops and vanilla. Pour into a prepared tin and bake for 50-60 minutes or until a skewer comes out clean. Cool in the tin for 10 minutes then turn out onto a rack. Dust lightly with icing sugar.

## SEVILLE ORANGE CHOCOLATE CAKE

*Seville Orange Chocolate Cake*

3 oz/75 g SR cake flour

3 oz/75 g fine cake plain flour

1 teaspoon bicarbonate of soda

2 oz/50 g ground almonds

2 Seville oranges (or sweet) zest and juice

4 oz/125 g caster sugar

3 oz/75 g butter, softened

2 eggs

5 fl oz/142 ml carton soured cream

*Orange Syrup:*

2 tablespoons caster sugar mixed with the orange juice

The theory behind this cake is more complicated than for the other Easy-Cream cakes since it makes use of a chemical combination more common in soda breads i.e. an acid-alkali mix which provides a special soft, velvety denseness. The acid in the sour cream and the orange juice also balances the richness of the other ingredients, making a unique cake which is hugely satisfying.

Preheat the oven to 350F/180C/Gas 4.

Line or grease and flour a 7-in (19-cm) round tin or deep metal ring mould.

### To bake

Follow the Basic Easy-Cream method (see p.207). Put into a bowl: both flours sifted with the bicarbonate of soda. Add the almonds, orange zest, caster sugar and beat for 60 seconds. Add the butter, eggs and soured cream. Beat for another 60 seconds. Stir in the chocolate drops. Put into the tin and bake for 50-60 minutes. Test with a skewer which should come out clean.

Make up the orange syrup and pour over the cake while still warm.

# Biscuits

## To eat with sweets and puddings or serve with tea

*...The drop biscuits and almond biscuits that so often appeared heaped high between dishes of jelly, cream and syllabub on the dinner table, at dessert, might also be offered at tea.*

Marion Lochhead,
*The Scots Household in the Eighteenth Century*, 1948.

## ALMOND BISCUITS

These plump little almond-flavoured balls are more of a confection than a biscuit. They are rolled in icing sugar and can be made with other nuts such as walnuts and pecans.

Mix all the ingredients together in a large bowl.

Pre-heat the oven to 350F/180C/Gas 4.

### To bake

Knead all the ingredients into a smooth, firm paste and roll into small balls the size of a walnut. Place on a greased baking sheet about 1 in (2½ cm) apart. Bake for 15 minutes. They should not brown. Roll in icing sugar when almost cool.

*Almond Biscuits*

½ lb/250 g plain flour (2 c)

4 oz/125 g granulated sugar (½ c generous)

½ teaspoon salt

½ lb/250 g butter (2 sticks)

2 teaspoons vanilla essence

½ lb/250 g finely chopped flaked almonds (2 c)

## BROKEN-BISCUIT CAKE

A popular no-bake cake which we made as children with a bag of cheap broken biscuits from the grocers, in the days when biscuits were sold loose from tins.

### To make

Melt together the chocolate and butter.

Add the broken biscuits, nuts and vanilla essence.

Pour into a baking tin, 10 x 15 in (25 x 37 cm), lined with greaseproof paper, level on top and cover with a weight. Leave to set overnight. Cut in slices. It can also be made into a loaf shape, poured into a lined loaf tin (1 x 2 lb/1 kg or 2 x 1 lb/½ kg), covered and pressed overnight till set.

*Broken-Biscuit Cake*

1 lb/500 g good plain chocolate

1 lb/500 g butter (4 sticks)

1 lb/500 g broken biscuits, any kind

½ lb/250 g chopped, mixed, toasted nuts (4 c)

1 teaspoon vanilla essence

## OTHER BAKING SPECIALITIES—ABERDEEN ROWIE, ABERNETHY BISCUIT, BORDER TART, CUMNOCK TART, GLASGOW ROLL, KIRRIEMUIR GINGERBREAD, PARKIN, SOFTIE, SQUARE LOAF AND WATER BISCUIT

**Aberdeen Rowie or Butterie**: A handmade roll (rowie), it is a roundish, high-fat, crisp, misshapen roll about half an inch thick. In and around Aberdeen they tend to be much crisper and saltier than they are elsewhere where they become more 'bready' than crisp. They are thought to have been made originally for fishermen as a long-keeping roll. An East Coast product seldom made on the West Coast.

**Abernethy Biscuit**: Pale-golden, shortbread-type biscuit, pricked on top, which contains less butter and sugar. Its name comes, not from the town of Abernethy, but from a Scots surgeon John Abernethy (1764-1831) who suggested the recipe to his local baker.

**Border Tart**: Variants are Eyemouth Tart and Ecclefechan Butter Tart. A shortcrust pastry flan is filled with a mixture of dried fruit, sugar, melted butter and egg. When baked it is usually coated with white water icing.

**Cumnock Tart**: A regional and sweet variation of the Scotch pie which is made with apples or rhubarb. It was originally made by an Ayrshire baker, Mr Stoddart, around 1920 and is presently made by Hugh Bradford of Glasgow, whose father was apprenticed to Mr Stoddart. It is a hand-crafted, oval, double-crust individual tart with a sugary browned surface and lightly burnt edges and they make about 800 a week.

**Glasgow Roll**: A morning roll with a hard outer surface with a light and very open, well aerated texture inside. Sometimes described as a 'chewy' roll. Specially designed as a roll for hot fillings with its hard crust and airy centre, the traditional filling was bacon and egg. It is made with a high-gluten flour and is entirely hand-crafted. The largest bakery in Glasgow makes 300,000 a night.

**Kirriemuir Gingerbread**: This was first made by Walter Burnett in Kirriemuir who sold his recipe to a large plant baker in East Kilbridge near Glasgow in the 1940s. It was made in this bakery until 1977 when the recipe was sold again to Bell's of Shotts who continue to make it. It is a light-textured, dumpling-type gingerbread which is sweetly malted and lightly spiced.

**Parkin**: Also known as 'perkin'. The recipes vary according to the baker, but they range from thick, biscuity cakes to thin, hard biscuits. They are a light, ginger-brown, with a sweet ginger flavour and most have some oatmeal added.

**Softie**: This is the description for a round bun on the East Coast, the name used to distinguish it from a hard, crisp 'rowie'. It contains double the amount of sugar in a plain bap.

**Square Loaf**: A loaf specially designed for making 'pieces', sandwiches which fit into a square lunch box. It is also known as a 'plain' loaf (distinguished from a 'pan' loaf which used to be considered a posher version, since it was made in a tin, and became used as a description for those who had aspirations above their station). It is also known as 'batch bread': a system of baking bread when the loaves are tightly packed on a tray and rise upwards rather than outwards which gives them their tall shape. It is the half slice which is square.

**Water Biscuit**: A thick circular biscuit which is made in Orkney, they are irregular cream to pale golden, blistered in places with gold-brown bubbles and docked with small holes. They  have a rich, nutty flavour and are extremely crisp with a flaky texture. Developed from the ship's biscuit, they were originally used as bread substitutes in remote areas.

# Sweeties

*The ecstasy of acquiring a 'Sugar hert' a handful of 'Curly Murlies' or a bottle of 'Treacle Ale' and a slab of 'Gingerbread' is impossible to describe.*
  G.M. Martin
  *Dundee Worthies*, 1934

Sugar hearts were, as you might imagine, fondant shapes, but the Curly Murlies were a more specialised Angus delicacy. They are described by Martin as 'mixed sweets of various shapes and sizes of the texture of

213

pandrops although the Curly Murlie proper had a rather gnarled exterior. They were formed on a seed or other foundation such as a carvie [caraway], clove or almond. The nucleus of the Curlie Murlie proper was probably aniseed. It was about the size of a large pea. These sweets were popular on feeding-market days when Jock was expected to give Jenny her "market" in the form of a pockie of market sweeties or Curlie Murlies.' (Murl means a crumb or fragment and pockie a paper bag.)

# BASIC SUGAR BOILING PROCESS

This can be done easily without professional equipment such as a sugar thermometer since the practical test of putting a few drops of the boiling sugar into a cup of cold water will tell you exactly what stage the sugar is at. If the result is a little past the desired stage, remove the pan from the heat, add a little warm water to lower the temperature and continue.

Dissolve the sugar over a low heat in the liquid, stirring with a wooden spoon until no particles of sugar are left. To test—examine the back of the spoon for any sugar crystals. Brush the sides of the pan with water to remove any crystals.

When all is dissolved, bring gradually to the boil and simmer gently till required stage is reached.

*Basic Sugar Boiling*

**1 lb/500 g granulated sugar (2¼ c)**

**½ pt/300 ml water (1¼ c)**

**Pinch of cream of tartar to prevent granulation**

## Stages in Sugar Boiling

**Smooth/Transparent Icing** (108C) for crystallising purposes and fondant. The mixture begins to look syrupy. To test, dip finger in water and then very quickly into the syrup, the thumb will slide smoothly over the fingers, but the sugar will cling.

**Soft ball** (115C) for soft caramel, candy, fudge and tablet. To test, drop a little syrup into cold water and leave for a few moments. Pick up between the finger and thumb when it should roll into a small soft ball.

**Firm or hard ball** (121C) for caramels, marshmallows, nougat, Edinburgh Rock and soft toffee. Test as above when the syrup should roll into a hard ball.

**Small crack** (138C) for toffees and rock. Test as above, when the thread of syrup should break lightly.

**Hard crack** (154C) for hard toffees, boiled sweeties and drops, pulled sugar and rock. Test as above, when the thread of syrup should break sharply.

**Caramel** (160C upwards). When the syrup begins to discolour, turning a darker brown colour, caramel stage is reached. If it is allowed to become too dark, the taste will be bitter.

# TABLET

'Taiblet for the bairns,' says Lady Grisell Baillie in her shopping list (*circa* 1692-1733).

Slightly harder than fudge, but not chewy like toffee, tablet has a slight 'bite' to it. In its plain form it has a special flavour to it which comes from boiling sugar and milk together. Its early versions were medicinal, carrying plant remedies (see p.187) though now it has many other flavourings added. The earliest Scots recipe, in Mrs McLintock (*circa* 1736), is flavoured with oranges, which at that time were taken as a medicine, but make a superbly flavoured tablet.

## Basic recipe

Follow the basic sugar-boiling process till soft-ball stage is reached. Keep stirring throughout since this rich mixture will burn easily. Remove from the heat, place the pan on a cool surface and beat for a few minutes. Pour into a greased tin and mark just before setting.

## Flavourings and colourings

Orange—Add **¼ pt/150 ml fresh orange juice** instead of water and before pouring, mix in the **orange zest**.

Vanilla and Walnut—mix in **2-3 drops of vanilla essence** and **2 oz/ 50 g finely chopped walnuts (½ c)** when the sugar is removed from the heat.

Coffee and Walnut—Add **¾ oz/20 g instant coffee powder** and **2 oz/50 g finely chopped walnuts** before pouring.

Cinnamon—Add **1 teaspoon cinnamon oil** before pouring.

Ginger—Add **2 oz/50 g chopped preserved ginger** before pouring.

Peppermint—Add **2-3 drops of peppermint oil** before pouring.

Fruit and Nut—Add **2 oz/50 g finely chopped nuts (½ c)** and **2 oz/ 50 g seedless raisins (½ c generous)** before pouring.

*Tablet*

**2 lb/1 kg granulated sugar**

**4 oz/125 g unsalted butter (½ stick)**

**1 tin condensed milk**

**¼ pt/150 ml water (¾ c generous)**

# TOFFY FOR COUGHS

Melt the butter and treacle together in a pan, stir and add the sugar. Increase the heat gradually until it bubbles. Keep stirring all the time to dissolve the sugar. Test in a cup of cold water. When it forms a firm ball, remove from the heat and add the lemon and ginger. Pour out very thinly into a buttered baking tin. Crack into pieces when cold. Store in an airtight tin.

From *The Cookery Book of Lady Clark of Tillypronie*, 1909.

*Toffy for Coughs*

**4 oz/125 g butter**

**4 oz/125 g black treacle**

**1 lb/500 g granulated sugar**

**1 teaspoon ground ginger**

**1 teaspoon grated lemon zest**

# Traditional Scottish Sweeties Past and Present

**Almond Cake**: a rich, buttery, toffee mixture, poured into a tin which has a thick layer of flaked almonds on the base. A version of this is made in Orkney.

**Barley Sugar**: usually made into a twisted stick of hard rock, flavoured with barley water and liquorice.

**Berwick Cockles**: peppermint flavoured boilings, white with pink strips and shaped like the cockle shells which used to be fished up near Tweedmouth harbour. Sold in tins.

**Bon-Bons**: strips of candied lemon or orange peel which are dipped into barley sugar.

**Black Man**: treacle toffee. Also known as **Treacle Gundy**.

**Black Striped Balls**: black and white striped balls of hard toffee with a strong peppermint flavour.

**Butterscotch**: a hard boiling with a buttery flavour. Made as a quality sweetie by Keillers in Dundee, shaped into a rectangular shape and wrapped in silver foil with a dent in the middle where it broke into two pieces. Packaged in cigarette-sized packets.

**Cheugh Jeans**: chewy (cheugh) toffee which was made in different flavours—clove, cinnamon, peppermint, ginger or chocolate.

**Coltart's Candy**: pronounced Coolter, and made famous by the song which the sweetie man sang as he travelled round the country selling his wares. The candy was aniseed flavoured but the recipe and the custom were lost when Coltart died, greatly lamented, in 1890.

**Claggum** or **Clack**: made with treacle and water, boiled till the soft-ball stage and then pulled into long sticks of rock.

**Curly Andra**: a white coral-like sweet with a coriander seed in the centre. The name comes from the Scots corruption of coriander which is 'curryander'.

**Curlie Murlies** also known as **Curly Doddies**: see p.213.

**Edinburgh Rock**: not the customary solid stick with letters down the centre, but a light, pastel-coloured, sugary confection, delicately flavoured. It was discovered by accident when Alexander Fergusson, popularly known as Sweetie Sandy, came across a piece of confectionery which he had overlooked and left lying for several months. He became one of Edinburgh's most successful confectioners in the nineteenth century and the rock is now exported all over the world.

**Glessie**: 'But the glessy! Who that ever tasted it can forget the stick of sheeny, golden rock, which stretched while you were eating it to gossamer threads of silver glistening like cobwebs in the sun.' *Scots Magazine*, 1925.

**Gundy**: toffee, also an aniseed or cinnamon-flavoured hard boiling.

**Hawick Balls**: cinnamon-flavoured hard toffee with a subtle hint of mint.

**Helensburgh Toffee**: more of a fudge than a toffee, it has a rich, creamy flavour which comes from the use of condensed milk.

**Horehound Boilings**: well-loved by Dundonian jute workers who sucked them to relieve their dry throats from jute dust in the factories. Still a popular sore-throat boiling.

**Jeddart Snails**: dark-brown toffees, mildly peppermint flavoured. The name and shape were given to them by a French prisoner-of-war from Napoleon's army who made them for a Jedburgh baker.

**Lettered Rock**: long sticks of hard rock with a strong peppermint flavour, bright pink on the outside, white in the middle with red letters down the middle spelling the name of the appropriate town.

**Mealie Candy**: a hard boiling flavoured with treacle and ginger and with oatmeal added.

**Moffat Toffee**: a hard toffee, amber and gold striped with a sherbet-like tangy centre. It is now made commercially by a local Moffat family who have been making toffee for generations. One of its early names was **Moffat Whirlies**. The Moffat Toffee shop in the town is Mecca for sweetie lovers.

**Oddfellows**: soft lozenges which are made in delicate colours and aromatic flavours such as cinnamon, clove and rose geranium. Made commercially by confectioners in Wishaw.

**Pan Drops**: mint imperials, or Granny Sookers. The sweetie your granny slipped you in church for the minister's sermon.

**Soor Plooms**: originated in the Borders where they were made to celebrate an incident in local history when a band of English marauders were surprised and overcome while eating unripe plums. They are round, bright-green balls with an acid astringent tang.

**Starrie Rock**: available from the Star Rock shop in the Roods in Kirriemuir, Angus. It was made originally by a stone mason who was blinded in 1833. The sticks are short and thin, slightly chewy and with a delectable buttery flavour. (They also continue to make excellent horehound boilings.)

**Sugar-ally-water**: liquorice water. Hard block liquorice is mixed with water in a lemonade bottle and shaken until it dissolves.

**Sugar-bools**: small round sugar plums like marbles.

**Sugar-hearts**: pink, heart-shaped fondants.

# Preserves

*For fifteen shillings a quarter Mrs McIver taught cookery, preserving and pickling. In her earlier...days she sold preserved cherries and raspberries, and also 'plumb-cake'.*
Alexander Law
*Education in Edinburgh in the Eighteenth Century*, 1965

## MARMALADE

To his delight Henry VIII was given a 'box of Marmalade' as a present in 1524. It was a box of preserved quinces, however, which so pleased the greedy Henry, and not marmalade as we know it today. The first mention of this confection is in port records at the end of the fifteenth century. The name, it seems, came from Spain and Portugal where quinces were known as 'Marmelos'. Marmalade, however, became the generic term for any kind of thick preserved fruit. Cherries, plums and apricots were popular early marmalades. The first English recipes appear in the seventeenth century (almost a century before a Scottish cookery book was published). A recipe for marmalade using oranges is given by Sir Kenelm Digby (1602-1665). He had travelled widely in Italy and Spain and had clearly developed a taste for the preserve.

The Scottish claim to marmalade history is through the Dundee Jam and Confectionery Company, Keillers. This began in a small way in the late eighteenth century with the founding husband-and-wife team, who had a grocery business in the city, seeing the potential of this bitter Seville orange in a sweet conserve. What they also recognised was the need for something a little less intense than the solid boxes of preserves which were expensive to make, as the fruit pulp was reduced in quantity as it boiled down.

What the Keillers are credited with inventing is a better marmalade recipe, in which the peel is cut into 'chips' and set in a jelly. It was this product which made the Keillers' fortune in the nineteenth century as they perfected the process and developed links with growers in Spain where they bought the best Seville oranges, aiming for the highest quality in marmalade, as they did in all their other products. The best of everything went into Keiller products and for them there were no shortcuts to quality.

Now the firm itself has become history, as the last marmalade was made in 1992. The Keiller family lost control in the closing years of the nineteenth century and though the name and the marmalade continued, it became a victim of takeover and asset-stripping by multinational confectionery companies. The Albert Museum in Dundee has a rich archive of Keiller memorabilia and the history of the family has been researched and written by W.M. Mathew in *Keiller's of Dundee* and *The Rise of the Marmalade Dynasty* (Dundee 1998).

## CHIP MARMALADE

This is an old-fashioned thick, bitter marmalade using lemon for added sharpness which includes all the bitter white pith. Alternatively, you can omit the pith and make a sweeter, more jelly-like version.

The pips are the main source of pectin (gelling material) in oranges and should be put in a bag and boiled with the rest of the oranges and sugar.

### Preparing the fruit

Wash the oranges well and put in the preserving pan. Pour over boiling water to cover.

Simmer until the fruit softens. It should take between one and two hours.

When cool, cut in half, remove the pulp with a spoon and put into a bowl. Cut up the skins into chips. Size is a personal taste. Put the pulp through a sieve. It goes through easily and you can decide at this point whether you want to put all the bitter pith through or not. Extract the pips and put into a muslin bag and tie up.

### Finishing the marmalade

Put the chips and pulp into the water the fruit was boiled in. Measure and add **1 lb/500 g preserving sugar** (2½ c) for every **1 pt/600 ml (2½ c) water**. Put into the pan with the zest and juice of the lemons.

Bring to the boil and simmer till set. Test by putting a teaspoonful on a chilled saucer and placing in the deep-freeze compartment for a few minutes to chill and give you a quick result. The surface should set and crinkle when pushed with the finger. Do not boil too vigorously while the test is being made otherwise the setting point may be missed.

Remove from the heat, skim with a slotted spoon, and leave for ten minutes to cool before potting—this prevents the chips sinking. Pour into clean hot jars.

*Chip Marmalade*

**2 lb/1 kg Seville oranges**

**2 lb/1 kg sugar (3 c)**

**2 lemons**

## Adding other flavours

Spirits or liqueurs can be added to the marmalade at this point before it is set. Leave a space at the top of the jar and add a tablespoonful to a 1 lb/500 g pot size. Stir well, cover and seal. Whisky and brandy are good, but for a flavour that really seems to heighten the sharp Seville orange flavour I find rum best. Orange-flavoured liqueurs like Drambuie and Glayva may also be used.

# FORTINGALL MARMALADE

*During the time I was the lessee of the Fortingall Hotel, about thirty-four years, we always made our own Orange Marmalade, rising at the end to a quarter of a ton every spring.*
> William Heptinstall,
> *Gourmet Recipes From a Highland Hotel*, 1967.

*Fortingall Marmalade*

4 lb/2 kg Seville oranges
Juice of 4 lemons
9 pts/4½ L water
9 lb/4½ kg preserving sugar

This is a less time-consuming recipe than the previous one since a processor is used to cut the skins and pulp. It is also a sweeter marmalade, and not so thick as the previous recipe.

## The day before

Halve the oranges and squeeze out the juice. Soak the pips in 1 pint/500 ml water (2½ c). Shred the orange skins in a food processor and soak them in the remainder of the water.

## Making the marmalade

Put the shredded peel with the water on to boil and when soft (1-2 hours) add the sugar, orange and lemon juice and the water in which the pips have been soaking. Boil to 218F/105C; test for a set. Pot, seal and cover.

# RASPBERRY OR TAYBERRY JAM

*Raspberry or Tayberry Jam*

3½ lb/1.6 kg fruit
4 lb/1.8 kg caster sugar (5 c)
4 tablespoons lemon juice
8 fl oz/250 ml liquid pectin (1 c)

The full, fresh raspberry flavour is preserved in this non-cooked jam which is thickened with liquid pectin then deep-frozen. It can be stored in the refrigerator for several weeks.

## To make

Put the fruit into a bowl with the sugar and lemon juice and stir till the sugar is dissolved. Add the pectin and mix in well. Ladle into small plastic containers. Cover with lids and put into the freezing compartment if you want to store for some time. Otherwise it can be kept in the refrigerator for several months but will not keep for more than about two weeks at room temperature.

# STRAWBERRY JAM

**Makes 5 lb**

Strawberries lack both pectin and acid so both have to be added to make the jam set. To keep the berries whole, it is necessary to use small fruit rather than large.

## To make

Put the fruit and lemon juice into a preserving pan and add the sugar. Heat gently till all the sugar is dissolved. Add the pectin and bring to the boil. Boil rapidly till the setting point is reached (see p.219 for test). Remove from the heat, skim with a slotted spoon and leave to cool for a few minutes before potting. Stir before pouring into hot jars, cover and seal.

*Strawberry Jam*

**3 lb/1½ kg strawberries**

**3 lb/1½ kg granulated sugar (2½ c)**

**8 fl oz/250 ml liquid pectin (1 c)**

**Juice of 1 lemon**

# ROWAN JELLY

An indispensable accompaniment with its sharp, astringent tang to roasts of venison and game birds. For a more intense flavour use rowans only or halve the amount of cooking apples.

## To make

Chop apples roughly and remove stalks from berries. Put into pan with just enough water to cover and bring to the boil. Simmer the fruit till soft and put into a preserving bag or muslin to drip overnight. Measure the juice and add **1 lb/500 g of sugar (2½ c)** to every **1 pt/600 ml liquid (2½ c)**. Put into the pan and bring to the boil, simmer till set (see p.219 for test). Pot, seal and cover.

*Rowan Jelly*

**2 lb/1 kg slightly under-ripe rowan berries**

**2 lb/1 kg unpeeled cooking apples**

# HERB JELLY

This apple-based jelly is usually made with mint but cinnamon is also very successful.

## To make

Place the coarsely chopped cooking apples in a pan. Just cover with water and cook till soft and pulpy. Pour into a jelly bag and drip overnight without squeezing.

Measure juice and weigh out **1 lb/500 g sugar** to each **1 pt/600 ml juice**. Stir over a low heat till the sugar is dissolved. Add the fresh herbs tied in a muslin bag, or 3-4 whole cinnamon sticks. Bring to the boil and simmer till set. Remove from the heat and allow to stand for about 5

*Herb Jelly*

**3 lb/1½ kg coarsely chopped cooking apples**

**4 oz/125 g fresh herbs or 3-4 whole cinnamon sticks**

**Water**

**Sugar**

minutes. Add one or two whole herb leaves to each of the pots once they have cooled or a 1-in piece of cinnamon. Pot, cover and seal.

# SPICED DAMSONS

*Spiced Damsons*

1 pt/600 ml full-bodied red
    wine (2½ c)

2 lb/1 kg ripe damsons

2 x 4 in (10 cm) sticks cinnamon

5 oz/150 g sugar (¾ c)

I never make enough of this remarkable preserve with its mulled wine flavour and deep crimson colour which enlivens both cold meats and roasts, particularly game.

## To make

Dissolve the sugar in the wine, add the cinnamon and bring to the boil for 1 minute. Add the damsons and simmer for 2–3 minutes or until they are just soft. Pack the damsons into jars and pour over the syrup.

# MINCEMEAT

*Mincemeat*

1 lb/500 g cooked beef (boiled
    or roast) or cooked fresh
    tongue, minced or finely
    chopped (optional)

¾ lb/350 g beef suet, finely
    chopped (3 c)

1 lb/500 g seedless raisins (1/¾ c)

1 lb/500 g sultanas (1¾ c)

1 lb/500 g currants (1¾ c)

8 oz/250 g mixed peel (2 c)

8 oz/250 g moist brown sugar
    (1½ c)

8 oz/250 g strawberry jam

1 dessertspoon salt

1 dessertspoon each—ground
    cinnamon; allspice; mace

1 grated nutmeg

½ teaspoon ground cloves

Juice and rind of 4 lemons

1 bottle sherry or sweet white
    wine

½ bottle brandy

From all accounts in early cookery books, large quantities of mincemeat were actually made using cooked meat. James Beard revives this idea in *Delights and Prejudices* (1964), using both freshly cooked tongue and boiled beef. It was late into the nineteenth century before the meat was being omitted from mincemeat—sometimes it was added when the mince pies were being made rather than in the original mix. But there is no doubt that meat adds an extra dimension to the texture and flavour. Of course it is also preserved in the high spice and alcoholic mix, so there is no danger of it spoiling. Well covered, it was often kept from one year to the next.

## For mincemeat, with or without meat

Combine together in a large earthenware crock or large pot with a lid which is not in constant use (it is easier to have the mixture in one large container to begin with). The fruit takes some time to absorb the liquid and more may have to be added while it is maturing. Once thoroughly matured it can be potted.

Cover well and keep checking once a week, add more sherry/wine/brandy if necessary. Pot, cover and seal after 1–2 months.

# MINCE PIES

Sometimes apples were added to the basic mix but usually they appeared when the mince pies were made, either mixed through the mincemeat, or arranged in layers in the pie, or simply placed on top of a mincemeat base (see recipe for Mincemeat Sandwich Cake p.209). A spoonful of sherry or claret was often added through the hole in the top as they went into the oven. They were served with 'burnt' brandy poured over as they were sent to the table, rather as we flame a Christmas pudding.

## MINCEMEAT TART

Make a 10-in x 1½-in (25-cm x 3½-cm) flan case (see p.55). Fill first with a layer of stewed apples then with mincemeat and cover the top thickly with flaked almonds. Bake in a moderate oven till the almonds are nicely toasted. Finish with some thinnish water icing laced in thin threads over the almonds. Serve warm or cold.

## APPLE CHUTNEY

The taste and aroma of this chutney depend on a subtle blending of spices, cinnamon, cloves and ginger, cooked in orange juice and cider vinegar.

Bring to the boil and simmer uncovered, stirring occasionally, for about 45-50 minutes. Cool and store.

### *Apple Chutney*

1½ lb/750 g cooking apples, coarsely chopped

1 tablespoon chopped ginger root

4 fl oz/125 ml orange juice (½ c)

1 teaspoon ground cinnamon

1 teaspoon ground cloves

1 teaspoon salt

8 fl oz/250 ml honey—to taste (1 c)

8 fl oz/250 ml cider vinegar (1 c)

## RAISIN CHUTNEY

Plump raisins cooked slowly in tomatoes blended with cinnamon and cloves make this outstandingly good chutney which combines well with a variety of cold meats and game as well as mature hard cheeses.

### To make

Melt the butter in a large wide pan and add the raisins. Sauté the raisins for a few minutes then add the tomatoes, water, cloves, cinnamon, salt and pepper. Cook uncovered for about 1 hour, stirring occasionally, till very thick.

Add the brown sugar and cider or wine vinegar.

Mix through, simmer for a few minutes. Taste for flavour. Remove cinnamon, pot, cover and seal.

### *Raisin Chutney*

2 oz/50 g butter (½ stick)

1 lb/500 g seedless raisins (2½ c)

2 x 200 g tin chopped tomatoes

½ pt/300 ml water (1¼ c)

4 whole cloves

2 sticks cinnamon bark

2 teaspoons salt

Ground black pepper to taste

5 oz/150 g brown sugar (1 c)

5 tablespoons cider or wine vinegar

## *Mrs Beeton's Plum Chutney*

3 lb/1½ kg stoned plums

2 medium onions, chopped

2 medium apples, chopped

4 tablespoons each—ground
   ginger, cinnamon, allspice

1½ tablespoons salt

1 pt/600 ml vinegar (2½ c)

¾ lb/375 g sugar (1¾ c)

## *Store Mustard*

1 x 4 oz/125 g tin Coleman's
   mustard

Same volume of double
   cream and caster sugar (i.e.
   8 fl oz/250 ml double cream
   and 9 oz/250 g caster sugar)

2 eggs

½ teaspoon potato flour

1 tablespoon acetic acid (or
   use non-brewed condiment,
   vinegar is too sharp)

## *Pickle Vinegar*

7 pts/4 L white wine vinegar

5 oz/150 g black mustard seeds

2 oz/50 g fresh ginger root

3 oz/75 g whole allspice

½ oz/15 g cloves

2 oz/50 g black peppercorns

½ oz/15 g celery seeds

1½ lb/750 g brown sugar

1¾ oz/40 g grated horseradish

1 head garlic

1½ sliced lemons

# MRS BEETON'S PLUM CHUTNEY

A highly spiced chutney which ought to be stored for at least six months to allow the flavours to mature. After two years the flavours grow and mellow with unique results.

## To make

Put all the ingredients except for the sugar into the pan and cook for half an hour.
   Add the sugar.
   Boil to the consistency of thick jam. Pot, cover and seal.

# To make a
# STORE MUSTARD

This recipe makes a lovely creamy mustard, rich and glossy with a faint sweetness which also keeps very well. It is Scandinavian in origin and is served with dill-cured salmon known as 'gravlax'.

## To make

Empty the contents of the mustard tin into a pan. Then fill up the tin with sugar, empty into the pan and then finally fill with cream and add to the pan. Add the eggs, mix in the potato flour and cook gently till it thickens. This can be done in a double boiler. When cold stir in the acetic acid and pour into pots. Cover and seal.

# PICKLE VINEGAR

The outstanding flavour of this vinegar is entirely dependent on the many spices and flavourings together with a long, slow maturing in the summer sun.

## To make

Combine all the ingredients in a large glass jar and leave in the sun all summer or at least four months. Strain and pour over parboiled or raw fruits and vegetables or use in salad dressings.

# 9
# CHEESE

*Many's the long night I have dreamed of cheese toasted mostly, and woke up again and here I were. You might not happen to have a piece of cheese about you now?*
  Robert Louis Stevenson
  *Treasure Island*, 1882

Poor Ben Gunn's first words to his rescuers, after being marooned for three years on Treasure Island, are echoed by Patrick Rance, cheese expert and author of *The Great British Cheese Book* (1982), when he says, 'If you offered me a desert island with just one kind of food, a farmhouse cheddar would be my unhesitating choice.'

Cheese is a rich area of gastronomy where passions run high. Its value in the past, however, was not just for pleasurable eating but also for its rich supply of preserved protein and its quality of portability. Much transfer of cheese went on, particularly from the Highlands to the Lowlands, in exchange for grain. Highlanders are said to have survived, at certain times of the year and during bad harvests, solely on cheese, fish and milk. The Highland cheeses were mostly of the soft variety made usually from skimmed milk and from ewes', cows' and goats' milk. They were made into a light, soft cheese with a sharp citric tang which became known as 'crowdie', also known as 'hangman cheese' or 'hangie' since the curds were tied in a cheesecloth and left to drain, usually from the branch of tree in the open air, for two or three days. To make a longer-keeping cheese, crowdie was mixed with butter and packed it into wooden barrels or stone crocks. This was called 'Crowdie Butter' and is still a well-remembered treat by the generation who ate it as children in the early decades of the twentieth century. It was kept cool in the barn and throughout the winter made a useful spread for oatcakes. 'The great treat, though, was to have crowdie mixed with fresh cream and piled on an oatcake with fresh salted butter. Then you had a royal feast of flavours—acid, sweet and salt, and, better perhaps, a royal mixture of textures, soft, crisp and crunchy,' says Wallace Lockhart in *The Scot and his Oats*, 1983.

225

'The unusual thing about crowdie,' says farmhouse cheese revivalist Susannah Stone, of Highland Fine Cheeses in Tain, 'is that it is semi-cooked. The fresh milk is soured naturally beside the stove and then "scrambled" over the heat and hung up to drip in a muslin cloth. This ancient cheese is unique to the Highlands and Islands of Scotland, and as far as we know was made nowhere else in Europe—it has special qualities. Firstly, because of the natural curding (12 hours) it has a lovely citric flavour. Rennet was not traditionally used to speed the souring. We use no rennet on our large scale, lactic cultures, and stick rigidly to the old recipe and method. Secondly, this semi-cooked cheese (believed to go back to Viking and possibly Pictish times) is very low in certain elements that are bad for kidney patients, among them potassium and sodium. Lactic or acid curd crowdie has a more refreshing, sharper flavour than rennet-started crowdie.'

While the crofter's crowdie was a short-keeping cheese made for fairly rapid consumption, other areas of the country became known for the quality of their longer-keeping cheeses. The special dairying areas of the country, where surplus cheese was bartered for other goods, included Rosshire, Caithness, Orkney and the Borders. But it was Ayrshire, Dumfries and Galloway, Arran, Bute, Kintyre and Islay which had become the major cheesemaking areas by the end of the nineteenth century. These warm, wet lowlands with their rich, heavy loam soil, most suitable for grass growing, provided the best conditions for dairy cattle and milk production. This is home to the native dairying breed of Ayrshire cows, prized for their milk, which is now being marketed commercially as 'Ayrshire Milk' to distinguish it as a milk of special quality.

Until the late seventeenth century, however, cheese had been essentially a short-keeping by-product of buttermaking, made from the skimmed milk of both cow and sheep. Then in 1690 a farmer's daughter from Ayrshire, Barbara Gilmour, returned home after fleeing to Ireland from religious persecution at the time of the Covenanters, bringing back with her a recipe for making cheese which revolutionised the old cheese methods. The new method from Ireland used full cream cow's milk, pressing the cheese until it was quite hard to improve both the keeping quality and the flavour. While the old cheese was called 'common cheese' the new one was described as 'sweet-milk cheese'. Around a century later, in the 1790 Statistical Account of Scotland, it is described as Dunlop cheese and was being made in five Ayrshire and two Lanarkshire parishes.

The rise of Dunlop manufacture to more than local significance virtually drove out all other cheeses, and the old traditional milking of ewes for cheese came to an end. It was the growth of the urban industrial markets of Central Scotland, which led to Dunlop's success as Scotland's premier cheese. By the end of the nineteenth century its recipe had been greatly improved with helpful advice coming from the Cheddar-making areas of England. Though it was now made in some larger creameries, it was still being made by single farmers in Ayrshire and the south-west in the 1930s. 'Each farm has a fully matured cheese open for cooking, and a softer one for eating,' says Patrick Rance. 'At breakfast, porridge was followed on alternate days by bacon and eggs or toasted cheese on a scone made from home-ground flour, eaten in front of the fire.'

The subsequent demise of Dunlop was due to the general decline in farmhouse cheesemaking, during and after World War II, when milk was bought in bulk by Milk Marketing Boards and taken in tanks to large creameries to make factory cheddar. Its position was further undermined when the MMB decided that their creameries should make cheddar rather than the old Dunlop. It has been admitted that one of the reasons for this was that the MMB considered it inappropriate to have a cheese named after a leading rubber tyre company of the day. Only in a few creameries did the old Dunlop survive while the tyre company no longer exists. With the late-twentieth-century revival of farmhouse cheeses, however, a new cheesemaker in Ayrshire, Ann Dorward at Dunlop Dairy, has recently started making Dunlop again with unpasteurised milk in the old way. It is distinguished from Scottish Cheddar by its mellower flavour and softer, creamier texture. Cheesemakers often describe it as a 'meatier' cheese.

## METHODS OF CHEESE PRODUCTION

Post-World War II saw a decline of traditional farmhouse cheese and an increase in block Cheddar cheese made in creameries. This now amounts to 80 per cent of cheese eaten in Scotland today. But the advantages of traditional farmhouse cheeses—clothbound, cylindrical and made from unpasteurised single-farm milk—are of flavour and texture. 'Pasteurisation eliminates 99 per cent of the worthwhile organisms, including the bacteria and esters vital to the character of cheese,' says Patrick Rance, *Good Food Guide*, 1985. Those who make cheese from unpasteurised milk make it from one farmer's milk, which means they can ensure high levels of management and hygiene. Some farmhouse cheesemakers, though not all, are also farmers with their own milking animals. Making cheese from one farm's milk provides the cheese with natural differences of locality and breed of cow, a distinction which is lost in the factory product when milk from numerous farms, covering a wide area, is mixed together in 3,000-gallon tankers.

Cheesemaking methods today are highly scientific. The cheesemaker carefully controls the process of curd-making by manipulating the recipe with lactic acid starters and bacterial cultures which will give the cheese much of its character. And yet there will always be differences in the milk caused by the breed of the milking animal, the time of year and the soil and ecology of the region. Animals feeding on fresh grass and wild clover from unspoilt meadows will produce different milk to those fed silage, turnips and straw. When they eat the fresh, young spring grasses, the milk will taste different from milk from mature autumn grass. All of which makes for a subtle, but fascinating, variety in cheese.

Moulding, pressing, coating and storing cheese also affects its flavour and quality. The clothbound, traditional cheese has the advantage of being able to breathe, mature and ripen to a fuller flavour. Vacuum-sealed, rindless blocks, however, must be kept at a lower temperature, to prevent the cheese from 'blowing' the wrap, with a consequent loss of mature flavour.

## USES/BUYING AND STORING CHEESE

*Cheese is capital in the forenoons, or the afternoons either, when you've had nae ither denner, especially wi' fresh butter and bread; but nane but gluttonous epicures wad hae recourse to it after they hae been stuffing themsels, as we hae noo been doin for the last hour, wi three coorses, forby hotch-potch and puddins.*

Christopher North
*Noctes Ambrosianae*, 1822-1825

Less gluttonous modern epicures would disagree with these remarks. But then it's all a question of the size and content of the dinner. North, and his tavern cronies, are to be found on another night ringing the bell for some toasted cheese. 'It's a gude while now sin' dinner and I'm getting roun' again into hunger.'

Cheese is one of the best stand-by foods, available at a moment's notice, it also fits into any meal. Its endless variations of texture, flavour and aroma mean that all palates can be satisfied. Buying from specialist shops allows a tasting before you buy, which means a better choice. A specialist cheese shop buys its own whole cheeses, maturing them, checking on their ripeness and selling when they reach their peak. This kind of cheese shop will provide the best cheese quality, because it is being carefully controlled. But there is time and effort involved in this, and also a moisture loss in the cheeses, which can be up to 15 per cent. For these reasons this cheese will be more expensive than others, but it will provide value in the extra flavour-punch which it contains.

While there have been attempts to distinguish cheddar, and other cheeses, according to strength, this is regarded by cheese experts as a poor way of judging. The strongest cheese is not always the best. In cheese-speak 'cleanness' is described as the level of acidity balanced against other flavours. The acidity should not be too high, but at the same time there should be enough there to provide a tang. Badly matured cheese may have a dull, muddy flavour or it might have sharpness at the first taste, but then no follow-through.

Cheese should be served at room temperature (it is best stored in cling film or waxed paper, in the vegetable compartment at the bottom of the fridge). It needs about half an hour to an hour at room temperature before serving, unwrapping just before eating and re-wrapping just after. Oatcakes with crowdie is the classic combination, but scones with Dunlop is another good partnership, also tangy farmhouse cheddar and cox's pippins. Crusty bread goes with all cheese. The French, who eat three times more cheese than the British, serve cheese immediately after the main course and before the dessert, usually with some of the main course's red full-bodied wine, when *le fromage* becomes a special course, a relaxing break for the cook, emphasising the unhurriedness of the eating occasion.

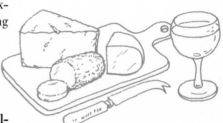

# Cheese Types

**1. Fresh-Soft Cheeses** (no visible rind or growth of mould) and **Natural-Rind** (may have a light mould) cheeses and **Whey Cheeses** (no mould).

Made from milk which has been turned into floppy curds and whey by using rennet to form the curd. Or a curd is formed naturally by the lactic acid in the milk as it sours which is the traditional method for crowdie. Such cheeses are known as Lactic Cheeses. The curds are separated from the whey by draining. For crowdie it is hung up in a muslin bag. No pressing is involved. Or it may be put into a perforated mould and allowed to drain naturally.

Another type of fresh cheese is Natural-Rind, a term which applies to fresh cheeses which have been left to drain longer and in a drier atmosphere than Fresh-Soft cheeses.

Whey cheese is made from the boiling the whey, when remaining particles of curd float to the surface and are scooped off and put into moulds to drain for a few days. The most common whey cheese is Ricotta.

## Cheesemakers and Varieties

Highland Fine Cheeses (Tain, Easter Ross): their varieties of **CROWDIE** made from pasteurised cows' milk as lactic cheeses, include: **CABOC**, a rich double cream cheese with a buttery texture, made in a small, 125 g cylinder shape, rolled in toasted pinhead oatmeal; **HRAMSA** is crowdie mixed with wild garlic and white and red pepper; **GALIC** is hramsa rolled in crumbled, flaked hazelnuts and almonds; **GRUTH DHU** (Black Crowdie) is a crowdie and cream-cheese mixture rolled in crushed peppercorns and toasted oatmeal, giving it a unique flavour. Cheesemakers: Susannah, Jamie and Rhuraidh Stone.

The Island Cheese Company (Creamery and Cheese Shop at Home Farm, Brodick, Isle of Arran): **CROTTIN** is a small round soft cheese from local goats' milk. Cheesemaker: Ian McChlery.

Loch Arthur Creamery (Camphill Village Trust Creamery and Shop, Beeswing, Dumfries): **CRANOG** is a small round, unpasteurised cows' milk cheese made plain or with herbs. Cheesemaker: Barry Graham.

Hilda Seater (Grimister, Finstown, Orkney): **GRIMISTER ORKNEY FARMHOUSE** is made throughout the summer months from unpasteurised cows' milk.

East Lairo Farm (Shapinsay, Orkney): **LAIROBELL**, semi-soft, goats' milk cheese, unpasteurised, natural-rind.

Galloway Farmhouse Cheese (Dumfries and Galloway): fresh soft **RICOTTA** cheese is made with leftover, unpasteurised whey from ewes' milk cheesemaking of **CAIRNSMORE,** which is a natural-rind cheese also available clothbound. Cheesemaker: Alan Brown.

Brenda Leddy (Garden Cottage Farm, Stitchill, Kelso): **KELSAE** is an unpasteurised, Jersey cows' milk cheese similar to a Wensleydale but a stronger, richer flavour. **STITCHILL** is from the same herd of Jersey cows but is more crumbly and less tangy.

**2. Soft-White Cheese** (with white, penicillium candidum rind).

Made with full-cream milk, the floppy curd is put into perforated moulds and the whey drains out naturally, without pressing, in an atmosphere of high humidity so that the curd does not lose too much whey. The high moisture content, plus the high humidity, encourages the growth of the mould. Maturity is usually reached in about a month. The mould spore is mostly sprayed on commercially now. The cheese is creamy and fairly mild in flavour—the texture buttery. There is a short period during which the cheeses are considered 'ripe', before they begin to start softening too much. This is a matter of taste; some like them quite runny. When they begin to smell too highly of ammonia, it is not wise to eat.

A variation of this is the **Washed-Rind** cheese (orangey-brown, sticky rind) which was brought to Scotland in the 1990s by a French cheesemaker who made them for Howgate Cheeses. They were invented by Trappist monks, the soft-white cheeses dunked into, or rubbed with, a brine and/

or alcoholic liquid when the moulds began to form. This produces a robust cheese, the sticky bacteria on the outside helping to break down the curd inside and becoming an important part of the distinctive flavour of the cheese.

## Cheesemaker and Varieties

Howgate Cheeses (Kinfauns Creamery, Perthshire): **BRIE** and **CAMEMBERT** are made from pasteurised cows' milk. **BISHOP KENNEDY** is a pasteurised, full-fat, rind-washed cheese with a strong, yeasty aroma. The rind is washed with whisky. **ST ANDREWS** is also a rind-washed cheese made from unpasteurised cows' milk.

**3. Blue Cheeses** (the rind varies from a fine bloom to thick rind, but usually they are wrapped in foil).

The blue mould, a strain of penicillium, is added to the cheeses at the beginning of the process. They are neither pressed nor cooked. The floppy curd is ladled into the moulds and left to set naturally. Turned frequently, it is the weight of the curd which presses out the whey. Once they can stand on their own they are rubbed with salt and put in a controlled atmosphere (in the case of Roquefort in underground caves) for the blue mould to develop.

## Cheesemakers and Varieties

Island Cheese Company (Arran): **BRODICK BLUE** made from pasteurised cows' milk.

Humphrey Errington (Ogscastle, Carnwath, Lanarkshire): **LANARK BLUE** is a revival—blue-veined ewes' milk cheese, unpasteurised, it is made from a Friesian-cross ewe in an area which was once noted for ewes' milk cheese. A Roquefort-style cheese. **DUNSYRE BLUE** is an unpasteurised, blue-veined cows' milk cheese made from a single herd of Ayrshire cows.

**4. Hard Cheeses** (thick-rind, often waxed, oiled or clothbound).

The curd must be cut more finely so that more whey can be extracted. It is then gently heated to force out more moisture, before the whey is drained off and the curd left to set. Then it is cut into blocks, and turned, until it reaches the correct acidity when it is cut again (cheddaring) before salting and putting into moulds. The final hardness will depending on how much pressure is put on the cheese at this point.

Hard block cheeses are produced in varying sizes of rounds, both plastic-wrapped and dipped in wax. The special plastic wrap allows the cheese to age without the development of either moulds or rind. Most of the moisture (up to 15 per cent) which would have been lost during maturation is retained making it a softer texture than traditionally clothbound matured hard cheese.

'Mild' creamery cheddar is matured for about 4-5 months while 'mature' is usually 9 months-1 year old, with some, 'extra mature', matured even longer for a stronger flavour.

Grades of cheddar include 'Choicest', which is the same as 'First Grade' but must be capable of keeping for more than one year. 'First Grade' is cheese with a clean flavour, firm body and close texture, with bright colour, no gas holes, free from mould and of a regular shape. 'Graded' is a description given when there is a slight fault, possibly weak 'body' or over-acid, which means that the cheese will not mature well and should be eaten young. 'No grade' is unsuitable for counter sale and will be used for processing.

## Farmhouse Cheesemakers and Varieties

Dunlop Dairy Products (Ayrshire): **DUNLOP** is made from unpasteurised cows' milk in both small clothbound truckles and in a large thirty-pound size similar to the original farmhouse Dunlop. **BONNET** is made from goats' milk and **SWINZIE** from ewes' milk. Cheesemaker: Ann Dorward.

Sgriob-ruadh Farm Dairy (Tobermory, Isle of Mull): **ISLE OF MULL CHEDDAR** is a long-matured, clothbound truckle made from unpasteurised cows' milk. Cheesemakers: Christine and Jeff Read.

Loch Arthur Cheeses (Dumfries and Galloway): **LOCH ARTHUR CHEDDAR** is a long-matured, clothbound truckle made from a single herd of organically reared Ayrshire cows, unpasteurised. Cheesemaker: Barry Grahame.

## Creamery Dunlops and Cheddars

While the farmhouse cheesemakers' output accounts for around 10 per cent of cheese production, the rest comes from larger-scale creameries using pasteurised milk collected from the surrounding area.

Large scale creameries incude: Stranraer, where they make **GALLO-WAY CHEDDAR**; Campbeltown, where they make **MULL OF KINTYRE CHEDDAR** and **HIGHLAND CHEDDAR**; Lockerbie, where they make **LOCKERBIE CHEDDAR**; Kirkwall on Orkney, where they make **ORKNEY MATURE CHEDDAR**, which won the Best Scottish Cheese at the 1996 British Cheese Awards; Rothesay, where they make **ISLE OF BUTE CHEDDAR**; Isle of Arran, where they make **ARRAN DUNLOP** and **CHEDDAR**; Isle of Islay, where they make **ISLAY DUNLOP**.

# TOASTED CHEESE

*'Toasted mostly'*—Ben Gunn's Dream.

The cheese of Ben Gunn's dream would have been toasted on a plate in front of the fire and left to melt slowly. The toast was made separately, on a toasting fork also in front of glowing embers, and then the runny cheese was poured over it. Often, things were mixed into the cheese, and frequently the toast was soaked in wine or beer and the dish properly described as 'Toast and Cheese'.

The Welsh can lay claim to making it a national dish. It appears that their description was entirely appropriate when they called it a 'rare bit' meaning something splendid. 'Rabbit' is a shortening of the original word and has nothing to do with the animal. The OED's definition of Welsh Rarebit is: 'A dish consisting of cheese and a little butter melted and mixed together, to which are added ale, cayenne pepper, and salt, the whole being stirred until it is creamy, and then poured over buttered toast: also simply, slices of toasted cheese laid on toast.' While Hanna Glasse has a 'Scots Rabbit' ( *The Art of Cookery made Plain and Easy*, 1747) as follows: 'Toast a piece of bread very nicely on both sides, butter it, cut a slice of cheese about as big as the bread, toast it on both sides, and lay it on the bread.' Her 'Welsh Rabbit' was similar but with mustard rubbed over the cheese while 'English Rabbit' had a glass of red wine poured over the toast before the cheese was put on top.

## JOHN THORNE'S TOASTED CHEESE

To toast cheese, you need a good knife, a long-handled fork (such as completes a barbecue set) and a fire in the fireplace that has burnt down to a nice set of coals. Sit yourself down before it with all necessary ingredients at hand: the cheese to be toasted, some paper-thin slices of onion, a pot of mustard or the butter dish, an unsliced loaf of bread and a mug of beer. Cut a thick slice from the loaf, spear it through the crust with the fork and toast on both sides over the coals. Place it on a plate, spread it with a little mustard or butter and set it in the hearth to keep warm.

Now cut a block of cheese about the size of a toothpick box (matchbox) and spear it through the one side with a fork, taking care not to let it crumble. Hold cheese over the coals, not too close, watching carefully. Turn the fork regularly, slowly, so that the heat penetrates all sides at approximately the same rate.

The surface will begin to sag as the cheese melts; twirl the fork to keep runny cheese from falling into the fire. The moment the whole piece begins to collapse, slip it onto the piece of toast, spreading it over the surface with the blade of the knife. Top with onion rings and eat when it has cooled a little, washing down with the beer.

From *Outlaw Cook*, 1994.

## CHEESE AND EGGS

*Cheese and Eggs*

8 oz/250 g grated Dunlop or mature cheddar (2 c)

1 teaspoon cornflour

4 tablespoons milk

3 eggs, beaten

Salt and pepper

Mustard to taste

**4 servings**

Originally a 'high tea', easy-and-quick dish (my granny's favourite) which was sometimes served with cauliflower. The procedure is the opposite to 'scrambled eggs and cheese' for it starts with melting the cheese with some milk then thickening this with a little cornflour and finally cooking gently with some eggs till smooth and creamy.

Dissolve the cornflour in the milk and put into a pan with the cheese. Heat very gently stirring all the time till the cheese melts.

Spoon some of the hot cheese mixture over the eggs and beat in, pour back into the pan and continue cooking, stir over a low heat till the mixture becomes thick and smooth. Taste and season, pour over buttered toast or cooked cauliflower and serve.

Note: In the *Household Book of Lady Grisell Baillie* (1692-1733) she frequently mentions 'Ramekins of Cheese' which referred to a kind of pie with a filling of cheese and eggs. The above mixture can be mixed with **8 oz/250 g cooked Finnan Haddock** (see p.52) and used to fill a prepared 7 in (18 cm) pastry flan. It sets well and can be served cold. See also Toast and Oysters (p.65).

# Milk-Related Traditions

*A dinner in the Western Isles differs very little from a dinner in England, except that in the place of tarts there are always set different preparations of milk.*

Samuel Johnson,
*Journey to the Western Isles of Scotland* (1775).

Besides the milk, buttermilk and whey, which was drunk by all classes, the Scots have a rich tradition of distinctive dishes made of milk. Travellers to Scotland, such as the good doctor above, often commented on this fact. A fuller explanation of the wide variety of these preparations, with their traditional names, is given in *The Scots Kitchen* by F. Marian

McNeill (1929). The main ones she describes, and gives recipes for, are Corstorphine Cream or Ru'glen Cream which was a buttermilk and sweet milk curd mixed, sweetened and flavoured with nutmeg and cinnamon; Oon or Frothed Whey and Bland or Sparkling Whey from Shetland. These were traditions based on a self-sufficient system of rural life where households had their own cows and were able to do things like milking the cow straight onto the buttermilk. It is true that many of these old traditions are obsolete but some will adapt and are worth preserving such as Hatted Kit (see below) which has strong similarities with the French *Coeur à la Creme*.

# HATTED KIT

## PLAIN

'Take equal parts whole milk and butter milk and place them in a small keg in a warm spot. After two or three days a thick white paste or curd rises to the top. Remove this and strain. If too thick, thin with whole milk and sweeten to taste. Best eaten as a dessert with oatcakes when preferred. Can be flavoured with whisky. This can be repeated several times by adding milk and buttermilk to the keg. Hence the name. A warm weather dish.'

Anon.

While the recipe quoted above flavours with whisky, F. Marian MacNeill suggests nutmeg and cinnamon.

Bring sweet milk almost to the boil and pour over buttermilk. Stir over the heat until the curd separates. Heat gently, it must not boil. Pour into a colander lined with a muslin and leave for 2-3 hours till most of the whey has drained off. While it is still quite soft, pour into a muslin-lined mould with holes in it, cover and leave to drain. When it has stopped dripping, turn out and serve with cream and fruit or oatcakes and bread.

## RICH

Beat together the butter and the caster or fine brown sugar.

Add the crowdie or cottage cheese, egg yolks, raisins, marmalade and almonds.

Mix all together thoroughly and pour into a lined mould, press down on top and lightly weight down overnight. Turn out and decorate with almonds and raisins. Eat as a spread for Plain Cookies or Hot Cross Buns or with a Special Yeast Cake (see p.201).

*Hatted Kit*

*Plain*

2 pt/1 L sweet whole milk

2 pt/1 L cultured buttermilk

*Hatted Kit*

*Rich*

7 oz/200 g unsalted butter (1¾ sticks)

7 oz/200 g caster or fine brown sugar (1 c)

1 lb/500 g crowdie or cottage cheese (2 c)

2 egg yolks

4 oz/100 g raisins

1 tablespoon thick bitter marmalade

1 tablespoon blanched chopped almonds

## Cheese Salad

*Cheese Salad*

2-3 handfuls of mixed salad
   greens (include pungent-
   flavoured rocket or
   watercress)

2 large tomatoes, chopped

1 sweet red pepper, chopped

½ cucumber, chopped

1 fennel bulb

8 oz/250 g semi-soft cheese
   such as Orkney farmhouse,
   cut into rough chunks

12 black olives

1 spring onion, finely chopped

Small bunch coriander leaves

3-4 tablespoons extra virgin
   olive oil

Juice of 1 lemon

Black pepper, freshly ground

# CHEESE SALAD

**4 servings**

A visually stunning platter with a pile of semi-soft cheese in the middle. The idea is to make a contrast of flavour, texture and colour. The choice of vegetables and cheese can be varied endlessly.

## Assembling the salad

In a large round earthenware dish, put the salad greens round the edge. Next, make a circle of tomatoes and red pepper, followed by the cucumber and fennel. Pile the cheese, mixed with the olives in the middle. Sprinkle over coriander and spring onion. Dribble enough oil over it to make it shine. Finally squeeze over the juice of a lemon and a few grindings of black pepper. Serve immediately.

## Cheesecake

*Cheesecake*

2 oz/50 g melted butter

6 oz/200 g digestive biscuits,
   crumbled finely

1 tablespoon muscovado sugar

8 oz/250 g crowdie or cottage
   cheese

3 medium eggs

10 fl oz/300 ml sour cream

3 oz/75 g caster sugar or
   flower honey

Juice of 1 lemon

# CHEESECAKE

This is a rich, tangy cheese mixture, set with eggs and flavoured simply with lemon.

Pre-heat the oven to 350F/180C/Gas 4.

Use a 7 in (18 cm) round springform cake tin or deep flan tin with a removable base, greased.

## To make

Mix the butter, biscuits and sugar (this can be done in a food processor) and spread in the base of the tin. Press down well. Spread flat with a spatula. Bake for 10 minutes to set it.

Combine the other ingredients in the processor, pour over the crumb base and bake for 45-50 minutes. Remove sides. Serve with fresh fruit and whipped cream.

# 10
# CULINARY
# INTERCHANGE

The late twentieth century has seen a flourishing of the ethnic restaurant in Scotland. Even as far north as the island of Lewis there are Asian restaurants run by an immigrant community. They are not only ambassadors for their distinctive cooking styles but also for the Scottish ingredients which they use daily. And they provide a fascinating supply of their authentic ingredients in Oriental supermarkets and Italian delicatessens.

Of the restaurants run by ethnic minorities, the highest percentage are Indo/Pak while Chinese come second. Mostly, they are run by men while women stay at home to look after children. Sometimes unable to communicate in English, the women can get cut off from the native community and it was to help these women integrate that International Centres were set up. The Centre in the Hillhead area of Glasgow during the 1970s and 80s was run by Stella Reekie, an ex-missionary and deaconess of the Church of Scotland. She made it open house for the women who came in the afternoons, sometimes to learn English and sometimes to cook. While they cooked their national dishes, I taught them some Scottish dishes. It was a two-way exchange which ranged the culinary globe: the speed and skill of the Indian women making chapati; the artistry of the Japanese; the correct Moroccan way to eat couscous in the desert. This chapter is dedicated to the women who were part of that group, who shared so freely and generously with their native culinary expertise. I hope some may still be making my shortbread, for I am still cooking their recipes.

*...For there is much, not only in the actual cookery but also in the Domestic Economy of our ingenious neighbours, worthy of profound attention. In the hope that the foreign graces transplanted into this volume may considerably enhance its value to the practical cook, and in the belief that a culinary system superior to either the French or the English, may be drawn from the combined excellencies of both countries.*
Meg Dods
*Cook and Housewife's Manual,*
1826

# Italians

## BIRTH OF A NEW CUISINE

Food historians credit Italy as the mother of the gastronomic renaissance, witnessed in the sixteenth century, which might never have moved out of Italy, had the fourteen-year-old Italian Caterina de Medici not married

237

the French Dauphin (later Henry II) in 1533. A special armada of ships took the Medicis from Livorno to Marseilles, where the ceremony took place officiated by the Pope. Part of the huge retinue which accompanied them were Caterina's Tuscan cooks and *gelatieri* (ice-cream makers), discovering the French court's out-of-date medieval food still being served. They set about changing the style to a culinary system which sought out the pure, unmistakable essence of each food, exalting it and presenting it with all the means suggested by nature and their experience.

It was mainly because of new plants, fruits and vegetables (particularly olives) which spread widely after the Crusades and voyages of discovery, that a new style evolved in the mild climate of North Italy. Florence was the centre of a type of Italian cooking which owed its superiority to the simplicity of internal order and the beauty of its natural appearance. It was the product of a new sense of art as well as new produce from the land. The French learnt quickly. Heavy spicing was laid aside and the mortar and pestle no longer ground ingredients to an indistinguishable pulp.

Three centuries later, migrating Italians came to Britain, many to Scotland. And while not exactly causing a renaissance, they certainly implanted many of their culinary traditions. Things like ice cream are now so well integrated that we hardly credit the Italians with bringing it to Scotland. Pasta and pizza are probably the two other Italian innovations which we eat most of today, their popularity directly related to their ability to satisfy the everyday need for fast-food.

## *O Ragu di Mama*

5 tablespoons olive oil

1 large onion, finely chopped

1 head of celery, chopped

2-3 large carrots, sliced thinly

8 oz/250 g button mushrooms

4 tablespoons tomato purée

4 x 400 g tins chopped tomatoes

1 tablespoon sugar

1 tablespoon wine vinegar

2 teaspoons sea salt

1 large head of garlic, crushed

1 tablespoon oregano

2 bay leaves

4 lb/2 kg fresh pork, preferably on the bone

Water to cover

## O RAGU DI MAMA

Eduardo di Fillipo wrote a poem of this title to celebrate the cooking women of Italy, emphasising that a *ragu* should never be described as just meat and tomato stew. It is a culinary system which provides many meals for many people, usually throughout the weekend. Friday is the shopping and cooking day, using the largest pot in the house. Saturday and Sunday there is meat—pork, meatballs and sausages—for eating with vegetables, while the constant supply of tomato sauce for pasta and pizzas means that mama can put her feet up.

### To cook

Heat the oil in a very large pot. Add the onions and cook till soft and transparent. Add celery, carrot and mushrooms and cook for about five minutes, stirring all the time. Add the tomato purée, stir in and cook for another few minutes before adding the tinned tomatoes, sugar, vinegar, salt, garlic, oregano, bay leaves and pork. Cover with water.

Bring up to a gentle simmer, cover and simmer very gently till the meat is tender, stirring occasionally. The time will depend on the cut: a shoulder joint will take longer than a prime cut of leg.

## To make the meatballs and/or sausages

Mix the mince, eggs, breadcrumbs, onion, parmesan, salt and pepper in a bowl to a stiff consistency. Roll into small balls the size of an egg. Heat the oil in a frying pan and add the meatballs and/or sausages. Fry on all sides until lightly browned. Add to the ragu. Season, add basil and serve.

*For the meatballs (optional)*

**1 lb/500 g minced beef**

**2 eggs**

**4 oz/125 g breadcrumbs**

**1 onion, finely chopped**

**2 tablespoons grated parmesan**

**2 tablespoons oil**

**1 lb/250 g fresh pork or beef sausages (preferably Italian *cotechino*)**

**Handful of fresh basil**

# French

The French-Scottish connection, which began with the Normans in the eleventh century, was consolidated when William the Lion took a French wife in 1186. The first treaty between the two countries was signed in 1295. Then a little over three hundred years later (1603) the Scottish monarch James VI went to London and the Scottish and English crowns were merged. In many ways this ended the close ties with France, though among some Scots, particularly the Highland Jacobites, the links with France continued. With the fall of the French aristocracy in 1789 many came to Scotland, and particularly influential were the talented French chefs who were welcomed by the aristocracy and upper classes.

The paradox for Scottish cooking is that though the country had important early links with the most sophisticated of European cuisines, and an influx of French chefs had created superior methods of cooking, there was also a force working against this attitude to eating for pleasure in the form of John Knox's doctrine. Regarding eating for pleasure alone as a sin, it encouraged theological extremists to take the 'sober-kail-and-brose' approach to food, reducing the Scottish diet to a frugal, joyless experience. Writing in the 1920s in *My Childhood in Scotland*, C. Miller makes it clear that this attitude survived even into the twentieth century: 'To question the taste of what one ate, or worse to question the quality, was almost as bad as studying one's face in the glass to find out whether one was pretty. As for my father, he thought that to be greedy showed weakness of character and something not to be tolerated, either in oneself or in one's children.'

Though there may not have been a wholesale acceptance of French gastronomy, nevertheless the French influence remains evident in words which have survived, such as Hogmanay which comes from the French *aguillanneuf*, a children's street cry for gifts on New Year's morning. Also from French comes ashet (*assiette*), meaning a large serving dish; dresser, meaning a kitchen sideboard, comes from the French *dressoir*; gean, meaning a wild cherry, comes from *guigne*; gigot, meaning a leg of mutton, comes from *gigot*; gout, meaning taste, comes from *gout*; grosset, meaning gooseberry, comes from *groseille*; hotch potch, meaning vegetable soup, comes from *hochepot*; howtowdie, meaning a young hen, comes from *hétoudeau*; rizzarded, meaning dried in the sun, comes from *ressoré*.

The early Alliance had a considerable effect on the Scottish soup tradition by strengthening and refining it. Henry MacKenzie (1745-1831) tells us in his *Anecdotes and Egotisms*: 'The Old English cookery was only roast and boil, the roasts very raw; blood and butter were the savage accompaniments of their cookery. Ours in Scotland was much improved by our constant communication and alliance with France. From France we got several excellent soups, such as Hodge Podge, Friers Chicken, Hare Soup, Lambs Stove, Cocky Leeky and a soup maigre called Pankail…made with greens, butter, and a small quantity of oatmeal.'

The French 'dessert' was common in Scotland by the time Mary Queen of Scots returned to Scotland in 1561. It was a more sophisticated form of service in which the table was 'disserved' after the main meal and fruits and confections were then eaten in a separate room. England did not adopt the habit till half a century later.

Drink in Scotland was also affected by its links with France and travellers frequently comment favourably on the excellent, and abundant, French claret and brandy which they enjoyed. Englishmen were surprised that the Scots did not put sugar into their wine, presumably because the French claret, which was shipped to Edinburgh, was less strong and finer flavoured than that sold in London. English wine connoisseurs regularly ordered wine from Leith. The history of this trade and links with France are explained in *Knee Deep in Claret* by Billy Kay and Cailean MacLean, 1983.

While the Alliance ties provided the country with a colourful early influence, the nineteenth-century importation of French chefs fleeing the Revolution and the upheavals that followed was an altogether different matter. '5,000 French cooks were distributed among the aristocratic houses, clubs, hotels and restaurants in Great Britain' says A. Suzanne in *La Cuisine Anglaise*, 1894. The great French masters in the kitchen—Carême (1784-1835), Francatelli (1805-1876), Soyer (1809-1858), Escoffier (1846-1935) and others established in printed form detailed information on the now classic French cuisine, while British cookery writers varied in their enthusiasm. Most, like Meg Dods (see p.262), agreed that we should welcome this culinary influence and turn it to our best advantage. Alexis Soyer, perhaps the most influential, and certainly the most colourful French personality among chefs in Britain, sums it up when he refers to the French word *sauter*—'…having found no means of translating it to my satisfaction, I see no other plan but to adopt it amongst us, and give it letters of naturalisation, not for the beauty of the word but for its utility.'

Following Soyer's advice has meant that we have now naturalised words like: purée, braise, larding, au bleu, roux, soufflé, vol-au-vent, consommé, rissole, compôte, mayonnaise, meringue and others. Whether we should also naturalise French words which have a perfectly good English translation is open to debate. 'Menu' is a more concise form than 'Bill of Fare' though there may be occasions when it is more appropriate to use the latter. A *gâteau* is a light creamy affair whereas cake has a more solid ring to it. Should a broth be called a *bouillon*; or fried bread a *croûton*? The last decade has seen a revolution in attitudes to menu French. French menu terminology is for French restaurants and those who continue to talk about their *soup du jour* are simply out of date.

## GRATIN DAUPHINOIS
### Potatoes baked in Cream

**4-6 servings**

In the Dauphiné area on the Alpine border of France, cooks developed this gratin with its golden-brown top and rich, soft potato layers underneath.

Choose firm, waxy potatoes which will hold their shape. The milk serves as the cooking liquid while the double cream poured on top browns in the oven to form the crust. Complications, such as cheese and eggs, compete with the natural cream and potato flavour.

Preheat the oven to 425F/220C/Gas 7.

### Preparing the dish

Peel potatoes and slice finely (⅛ in-3 mm). Use a mandolin if you have one. Rub the inside of a gratin dish with the cut garlic clove. Leave to dry, then butter the dish thickly. Arrange the potato slices in overlapping rows and season between each layer. The dish should be about two-thirds full. Pour in milk and put a layer of cream on top. Scatter the remaining butter in pieces on top.

### Baking

Put the dish into a hot oven to begin with. Then after 15 minutes reduce to moderate (350F/180C/Gas 4) and bake for another 45 minutes until

*Gratin Dauphinois*

**2 lb/1 kg large waxy potatoes**

**Salt and pepper**

**Grated nutmeg**

**2 oz/50 g butter (½ stick)**

**1 clove garlic (optional)**

**1 pt/600 ml milk (2 /12 c)**

**¼ pt/150 ml double cream (¾ c)**

the potatoes are soft and have absorbed all the milk and the cream has formed a golden crust on top. Serve.

# TARTE TATIN

This is the classic French method of cooking an apple tart with the pastry on top rather than underneath, then turning just before serving. It has the advantage of keeping the pastry crisp but at the same time allowing a thick, moist, syrupy layer of apples for the filling without sogging-up the pastry. It is a Sologne dish which takes its name from Mademoiselle Tatin, who first delighted her customers by this inventive method of making a tart.

*Tarte Tatin*

*Apple filling*

**2 oz/50 g unsalted butter (½ stick)**

**3 tablespoons caster sugar**

**2 lb/1 kg small eating apples**

*Pastry*

**4 oz/100 g flour (1 c)**

**2½ oz/65 g butter (½ stick generous)**

**1 tablespoon caster sugar**

**1 egg yolk**

## Apple Filling

Melt the butter in an 8 in (20 cm) round pan which will go into the oven, sprinkle with sugar and heat over a very low heat till the mixture begins to caramelise slightly. Peel and core apples and arrange side by side close together. They may be halved if large. Cook over a low heat till the apples are just soft, turning once; if halved the flat surface should be uppermost. Remove from the heat and then leave to cool.

## Pastry

Bake at 375F/190C/Gas 5.

Sift the flour onto the board and rub in the butter. Add the sugar and make a well in the centre. Drop in the egg yolk and work in the flour with your fingers till it is all incorporated and you have a smooth, firm paste—or blend together in the processor. Roll out to fit the size of the pan and lay over apples, turn in any surplus to make a double thickness around the edge. Bake 15-18 minutes till the pastry is cooked. Turn upside down onto a round dish.

Put 2 tablespoons of sugar in a pan and heat to make a very light-brown caramel in a small saucepan with 2 teaspoons water and 2 teaspoons lemon juice.

Pour the caramel, which should be soft and smooth, over the apples. Serve warm.

# English

On my first visit to London I stayed with some English relatives who thought they would make me feel more at home with a plate of porridge for breakfast. It was made with fine oatmeal, sweetened with sugar and looked like pale grey custard. 'What is it?' I asked politely.

Ham is another area of difference. The Scots use the word 'ham' for what the English call 'bacon', which in Scotland is cut in very much thinner slices—and there are lots more differences.

When the Scottish and English crowns were joined in 1603, the Scots feared that they might lose identity and made a special effort to preserve all things Scottish, including their food traditions. Of course there were differences in indigenous raw materials which meant that natural variations existed. This had made Scotland into more of a fish/oat eating country rather than a meat/bread one. Also, centuries of feuding between the two countries had built up barriers of suspicion and mutual hostility which did not encourage culinary interchange, and it was not until Sir Walter Scott set about selling Scotland to the English that a better understanding developed. But even so, Scots have borrowed least from their nearest neighbours.

Much Scottish produce was exported to English markets and the traditional Roast Beef of England was established on the strength of prime Scottish beef. Meat eating in England was synonymous with manliness in a way which was never universal in Scotland. The fictitious John Bull owed his vigour to meat, while the Marlborough wars were said to have been won by sturdy Englishmen fed on roast meats. Scots vigour, on the other hand, was attributed to a frugal fish/oatmeal diet. When Carême (1784-1835) spent a brief period working in England, he was quick to realise the contrast between England and France. 'The cattle', he says, 'are fat and of very good quality, as is the mutton, veal and lamb; the roast beef is succulent much more so than ours in France. The English housewives are all experts at this roast beef, and this, and roast veal, mutton and lamb are the mainstay of the English table.'

Eating a pudding with meat is an English tradition which goes back to before the days of potatoes, when a boiled pudding was eaten with boiled meat (Boiled Pork and Pease Pudding) or a batter pudding cooked under the spit was eaten as a prelude to the roasted meat (Roast Beef and Yorkshire Pudding). As with the English version of porridge which I had found so difficult to identify, Yorkshire friends have difficulty in recognising some of the Yorkshire Puddings served in Scotland.

When George of Hanover became George I of Great Britain in 1714, he brought with him from Germany a taste for sweet, boiled puddings

*Today our Scots porridge and barley broth and scones and orange marmalade are as popular south of the Tweed as are ham and eggs, bath buns, and Yorkshire pudding in the north. But native dishes have a habit of deteriorating on alien soil, and despite their similarity to a casual observer, the cuisines of the two countries remain, in many respects, curiously distinctive.*

F. Marian McNeill
*The Scots Kitchen*, 1929

and earned himself the title 'Pudding George'. It is said that he was responsible for introducing the 'plumb pudding' as we know it today. While it was eaten with other meats its associations with Christmas and with Roast Beef are indicated in the Norfolk *Diary of a Country Parson* by James Woodforde when he writes that on the 25th December 1782 there was 'For the poor of the Parish, Surloin of Beef Roasted, Plenty of Plumb pudding, Mince pies for the first time today.'

## ROAST ENGLISH SIRLOIN OF BEEF
### and Yorkshire Pudding

There are three types of rib roast. The sirloin end has the fillet on the inside of the bone—this is not an advantage since it will cook in a much shorter time than the meat on the outside of the bone, so should really be removed and cooked separately. Next up from the sirloin is the Wing Rib, also known as an English Cut Sirloin. On the bone it looks like a giant cutlet and is easy to carve—this would be my choice for roasting. Further up, nearer the head, are the Fore Ribs which have an excellent flavour but they also have a thick 'lip' of meat and fat on the outer edge which tends to be slightly tougher than the rest of the meat and will take longer to cook.

Boned and rolled is perhaps easier to carve, but meat gains flavour from the bone; it protects the meat during the cooking and prevents it drying out and shrinking—it does not take any longer to cook either.

The English eat more meat on the bone than the Scots. Allow about 8 oz/250 g per person on the bone.

### Preparing the meat

For a **4 lb/2 kg piece of meat** to serve about 8-10, melt some **butter** and brush the meat, especially at the ends. Lightly brown **1 tablespoon flour** in a pan and mix with **1 teaspoon freshly ground black pepper** and **1 teaspoon powdered mustard**. Rub this into the meat all over and leave at room temperature for a few hours or overnight to absorb flavours before cooking. The fat surface may be salted lightly.

### Roasting

Pre-heat the oven to 400F/200C/Gas 6.

Place the meat on a rack in a roasting tin or on a bed of roughly cut up vegetables or chopped bones. Roast, basting occasionally, for 15 minutes per pound plus 15 minutes if you like the meat red and juicy in the middle, 20 minutes per pound plus 20 minutes if you prefer it medium to rare, and 30 minutes per pound plus 30 minutes for well done.

### Resting the meat

Remove from the oven, put on heated serving dish and keep in a warm place to allow the muscles to relax before carving. Remove vegetables or bones from the roasting tin and pour off excess fat—reserve the dripping for making the pudding.

### Making the Pudding

Make up the batter in advance—at least an hour before cooking.

Sift the flour into a bowl. Add the salt and make a well in the centre. Break in the egg and add the milk. Beat to a smooth consistency.

Pour 1 tablespoon of dripping from the roasting tin into each pudding tin and put into a very hot oven, 450F/230C/Gas 8. Leave for five minutes till the fat is really hot, remove and then add the batter. Bake for 10-15 minutes till the puddings are puffed and golden.

### Making the gravy

This can be made while the puddings are cooking. Add 2 cups of water to the roasting tin. Bring to the boil and scrape up all the residue in the tin, boil to reduce and concentrate flavours, season, strain and keep hot.

### Serving

In Yorkshire I have always had the puddings first with gravy and the meat and vegetables after, though it seems that this is not standard practice throughout the country. Serve with mustard (see p.224) and horseradish sauce (grated horseradish mixed with cream).

## SUSSEX POND PUDDING

This classic English steamed pudding depends for its excellence on the contrasts of flavour and textures from bland suet pastry to rich buttery sauce, melting and fusing during the long, slow cooking whilst absorbing all the sharp tangs from the lemon hidden within. There is also the surprise element, when you cut into it, and release its delectable aroma and buttery sauce which immediately spills out to make the 'pond'.

Use a 3½ pt greased pudding basin (1¾ L).

### Pastry

Mix all the ingredients with water to make a soft dough, divide into two thirds and one third and roll out the larger piece to fit the pudding basin.

### Filling

Put a layer of half the butter and sugar in the base, lay the lemon on top

*Yorkshire Pudding*

**4 oz/125 g plain flour**

**Pinch of salt**

**1 egg**

**½ pt/300 ml milk (1¼ c)**

**Dripping**

*Sussex Pond Pudding*

*For the pastry*

**12 oz/350 g self-raising flour (3 c)**

**1 level teaspoon baking powder**

**¼ teaspoon salt**

**6 oz/175 g beef suet, finely chopped (1 c tightly packed)**

**Cold water**

*Filling*

**7 oz/200 g butter (1¾ stick)**

**7 oz/200 g demerara sugar (1¼ c)**

**1 large lemon, well washed and pricked all over with a fork**

and cover with remaining butter and sugar. Put on the pastry lid, sealing well. Cover and steam for 3 hours. Turn out onto a deep serving dish, an ashet is ideal, but make sure there is enough room on the plate for the 'pond'. Cut up the lemon and serve a piece with each serving.

# Irish

*Amongst half a dozen families in the entry there was a broth exchange. Each family made a few extra quarts and exchanged them. Each can was emptied, washed, refilled and returned. 'Did ye ever think, Jamie, how like folks are to th' broth they make?'*

*'No,' he said, 'but there's no raisin why people should sting jist because they've got nothin' but nettles in their broth!'*

*The potatoes were emptied out of their pot on the bare table, my father encircling it with his arms to prevent them from rolling off. A little pile of salt was placed beside each person, and each had a big bowl full of broth. The different kinds had lost their identity in the common pot.*

Alexander Irvine
*My Lady of the Chimney Corner*, 1966

When St Columba sailed the Irish sea and settled in Iona he was one of many to make this crossing from one Celtic country to another, so that now the Irish find themselves today as much at home in Scotland as the Scots are in Ireland. Cultural similarities apart, they both share similar food traditions which have led to broadly similar eating patterns. Cooking food in a large iron pot over a slow-burning peat fire and baking with a girdle, rather than an oven, are only two cooking methods common to both countries. Both are also oat growing and fish eating and, in addition, in the past have reared cattle more for selling than eating.

One of the main differences, however, is that the Irish were more enthusiastic about potatoes than the Scots. Original and frequent use of potatoes in their diet was the result; they made bread with potatoes (Boxty); they made cakes with potatoes (Fadge, similar to Scots Potato Scones; also Potato Cakes which are more like a Scone, as well as Pratie Oaten which was a Potato Scone with oatmeal); and they developed interesting potato and vegetable dishes like Colcannon and Champ, which are also to be found in the Scottish repertoire. They combined their most common meat with potatoes and onions to make Irish Stew, which has had many variations throughout the Western world but originally depended on a combination of only three basic flavours, potatoes, onion and mutton, with some herbs as available. But the Irish peasantry gave up growing many other crops to concentrate on potatoes, with tragic results when the crop failed in 1845/46 and caused the deaths of so many during the Potato Famine.

## IRISH STEW

*The dish originated in the Irish cabin. In it utensils were scarce—a frying pan, a griddle, a kettle and a potato pot sometimes constituting the entire cooking apparatus. When a pig or sheep was killed at the 'big house' the griskin, spare-ribs, or scrag-end of the neck of mutton were shared with the peasants. Having limited vessels and more limited experience, the potatoes were peeled when meat was used, otherwise they were boiled in their 'jackets'; and meat, potatoes and onions were put in the pot, covered with water and all boiled together. So Irish Stew was made, and without much change has remained as a popular dish to this day.*

Florence Irwin,
*The Cookin' Woman*, 1949.

**6-8 servings**

Irish Stew should have a thick, creamy consistency similar to Scottish Stovies.

Put the meat into a heavy-based pan. Cover with water and bring to the boil briefly, skim. Slice about a third of the potatoes very thinly; these will disintegrate and thicken the stew. Leave the rest in larger pieces. Add the thinly sliced potatoes, onion, salt, pepper and herbs to the meat and stir well. Place the larger potatoes on top, cover and simmer gently till the meat is tender. Taste for seasoning and finish with more chopped parsley.

Often served in Ireland with **Pickled Red Cabbage**: Shred a large cabbage finely, spread out on a large tray and lightly cover with salt. Leave for 2-3 days, turning daily. Drain the cabbage and pack into jars, then cover with Pickle Vinegar (see p.224). Put a cayenne pod and a few peppercorns into the jars, cover and seal. Ready for use in a fortnight.

## Variation

Use a leftover joint, removing all meat from the bones. Cover the bones with water and simmer for about 2 hours to make a stock. Strain. Prepare the potatoes and onions as above and add to the stock, cook till tender, then add the cooked meat thinly sliced and heat through.

# COLCANNON

**6-8 servings**

You can make this into a main meal dish by adding crowdie (cottage cheese) and some sour cream. It is versatile and lends itself to many variations.

## Sautéing the onions and cabbage

Heat the butter and oil together in a large pan and add the onions. Cook till soft and yellow. Add the cabbage and sauté the cabbage till just tender.

## Preparing the other vegetables

Cook and mash the potatoes, turnip and carrots. Season and while still warm add crowdie and sour cream.

*Irish Stew*

**3 lb/1½ kg neck of lamb chops**

**3 lb/1½ kg mealy potatoes, peeled**

**1 lb/500 g onions, sliced**

**Salt and pepper**

**Parsley and thyme**

*Colcannon*

**3 medium onions, finely chopped**

**4 tablespoons butter**

**2 tablespoons oil**

**½ teaspoon salt**

**1 lb/500 g shredded cabbage (4 c)**

**4 medium potatoes**

**2 medium carrots**

**Half a small turnip**

**10 oz/375 g crowdie (cottage cheese) (1½ c)**

**4 fl oz/125 ml sour cream (½ c)**

*To finish*

½ **teaspoon ground caraway (optional)**

2 **tablespoons cider vinegar**

2 **tablespoons grated cheddar**

### Finishing the dish

Mix together the two lots of vegetables. Add ground caraway if desired and the cider vinegar. Taste for seasoning. Spread in a 2½ pt (1¼ kg) gratin dish and cover with 2 tablespoons grated cheddar cheese. Brown under the grill or finish in the oven (400F/200C/Gas 6).

# Scandinavians

*The Scandinavians are widely known as brilliant designers, and much of what they have designed, crafted and sent out into the world for the past three decades has been for the beautification of the table—porcelain, silverware, crystal, linen. It is not so widely known that they are excellent cooks as well. It should stand to reason, however, that a people who could care so much about the way a table looks would also care vitally about food, and the Scandinavians do.*
Dale Brown
*The Cooking of Scandinavia*
1969

While the Celtic Irish naturally had more contact with the West of Scotland, then the East and North were more influenced by Norse Scandinavia. They shared a strong fishing tradition which encouraged much interchange and as recently as 1469 the islands of Orkney and Shetland were still part of the Norwegian crown's lands. They were pledged for 58,000 florins, which was to be the unpaid dowry of their Princess Margaret when she married James III in 1470. From 1472 they were annexed to the Scottish crown, though the Norwegians frequently tried to get them back and only abandoned their efforts in 1749.

There was also strong Norse influence on all the islands of the Hebrides and the West Coast which can be still seen in the Norse place names like Ness ('nes'—Norse for headland) on Lewis.

Norse culture in Shetland remains strong and the islanders continue to celebrate the end of Yule by burning a Viking ship at the Up-Helly-A' ceremony. Interchange of food traditions with Scandinavia is frequent. The Shetlanders' extensive use of livers, heads and roes in the past, when they were a by-product of salting large white fish, is one similarity. They also shared with Scandinavians a liking for fermented fish, and while they no longer go in for things like Sookit Piltacks (Saith left in the open to ferment for 10 days) or Klossed Heads (Fish heads pressed between stones and left to ferment) they do still salt and eat herring. Salted mutton (Reested mutton) can also be bought in butcher's shops in Lerwick (I am not aware that it is available in any other part of Scotland) and Shetlanders use it to make an excellent broth.

Other evidence of Scandinavian influence is the extensive use of cabbage and the use of onions with herring which is not common in the rest of Scotland. At the Yule breakfast there was the tradition of Whipkull (see p.146) which is another tradition which they share with Norway. This is a light, frothy mixture of eggs and sugar beaten over heat and called Eggedosis in Norway. The Scandinavian tradition of salting and pickling herring and using it as a central part of the cold table (Smorgasbord), with many variations, has kept alive old herring cures.

## SALT HERRING WITH LEEKS

**4 servings**

This Finnish combination has a strong personality of contrasting flavours. It should be eaten with plainly boiled or baked potatoes.

### To assemble

Arrange the herring in a row up the centre of an ashet. Put the hard-boiled eggs on one side and the leeks on the other. Pour the very hot melted butter over everything and serve immediately with baked or boiled potatoes.

## MARINATED FRIED HERRING

The method is in two parts, first the frying then the marinading. In theory it is the same idea as sousing but frying the fish first gives it a firmer texture and fuller flavour.

### To cook

Coat the herring fillets in seasoned flour. Fry in butter till golden brown on both sides. Leave to cool.

Bring the cider vinegar and water, with the sugar, bay leaf, peppercorns and onion, to the boil and then cool.

When both are cold, pour marinade over the fish and leave overnight before using. Serve cold with brown bread and butter. The dish will keep in a cool place for about a week.

# Pakistanis/Indians

For a country with at least a hundred different spices known in its cooking it is not surprising that it was these spices which first stimulated British interest in India. Queen Elizabeth I began the association by founding the East India Company (EIC) in 1600, but it was not until 1773 that Lord North's Regulating Act began the process of transferring control of the EIC's possessions in India to the British Government. In the intervening years the British had beaten off attempts by the Portuguese, Dutch and French to take over India; and had taken control of Bombay, Madras and Calcutta. But the decisive battle was won against the French by Clive at Plassey in 1757.

*Salt Herring with Leeks*

8 salt herring, boned and skinned

3 medium leeks, white and pale green only, cleaned and finely sliced

2 hard-boiled eggs

2 oz/50 g unsalted butter, melted and very hot (½ stick)

4 large baked potatoes

*Marinated Fried Herring*

8 herring fillets

Seasoned flour

½ pt/300 ml cider vinegar (1½ c)

½ pt/300 ml water (1½ c)

6 tablespoons granulated sugar

1 bay leaf

6 peppercorns

1 medium onion, finely sliced

*Chana-jora-garam!*
*Brother, I have come from a long, long distance*
*To bring you this unimaginably tasty Chana-jora-garam.*
*I use the most excellent and secret masala—*
*You can know, because all kinds of famous people*
*Eat my chana-jora-garam.\**
Indian street seller's song

*\*A spicy, savoury snack.*

While there has been much use of spices in traditional British cooking throughout the centuries as a result of this contact, first attempts at a British version of an Indian curry often bore little resemblance to the real thing. It was not until the people of the Indian sub-continent gained their independence in 1947 and began coming to Britain to settle that we first sampled authentic Indian food. Restaurants throughout Britain now provide a sophisticated choice, exploiting the subtleties of this varied cuisine. Many source their herbs and spices from markets in India and Pakistan. The Scots' enthusiasm for good Indian food is not just seen in the proliferation of restaurants, but also in every Indo/Pak corner shop's selection of nan bread, pakoras and samosas, which have become part of everyday eating.

## PAKORA

*Pakora*

1 lb/500 g besan (gram) flour*
   (4 c)

½ lb/250 g onions

½ lb/250 g potatoes

1 lb/500 g fresh spinach or
   cabbage

1 tablespoon salt

1 tablespoon chilli powder—or
   to taste

1-2 tablespoons tomato paste

*Besan (gram) flour is made from grinding dried chick peas—it is widely available in specialist food shops.

These deep fried vegetables are traditionally eaten as snack food, though they may also be part of an Indian meal. Indians never eat them, as they are often eaten in restaurants by Westerners, at the start of the meal. In India they are sold at street corners or in bazaars for the people to nibble during the day. The same applies to Samosas, which are triangular meat-filled, deep-fried pastries. Every Indian or Pakistani woman I have known has made a different version of Pakora—the combination of vegetables and spices is a matter of taste and availability; the gram flour and the method of deep frying seem the only constant factors.

### To cook

Put the gram flour into a large bowl. Halve the onions and slice lengthways into paper-thin slices. Peel and slice the potatoes into very thin slices. Chop the cabbage or spinach finely. Put all the ingredients into the flour as they are prepared and mix well with the salt, chilli powder and tomato paste. Fry in spoonfuls in deep fat. Drain and serve hot or warm.

### Serve with Tomato Chutney

Blend together in liquidiser or processor: **2 green chillies; 1 onion; 2 cloves garlic; 2 tomatoes; sprig of mint; 1 tablespoon Mango chutney; ½ teaspoon salt.**

## MRS ANWAR'S CHICKEN

The subtleties of cooking chicken in yoghurt were revealed to me by Mrs Anwar when we made this dish together. The delicate spicing and the gradual evaporation of the yoghurt during cooking leaves the chicken moist inside but with a crisp, nicely flavoured skin. The crucial point is at the end of the cooking when the outer skin is crisping. Too long in the oven will dry out the meat, too short a time and the skin will still be soggy.

## Curry powder

Grind the curry powder spices in a blender till powdered.

## Marinading in yoghurt

Mix 1 tablespoon of curry powder with all the flavouring ingredients together in the yoghurt and add the chicken. Leave overnight and turn chicken once or twice.

## Roasting the chicken

Pre-heat the oven to 375F/190C/Gas 5.

Cut up **2 oz/50 g butter (½ stick)** into small pieces and place over the chicken which should be skin side up. Roast in the oven for about an hour or until the skin is brown and crisp and nearly all the yoghurt has evaporated.

## Serve with Chapati

Put the wholemeal flour into a bowl and rub in the ghee or melted butter. Make a well in the centre and add 3 tablespoons lukewarm water. Continue adding water, 3 tablespoons at a time, till the dough comes together into a firm, compact ball. Knead the dough till it becomes a smooth and elastic. Leave to rest for 30 minutes. Shape into small balls about the size of a small egg and roll out to a 5 in (12 cm) round. Cook on a heated, but ungreased girdle or large frying-pan till lightly brown on both sides. Serve warm.

# Chinese

*...One can compare Chinese cooking with Chinese painting and calligraphy, where the aim is to achieve a very high degree of delicacy and refinement within a traditional and sometimes stylized framework, but at the same time never lose sight of the need for character, quality and meaning which should be the foundation of every artistic expression.*

Kenneth Lo,
*The Chinese Cookery Encyclopedia*, 1974.

Like many others, Kenneth Lo came to Britain before the Second World War to study. When China joined the Allies, her diplomatic missions

## Mrs Anwar's Chicken

1 x 3½-4 lb/1¾-2 kg chicken, jointed (see p.172)

*Curry powder:*

2 oz/ 50 g coriander seeds

2 oz/ 50 g cumin seeds

4-6 small dried chillies

2 oz/50 g turmeric

5 cardamom pods

½ oz/15 g cinnamon

¼ oz/7 g each of cloves; nutmeg; mace

2 oz/50 g fenugreek

*Flavouring*

10 fl oz/300 ml natural yoghurt (1¼ c)

2 green chillies, finely chopped

1 in (2½ cm) piece of ginger root, peeled and grated

1 grated onion

Salt

*Chapati*

½ lb/250 g wholemeal flour (2 c)

2½ tablespoons ghee or melted butter

Water

abroad were enlarged and expatriate Chinese were employed (during the war he worked at the Chinese Consulate in Liverpool and was later vice-consul in Manchester). Many other new Chinese representatives arrived with their families and their cooks. When the war was over they stayed on and then the Revolution in China left them stranded. In 1951 Mao's regime was officially recognised by the British Government, which left the staff of the Nationalist Chinese Embassies out of a job. The cooks opened restaurants. Many more Chinese, fleeing the Revolution, went to Hong Kong and there discovered that they could get to Britain where there was an increasing demand for Chinese food. It was a similar sort of exodus to the one by French chefs in the aftermath of the French Revolution.

Though the first Chinese restaurant in Britain was the Cathay in Piccadilly Circus—opened in 1908—it was not till after the Second World War that demand for Chinese food really developed. American and Commonwealth troops had a liking for Eastern food and when the Far Eastern ports were occupied by the Japanese, large numbers of Chinese sailors used British ports where restaurants of a more humble variety than 'The Cathay' were to be found in dockland areas. During the war British forces serving in the East enjoyed the Oriental food and they also created a demand when the war was over.

Restaurant interpretation of this sophisticated and varied cuisine has not always given Westerners the correct impression of true Chinese dishes. Native Chinese will shop around carefully before deciding on the authenticity and quality of an establishment. But despite this, the Chinese influence has been considerable. While noodles and rice are now commonplace, the Chinese treatment of vegetables is a rich area of exploration for Western cooks. It was in the kitchens of Buddhist temples and monasteries that vegetarian cookery was most highly developed. They catered for large communities and the most frequent and popular method of cooking was stir-frying.

'Chow' or stir-frying is only one of forty different methods of cooking used by the Chinese and listed by Kenneth Lo. Only a small amount of oil is used and the usual practice is to stir-fry the stronger vegetables first (garlic, ginger, onions) so that the oil becomes impregnated with their flavour. The heat should be very high; the materials to be cooked cut into strips, or small pieces. The blending of flavours and textures is a skill learnt only by practice. Watching a good Chinese cook throwing together foods of widely different substance and texture to create a whole, with so many different facets, in the space of a few minutes is a great piece of theatre.

## CHINESE STIR-FRIED VEGETABLES

Cut vegetables on the thin side and in bite-sized pieces. Any combination can be used but allow about 2½ cups per person.

Separate vegetables into four groups:

**1. ONION, GARLIC, ROOT GINGER**

**2. HARDER, LONGER-COOKING TYPES**—turnips, carrots, celery, broccoli stems, cauliflower stems

**3. SOFTER, QUICKER-COOKING TYPES**—courgettes, sweet peppers, tomatoes, broccoli heads, cauliflower heads

**4. LAST MINUTE ADDITIONS**—herbs, spinach, watercress, lettuce, chopped spring onions, sesame seeds

### Cooking

Heat 2–3 tablespoons oil in a large sauté pan or wok for about 4 portions. Begin over a high heat by cooking the onions, garlic and ginger—this flavours the oil. Then add group 2 vegetables and toss till almost tender. Then add group 3 and finish cooking quickly with last-minute additions. Keep tossing the vegetables all the time, season with salt and pepper if necessary. Serve immediately.

# Jews

*The real crystallisation of Jewish cuisine took place in the sixteenth century, when the Jews were confined to ghettos by edict. It may seem surprising that interest in food should blossom in a ghetto, especially one devoted to religious worship: but people focused on their home lives as an antidote to the misery and degradation outside. Hospitality became a means of survival and the celebration of religious festivals...made it possible to remain indifferent to the world outside the gates. Banquets were held on top of the bakehouse which was the hub of bustling activity where housewives exchanged hints, stuffed necks and cabbage leaves, rolled meat balls and dumplings, fried potato pancakes and grated horseradish while they waited for their goose and chicken drippings to melt down and their pickled beef to boil.*

　　Claudia Roden,
　　*The Good Food Guide*, 1985.

Although there is a large Jewish population in Scotland, their food traditions have not had anything like the impact of the Chinese or Indians simply because they have not had an influence through restaurants. Since so much of Jewish food is related to religious ritual, it is not conducive to general restaurant eating, though there are some kosher restaurants in and around London which cater for the local Jewish population. It is for their baking skills, however, that immigrant Jews from East European became most appreciated by the native population. Post-war, they set up bakeries, some of which have grown into well-established quality bakers. Among the bagels and sourdough bread, is the plaited white bread known as Challah (pronounced halla) which is eaten on the Sabbath.

The bread takes its name from the Jewish 'act of Challah' in which the woman takes a small piece of the dough and puts it in the oven to burn as an offering, thereby re-enacting her origin at the Creation when she sprang from man's rib. The Hebrew law of Challah requires that the quantity of flour to be kneaded into dough be no less than the weight of 43⅕ eggs; or 2½ quarts; or 3½ pounds. The portion to be separated as the Challah offering is to be no less than the size of an olive.

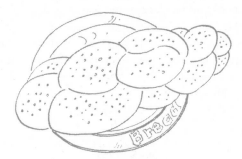

## *Challah*

1¼ lb/625 g strong white flour (5 c)

2 tablespoons sugar

1½ teaspoons salt

1 oz/50 g fresh yeast, or 1 tablespoon dried, or 1 pkt Easy Bake

2 oz/50 g butter at room temperature

½ pt/300 ml warm water (1¼ c scant)

3 eggs + 1 white

Glaze—1 yolk from egg white above with 1 teaspoon water

½ teaspoon poppy seeds

# CHALLAH

A handsome plaited white loaf, glazed and decorated with poppy seeds, it rises in the middle and tapers at the ends. Traditionally it is plaited with four strips (not difficult) to make an interesting weave, though it is equally attractive in the usual three-plait.

Pre-heat the oven to 400F/200C/Gas 6.

Prepare a greased baking tin.

## Making up the dough

Reconstitute the dried yeast by mixing in a little of the measured water. Leave till it froths. Mix the fresh yeast with a little sugar till a smooth paste. Add the Easy Bake with the flour.

Put into a mixing bowl a little less than half of the flour, sugar, salt, yeast and butter. Gradually add the water, do not add all at once since it may not all be needed, and beat by hand or with an electric beater for two minutes. Then add the eggs and beat for another two minutes. Add remaining flour gradually till the dough is fairly firm. Turn out onto the board and knead till it is smooth and elastic. Grease a clean bowl with oil.

Put in the dough and turn it in the bowl to coat the top surface. This will prevent it drying out. Cover with a piece of cling-film and leave in a warm place till doubled in size.

## Shaping the dough

Knock down the dough and knead out the bubbles. Divide in four. Roll out each piece into a rope about 12 in (30 cm) long, thicker in the centre and tapering at the ends. To make a four-plait loaf place the four pieces in the form of a cross, joining the four tapered ends together at the centre of the cross. Lift the ends of the two opposite ropes and twist them over the other pair to reverse their positions but still preserve the cross shape. Then lift and reverse the other pair. Repeat lifting and reversing one pair at a time to weave the four ropes into a compact plait rising in the middle. Tuck loose ends under the loaf and leave in a warm place to rise for 30 minutes. Brush with glaze, sprinkle with poppy seeds and bake for about 30-40 minutes till golden brown and crusty.

# Americans

The exodus of Scots to America over the years has developed strong cultural links and led to much culinary borrowing to and fro. This informal interchange was given new dimensions in the years since the Second World War. This arose firstly with the influence of thousands of American servicemen stationed in Scotland, then more recently with the development of American fast-food restaurants and take-away chains.

*Today American cookery is at a crossroads somewhere between technology and tradition.*
James Beard
*American Cookery*, 1980

The GIs enthralled their Scottish hosts during the war with such goodies as heavy, rich fruit cakes, brownies, cookies and sugar candies which had been sent from home in food parcels and which the Americans gave freely to the Scots in return for their hospitality. They were welcomed by the sweet-loving Scots, deprived as they were during war-time of such luxuries. But of more lasting significance was the American liking for fast foods. The first arrived in Britain after the war in the form of restaurant chains operating a franchising system where the native population ran the operation but had to conform to the brand image by producing standardised food in a form laid down by the parent company. The UK in general was introduced to the hazards of mass-produced hamburgers, hot dogs, fried chicken, pizzas and ice cream, et al. It is worth remembering, however, that the roots of this fast-food bonanza was in honest-to-goodness American home cooking.

## ORIGINAL SOUTHERN CRISP FRIED CHICKEN
### with Cream Gravy

### *Original Southern Crisp Fried Chicken*

3 lb/1½ kg roasting chicken, jointed (see p.172)

*For coating:*

4 tablespoons wholemeal flour

1 teaspoon salt

½ teaspoon ground pepper

½ pt/300 ml vegetable oil (1¼ c)

*For the sauce:*

4 tablespoons chicken or other suitable stock

¼ pt/150 ml single cream (¾ cup)

Salt and pepper

½ teaspoon fresh thyme

1 tablespoon lemon juice

**4-6 servings**

The colour should be an even golden brown, the crust crisp but tender and the meat moist and well flavoured.

### To cook

Heat the oil (or lard) in a 10-12 in (25-30 cm) frying-pan. Put the flour for coating, salt and pepper (some recipes add a teaspoon of cinnamon) into a polythene bag, mix well and then add the chicken pieces two or three at a time and toss in the bag till they are well coated. Remove and repeat with remaining chicken and shake off excess flour. Heat the fat till it is moderately hot—it should be about 2-2½ in (5 cm) deep, and add the chicken legs and thighs first since they will take longer. After about five minutes add the rest and brown evenly on both sides. Maintain the heat at a moderate temperature, allowing the crust to brown slowly—there should not be any smoking fat or spluttering. This frying process should take about three-quarters of an hour. Pile on a serving dish and keep warm.

For the sauce, use the leftover flour from coating, about 2 tablespoons.

Pour off all but about 2 tablespoons of fat in the frying pan and add flour. Stir for a few minutes, then add the chicken stock and cream. Simmer gently to reduce to the correct consistency. Add thyme and lemon juice. Taste for seasoning and serve with the chicken.

### Corn Fritters

Put **6 oz/150 g sweetcorn kernels (½ c)** into a bowl and add **4 oz/125 g self-raising flour (1 c)**; **1 egg**; **salt and pepper**; and **¼ pt/150 ml milk (¾ c)** to make a dropping consistency. Drop in spoonfuls into the hot oil and cook both sides till golden brown.

### Banana and Bacon Rolls

Roll some streaky bacon round a peeled banana and grill till crisp, turning once or twice.

### BROWNIES

Though they have no raising agent, these rise surprisingly well in the oven. When cooled, the centres are moist and pregnant with chocolate. Americans often cover them with icing and nuts, though I find this unnecessary. This version has no authentic American pedigree but is merely my own attempt to recreate the best Brownies I have tasted in America.

Pre-heat the oven to 350F/180C/Gas 4.

Use a 7 x 11 in (17-27 cm) Swiss roll tin, greased, or 2 x 9 in (22 cm) round sandwich cake tins.

### To cook

Cream the butter and sugar together till light and creamy, beat in the eggs gradually. Add the vanilla. Mix in and then sift in the flour and cocoa powder. Mix in well but do not beat. It should have a fairly thick consistency. Spread into the tin and bake for ¾-1 hour or until risen and firm on top. Remove from the oven. Leave to cool for about five minutes then cut into squares and take out, cool on a rack. They can be iced with chocolate icing and decorated with nuts. They may be served warm with vanilla ice-cream for pudding.

*Brownies*

12 oz/350 g butter (3 c)

12 oz/350 g soft brown sugar (2½ c)

4 eggs (large)

4 oz/125 g plain, super-refined cake flour (1 c)

3 oz/75 g cocoa powder (1 c)

1½ teaspoons vanilla

## STRAWBERRY SHORTCAKE

Pre-heat the oven to 425F/220C/gas 7.

Sprinkle the caster sugar and lemon juice over the strawberries. Marinate for a couple of hours.

Put the flour, salt, sugar into a bowl and make a well in the centre. Add the butter, milk and eggs. Mix to a soft dough. Turn out onto a floured board and shape into a large round about half an inch thick. Put onto a greased baking tray and bake for 20-25 minutes until cooked through. Cool slightly and split in half while still warm. Spread the base with half the cream and cover with half the strawberries. Spread over the rest of the cream and finish with the remaining strawberries. Put on the lid. More cream can be put on top or the whole shortcake dusted with icing sugar. It is correct for the strawberries to fall down the sides and onto the plate. Serve immediately while still slightly warm.

*Strawberry Shortcake*
*Berry mix*

1 lb 8 oz/750 g ripe strawberries

2-3 tablespoons caster sugar

juice of 1 lemon

*Shortcake mix*

8 oz/250 g self-raising flour

pinch of salt

2 tablespoons caster sugar

2 oz/50 g softened butter

4 fl oz/125 ml milk

2 egg yolks

*For serving*

10 fl oz/300 ml whipping cream

258

# Scottish Regional Recipes

The picture of Scottish food would not be complete without mention of the fact that the country has wide geographical differences which, along with some other cultural, social and political factors, have created different dishes in different areas. The following is an indication of the regions and the dishes which especially belong within them.

**Edinburgh and the Lothians**—Midlothian Oatcakes; Petticoat Tails; Edinburgh Gingerbread; Edinburgh Tart; Edinburgh Rock; Tantallon Cakes; Cock-a-Leekie Soup; Tweed Kettle; Stoved Howtowdie; Holyrood Pudding; Barley Pudding; Newhaven Cream; Musselburgh Pie.

**Angus and Fife**—Forfar Bridies; Lowland Game Pie; Dundee Marmalade; Dundee Cake; Montrose Cakes; Angus Fruit Cake; Angus Toffee; Arbroath Smokies; Angus Fish Soup; Large Potato Soup; Kingdom of Fife Pie; Fife Broth; Kilmeny Kail; Fife Bannocks; Aberdeen Angus Beef; Pitcaithly Bannock.

**Glasgow and Clydeside**—Glasgow Broth; Glasgow Tripe; Glasgow Toffee; Helensburgh Toffee; Glasgow Punch; Het Pint; Apple Frushie.

**Ayrshire**—Cheese; Aryshire Meat Roll; Cod with Mustard Sauce; Ayrshire Shortbread; Sweet Haggis.

**The Border Counties**—Friar's Chicken; Selkirk Bannock; Yetholm Bannock; Teviotdale or Benalty Pie; Rumbledethumps; Soup n'Stovies; Original Border Tart; Eyemouth Tart; Border Sweeties; Eyemouth Fish Pie.

**Dumfries and Galloway**—Roast Upland Lamb; Drumlanrig Pudding; Ecclefechan Butter Tart; Solway Scallops; Galloway Beef.

**The North East**—Finnan Haddock; Ham and Haddock; Fisherman's Stew; Findon Fish Pudding; Aberdeen Whiting; Aberdeen Sausage; Aberdeen Angus Steak; Sea Pie; Burnt Cream; Neep Bree; Kailkenny; Skirlie; Morayshire Apples; Aberdeen Preserved Apples; Mrs MacNab's Scones; Balmoral Shortbread; Portnockie Shortbread; Aberdeen Crulla; Butteries or Buttery Rowies; Fochabers Gingerbread; Aberdeenshire Rich Fruit Cake.

259

**The Highlands and Inner Hebrides**—Fried West Coat Herring; Islay Scallops; Limpet Stovies; Croppen Head; Sutherland Venison; Poca Buidhe; Roast Red Grouse; Roast Pheasant; Highland Game Soup; Nettle Kail; Chicken Stovies; Pan White Pudding; Tatties and Crowdie; Stapag Uachair (Crowdie Cream); Fuarag; Cranachan; Atholl Brose; Gromack; Highland Oatcakes; Highland Cakes.

**The Outer Hebrides**—Hebridean Shellfish; Whelks in Sauce; Whelk Soup; Lobster Hebridean; Fried Cockles; Carageen Mould; Fried Skate; Port of Ness Cod; Lewis way of frying Brown Trout; Boiled Fish Roe; Roe Cakes; Kale Soup; Lewis Kailkenny; Sweet Maragan; Greiseagan; Barley Bannocks; Bonnach Imeach.

**Orkney and Shetland**—Orkney Pork and Kale; Clapshot, Orcadian Oatmeal Soup; Tatties and Cream; Fatty Cutties; Sour Skons; Orkney Pancakes; Orkney Broonies; Shetland Fish Soup; Flats; Fried Herring and Onions; Sassermaet and Bronies; Roast Leg of Shetland Lamb; Boiled Mutton; Boiled Pork; Lentil Bro; Gooseberry Sauce; Potatoes with Milk; Bride's Bonn or Bridal Cake; Brunnies; Brunnies of Rye; Whipkull; Beremeal Bannocks.

# Early Scottish Cookery Writers

**Mrs McLintock**

*Mrs McLintock's Receipts for Cookery*, Glasgow 1736

Thought to be the first collection of Scottish recipes, it is a rare little book (only two copies are known to exist, both in Glasgow University Library) and Mrs McLintock has clearly been influenced by the need for preservation of food since more than half the book is taken up with recipes for pickling, potting, preserving and making wines. This perhaps explains why there are few Scottish national dishes. No Haggis, Barley Broth or Black Bun, though there is a recipe for Shortbread. She has one or two excellent soups, a Lobster Soup which is finished with oysters and mussels and a basic soup recipe which starts with, 'great whole onions stuck with cloves, a bunch of sweet herbs,' and lots of beef and veal bones. It is finished with toasted bread floating in the soup and a cooked marrow bone in the centre of the plate.

**Mrs Johnston**

*Mrs Johnston's Receipts for all sort of pastry, cream, puddings, etc.*, Edinburgh 1740

A small collection of recipes for plain basic fare thought to be either copied from Mrs McLintock or written by her under another name. Of the 117 pages in the book the first 92 are the same as in Mrs McLintock's 1736 edition.

**Elizabeth Cleland**

*The Practice of Cookery, pastry, pickling, preserving, containing...a full list of supper dishes...directions for choosing provisions: with two plates, showing the method of placing dishes upon a table etc.*, Edinburgh 1759

Mrs Cleland also had a cookery school in Edinburgh and her book has the feeling of an elementary manual of instruction—there is much emphasis on methods of preservation. A whole chapter is dedicated 'To pot and make hams' but Scottish national dishes are also well represented.

### Susanna MacIver
*Cookery and Pastry*, Edinburgh 1773

She began by selling cakes, jams, chutneys and pickles from her shop, but later opened a cookery school where she taught a sophisticated range of dishes to the well-to-do of Edinburgh. In 1773 her pupils encouraged her to publish her recipes. The collection is well mixed with French influence. Unlike many contemporary English books which are at pains to denounce the French as spoiling good English fare, possibly because of the long Scottish association with the French, she, like most Scots, seems to have had a more relaxed attitude to their incursions.

She includes a fair representation of Scottish dishes, like Scotch Haggis, Parton Pies, Rich Bun, Shortbread, Diet Loaf, Chip Marmalade, To Make Tablets and To Make Barley Sugar. It seems, though, that she was not a broth-lover since no recipe appears for the universal Scotch Broth which was considered so much of a national institution both at home and abroad that it is included in *The London Art of Cookery* by John Farley (1785).

### Mrs Fraser
*The Practice of Cookery and Pastry*, Edinburgh 1791

She helped to run Mrs McIver's cookery school, took over after her death and then published her own recipes. This is a more sophisticated and comprehensive collection than Mrs McIver's. Her aim was to 'reconcile simplicity with elegance, and variety with economy'. She has organised the book in a more logical structure, dividing it up into three parts—I cookery; II Pastry; and III Confectionery, which includes all the preservation methods. Plain simple fare predominates with all the basic Scottish dishes and little French or foreign influence besides the odd 'ragoo' and 'fricassy'. Curiously she also, like Mrs McIver, has no recipe for Scotch Broth among her nineteen soup recipes of which only three could be termed traditionally Scottish. In place of Cock-a-Leekie she has a poor version of Leek Soup with prunes but no chicken.

### Mistress Margaret (Meg) Dods of the Cleikum Inn, St Ronan's
*The Cook and Housewife's Manual*, Edinburgh 1826

Meg Dods was a fictitious character whom Sir Walter Scott created in his novel *St Ronan's Well*, but is said to have been modelled on Miss Marian Ritchie, the landlady of his local inn, the Cross Keys in Peebles.

Meg was a capricious and eccentric old landlady with a detestable bad humor. Potential guests were turned away if she disliked the 'cut of their jib', and the ones who stayed had to be prepared for her blunt couthy ways. Her saving grace, and the reason why gourmets flocked to her inn, was that she was a superb cook.

The real author of the cookery book was Mrs Isobel Christian Johnston, wife of an Edinburgh publisher. The connection with Scott and his novel is not made clear in the introductory 'The St Ronan's Culinary Club'. Mrs Johnston is the first Scottish cookery writer of the century to make an accurate assessment of the changes taking place, cutting her cloth accordingly, while at the same time carrying out the task with expert professionalism. Public horizons were widening far beyond the basics of Plain Roast and Boiled, although these were still important. Curiosity and the desire to learn were cultivating the made dishes of beef, mutton, veal and venison, etc. In the second chapter the whole system of French Cuisine is thoroughly explored while the next deals with national dishes—Scottish, Irish, Welsh, German, Spanish and Oriental. She is one of the first cookery writers to isolate these subjects, recognising the public interest in them. Both before, and after her, the tendency was to create a hotch-potch of foreign and national dishes with no clear distinction.

She was careful also not to adopt these dishes purely for their novelty, but claims that she has set out to embody 'all in Foreign culinary science that is considered really useful'. She was a very practical lady.

## Mrs Dalgairns
*The Practice of Cookery*, Edinburgh 1829

First published only three years after Meg Dods, and competing with her for popularity, this is a large cookery book with 1,434 recipes. It seems, however, that the public did not take to Mrs Dalgairns with the same enthusiasm they felt for Meg Dods, but her book is just as large and comprehensive. Despite this, there is a feeling of muddle about the structure of the book. There are all the basic Scottish national dishes but French, English, Irish and other foreign dishes occur randomly throughout the book. Apart from the lack of form she has a vague style of writing so that when you read the recipes you are constantly frustrated by lack of quantities and instruction. None of these criticisms apply to Meg Dods, which explains why her book was reprinted frequently throughout the century and Mrs Dalgairns' was not.

### Lady Clark of Tillypronie

*The Cookery Book of Lady Clark of Tillypronie*, arranged and edited by Catherine F. Frere, London 1909

Lady Clark was an obsessional collector of recipes. When she died her husband asked Catherine Frere to edit her manuscript collection. She took on the task of sorting out 'the gatherings of many years' which consisted of sixteen books of various sizes, containing nearly three thousand pages of manuscript, some of the page written on every available margin, plus recipes written on loose sheets pinned in; or on backs of envelopes; or on backs of paid bills; or any available piece of paper.

The collection begins in 1841 when emigrés from the French Revolution stayed with Lady Clark's family. Her culinary curiosity was aroused by them and consolidated when she travelled with her family to Italy and France. When she married in 1851, her husband was in the Diplomatic Service and they lived in both Paris and Turin. Her collection has a strong hidden implication that if you give fifty different chefs the same recipe they will all produce a different dish. She spent so much time gathering recipes from so many different people that there are many variations of the same recipe, reflecting always the personality of the individual. It makes interesting reading; especially since her roots were in the North East of Scotland, and it was to this part that she returned frequently, absorbing also the culinary traditions of her home.

### F. Marian McNeill

*The Scots Kitchen, Its Traditions and Lore*, Blackie 1929 (new edition Mercat Press, 1993)

Because she thought that our old national dishes were in danger of sinking into oblivion through modern standardisation of food she set about preserving everything hallowed by age.

She ranged the country from North to South and from palaces to island sheilings in her search for the authentic food of the people. Being by profession a historian, she also sketched the development of Scottish food throughout the centuries and set about showing how 'the pagent of Scottish History is shadowed in the kitchen.' She highlights the distinctive traditons and customs not out of 'antiquarian zeal' but from a 'healthy national sentiment' and our debt to her is infinite.

### William Heptinstall

*Gourmet Recipes From a Highland Hotel*, Faber and Faber 1967

In the 1920s when railway hotels were the only outposts of serious gastronomy in Scotland, an enterprising Yorkshire-born chef, with a formidable international reputation, bought Fortingall Hotel—eight miles from the nearest railway station and on a quiet back road in Perthshire.

During the thirty-five years of Heptinstall's reign at Fortingall he not only created an outstanding hotel off the beaten track, but stimulated, encouraged and trained many young chefs who continue to keep his cooking philosophy alive in hotels and restaurants in Scotland and further afield. He was particularly well known for his Cold Table, only offered once a week, preceding Sunday lunch. On an average Sunday, forty dishes could appear on the table, half of which probably had to be prepared before breakfast. He felt that the start to a meal was vitally important—'Just as a good or bad start may win or lose the race,' he said, 'so may hors-d'oeuvres make or mar a meal. Unless they are dainty, little, and tasty, they will dull the keen edge of your appetite.'

In *Gourmet Recipes* he exploits the natural produce of Scotland with originality and flair but mindful always of the practicalities—his infectious enthusiasm shines through.

*Fortingall menus were beautifully balanced and offered an astonishing mixture of haute cuisine and bourgeois dishes from all over Europe. At lunchtime there was a limited choice but at dinner the guests were obliged to take what was offered or do without. It was only in this way that 'Hep' as he was known, was able to offer such good food at such moderate prices, for no effort or ingredients ever needed to be wasted.*

Gregory Houston Bowden
*British Gastronomy*, 1975

# People who kept Records in Household Books; or wrote Journals of Travel; or Letters; or kept Diaries

### Lady Grisell Baillie

*The Household Book of Lady Grisell Baillie 1692-1733*, edited by Robert Scott-Moncrieff, 1911

Besides much information on household expenditure, Lady Grisell also kept a special book in which she recorded 'Bills of Fair'. Not all of the hundred and seventy in the book are meals in her own family home, but she recalls meals with friends and in other countries. The list of dishes give an indication of the types of foods which were popular at this level of society. She has carefully preserved the exact layout of the dishes on the table, so that the book shows clearly the type of eating in the days when they arranged everything on the table at once.

### Edward Burt

*Letters from a Gentleman in the North of Scotland*, 5th ed., 1822

Edward Burt was an English engineer who served with General Wade building roads in the Highlands from 1724-28. His letters are unique since he was travelling in the area before the very roads he was helping to build brought 'travellers' to the Highlands. His record of the manners and conditions of the people is vivid and detailed, interspersed with much humour—a good read ('I was invited to sup at a Tavern. The cook was too filthy on Object to be described: only another English Gentleman whispered me and said, he believed, if the fellow was to be thrown against the Wall, he would stick to it'). He lived for some time in or near Inverness and made a number of journeys along the Great Glen and into some of the adjacent country.

*Ochtertyre House Booke of Accomps 1737-1739*, edited by James Colville, Edinburgh 1907

While Grisell Baillie's bills of fare give an indication of the dinner party fare of sophisticated Edinburgh society, then the Ochtertyre House Book gives the picture of the standard of daily living in an average baronial establishment just before the 'Forty Five. It is a detailed catalogue of daily meals, purchases and home-grown or home-produced food. You can follow the rhythm of the seasons in the foods they ate and see the way they utilised all the odds and ends in a most economical way when beasts were killed.

### Thomas Pennant
*Tour in Scotland*, 1771 [Describes a journey made in 1769]

According to Pennant his book was such a success that Scotland was, as a result, '*inondée* with Southern visitors'. He was one of the most eminent naturalists of the eighteenth century and as a traveller showed a lively curiosity about people and customs as well as the natural things of the country. His comments on the things he saw growing, and which the people were eating, are an important record of the Scots diet. His 1769 *Tour in Scotland* went into five editions between 1771 and 1790. He made another tour round the West Coast and the Islands in 1772 but this was less popular with the public since these areas were much less accessible.

### Christopher North (Professor John Wilson)
*Noctes Ambrosianae* 1822-1835

Ambrosian nights in an Edinburgh tavern were brought to life by Wilson, a professor of philosophy, in a series of imaginary colloquies which entertained the readers of *Blackwood's Magazine* for more than a decade. They were so popular that Blackwood's allowed other writers besides Wilson to write the dialogues when, for one reason or another, he couldn't contribute. But none of them could match his style and the published collection in four volumes is confined only to Wilson's work.

His principal characters, Christopher North (Wilson himself), Timothy Tickler (Robert Sym) and James Hogg, The Ettrick Shepherd, only bear the slightest resemblance to the original people. They formed the prototypes, and Wilson's imagination expanded and developed them. Besides talking a great deal, they also ate.

Most of the vivid and detailed descriptions of what and how they would have eaten in early nineteenth century Edinburgh ring true. There is just the occasional doubt that Wilson's imagination has elaborated over much. His description of the 'Deluge of Haggis' likening it to a flood when the haggis was first burst open, while highly entertaining, goes well beyond the bounds of reality by the time he is finished.

His comments, though, on attitudes to food indicate current taste and style and occasional pieces on things like how they ought to eat these new things called 'pineapples' are both revealing and amusing:

*Shep*. And what ca' ye thae, like great big fir cones wi' outlandish-looking palm-tree leaves arching frae them wi' an elegance o' their ain…What ca' ye them?

*North*. Pineapples.

*Shep*. I've aften heard tell o' them—but never clapped een on them afore. And these are pines! Oh! but the scant is sweet, sweet—and wild as sweet…I'll join you noo in a pair o' pines.

[NORTH gives the SHEPHERD a pine-apple]

Hoo are they eaten?

*Tickler*. With pepper, mustard, and vinegar, like oysters, James.

*Shepherd*. I'm thinking you maun be leein.

*Tickler*. Some people prefer catsup.

*Shepherd*. Haud your blethers. Catchup's gran kitchen [relish] for a' kinds o' flesh, fish and fule, but for frutes the rule is 'sugar or naething',— and if this pine keep the taste o' promise to the palat, made by the scent he sends through the nose, nae extrawneous sweetness will he need, self sufficient in his ain sappiness, rich as the colour o' pinks, in which it is sae savourily enshrined.—I never pree'd ony taste half sae delicious as that in a' ma born days! Ribstanes, pippins, jargonels, peaches, nectrins, currans and strawberries, grapes and grozets, a' in ane!'

## Samuel Johnson and James Boswell

*Johnson's Journey to the Western Islands of Scotland*, 1775
*Boswell's Journal of a Tour to the Hebrides with Samuel Johnson*, 1785

The 64-year-old English lexicographer and the 33-year-old Scot spent four months together on a tour which took them round a large part of Scotland and into many different types of Scottish homes. They went from Edinburgh northwards to Aberdeen, then along the Morayshire coast to Inverness. This was the easy part. In Inverness they bade 'farewell to the luxury of travelling' and continued on horseback across to Glenelg, over to Skye, down to Coll, across to Mull and back to the mainland at Oban. From there they travelled south to Glasgow and then into Ayrshire before going back to Edinburgh.

Boswell's journal is more detailed and, according to literary experts, also a better travel book than Johnson's. Johnson seems to allow his prejudices about the Scots and their customs to influence his opinions, and his likes and dislikes, while interesting and relevant, perhaps don't always reflect the true nature of things. He was, after all, a brilliant critic and he naturally came, not like the Wordsworths in 1803, to see and feel, but to pass his own judgment. He was a colourful character, highly amusing, witty and notoriously rude, which was occasionally matched by his Scottish hosts. When he was eating Hotch Potch at his Edinburgh landlady's she is reputed to have asked him, 'And how do you like the Hotch Potch, sir.' 'Good enough for hogs,' replied Johnson. 'Shall I help you to a little more of it, then?' retorted the landlady.

Besides all kinds of opinions on all kinds of topics the two men both noted how the people lived. They described the conditions, the traditions and the diet of the people and have provided a revealing and valuable account of life in different parts of Scotland and at different levels of society in the late eighteenth century.

# Select Bibliography

## COOKERY BOOKS

Beard, James *Delights and Prejudices*, 1964
   *James Beard's American Cookery*, Little, Brown and Company, 1972

British Deer Society (Scotland) *Venison Recipes*

Boyd, Lizzie (Ed.) *British Cookery*, Croom Helm, 1976

Brown, Catherine *Scottish Regional Recipes*, Molendinar, 1981/Penguin 1983

Clayton, Bernard *The Complete Book of Breads*, Simon and Schuster, 1973

Clifton, Claire *Edible Flowers*, Bodley Head, 1983

Craig, Elizabeth *The Scottish Cookery Book*, Deutsch, 1956

David, Elizabeth *English Bread and Yeast Cookery*, Allen Lane, 1977

Davidson, Alan *North Atlantic Seafood*, Macmillan, 1979

Dods, Meg *The Cook and Housewife's Manual*, 1826

Drysdale, Julia *The Game Cookery Book*, Collins, 1975

Escoffier, August *Ma Cuisine*, first edition Flammarion, 1934, Paul Hamlyn, 1965

Fitzgibbon, Theodora *A Taste of Scotland*, Dent, 1970

Fletcher, Nichola Venison, *The Monarch of the Table*, Nichola Fletcher, 1983

Fulton, Willie *The Hebridean Kitchen*, Buidheann foillseachaidh nan Eilean an Iar, 1978

*The Glasgow Cookery Book: Queens College Glasgow*, John Smith, Revised Edition, 1962

Grigson, Jane *Good Things*, M. Joseph, 1971
   *Fish Cookery*, Penguin, 1975
   *Jane Grigson's Vegetable Book*, M. Joseph, 1978
   *Jane Grigson's Fruit Book*, M. Joseph, 1982

Harben, Philip *Cooking*, Penguin, 1960

Heptinstall, William *Gourmet Recipes from a Highland Hotel*, Faber, 1967

Katzen, Mollie *The Mosewood Cookbook*, Ten Speed Press, California, 1977
   *The Enchanted Broccoli Forest*, Ten Speed Press, California, 1982

King, A. and Dunnet, F. *The Home Book of Scottish Cookery*, Faber, 1967

Mabey, Richard *Food For Free. A guide to the edible wild plants of Britain*, Collins, 1972

Mabey, David and Rose *The Penguin Book of Jams, Pickles and Chutneys*, Penguin 1975

Menhinick, Gladys *Grampian Cookbook*, Aberdeen University Press, 1984.

Murray, Janet *Wartime Cookery Book*, Fraser, 1944
   *Janet Murray's Cookery Book*, London, 1950
   *Traditional Recipes from Scotland*, BBC, 1964
   *With a Fine Feeling for Food*, Impulse, 1972.

Nelson, Janet M. (Ed.) *A Mull Companion*, Mull 1977

Nice, Jill *Home-Made Preserves*, Collins, 1982

Olney, Richard *Simple French Food*, Penguin, 1983

Phillips, Roger *Wild Food*, Pan, 1983

Reid, Nancy (Ed.) *Highland Housewives' Cook Book*, Highland Printers, 1971

*Scottish Women's Rural Institutes Traditional Scottish Recipes Cookery Book* 6th Edition, 1946

Simmons, Jenni *A Shetland Cook Book*, Thuleprint, 1978

Stout, Margaret B. *The Shetland Cookery Book*, Manson, 1968 (first published in 1925 as *Cookery for Northern Wives*)

Taste of Scotland Ltd. and Catherine Brown *Chef's Manual*, 4th edition, 1985

Troisgros, Jean and Pierre *The Nouvelle Cuisine*, edited and adapted by Caroline Conran, Macmillan, 1980

Whyte, Hamish *Lady Castehill's Receipt Book, A Selection of Eighteenth Century Scottish Fare*, Molendinar, 1976

Wolfe, Eileen *Recipes from the Orkney Islands*, Gordon Wright, 1978

## GENERAL

Anderson, W. *The Poor of Edinburgh and Their Homes*, Menzies, 1867

Brown, P. Hume (Ed.) *Early Travellers in Scotland*, Edinburgh, 1891

Burt, Edward *Letters from the North of Scotland* 5th ed., London, 1822

Campbell, John *An Exact and Authentic Account of the Greatest White-Herring Fishery in Scotland, carried on yearly in the Island of Zetland*, Edinburgh, 1750

Chambers, Robert *Walks in Edinburgh*, Edinburgh, 1825
  *Traditions of Edinburgh*, 2nd ed. Edinburgh, 1868
  *Domestic Annals of Scotland*, Edinburgh, 1859

Chapman, R.W. (Ed.) *Johnson's Journey to the Western Islands of Scotland and Boswell's Journal of a Tour to the Hebrides with Samuel Johnson*, Oxford University Press, 1961

Cheke, Val *The Story of Cheese Making in Britain*, Routledge, 1959

Colville, James (Ed.) *The Ochtertyre House Booke—1737-1739*, Scottish History Society, Edinburgh, 1907

Cutting, Charles L. *Fish Saving*, (Leonard Hill, 1955)

Edmonston, Elizabeth *Sketches and Tales of Shetland*, Edinburgh, 1856

Faujas de Saint-Fond, B. *Travels in England, Scotland and the Hebrides etc.*, London, 1799

Fenton, Alexander *Scottish Country Life*, John Donald, 1976.

Foulis, Sir John *Foulis of Ravelston's Account Book, 1671-1707*, Scottish History Society, 194

Fyfe, J.G. *Scottish Diaries and Memoirs*, Volume I (1550-1746), Volume II (1746-1843), Maclean, 1928

Grant, Elizabeth *Memoirs of a Highland Lady*, London, 1898

Hodgson, W.C. *The Herring and its Fishery*, Routledge, 1957

Jamieson, John *Etymological Dictionary of the Scottish Language*, new ed. 1879-82

Jamieson, J.H. *The Edinburgh Street Traders and their Cries*, in *Book of the Old Edinburgh Club*, Volume II, Constable, 1909

Kitchen, A.H. *The Scotsman's Food*, Livingston, 1949

Lochhead, Marion *The Scots Household in the Eighteenth Century*, Moray Press, 1948

Lockhart, G.W. *The Scot and His Oats*, Luath Press, 1983

MacCarthy, Daphne (Ed.) *Prodfact 1985, a Comprehensive Guide to British Agricultural and Horticultural Produce*, British Farm Produce Council, 1985

MacClure, Victor *Scotland's Inner Man*, Routledge, 1935
  *Good Appetite, My Companion*, Odhams Press, 1955

Martin, Martin *A Description of the Western Islands of Scotland, etc.*, 1703, Stirling, 1934

Mitchison, Rosalind *Life of Scotland*, Batsford, 1978

Newton, Lily *A Handbook of British Seaweeds*, British Museum, Natural History, 1931

    *Seaweed Utilisation* Sampson and Low, 1951

Page, E.B. and Kingsford P.W. *The Master Chefs*, Arnold, 1971

Plant, Marjorie *The Domestic Life of Scotland in the Eighteenth Century*, Edinburgh University Press, 1952

Pococke, Richard *Tours in Scotland, 1747, 1750, 1760*, Scottish History Society, 1887

Ramsay, Dean *Reminiscences of Scottish Life and Character*, first published 1857, Robert Grant, 1947

Robertson, Una A. *Let's Dine at Hopetoun*, published in aid of the Hopetoun House Preservation Trust, 1981

Salaman, Redcliffe N. *The History and Social Influence of the Potato*, Cambridge University Press, 1970

Samuel, A.M. *The Herring: Its Effect on the History of Britain*, Murray, 1918

Sibbald, Sir Robert *What the Poor might eat; Provision for the Poor in time of Dearth and Scarcity*, Edinburgh, 1707

Sinclair, Sir John (Ed.) *The Statistical Account of Scotland*, Edinburgh, 1791-99

    *General View of the Agriculture of the Northern Counties and Islands of Scotland*, Edinburgh, 1795

Southey, Robert *Journal of a Tour in Scotland in 1819*, The Mercat Press, 1972

Steven, Maisie *The Good Scots Diet*, Aberdeen University Press, 1985

Stuart, Marie W. *Old Edinburgh Taverns*, Hale, 1952

Sutherland, Douglas *The Salmon Book*, Collins, 1982

Tannahill, Reay *Food in History*, Stein and Day, 1973

Thornton, R. and Sieczka J.B. *Potato Atlas*, International Potato Centre, Lima, 1978

Torry Research Station *Fish Handling and Processing*

Victoria, Queen *Leaves From a Journal of Our Life in the Highlands, 1846-1861*, 1867

Wilson, C. Anne *Food and Drink in Britain*, Constable, 1973

Youngson, A.J. *Beyond the Highland Line, Three Journals of Travel in Eighteenth Century Scotland*, Collins, 1974

# GENERAL INDEX

Aberdeen Butterie 212
Abernethy Biscuit 212
Almond Biscuits 211
Almond Tart 206
American
  brownies 256
  cooking vocabulary xix
  culinary interchange
    255
  measures xv-xviii
Apple
  cake 208
  chutney 223
Arbroath Smokie 55
  with baked potato 56
  poached in milk 56
  potted with oatcake 57
Arisaig seafood pastry 95
Arran Cheddar Cheese
  232
Arran Dunlop Cheese 232
Ashet of Fresh Fruit 143
Atholl Brose 11

Baillie, Grisell 266
Bannocks 12
  barley 13
  modern barley 14
  oatmeal 14
  old fashioned 13
  Selkirk 205
Baps, white floury 201
Barley 20
  bannocks 13
  flour 20
  modern bannocks 30
  pearl 4
  sugar 216
Bawd Bree 101
Beef 121
  boiled whole piece 105
  breeds 105
  cooked in claret 116
  Forfar bridies 117
  grilled beefsteak 114
  minced collops 112

olives 113
pieces boiled 110
roast English Sirloin
  244
Scotch Collops 112
spiced 114
Beefsteaks, charcoal
  grilled 114
Beremeal 4
  bannock 13
  stoneground Orkney 4
Biscuits 211
  almond 140
  and cream 154
  broken cake 211
  origins 5
  walnut oat 23
Black Bun 204
Black Striped Balls 216
Blackcurrant and Apple
  Pudding 156
Blawn Whiting 52
Border Tart 212
Boswell, James 268
Brandied Fruit Cup 145
Bread
  barley 36
  buttermilk with oatmeal
    19
  challah 254
  oatmeal bread rolls 16
  oatmeal with molasses
    32
  sour dough oatmeal 17
Broccoli 182
  creamy salad 182
  varieties/buying 182
Broken Biscuit Cake 211
Brose 10
  Atholl 11
  mixed grain 12
  oatmeal 11
  pease 11
  traditions 10
Brownies, American 256
Brown Trout Baked 36
Burt, Edward 266

Buttered Oats 22
Butterscotch sauce 156

Cabbage 178
  rumbledethumps 178
  varieties 178
Caboc 229
Cakes
  apple 208
  basic easy-cream
    method 207
  Chocolate drop 210
  Dundee 207
  easy-to-make 206
  maple syrup 209
  mincemeat 209
  Seville orange 210
  yeast 201
Calabrese, see Broccoli 182
Caledonian Cream 154
Campbeltown Cheddar
  232
Carragheen 84
  chocolate pudding 84
  identification 83
Carrots 174
  buying 175
  cake 176
  glazed 177
  soup 175
Challah 254
Chappit Tatties 167
Charcoal Grilled Beefsteaks
  114
Cheese 225
  and eggs 234
  Arran Dunlop 232
  Arran Cheddar 232
  Bishop Kennedy 231
  blue 231
  Bonnet 232
  Brodick Blue 231
  buying/storing 228
  Caboc 229
  Cairnsmore 230
  Campbeltown Cheddar
    232

cheesecake 236
Cranog 230
creamery dunlops and
  cheddars 232
Crottin 230
crowdie 229
Dunlop 232
Dunlop, origins 226
Dunsyre Blue 231
farmhouse cheeses 232
Fresh soft 229
Galloway Cheddar 232
Galloway Ricotta 230
Galic 230
Grimister Orkney 230
Gruth Dhu 230
hard 231
hatted kit 235
Highland Fine 229
Highland Cheddar 232
Hramsa 230
Howgate brie and
  camembert 231
Isle of Bute cheddar
  232
Isle of Mull cheddar
  232
Islay Dunlop 232
Kelsae 230
Lairobell Orkney 230
Lanark Blue 231
Loch Arthur 232
Lockerbie Cheddar 232
methods of production
  227
Mull of Kintyre
  cheddar 232
natural rind 229
Orkney Cheddar 232
salad 236
soft white 230
St Andrews 231
Stitchill 230
Swinzie 232
toasted 233
washed rind 230
whey cheeeses 229

Cheugh Jeans 216
Chicken
    Mrs Anwar's 250
    sauteed with skirlie and
        leeks 172
    southern crisp fried 256
Chinese culinary inter-
    change 251
    stir-fried vegetables 253
Chocolate drop cake 210
Chutney
    apple 223
    Mrs Beeton's Plum 224
Clabbie Dubhs 66
    identification/buying/
        preparing 66
    with leek and tomatoes
        68
Claggum 216
Clams 70
Cleland, Mrs 261
Clootie Dumpling 20
Cock-a-Leekie 170
Cockles 70
Colcannon 247
Coltart's Candy 216
Cookies 198
    cream 200
    currant 200
    iced 200
    plain 190
    Scottish 198
    spice 200
Crab 71
    identification/buying/
        preparing 71
    partan bree 73
    partan pies 72
Cranachan 150
Crowdie 225
    butter 225
    crofter's 226
    varieties 229
Crumpets, Scottish 197
Cullen Skink (East Coast
    Fishwife's Broth) 53
Cumnock Tart 212
Culinary Interchange 237
Curlie Murlies 216

Curly Andra 216

Dalgairns, Mrs 263
Damsons, spiced 222
Dods, Meg 288
Dublin Bay Prawns/
    Scampi 76
Duck, seasons 104
Dulse 85
    broth 85
    cakes 86
    uses 85
Dundee Cake 207

East Coast Fishwife's
    Broth 53
Ecclefechan Butter Tart
    206
Edinburgh Rock 216
English, culinary inter-
    change 243
Ettrickshaws Ice Cream 149

Finnan/Smoked Haddock
    52
    baked with cream and
        poached egg 54
    cures 53
    flan 52
    speldings 52
    variations 53
    with melted cheese and
        eggs 54
Fish 25
    place in the Scottish
        diet 25
    varieties 26
Forfar Bridies 117
Fortingall Marmalade 220
Fraser, Mrs 262
French, culinary inter-
    change 239
Fruit Pudding, whipped
    147
Fruit with Cream, five
    ways 142
Fruit 137
    varieties 137
Fruits of the sea 79

Galloway Cheddar Cheese
    232
Game 87
    place in the Scottish
        diet 87
    stew, rich 103
Galic Cheese 230
Gigot, to boil with
    turnips 124
Gingerbread 201
    dark 203
Girdle Oatcakes, Tradi-
    tional 53
Glasgow roll 212
Goose, seasons 104
Gourmet Strawberries 144
Gratin Dauphinois 241
Grilled Herring with
    Mustard 40
Grouse 95
    judging age/hanging 95
    roast young 96
    soup 96
Gruth Dhu Cheese 230

Haddock 49
    and chips 49
    in mustard sauce 50
    grilled fresh with
        lemon 51
    other white fish 48
    rizzared 52
    seasons and buying 48
Haggis 133
Hare 99
Hatted Kit 235
Hawick Balls 217
Hazelnut Meringue Cake
    158
Helensburgh Toffee 217
Heptinstall, William 264
Herb Jelly 221
Herring 36
    fresh at Inverary 39
    fresh fried in oatmeal 38
    grilled with mustard 40
    landings 36
    marinated fried 249

Open Arms, with
    Drambuie butter 39
    salt marinated 47
    salt pickled 45
    salt salad with beetroot
        47
    seasons and buying 37
    soused or potted
        (whole) 40
    soused or potted
        (filleted) 41
    sweet spiced 42
    tatties and 46
Highland cheddar 232
Highland Fine Cheeses
    229
Honey, types/buying and
    storing 189
Honeyed Rabbit 102
Horse Mussels 66
Hotch Potch 184
Hough, Potted 122
Hramsa Cheese 230

Ice Cream 147
    Ettrickshaws 149
    Italians and 238
Irish Stew 246
Irish, culinary interchange
    246
Islay Dunlop Cheese 232
Italians, culinary inter-
    change 237

Jam
    raspberry 220
    strawberry 221
    tayberry 220
Jeddart Snails 217
Jelly
    herb 221
    rowan 221
Jews, culinary interchange
    253
Johnson, Samuel 268
Johnston, Mrs 261
Kale 180
    and crowdie pie 181
    buttered 181

buying/preparing 181
soup with bacon 182
Kidney puddings 118
Kipper 43
    baked 45
    cures/dyes 43
    fried 45
    grilled 44
    jugged 45
    potted 44
    uncooked 45
Kirriemuir Gingerbread
    212

Lamb
    and kidney pie 130
    availability 127
    boiled gigot 128
    braised shoulder 130
    breeds 124
    fry 133
    grilled flank with
        tomato sauce 132
    grilled or barbecued leg
        129
    haggis 133
    Irish stew 246
    Roast rack of 128
    using whole sheep 131
Leeks 169
    and bacon pie 173
    and hard boiled eggs
        174
    and sauteed chicken
        with skirlie 172
    buying/preparing 169
    roasted 174
    salad 173
    salt herring 249
Lemon Pudding/Tart
    158
Lentil Soup 185
Lettered rock 217
Limpets 70
Lobster 73
    boiled 75
    grilled 74
    identification/buying/
        killing 74

soup 91

MacIver, Mrs 262
Mackerel 42
    hot smoked 43
    potted 43
McLintock, Mrs 261
McNeill, F. Marian 264
Maple syrup cake 209
Marinated Salt Herring
    fried 249
Marinated Strawberries
    146
Marmalade 232
    Fortingall 234
Mealie Puddings 14
Mince and Tatties 112
Minced Collops 112
Mincemeat 209
    cake 222
Moffat Toffee 217
Mussels 65
    in garlic and olive oil
        67
    grilled in their shells
        with wine 67
    identification/buying/
        preparing 66
    stew with crusty bread
        and butter 67
Mustard, store sauce 224

North, Christopher 267
Norway Lobster 76
    identification/buying/
        preparing 77
    serving cold as a salad
        78
    serving hot in their
        shells 78

Oatcakes 7
    in the diet 7
    oven 8
    shape and flavour 6
    traditional girdle 7
Oatmeal
    bannocks 14
    bread rolls 16

bread with molasses or
    treacle 16
brose 11
fresh herring fried in
    38
grades 3
other recipes 24
potatoes 167
sour dough bread 17
sweet oaten pudding 21
Oats 1
    buttered 22
    origins 1
    place in the Scottish
        diet 1
    rolled 3
    varieties/flavour 2
Oddfellows 217
Offal
    haggis 133
    kidneys 130
    lambs fry 133
    sweetbread pie 120
    tripe suppers 118
    veal sweetbreads 119
O ragu di mama 238
Open Arms Herring with
    Drambuie Butter 39
Orkney Squid 81
Oysters 62
    eating 63
    farmed 63
    identification/buying/
        opening 62
    in a crust 65
    on skewers 65
    traditions 62
    with whelks 64

Pakistanis/Indians,
    culinary interchange
    249
Pakora 250
Pan Drops 217
Pancakes Scottish 197
Parkin 213
Partan 71
    bree 73
    pies 72

Peach Highland Cream
    150
Peas 183
    buttered with mint 183
    puree baked in a mould
        184
    pease brose 11
    peasemeal 4
Pennant, Thomas 267
Periwinkle 69
    cooking/eating/
        identification/
        preparation 97
Pheasant 97
    braised with whisky 99
    judging age/hanging 97
    roast with fresh herbs
        98
Pickle vinegar, spiced 224
Pick-your-own 141
Pies
    kale and crowdie 181
    lamb and kidney 130
    partan 72
    Scotch 131
    sweetbread 120
Pitcaithly Bannock 193
Plum Chutney, Mrs
    Beeton's 224
Poca Buidhe 94
Porridge 9
Potatoes 160
    and hardboiled eggs
        169
    buying/varieties/
        properties 163
    chappit tatties 167
    dripping 167
    gratin Dauphinois 241
    fried potato cake 168
    Irish consumption 246
    mealy 165
    oatmealed 167
    origins 160
    place in the Scottish
        diet 160
    scones 168
    soup 183
    stovies 165

stovies in the oven 166
Potted
hough 122
mackerel 43
salmon 30
tongue 122
Prawn, Common 79
Prawns/Dublin Bay
Prawns/Scampi 77
Preserves 218
apple chutney 223
Fortingall marmalade
220
herb jelly 221
marmalade 218
mincemeat 222
mustard, store 224
pickle vinegar 224
plum chutney 224
raspberry jam 220
rowan jelly 221
spiced damsons 222
strawberry jam 221
Puddings
ashet of fresh fruit 143
biscuits and cream 154
blackcurrant and apple
pudding 156
brandied fruit cup 145
Caledonian cream 154
carragheen chocolate 84
clootie dumpling 20
cranachan 150
Escoffier's strawberries
144
Ettrickshaws ice cream
149
Gourmet strawberries
144
hazelnut meringue cake
158
lemon pudding/tart 158
marinated strawberries
146
peach Highland cream
150
rhubarb and bananas
155
rhubarb custard tart

155
rich ice cream 148
strawberry tart 157
Sussex pond 245
syllabub 156
sweet oaten 22
trifle 151
water ice 149
whipped fruit pudding
147
wine with fruit 146
Yorkshire 245

Rabbit 101
buying 102
honeyed 102
Elsie's with onions 102
Raspberries 139
marinated with
whipkull 146
vinegar 145
Razor Shells 69
Regional recipes
Angus and Fife 259
Ayrshire 259
Borders 259
Dumfries and Galloway
259
Edinburgh and the
Lothians 259
Glasgow and Clydeside
259
Highlands and Inner
Hebrides 260
North East 259
Outer Hebrides 260
Orkney and Shetland
260
Rhubarb and Bananas 155
Rhubarb Custard Tart
155
Rich Game Stew 103
Rizzared Haddock 52
Rolled Oats 2
buttered 22
Swiss/Scots breakfast
24
walnut and oat biscuits
23

Rowan Jelly 221
Rumbledethumps 178
Rutabaga, see Turnips 178

Salad, cheese 236
Salmon
Atlantic 26
baked in butter 28
farmed 28
grilled steak 29
life cycle 26
Pacific 34
potted 30
season 27
smoked Scottish 32
soup 31
Tay salmon in pastry
32
wild Scottish 27
Sassermaet 123
Sauces
butterscotch 156
shellfish 81
Scallops 59
identification/buying
60
sauteed in butter with
shallots 60
steamed in a creamy
white sauce 61
Scandinavia, culinary
interchange
Scones 193
basic information 193
basic recipe 195
cheese 197
cream 196
fresh fruit 197
herb 197
honey 196
onion 197
potato 168
soda 195
sultana 196
treacle 196
Scotch Barley Broth 110
Scotch Collops 112
Scotch Pies 131
Scottish Baking 186

Scottish Cream Sweets
142
Seaweeds 82
carragheen 83
dietetic value 82
dulse 85
gathering/buying 83
sloke 86
tangle 85
Selkirk Bannock 205
Seville orange chocolate
cake 210
Shellfish 58
broth 80
Shortbread 190
basic recipe 191
origin 190
Pitcaithly bannock 193
rich 192
types of flour/butter/
sugar 190
Shrimp, Brown 79
Skirlie 14
Sloke 86
Smoked Haddock Flan 55
Smoked Scottish Salmon
32
buying/preparing 33
cures 33
fresh/frozen 34
serving 35
Soda Scones 195
Soor Plooms 217
Sorbet 149
Soups
bawd bree 101
carrot 175
cock-a-leekie 170
dulse broth 85
green kale with bacon
182
grouse 95
hotch potch 184
lentil 185
lobster 76
partan bree 73
potato 183
salmon 31
Scotch barley broth 110

shellfish 80
turnip 175
Southern Crisp Fried
    Chicken 256
Spiced
    beef 114
    damsons 222
Spices 188
    buying and storing 189
    Indian trade 249
Spiny Lobster (Crawfish)
    79
Spoots 69
Square loaf 213
Squid, Orkney 81
Starrie Rock 217
Stovies 165
Strawberries 140
    gourmet 144
    Escoffier, at the
        Carlton 144
    jam 221
    marinated with
        whipkull 146
    rich tart 157
    shortcake 257
Suet 123
Sugar 188
    ally water 218
    bools 218
    boiling, basic process
        214
    hearts 218
Sussex Pond Pudding 245
Swedes, *see* Turnips 178
Sweet haggis 21
Sweet Oaten Pudding 21
Sweetbread Pie 120
Sweeties 213
    almond cake 216
    barley sugar 216
    Berwick cockles 216
    bon bons 216
    black man/treacle
        candy 216
    black striped balls 216
    butterscotch 216
    cheugh Jeans 216
    Coltart's candy 216

claggum or clack 216
curly Andra 216
curly murlie 216
Edinburgh rock 216
glessie 217
gundy 217
Hawick balls 217
Helensburgh toffee 217
horehound boilings 217
Jeddart snails 217
lettered rock 217
mealie candy 217
Moffat toffee 217
Moffat whirlies 217
oddfellows 217
pan drops 217
soor plooms 217
starrie rock 217
sugar ally water 218
sugar bools/hearts 218
tablet, traditional 215
toffy for coughs 215
Swiss/Scots Breakfast 24
Syllabub 156

Tablet 215
Tart
    lemon 158
    mincemeat 222
    strawberry 157
    tatin 242
Tatties and Herring 46
Tay Salmon in Pastry 32
Tillypronie, Lady Clark
    of 264
Toasted Cheese 233
Toffy for coughs 215
Tongue, potted 122
Trifle origins/flavourings
    151
Tripe Suppers 118
Trout
    baked brown 35
    brown baked with
        herbs and lemon 36
    sea/salmon 35
Turnips 178
    buying/preparing 179
    mashed 180

Orkney Clapshot 180
    soup 175
    varieties 178

Veal Sweetbreads and
    Kidneys 119
Vegetables 160
    Chinese stir-fried 253
Venison 88
    braised shoulder of red
        deer 91
    collops with lemon and
        port 92
    fallow deer seasons 89
    farmed 88
    liver 94
    pasty 93
    poca buidhe 94
    red deer seasons 89
    roast saddle 92
    roe deer seasons 89
    sika deer seasons 89
    tripe 94
Vinegar 224
    pickle 23
    raspberry 145
    spiced 224

Water biscuits 213
Walnut and Oat Biscuits 23
Water biscuits 213
Water Ice 149
Weights and Measures xv
Wheat 4
Whelks 69
    identification/
        preparation 69
    oysters with 64
Whipkull 146
Whipped fruit pudding
    147

Yeast Cake, special 201
Yorkshire Pudding 245